Qualitative Analysis

QUALITATIVE ANALYSIS

Historical and Critical Essays

PAUL F. LAZARSFELD

Professor of Sociology
Columbia University

Allyn and Bacon, Inc.
Boston

For Professor Patricia Louise Kendall

Contents

v

Part Four/   Exchange With Neighbors

Part Five/   Organizational Issues

Part Six/   Expert Witnesses

Introduction

It is sometimes useful to distinguish three main areas of inquiry: (1) the natural sciences; (2) the humanistic social sciences (history, literary studies, philosophy); and (3) the "law-seeking" social sciences, to borrow a term recently introduced by a UNESCO committee reviewing recent trends in economics, psychology, linguistics and sociology. Two disciplines present difficulties, namely anthropology and sociology. Where does anthropology belong? In the UNESCO report, it was defined, almost by administrative accident, as a humanistic topic. And what about sociology? UNESCO classified it as "law-seeking," although it was taken for granted that even highly quantitative sociological inquiries are likely to include humanistic elements.

To debate in general terms the proper balance between these two sociological strands seems rather futile. Instead, Professor Etzioni had the idea of turning the issue into an empirical question. Why not take the writings of a sociologist generally identified with the quantitative tradition and see to what extent they had humanistic and qualitative aspects? I am flattered to be chosen as a case in point. Reviewing my work as it was written and published over the years, I found that it permitted a rough classification which helped to bring out some of the main humanistic features in the setting of empirical social research.

PART ONE/ HISTORICAL ESSAYS

Working in a field that is relatively new almost inevitably leads to interest in its history; yet it is rather difficult to explain why this is so. Partly, one hopes to demonstrate an honorable pedigree. In working on the mathematical foundations of measurement in the social sciences, I wanted to show that the basic elements of these mathematical foundations were rooted in the classical writings of philosophers and psychologists. This review became "Historical Notes on Concept Formation in the Social Sciences" (Chapter 1).

It is sometimes surprising to see the difference in approach taken by two authors working on similar problems. A desire to explain the reasons for one's focus can then become a second motive for interest in historical emphasis. I have always been concerned with the application of social research. When I first came to this country, I reviewed work in the field of consumer studies. This resulted in a paper on "The Psychological Aspects of Market Research" (not reproduced in the present volume). In this paper, I made the point that the notion of "action" should be central to all study of human behavior. Shortly thereafter, Talcott Parsons' famous book *The Structure of Social Action* appeared. He took his lead from Weber's emphasis on *Handlung,* but he was apparently unaware that parallel to Weber's more speculative use of the term, a broad empirical tradition had developed, especially in Germany. In view of this, I wrote a rather elaborate essay entitled "Historical Notes on the Empirical Study of Action." The paper was not previously published because it was too long for an article and too short for a book. The historical material has not lost validity, but I have added a few paragraphs on papers that have appeared more recently (Chapter 2).

The above essays were addressed primarily to professional colleagues. But for many years research on the media of mass communication brought me in close contact with practitioners and their controversies. It was apparent that their arguments were usually custom-tailored to the exigencies of the moment. I felt it would be helpful to show that at various earlier periods the same issues were debated and that the positions taken shifted with the historical situation. The mass media today present a very different problem of "freedom of the press" than confronted the isolated editor during the American Revolution. Thus, to suggest greater flexibility in contemporary controversies was a third motivation which made me turn to historical material. A typical example is a speech made during Columbia University's bicentennial celebration, "Mass Media of Communication in Modern Society." It is reproduced here partly because it is not easily accessible and partly because it reflects the humanistic element I tried to introduce into the graduate courses I gave at the time (Chapter 3). Whenever I had the opportunity, I also supported historical studies on mass communications carried out by colleagues; the work of Leo Lowenthal was especially fruitful.

One paper is not included in this collection because it has not been written. In spite of my interest in the historical aspects of my work, I never was able to give it a satisfactory rationale. I simply had a vague sense of some of the strands involved. An astute analysis of what the historical dimension adds to contemporary social research would represent a much-needed contribution to the field.

PART TWO/ CRITICAL SOCIOLOGY

Empirical studies are often undertaken to help decision makers in the private or governmental sectors of society. Columbia's Bureau of Applied Social Research, which I directed for many years, did a great deal of such work; it is not surprising, therefore, that we were often confronted with the danger of "selling out." In retrospect I notice how often I pondered the relation to what loosely can be called critical sociology. In view of recent discussions, it seems reasonable to devote a special section of this volume to papers that emerged from this concern. The first is an address delivered at a convention of journalism schools more than thirty years ago. I was struck by the sensitivity and aggressiveness with which the mass media countered criticism by intellectual groups, and suggested how balanced reaction to criticism, including self-criticism, could be incorporated into the training of journalists and broadcasters (Chapter 4).

Fifteen years later I presided over a two-day meeting of writers, social scientists, and professionals from the mass media. The central theme of this symposium was the relation between intellectuals and the communications industry. When the papers were published, I summarized their content and tried, in an introduction, to point out the complexity of the problem. It is included here because it gives a good picture of a continuing debate and of the way I myself tried to mediate. Criticism should be based on actual research but, of course, in the end there remains a normative area where each individual must take his own stand. I summarized mine in the final sentence: critics will never fully win over technological, commercial and political forces, but without them, society would be much the poorer (Chapter 5).

The political events of recent years have pushed the mass culture debate into the background, and the appearance of cable television and of satellites will certainly change its technological base. But the relation between social research and a public controversy should be a perennial source of concern. Several years ago I headed a committee of the American Sociological Association which edited a volume on the uses of sociology. Colleagues competent in a variety of fields reported on how their kind of research was related to the stream of practical decision making. None of the contributors could go into details, but it became clear that in the field of poverty legislation, educational reform, public health and many other fields debates are going on which are alike irrespective of the subject matter. A more detailed record concerning one such episode as seen from my vantage point therefore seemed well justified.

Concern with critical sociology was greatly enhanced by my contacts with a group of German philosophers, especially Horkheimer and Adorno, who opposed the notion of "critical theory" to the activities of empirical sociologists. I published in their journal a paper, "Administrative and Critical Communications Research," in which I tried to justify both approaches (Chapter 6). The Frankfurt group has played a considerable role in recent student protests. Perhaps it is worthwhile to listen to the way the debate sounded in a more detached context. T. W. Adorno and I each told our side of the encounter in our contribution to the Harvard collection on "Intellectual Immigrants."

With some hesitation I add a section of the UNESCO report mentioned above. As the sociological member of the group, I had to sample major issues in my field. Writing in 1968, I could not overlook the interest of some students in the literature on "dialectics." It was of course not possible to cover the whole literature, so I selected a few writers with whom I had personal acquaintance and whose names would be familiar to most members of an international committee. In reviewing what I finally wrote, I oscillate between the feeling that I was not up to even this limited task, and doubt that it was worth doing at all. Still, the piece contains material not easily available to an English-speaking audience, and therefore, its inclusion in this collection seems justified (Chapter 7).

PART THREE/ QUALITATIVE RESEARCH TECHNIQUES

Thus far, my retrospections have been directed toward some of the conceptual and substantive problems I've encountered. But qualitative problems also enter into all technical phases of social research—the collection of data, their classification and their analysis.

The methodology of these qualitative procedures is still very little developed. While there are numerous books and collections on quantitative research, only recently a few readers on qualitative procedures have appeared. From time to time polemical monographs opposing the two approaches have been published, but balanced discussions are rare indeed. I have returned to the task of explicating qualitative procedures whenever I had an opportunity to work on a specific issue. But I am still working on a more comprehensive presentation. In the meantime, I can only include samples of my efforts.

Critics of empirical studies often scoff at the use of questionnaires because they do not realize how much analytical thinking goes into the construction of a good instrument. This is especially the case when people are asked to account for a personal decision—why they bought a book, voted for a candidate or went to a psychiatrist. When I came to this country, I summarized my Austrian work on this technique in a paper, "The Art of Asking Why" (Chapter 8). Its ideas have been followed up by many students, and the present state of the art has been ably summarized by Professor Charles Kadushin in his essay, "Reason Analysis," in the new *International Encyclopedia of the Social Sciences*.

Derivative from my early approach is the work, now known as motivation research, of some of my Austrian collaborators. I refer especially to Herta Herzog and Ernst Dichter who, like me, belonged to the Karl and Charlotte Bühler group. Their imaginative interpretations have occasionally suffered from overpopularization, and consequently from academic mistrust. I have on one occasion tried to locate their approach in a broader programmatic frame of qualitative research (Chapter 9).

It might surprise today's reader that the papers in Chapters 8 and 9 took their main examples from the study of consumer behavior. One of my main interests as an instructor at the Psychological Institute in Vienna was the empirical analysis of decisions, and one of my first books written in Vienna dealt with the occupational choices of adolescents. Consumer choices also provided interesting material, and they had the additional advantage that one could mobilize funds to pay interviewers and analysts. (See Chapter 12 in this connection.) But all this was conceived as part of a broad program to study social action, which I have traced in the essay included as Chapter 2 in this collection. When I came to this country my academic colleagues were not much impressed by this kind of pursuit. It was not experimental enough for the psychologists and not dignified enough for social theorists. As a result, my first American publications were of rather hybrid form. They would be published by business school journals which were willing to let me include pages filled with European concern with *"Handlung."* The ending of the paper reproduced in Chapter 8 is a typical example. Incidentally, notice the continuous use of the term "psychology." Forty years ago the term "sociology" would hardly have made any sense outside of academic circles.

Concomitant to this whole trend is the problem of how to summarize "open-ended" interview questions. This is a problem of classification for which standard manuals on logic do not suffice. A paper written in collaboration with Professor Allen H. Barton attempted to develop some additional principles of classification especially applicable to the qualitative data obtained from a study of the leisure-time problems of young workers (Chapter 10). A more complex aspect of classification is the development of typologies based on the scrutiny of unstructured material. Letters, diaries and field reports are typical sources. At one point I tried to organize the vast supply of terms that each language has to describe goal-directed experiences. I again chose as a general tag the term "disposition concepts" and "substructed" to my linguistic inventory a three-dimensional-attribute space (Chapter 11). The reader will get a general idea of this procedure; if he becomes interested, he can consult additional material included in a paper that Barton and I wrote fifteen years ago, the "Role of Qualitative Analysis in Empirical Social Research." The paper has been reprinted often and therefore, is not included in the present collection.

It is fairly clear what I mean by a typological analysis of qualitative material. But another idea presented in that paper is much more difficult to articulate. Often a study, or for that matter one's own experience, can provide one with various bits of information: a remark by an informant, a field observation, a revealing document all on the same topic. These elements must be integrated by some conceptual "formula" which makes them part of a more general imagery. From my own writings, I might refer to two such protoconcepts: (1) the notion of "effective scope" used in the *Academic Mind* (pp. 262–5) and (2) the idea of "half knowledge" in the introduction to the *Uses of Sociology* (p. 27). Sometimes such tags are quickly forgotten; other times they grow to become permanent members of the sociologists' conceptual store. The "marginal man," "relative deprivation" or "reference group" are familiar examples of such survivors. Little work has been done to clarify the "conception of concepts," and I cannot offer any general ideas.

As a concrete example, however, I have included in this collection a chapter on the way in which I tried in retrospect to structure my experiences at the time I moved to this country—my Atlantic transfer. The introduction to this selection formulates the general problem of analysis; it is followed by a brief description of external events. I then organize the available documents and memories around the two integrating formulas of "anticipatory cues" and "latent strategies" (Chapter 12).

In one case, such a qualitative analysis of mine had considerable consequences. *The People's Choice*, a study of the role of mass media in the presidential campaign of 1940, made me feel that personal influence played a great role in the way people make up their minds how to vote. Not having anticipated this issue I had no data to pursue it quantitatively. I therefore attached to our book a chapter on "The Nature of Personal Influence" which was based only on a few qualitative observations. Some of the concepts I derived—the two-step flow of communication and the idea of horizontal opinion leaders—have since entered the sociological general literature. I have not included the last chapter of *The People's Choice* in the present collection because the original study is still being reprinted and is currently included in reading lists at many colleges.

PART FOUR/ EXCHANGE WITH NEIGHBORS

Progress in qualitative methodology will come from careful scrutiny of successful work. As in literary criticism, we have to wait for the creative work of the innovator before we can analyze what it consists of. Modern philosophers of science take this position when they explicate the procedures of the natural sciences. But when it comes to the social sciences, they rather give us advice as to what we should do, since they don't have the patience or the interest to start from the study of concrete investigations.

Actually, qualitative research procedures comprise a sector of methodology sorely in need of more work. Philosophers of science neglect these techniques because they find it more prestigious to explicate what natural scientists do. When I was invited to address an international congress of philosophers, I used the occasion to give a hortative paper on "Philosophy of Science and Empirical Social Research." I took my own medicine and dissected carefully what some members of the audience had written about typologies and definitions in the social sciences. Previously, the paper was published only in the minutes of the congress; I hope that wider circulation will mobilize some collaboration from our philosophical colleagues (Chapter 13).

What the French call *explication de texte* should be helpful in facilitating communication with other disciplines. Thus, for example, historians wrote about the medieval mind and the spirit of the Renaissance long before there were attitude scales or opinion polls. A confrontation of such material with techniques of quantification should clarify their relation to qualitative analysis. Twice I had occasion to stress this position by addressing simultaneously my own co-professionals and neighbors in related fields. My presidential address to the American Association for Public Opinion Research dealt with "History and Public Opinion Research." I advocated a mixed commission of historians and public opinion researchers to select questions for periodic public opinion polls which would be of interest fifty years hence (Chapter 14). For the twentieth anniversary of the *Public Opinion Quarterly* I wrote a paper, "Public Opinion Research and the Classical Tradition," which urged the translation of some of the classical writings of political scientists into the language of empirical research (Chapter 15). In a somewhat circuitous way, both Chapters 14 and 15 show how the call of the humanist is never very far away from that of the quantitative scholar.

PART FIVE/ ORGANIZATIONAL ISSUES

The theme of this entire volume has one more facet. Major research projects require rather complex administrative arrangements.

Anyone guiding such work is confronted with problems very like a continuing series of cases in organizational analysis. The core of such experiences can be gleaned from the selections in this section.

In my address as president of the American Sociological Association, I discussed the problems that arise when empirical social research begins to be integrated into the university structure. The correct balance between a humanistic tradition and newly developing professional technology is the pivot of the matter (Chapter 16). In a paper written in collaboration with Ruth Leeds, the same theme reappears. When welcoming visitors to an international sociological congress, I urged my American colleagues and our foreign visitors to listen to each other "with a third ear" in order better to bridge and profit from different intellectual and cultural traditions (Chapter 17).

The final paper represents a somewhat hopeful look into the future. Twenty years ago, in collaboration with my colleague Robert Merton, I worked out the idea of a professional school that would train people in the methods of studying human affairs and would, at the same time, keep students attuned to basic intellectual developments in a specific discipline. This school thus far has not materialized; but a recent report on "The Behavioral and Social Sciences" ought to revive the whole idea. It was written by a committee appointed jointly by the National Academy of Science and the Social Science Research Council. A major recommendation is to create "a graduate school of applied behavioral sciences" (p. 201 ff.). In ten detailed pages, the implementation of the plan is spelled out. Change and continuity in this whole area become highly visible in comparison with the earlier project (Chapter 18).

PART SIX/ EXPERT WITNESSES

Ever since Professor Etzioni suggested this undertaking, I have wondered how it might emerge different from the usual cliché of "selected papers." It occurred to me that the inclusion of comments by others might provide a useful perspective. Like most of us, I have been the object of criticism and friendly appreciation. From three occasions, rather detailed comments are available from collaborators who themselves have made major contributions to sociology; their observations regarding my work express ideas that by themselves are contributions to current problems in our discipline.

Raymond Boudon's pages are closest to the content of this volume.

He edited a French translation of some of my papers, which partly overlaps with the present collection. From his over-generous remarks one can glean three ideas which definitely add to the repertoire of my own thinking. For one, his observations on the relation between historical and methodological analysis go well beyond what I had sketched for this introduction; it was written before Boudon's text appeared, and I have purposely not made any changes since. Secondly, Boudon brings out with great clarity the importance of the *explication de texte*—no wonder, as I owe much of this idea to my long association with the French educational system, as a student as well as a teacher. And finally, my French colleague puts his finger on a major shortcoming of my qualitative efforts: the psychologistic bias. That this criticism fills the last pages of his essay makes it the more important—as everyone who knows French literary tradition will recognize (Chapter 19).

Characteristically, James S. Coleman makes the same point. His paper was read as part of a lecture series which my friend Hanan Selvin organized on the occasion of my 65th birthday. Coleman does rescue me from the reputation of a "mere" quantitative craftsman. The context of his review required comments on my mathematical work, which of course is excluded from this volume. But his remarks on this point also single out the lack of a truly sociological approach to model building. I have been greatly impressed by the parallel of Boudon's and Coleman's criticism. I obviously cannot change the past, but in some recent work I am seriously trying to build some kind of bridge between it and the admirable work through which these two younger colleagues are now pioneering in the promised land of a precise and yet non-atomistic sociology (Chapter 20).

Finally, we obtained permission to reprint a piece from C. Wright Mills' famous *Sociological Imagination*. He describes me there—with courtesy but with firmness—as the prototype of an "abstracted empiricism" (Chapter 21). For one, this is a good antidote in a book where I might have overplayed the humanistic strain in my work. A former student of Mills and mine once published the following remark:

> One of my favorite fantasies is a dialogue between Mills and Lazarsfeld in which the former reads to the latter the first sentence of the *Sociological Imagination:* "Nowadays men often feel that their private lives are a series of traps." Lazarsfeld immediately replies: "How many men, which men, how long have they felt this way . . . ?"

I probably would have been marginally interested in such a count. But my real query would have gone in a different direction: What does Mills mean by "alienated"? How would he decide whether a specific person should be classified as more alienated than another person? Only the answer to such questions would make a count possible. But even then I would have passed over the count very quickly to investigate the biographical or social factors that would explain varying levels of alienation. Before I was through, the whole arsenal of qualitative techniques would have come into play, including a detailed interview with Mills and a scrutiny of the place the quoted sentence had in the structure of his text.

I always believed in the interdependence of quantitative and qualitative work; but I was also aware that whatever talent I had was weighted on the quantitative side. Therefore, in the choice of my associates I continuously looked for balance. My relations with the Horkheimer group, my joining forces with David Riesman and the late Ludwig Wagner, and my long and gratifying collaboration with Robert Merton, are examples as well as symbols.

Qualitative Analysis

Part One

Historical Essays

CHAPTER *1*

NOTES ON THE HISTORY OF CONCEPT FORMATION

INTRODUCTION

All the social sciences deal with concepts that seem to have a certain vagueness. Who can precisely say what a folk society is? Who has not read many discussions as to the real meaning of public opinion? Who can, in practice, recognize an extrovert personality? There are various reasons why the social scientist's language has so many of these terms, which at first sight seem to be ill defined and even at their best are so "fuzzy at the fringe." In some cases we can, by the nature of concept, only observe symptoms, behind which we assume a more permanent reality: this would be true, for example, in the case of personality notions. In other matters the object of investigation is so vast that we can only analyze certain aspects of it: notions like patterns of culture or Zeitgeist belong here. For still other purposes the problem itself seems to require a looser kind of formulation: wherever we study adjustments—e.g., in marriage, in job performance or in standard of living—we find that large numbers of actual solutions may serve the same functional purpose.

This peculiarity of the social scientist's intellectual tools has been deplored by some, considered as unavoidable by others. Most of all, however, it has been covered with nomenclature. Syndromes, genotypes, underlying concepts, hypothetical constructs and many other

Reprinted from *Concepts, Theory,* and *Explanation in the Behavioral Sciences* (1936), pp. 144–186, by permission of the publisher. Copyright © 1966 by Random House, Inc.

terms have been used. It is hard to say to what extent we have today a clear formulation of the problem behind all these terms, let alone clear directions on how to deal with them in the pursuit of empirical research. And yet it is in the course of actual investigations that some clarification is most needed. For if we have to decide whether there is in government increased bureaucratization or whether city life makes people progressively neurotic, we have to get some measure of these tendencies. And whatever index we use, we make implicit assumptions on the meaning of the kind of terms which we have just exemplified.

Thus, problems of measurement, of meaning and of concept formation fuse necessarily into each other. No empirical procedure of classifying social objects can be understood without reference to general logical discussions. And philosophical disquisitions about the nature of the social sciences are not likely to be fruitful without an incisive analysis as to how empirical social research does actually proceed.

The present monograph will analyze one special procedure by which it is possible to make what one might call inferential classifications. Any number of well known topics are covered by this provisional name tag: a person's attitude as inferred from his behavior; the intention of a document as inferred from certain linguistic characteristics; the morale of a group as inferred from its various performances, and many others. No exhaustive listing or explicit definition will be given of the applications which we intend to cover. If it were possible to clearly state at the beginning the purpose of the procedures to be described, the whole monograph—even the procedure itself— might be superfluous. But the basic thesis to be developed is exactly this: measurement, classification and concept formation in the social sciences exhibit special difficulties; they can be met by a variety of procedures, and only a careful analysis of the procedure and its relation to alternative solutions can clarify the problem itself, which the procedure attempts to solve.

This presentation, then, will necessarily take on the character of a slowly unfolding story. I shall first review some literature because the authors saw the problem and discussed it from their different points of view. This will give the reader, I hope, a feeling for the general intellectual intention to which his attention should be directed. Then I shall try to single out more precisely the elements involved in this discussion. This will enable me to state clearly the specific way in which I have combined these elements into an empirical procedure called latent structure analysis. And, finally, the limitation of this procedure and its relation to other approaches will be brought out.

It is especially at the beginning of such a form of presentation that the patience and cooperation of the reader have to be solicited. Because latent structure analysis has a mathematical foundation, it would be possible to start right out with a precise formulation of what it is and what it can be used for. But this would becloud the connection of this specific research operation with an important and much more general intellectual problem. Conversely, by starting with this broader tradition, the presentation appears at first unprecise and the selection of references somewhat arbitrary. This, however, is inherent in any effort to show the progressive crystallization of a problem area. And it is especially true that the contemporary stage of methodology in the social sciences has a transitional character. Until recently, the philosophy of the social sciences was discussed in very general terms. Now the number of specific methods of investigation is rapidly increasing. As a result, we see that problems, as they were stated before, need reinterpretation in more concrete terms; and we find, as usual, that the broader formulations are somewhat vague and that each permits several translations into the terms of actual research procedure.

The present section, then, is given over to a review of some recent efforts to bring out the role of inferential concepts in the social sciences. As my report proceeds, the reader will see better and better what kind of problems I have subsumed under this term. And at the end of the section he will be asked to forget the words "inferential concept" again; it was merely chosen as a placeholder until my review should lead to a more precise terminology, derived from the subject matter itself.

My starting point will be certain discussions among professional psychologists. This is not to say that I shall be more interested in psychological concepts as compared to the notions of sociologists, anthropologists, or political scientists; but psychologists have been the first to be systematically concerned with the logic of their empirical procedures. And in their field, too, the problem of inferential concepts can be most clearly demonstrated. In general, such notions originate if we observe what one might call permanencies under variation. If under similar circumstances one social group survives and another disintegrates, concepts like cohesion develop. If the objects created in two periods of history are markedly different, we introduce notions of style, distinguishing between, say, Gothic and Baroque. But we will always be concerned as to how to justify the choice of just those concepts. The psychologist seems to have an easier task; he does not only notice that a man behaves more restlessly the nearer he comes to a moment of danger; he has himself experienced anxiety and the subject under observation is himself likely to say that he feels anxious. Actually, this advantage of psychological concept formation has turned out to be a more tantalizing gift than it would seem to be at first sight. But it is just for this reason that certain methodological discussions among psychologists seem to furnish a paradigm for the other social sciences.

Actually, this very idea needs careful formulation and scrutiny. Not only do we have to see whether it is true; we have to make sure that it is taken as a formal proposition about the social scientist's language, and not confused with ideas on the substantive relationship between psychology and the other social sciences. I shall therefore examine in some detail empirical findings, the subject matter of which are groups and social institutions. I will select such cases where these groups are characterized as units in their own right, where processes within the group are considered by inference, in clear parallel to the inferences made by the psychologist. From there, I shall turn to some discussions by modern logicians who have themselves taken cognizance of the area that we have selected for review. Then finally, at the end of this section, I will be prepared to look back and suggest a precise formulation of the problem.

THE INTERVENING VARIABLE

THE SHIFTING ROLE OF INTROSPECTION

At the beginning of this century it was generally agreed that psychology was the "study of man's mind." The approved method of study was introspection, either performed by the psychologist himself or by a few students well trained in the art. Complex experiences such as thoughts, emotions, and mental attitudes were described, analyzed into their different elements, and compared with each other.

But about this time "animal psychology" began to develop as part of that Darwinian tradition which stressed the continuity of all biological phenomena. The rise of animal psychology confronted the traditional systematic psychologist with a necessary choice. Was it possible for the introspectionist to accept observations on animals as any part of "psychology" at all? Titchener, the most rigorous of all the introspectionists, considered the matter carefully in his major work, a textbook of psychology completed in 1910. He answered the question in the affirmative: observations on animals could be regarded as "psychology." Here, in selected quotations, is the gist of his argument:

> We have agreed that the psychologist is not confined to a knowledge of his own mind . . . he can apply the method (of experimental introspection) to any number of minds. Psychology is based upon the introspection of a large number of trained observers. . . .
>
> At the same time language is not the only possible means of expression. . . . We can express our ideas by a grimace or a shrug of the shoulders, as well as by spoken words or a written paragraph.
>
> Now the psychologist argues by analogy, that what holds of himself holds also, in principle, of the animal . . . He argues that the movements of animals . . . record the animals' mental processes. He places the animal in circumstances which permit of the repetition, isolation and variation of certain types of movement or behavior. The animal is thus made, so to say, to observe, to introspect; it attends to certain stimuli, and registers its experience by gestures.[1]

In short, the grand old man of introspective psychology accepted introspective psychology as legitimate because animals were enough like college professors to make possible a valid analysis of their experiences.

But the fledgling science, to which Titchener so generously gave the nod, rewarded him with scant gratitude. As animal psychology continued to gain ground, it became more aggressive. By the mid-twenties the behaviorists were denying that introspection had any place in psychology at all. The study of human nature, it was held,

---

[1] E. B. Titchener, *A Textbook on Psychology* (New York: The Macmillan Company, 1910). The entire first chapter of Titchener's *Textbook of Psychology* deals with this kind of argument. Our quotations are taken from pp. 30 and 31 of a 1921 reprinted edition. Similar ones can be found on pp. 26, 27, 28, 32, 33 and 34.

could be scientific only to the extent that it emulated the "non-mentalistic" assumptions and methods of animal psychology.

A few more years passed and psychology entered upon a new era. Now another great figure, Tolman, surveyed the scene. In his presidential address to the American Psychological Association (*1935*) Tolman developed his notion of the role of introspection in systematic psychology. He began by declaring proudly, "I am a behaviorist." How, then, could he go on to say that a rat has "bias," "vigilance," and "demands"? Here is his answer:

> . . . I am at present being openly and consciously anthropomorphic about it as I please. For, to be anthropomorphic is, as I see it, merely to cast one's concepts into a mold such that one can derive useful preliminary hunches from one's own human, everyday experience. These hunches may then, later, be translated into objective terms. But there seems to me every advantage in beginning by conceiving the situation loosely and anthropomorphically . . . I in my future work intend to go ahead imagining how, *if I were a rat,* I would behave as a result of such and such a demand combined with such and such an appetite and such and such a degree of differentiation; and so on. And then, on the basis of such imaginings, I shall try to figure out some sort of rules or equations. And then eventually I shall try to state these latter in some kind of objective and respectable sounding terms such as vectors, valences, barriers, and the like.[2]

We see that between the era of Titchener and that of Tolman, psychology had come full circle. Now the behaviorist declared that introspection could have some usefulness. It facilitates the development of animal psychology, says Tolman, because college professors are enough like animals so that their experiences can lead to useful categories of behavior analysis.

And yet in the course of all this a useful notion had been developed: the intervening variable (I.V.). This turned out to be a very stimulating idea: it never got quite clarified; various authors adapted it differently to their specific kind of work; and still the way it "tagged" and focussed on a common fund of methodological problems

---

[2] Edward C. Tolman, "The Determiners of Behavior at a Choice Point," *Psychological Review,* XLV (1938), 24. Italics from Tolman.

made their discussion fruitful and coherent. It will help us to trace the development of the I.V. idea in more detail.

THE FUNCTION OF INTERVENING VARIABLES

Everyone wants to know why people behave as they do. In this generality, however, the question cannot be answered; as a matter of fact, it makes no sense. So all the social sciences have to limit it in some way: what differences come about through varying childhood experiences, through application of drugs, through propaganda, etc.? One formulation became of special interest to American psychologists: why do people behave differently than they have behaved just before in similar situations? How does repeated experience affect behavior? how do people (and animals) learn? From one point of view "learning theory" is best described as attending to the following type of problem:

a) There are subjects (animals and people) characterized by heredity, age, previous experiences, and so on.

b) They are brought into specific situations under specific conditions: a hungry rat in a maze, a Catholic worker in a radical union; they are supposed to make some kind of decision repeatedly.

c) Their decisions have certain consequences for the subjects either in terms of their own satisfactions or in terms of observable changes in the outside world.

Query: What will subjects of type a) do under conditions b) as the result of their experiences c)?

The experimental psychologist thus divides the factors which might account for his subjects' behavior into three groups and handles them differently: the antecedents going back a long time are averaged out; the antecedents just preceding the experiment are systematically varied; the events during the experiment are watched and explained in the light of the other two groups.

It is understandable how this emphasis grew out of a desire to get findings applicable both to animals and to people. The rat runs repeatedly through a maze until it knows where to find food; the child hears repeatedly a list of words until it knows them by heart. It also became possible to formulate more clearly what "explaining" meant under the circumstances. Here are subjects exposed to various stimuli,

S_1 S_2 . . . the term stimuli combining the experimental conditions b) and the experiences in the experimental sequence c) mentioned in our preceding list. The subjects make certain responses R to these stimuli. The experimental work shows certain "functional" relations[3] between S and R, say

$$R = f\ (S_1, S_2 \dots)$$

But the S_i and R are separated in time; the form of the function f varies greatly from one situation to another, and seems in all cases quite complicated; additional stimuli might play a role at any time. So the idea is to simplify the approach by interposing between the S_i and R "intervening variables" according to the following scheme. The stimuli S_i are related to the I.V. and they in turn are related to the responses:

$$R = f_i\ (S_i) \text{ becomes}$$
$$R = f_2\ (\text{I.V.}) \text{ and, therefore } (\text{I.V.}) = f_3\ (S)$$

The I.V.'s are so chosen that they are less numerous than the S_i and the functions f_2 and f_3 are supposed to be simpler than f_1. The schematic examples should make the general idea more concrete.

A dog is being trained to give the paw when he is asked to. The trainer says "Give the paw," takes the dog's leg and gives him a piece of food. After a while he says the word, waits, and then gives the food if the dog happens to extend his paw. In the end the dog will give the paw most of the time when the trainer utters the request. How long will it last until this end is reached and how successful (in terms of a number of failures) will the training be? The psychologist would still need about a dozen intervening variables to analyze the situation, but we will just select three of them for the sake of illustration. The oftener the dog is rewarded by food, the stronger a habit (H) does he develop. So $H = f(N)$ where N is the number of rewarded trials. But it also depends upon the food used. If the dog has a great desire (D) for the food, the training proceeds more quickly. This is taken account of by introducing the notion of excitatory potential E, which is a measure of readiness in the dog's organism to perform the required

---

[3] For the time being the mathematically untrained reader may think of a functional relation in terms of simple examples; the longer an egg is boiled, the harder the yoke becomes; the more a bar of iron is heated, the longer it becomes; the more often we read a text, the more of it we remember, etc. Later we shall give a more precise definition.

task. $E = g(D,H)$, which expresses the idea that this readiness depends upon the product of desire D (which is presumed constant for the experiment) and habit strength H which is built up by repetitive reward during training. Finally, we have the probability p that the dog performs correctly in a given number of exhibitions.

So, $p = h(E) = h[g(DH)] = h(g[D,f(N)])$. In the end we have a relationship between p and N which can both be observed empirically; but this function was derived from the mediating relationships just mentioned. The choice of such intervening variables like habit strength and excitatory potential is the result of elaborate systematic analysis of a great variety of experiments. The claim is implied that these concepts are likely to best organize existing knowledge and to lead to new studies with predictable results.[4]

But obviously the choice of the I.V.'s is arbitrary and especially in the early stages of a science a great variety of them can be tried out. Tolman, who introduced the notion of I.V., certainly had different ideas from Hull, who adapted the term to his experimental work. Here is a condensed quotation from one of Tolman's earlier papers, where he still had to argue for the acceptance of I.V.'s as legitimate notions in systematic psychology:

> Suppose a rat be run in a successive discrimination box. Such a box is an apparatus in which the animal has to choose one of two doors at each of four successive choice points. One of the two doors at each such point is lighted and one is dark. The lighted door may be either the one on the left or the one on the right in chance order. Thus at each such point the animal has the possibility of responding either on the basis of light-darkness or on that of right-leftness. . . . Under these conditions it was found . . . that the rat will pick up one systematic way of behaving after another. In the first two or three days he may pick up, say, the propensity of choosing always the right-hand doors. But then he will shift sooner or later to some new propensity, to that say, of choosing only the left-hand doors; and then still later to that of choosing alternate right and left doors; . . . we may now define each such intervening condition (or "I") in the organism, behind any one such systematic way of behaving, as a hypothesis.

[4] The main papers on intervening variables are reprinted in Melvin H. Marx (ed.), *Theories in Contemporary Psychology* (New York: The Macmillan Company, 1963).

*A hypothesis, behavioristically, in other words, is to be defined
as nothing more nor less than a condition in the organism which,
while it lasts, produces just such a systematic selectivity in behavior* . . . The rats assert—hypothesize—that it is the right-
hand doors, or the left-hand doors, or alternate right and left
doors or dark doors, or whatever, which, as such, lead on. And
when any one such assertion proves incorrect, an animal sooner
or later drops it for a new one. (Emphasis supplied.)[5]

The rat's hypothesis is an inferential concept of considerable complexity. A situation is observed in which the animal can behave in a
variety of ways; it is found that he picks one alternative rather consistently. His choice can be affected by changes in the experimental
situation. So the "model" is developed that the rat "wants" the food
reward offered to him and forms "ideas" as to how he is likely to get
it. The theoretical psychologist infers these wants, ideas, etc., from
observations and introduces them into his system as explanatory I.V.'s.

It is unnecessary to go into further detail. All that was needed
here was a general understanding as to the role which I.V.'s play in
psychological research work. By now a fairly standardized doctrine
has developed to which authors adhere when they judge the merit of
a specific I.V. It has to be linked to the antecedent stimulus conditions
by one set of functions; it has to be linked to subsequent overt responses by another set of relations; and its connection with previously
established I.V.'s has to be clarified.[6] But in the two examples I just
gave, there is a difference in "intellectual style" which for my purpose
I should try to make more explicit.

TWO MODES OF DEALING WITH INTERVENING VARIABLES   When I described the training of a dog in simplified Hullian language, all the
intervening variables were introduced in terms of equations, either
relating I.V.'s to empirical observations or to each other. The functions f, g, h, defined the I.V.'s in principle. In Tolman's example of
the rat's hypothesis such connections were not mentioned explicitly.

[5] Edward C. Tolman, "Psychology versus Immediate Experience," in *Collected Papers in Psychology* (Berkeley: University of California Press, 1951), pp.
109–110.

[6] A systematic and instructive job was done on the concept of frustration
as an I.V. It will be found in J. S. Brown and I. E. Farber, "Emotions concep-
tualized as intervening variables—with suggestions toward a theory of frustration." *Psychological Bulletin* (November, 1951), XLVIII, especially pp. 480–492.

It is true that Tolman in his general writing stresses their importance. But, as many writers have observed, Tolman—in contrast to Hull—has never proposed any specific equations. He usually refers to a broad class of experimental observations and allocates to them a vivid term taken from general language; the term stimulates the reader to visualize the animal behavior by implicit reference to general experiences with living beings. The preceding story on hypotheses is a typical example. The clue for this procedure might be found in an almost offhand remark which Tolman made in comparing his and Hull's work:

> But what is a theory? According to Professor Hull, a theory is a set of definitions and postulates proposed by the theorist (on the basis presumably of some already found facts) from which other empirically testable facts, or as he calls them, theorems, can be logically deduced. These deduced theorems will be new empirical relationships which the theorist—or more often, his research assistants—can, then and there, be set to look for.
>
> For my own nefarious purposes, however, I wish to phrase this matter of the relationship of a theory to the empirical facts out of which it arises and to which it leads in somewhat other terms. A theory, as I shall conceive it, is a set of "intervening variables."[7]

This paper appeared in 1937 when Tolman was still fully immersed in animal work. For him, even then, the construction of the I.V.'s themselves was important theoretic business irrespective of the propositions into which they were to be fitted. He seemed to feel that at an early stage of a science concept formation is as important as the establishing of relationships between them. Fifteen years later, when we know in which direction Tolman's interest turned, we understand his emphasis even better. The man who advocated an anthropomorphic approach to rats joined, in 1949, with a group of sociologists to apply his notion of I.V. to a joint "theory of action." His contribution consisted of an 80-page discussion "which contains, it is believed, all the descriptive and theoretical constructs necessary for explaining and predicting the action or behavior of individual persons."[8] In such a program, ob

---

[7] Tolman, *op. cit.*, "The Determiners of Behavior at a Choice Point," p.

[8] Edward Tolman, "A Psychological Model," in Talcott Parsons and Edward Shils (eds.), *Toward a General Theory of Action* (Cambridge: Harvard University Press, 1951), pp. 279–361.

viously, general propositions can hardly play any role because they just don't yet exist in any area where human relations are being studied. In a very consistent vein, then, this monograph just presents a system of intervening variables which is called a "model," probably because it makes elaborate and skillful use of graphical presentations. The definition of an I.V. is the same as Tolman gave it in his original paper. But obviously the scope of references and examples is now much more vast than when I.V.'s were only linked up to the behavior of animals under experimental conditions. As a result the sources of suggestions are greatly enlarged. Tolman states the turn of affairs as follows:

> (3) Theories which exhibit the *trend toward a sui generis model* invent a set of explanatory structures and processes (hypothetical constructs) which draw on analogies from whatever other disciplines—mathematics, physics, mechanics, physiology, etc.—as may be deemed useful. Freud's water-reservoir concept of the "libido," Lewin's "topological and vector" psychology, and the theory to be presented in the following pages belong primarily in this third category.
>
> The theory to be presented here will then be quite frankly one which develops (by various analogies drawn from simple physics and mechanics, from Lewin's "topological and vector" psychology, and from common experience) *a sui generis* model. This model has its own (tentatively) ascribed intervening constitutive structures and processes and its own variety of interconnecting causal functions.[9]

We have now before us I.V.'s like belief-value matrices, locomotion in psychological spaces, etc. When complex matters like identification and repression are discussed, additional I.V.'s are suggested or new features are added to ones introduced before.

The merit of such procedures can, of course, be judged only by reading the original text and it would be out of turn here to even attempt an evaluation. But it is clear that this development in the use of I.V.'s is quite different from Hull's use where all the emphasis was on just one idea: the systematic organization of experimental results in a limited field of learning with the help of a minimum number of I.V.'s and their interconnection. In retrospect, then, the difference between Hull and Tolman becomes much more significant than at the time when contemporary critics thought that both scholars used the notion

[9]   *Ibid.*, p. 283.

of an I.V. in the same way and for the same purpose. I shall come back to this point once more.

HOW TO "MEASURE" AN INTERVENING VARIABLE

One element in this difference is especially significant for our discussion. Hull was never much concerned with problems of measurement. The dimension of his concepts, like habit strength or excitatory potential, grew necessarily out of his basic equations. But Tolman, from the beginning, was concerned about how the intervening variables are arrived at, operationally defined, measured or whatever other terms he used to apply in pointing to the problem.[10]

The answer Tolman gave 15 years ago, when he was concerned with the behavior of a rat at a choice point, is the same he gave recently when the whole system was "elaborated for the specific case of a hungry actor going to a particular restaurant and ordering and eating a particular food."[11]

In certain carefully chosen, controlled and 'standard' experimental setups, one tries to hold all but one, or one small group, of the independent variables constant and studies the functional connection between the variations in this one independent variable, or this one limited group of independent variables on the one hand, and the correlated variations in quantitatable feature of the final behavior on the other. For example, one holds all the independent variables but, say P_1 (time since last feeding) constant. And in doing this, one chooses certain 'standard' values for all the other independent variables such as P_2, S_1, S_2, etcetera. And then, under these conditions, one observes the correlations between the variations in P_1, on the one hand, and the resulting variations in some aspect of the behavior B, on the other.[12]

By an operational definition of an intervening variable I shall mean, first, a statement about a standard defining experiment in which a certain measurable variation in some feature of the observed behavior will, by definition, be assumed to be a direct

[10] *See* Edward C. Tolman, "Operational Behaviorism and Current Trends in Psychology," in *Collected Papers in Psychology* (Berkeley: University of California Press, 1951), p. 123 ff. and p. 158 ff.

[11] Parsons-Shils, *op. cit.*, p. 288.

[12] Tolman, *op. cit.*, p. 122.

measure of corresponding variation in the magnitudes of a given intervening variable. Second, such a definition will involve an assumption about the linear or nonlinear nature of this mathematical function connecting the measured feature of the dependent behavior to the intervening variable. And, third, the specific constants in this form of mathematical function must also be known, or assumed, before such definitions will be final.[13]

The idea is about as follows. We can find certain indicators for intervening variables. Everything else being constant, the variations in the indicators correspond to the variations in the I.V. We shall meet this general idea repeatedly and will finally examine it in considerable detail. For the moment, we rather need a more concrete idea as to how it works in actual research. Let us look at one set of intervening variables, an "actor's" belief-value matrix which consists of his opinions about various restaurants, his food preferences, etc. How will we find out about this I.V.? One way is through

> . . . mere questionnaires or interviews. Thus, for example, one could ask the subjects: 1) 'What are you ready to do when you haven't eaten for a considerable length of time?' 2) 'What kinds of food do you like? Name six varieties of food in order of preference. What do you like about each of these six?' 3) 'For each of these six foods what types of restaurant would you go to and in what order? List all the considerations you would take into account in choosing the one kind of restaurant or the other.'[14]

The repeated references to questionnaires in this monograph[15] make it easy to predict what problems Tolman would face if he were really to develop measurements along his line of argument: the student experienced in social research knows that answers to questionnaires vary considerably, if wordings are slightly changed, if the interview is done under slightly varying conditions, etc. There just is no way to develop a "standard experimental set up" or "standard defining experiment." We will have to face the fact *that to an intervening variable there will correspond a variety of indicators and that they will have*

---

[13]   Parsons-Shils, *op. cit.,* p. 333.

[14]   *Ibid.,* p. 295.

[15]   *See* e.g., Tolman, "A Psychological Model," p. 336 ff.

to be reconciled in some way. We suspect that the same will be true if one were to examine more carefully laboratory experiments which were proposed to define other I.V.'s like needs or valences. But this goes beyond the scope of the present discussion.

Our short look at the history of I.V.'s had three purposes: to give a first example of the type of thinking which we tagged as "concern with inferential concepts"; to show how closely it is related to "problems of measurement," this again remaining for the time being a rather vague notion; and how these problems lead to the use of indicators which in some way are supposed to correspond to or to express the inferential concept. We came to the conclusion, in the case of the I.V., that, in some cases at least, there could come up several indicators and that they would have to be reconciled or combined in some way. This fact needs further exemplification. We will find it in another area of psychological discussion, where the multiplicity of indicators is actually the central theme.

THE TRAIT

In the preceding section I tried to sketch how introspection becomes a source for inferential concepts. We experience, say, anxiety, and its role in our own course of action (R). We observe how other people act in situations (S) which would, we know, bring on our anxieties; we notice that their reaction R is similar to ours. As a result, we file away in our minds that as a rule such a "stimulus" S is likely to be followed by response R. We "explain" such S-R sequences with the help of an intervening variable: anxiety. The value of this I.V. becomes particularly apparent if many S-R situations are observed where the S and the R vary, but where the same I.V. (anxiety) seems appropriate. We can then organize our observations in a somewhat more economical way: we remember the series of x situations which create anxiety and the series of y responses by which anxiety is expressed. Instead of registering x times y relationships of the S-R type, we need only remember $(x + y)$ findings: the x prompters to and the y indicators of anxiety.

In this schema one element is still missing. As we transferred from our own experience to the observation of other people we undoubtedly noticed something else: in a given situation different people show varying amounts of anxiety. Some are prone to quickly lose their heads; others are able to maintain their balance. Individual variations of this kind lead to the notion of "traits."[16]

If we are willing to accept an oversimplification, we can put the matter as follows: the notion of I.V.'s serves the purpose of making introspective material accessible to scientific treatment; the notion of traits serves the same purpose for our observation that other people vary in their responses to the same situation. In this sense, the "trait" is likely to lead us farther afield: we can organize other people's responses into conceptual clusters even if we can find nothing that corresponds in our own experience.

THE PRAGMATISTIC TRADITION

Traits became the topic of more systematic reflection in connection with moral problems—at least as far as American psychological literature goes. One starts naturally with William James' *Principles of Psychology (1890)*; there one does not find the term trait in the index. In the chapter on habits, however, (Chapter X) there is an extensive discussion on how people can acquire desirable habits, like industriousness, or lose undesirable ones, like drunkenness. This intertwining of ethical problems with the question of traits, their acquisition and change is still equally strong in John Dewey; it is the main theme of his *Human Nature and Conduct (1922)*. Dewey also uses "habit" as his central term; he considers it interchangeable, however, with terms like trait, characteristic, attitude and tendency.[17] Dewey's concern with the changing of habits, the examples he chooses, and the advice he gives are often very similar to James' treatment.

[16]   There is also the experience, of course, that other people, as well as ourselves, vary in their responses under varying circumstances—as they grow older, for example, or move to another part of the country. For the time being, we shall not make a distinction between this and the more strictly inter-individual kind of variations.

[17]   John Dewey, *Human Nature and Conduct* (New York: Henry Holt and Company, 1922; New York: Random House, Inc., 1957). He explains at one point why the word "habit" seems to him slightly preferable in view of common language usage (p. 41). But this term clearly covers such things as honesty, peevishness, courage, etc. (p. 16).

The moralist observes differences in his and other people's conduct, tags them as good or bad, and reflects on how valuable traits can be strengthened. The methodologist starts from the same observations but is more interested in defining, classifying and measuring these traits. The pragmatists were a combination of moralist and logician and they found a way to fuse their double motivation into a view which combined their activistic philosophy and their operational idea of scientific work. James' main maxim on self-improvement—which he derived from physiological considerations of habit—read as follows: "Seize the very first possible opportunity to act on every resolution you make and on every emotional prompting you may experience in the direction of the habits you aspire to gain."[18] He was convinced that the "expression" of a trait would in turn reinforce its "existence" —for better or for worse. On the negative side, he was of course sure that every drink reinforced the trait of drunkenness. But he thought that "even the excessive indulgence in music *for those who are not performers themselves* has probably a relaxing effect upon the character."[19] In his later career as a philosopher he paralleled this relation between a trait and its expression on a logical plane. He was, as is well known, much concerned with meanings and it is in his last book on the meaning of truth that we find the following passage:

> . . . Suppose, e.g., that we say a *man is 'prudent'*. Concretely, *that means that he takes out insurance, hedges in betting, looks before he leaps* . . . As a constant habit in him, a permanent tone of character, it is convenient to call him prudent in abstraction from any one of his acts. . . . There are peculiarities in his psychophysical system that make him act prudently. . . . (Emphasis supplied.[20])

We are not surprised to see that James is very explicit on the relation between an inferential concept and the indicators connected with it. He is, after all, the one who coined the phrase "concepts signify consequences." He felt that abstract descriptions are often

[18] William James, The *Principles of Psychology* (New York: Henry Holt and Company, 1890), p. 147.

[19] *Ibid.*, p. 148.

[20] William James, *The Meaning of Truth* (New York: Longmans, Green, and Company, 1909), pp. 149–150.

useful enough, yet they are "sucked up and absorbed without residuum into the concrete ones, and contain nothing of any essentially other or higher nature which the concrete descriptions can be justly accused of leaving behind." Here is picturesque language, the precise meaning of which is not easily checked. But it is safe to assume that James inclined toward identifying the concept and its indicators. Now this leads to obvious difficulties. Do all prudent people always look before they leap? Where do we take account of the amount of insurance taken out? How about people who show some but not all the symptoms mentioned by James? Inversely, shouldn't other indicators have been included?

Dewey was obviously aware of these difficulties. As a moral philosopher he was not less convinced than James of the mutual interaction between "disposition" and "doing"; today's tradition of progressive education is testimony to his point of view. But as a logician, he saw a looser connection between concepts and indicators. He warned that one should *not* "assume that there is or ever can be an exact equation of disposition and outcome."[21]

It was characteristic for habits

> that their outworking in any particular case is subject to contingencies, to circumstances which are unforeseeable and which carry an act one side of its usual effect.[22]

At the end of the previous section we noticed the emergence of one idea: to an inferential concept there will correspond a variety of indicators. Now a second idea comes to the fore, although rather shadowy at first: the notion of probability. It is easy to see how the progress from James to Dewey can be reformulated. The prudent man is *likely* to look before he leaps because any specific behavior item is only a probable but not a necessary condition of a related trait.

I shall now show how the probability character of indicators was elaborated as traits became part of a more specialized discipline: personality research. In the 1930's the first textbooks on personality began to appear in this country. Two of these authors, Allport and Cattell, are especially significant for my survey.

[21] John Dewey, *op. cit.*, p. 48.
[22] *Ibid.*, p. 49.

TRAIT AND INTERVENING VARIABLE

In an early systematic discussion Allport tried "with the aid of eight criteria to define trait and to state the logic and some of the evidence for the admission of this concept to good standing in psychology." Two of his criteria, numbers 4 and 7, are pertinent here.

> 4) The evidence of a trait may be established empirically and statistically . . . in order to know that an individual has a trait it is necessary to have evidence of repeated reactions, which, though not necessarily constant in type, seem nonetheless to be consistently *a function of the same underlying determinant.* (Emphasis supplied.)

> 7) Acts and even habits that are inconsistent with a trait are not proof of the non-existence of the trait . . . there are in every personality instances of acts that are *unrelated to existent traits, the product of the stimulus and of the attitude of the moment.* Even the characteristically neat person may become careless in his haste to catch a train.[23]

Here both elements necessary for the diagnosis of an inferential concept are used: multiplicity of criteria and probability relation between criterion and trait. Allport later gave a rather complicated definition of trait, the core of which was that it would render "many stimuli functionally equivalent" and would initiate "equivalent forms of adaptive and expressive behavior."[24] At that time (*1937*), personality theorists were engaged in debates which have no bearing on this essay. But Allport's definition was "translated" by a subsequent writer into a form which is very interesting from my point of view. J. C. McClelland, in a 1951 textbook on personality, quotes Allport's definition and adds:

> What Allport appears to be saying is that a trait, on the one hand, renders stimuli equivalent and, on the other, initiates

[23] Gordon W. Allport, "What Is a Trait of Personality?" *Journal of Abnormal and Social Psychology* (1931), pp. 368–372.

[24] Gordon W. Allport, Personality: *A Psychological Interpretation* (New York: Henry Holt and Company, 1937), p. 295.

equivalent responses. These two functions of a trait can be
illustrated by a simple diagram:

$$
\begin{array}{llll}
 & S_1 & & R_1 \\
 & S_2 & \textit{trait} & R_2 \\
\text{Situations} & & & \text{Responses} \\
 & S_3 & \text{hypothetical} & \cdot \\
 & & \text{construct} \\
 & \cdot & & \cdot \\
 & \cdot & & \cdot \\
 & S_n & & R_n
\end{array}
$$

> This figure shows how a trait for Allport is a kind of inter-
> vening hypothetical state which serves to unite or knit together
> what might otherwise be dissimilar stimuli and responses. He
> apparently feels that a trait is both an inference the observer
> finds necessary to explain equivalences (on the *S* or *R* side) and
> a living reality or force which acts within the individual to pro-
> duce the equivalences.[25]

It should be obvious why I find this formulation revealing. In the
twenty years since Allport's original formulation, the "intervening
variable" had made its victorious appearance on the academic scene.
McClelland's scheme is practically identical with the one Tolman
used to introduce this concept. Traits, in this analysis, turn out to be
special kinds of intervening variables.

The last sentence in McClelland's analysis points to a disturbing
intertwining of ideas which we had best unravel at this point. It was
remarked before that the pragmatists had a tendency to condense two
arguments: that habits are expressed and in turn affected by actual
behavior, and that habits, as inferential concepts, have somehow to be
defined and "measured" by behavioral items. It seems that this remains
a tradition in the experimental area of personality research. Even after
McClelland has remarked on the double content of Allport's definition,
he himself defines trait as a learned tendency of an individual as he has
reacted successfully in the past in similar situations.

There is nothing basically wrong in stating within one sentence
what a trait is supposed to be, what its function is and how it has
developed. But for a general discussion of inferential concepts, it is

[25] David C. McClelland, *Personality*, p. 202. Copyright © 1951 by David C.
McClelland. Used by permission of Holt, Rinehart and Winston, Inc.

probably better to isolate the definitional element from all the others. If this is done carefully then it turns out that one topic is still unsettled. Differential concepts come into play where we intend to characterize a set of objects in an indirect way. We assume that the intended classification can be reached through a number of indicators. Each of them has only a probabilistic relation to the "underlying characteristic." But by using a number of them we hope that our classification will be "correct"—which at the moment shall mean only that it conforms to whatever theoretical or practical goal the investigator has set himself. Using an obvious analogy from medicine, I will call this relating of indicators to intended classification the diagnostic procedure. It deserves some further reflection.

THE DIAGNOSTIC PROCEDURE

One can distinguish at least four ways in which our inferential classification can make use of indicators. It could be that independent laws are known which link the observed properties with those the investigator really wants to know about. A Geiger counter indicating radioactivity, or a bacillus in the sputum indicating tuberculosis would be examples. Such cases don't exist yet in the social sciences and therefore don't need further discussion.

In a second type of procedure, while such laws are not known, they are at least temporarily—and often in a vague form—assumed. A psychoanalyst who has an image of unconscious desires and their repressions uses dreams and slips in everyday life for diagnostic purposes. There the methodologist has the task of spelling out the assumptions implicit in the diagnostic procedures. Lindzey's analysis of the use of thematic apperception tests to judge people's anxieties or ambitions is an excellent example of such work.[26] But it too is outside of our scope for this monograph.

For the third type take as an example an experimenter who wants to know how hungry a given rat is at a certain moment; he uses as a measure the amount of electric shock the rat is willing to endure in its effort to get food. There obviously the diagnosis of hunger is based on

[26] Gardener Lindzey, "Thematic Apperception Test: Interpretive Assumptions and Related Empirical Evidence," *Psychological Bulletin*, (1952), XLIX, No. 1, pp. 1–25.

the kind of intervening variable which was reported above as characteristic of Hull's work. K. Spence has called it the *S-R* kind; for while
it is conjectural it is derived from previous experiments where stimuli
were varied and the consequent variations of responses were observed.[27]

In distinction from the *S-R* mode Spence then introduced the *R-R*
kind of intervening variable. Here inferences are drawn from the fact
that a variety of responses are sometimes likely to vary together. We
notice that under certain conditions people have a heightened pulse
rate, they bite their nails, they pace up and down; therefrom we derive
the notion of anxiety. It is the covariance of indicators which is the
source for our intervening variable and not the variation of a response
subsequent to the variation of a stimulus. This is the fourth type of
diagnostic procedure and as it will turn out, it is for our purpose the
most important one. It is in these terms that we can also relate the
trend from Tolman's earlier to his latest writings: they represent an
increasing shift from an *S-R* to an *R-R* conception of intervening
variables.

Spence properly gave as one example the work of factor analysts.
Among them R. Cattell has provided the most articulate description of
their intention and so a brief reference to his formulations should be
helpful.

If a trait is expressed by a variety of indicators, then these indicators are bound to be related to each other in a variety of ways. If
upon repeated observation a person exhibits one indicator frequently,
the others are also likely to be observed frequently; this is what is
meant when authors talk about *intra*-individual covariance. But if we
have observations on many people at one time we will expect also an
inter-individual covariance; people exhibiting one indicator will also
be more likely to exhibit all the others. It is such considerations which
have made correlation analysis the main tool of modern trait research.
As an outstanding representative of this approach is R. Cattell, who has
no doubt that "a unity can be detected from the fact that the consistent
elements in a trait covary."[28] He has devoted a life's work to the
systematic survey of all the correlations which turned up in empirical

[27] K. W. Spence, "Types of Constructs in Psychology," in Melvin Marx
(ed.), *Theories in Contemporary Psychology* (New York: The Macmillan Company, 1963).

[28] R. B. Cattell, *Description and Measurement of Personality* (New York:
World Book Company, 1946), p. 12.

studies. From them he has derived a system of basic personality traits: the essence of the idea is the inference from covariation of responses to the "existence" of underlying units. He puts it drastically, as follows:

> . . . what the psychometrist has to deal with is a series of actual behavior manifestations. He is like a plumber who is given no map of the underlying conditions but is asked to deduce, from the rates of flow from many faucets—and their mutual interferences—what conduit system exists.[29]

Cattell does not use the term "intervening variable" in his extensive writings on the theory of traits. But his "underlying conditions," his image of a "conduit system" controlling observable flows serves the same conceptual purpose. It will turn out that the covariance of a set of probabilistic indicators and its relation to inferential concepts are a crucial issue of this whole discussion. But I shall interrupt the sequence of my argument and raise a question which might have come to many a reader's mind. Are the problems reviewed so far peculiar to psychologists or do they also arise for sociologists who are more interested in persons collectively than in individual persons? I shall try to make a case for the affirmative side.

THE SOCIAL FACT

At the end of the preceding section we got the first signal that statistical procedures could be basic for the formation of concepts. The diagnostic procedure it uses belongs to the type that focuses on the covariance of indicators. It requires observation of a large number of units and a study of how they change together; therefrom inferences then are made as to the "underlying structure" and the position of a specific unit in it. For a sociologist the appropriate units would be a collective rather than a person. But for quite a while the objects of sociological interest were either specific communities or society as a whole. Only recently has there emerged a study of small groups, of

[29] *Ibid.,* p. 110.

cities and of primitive cultures which is logically comparable to the statistical analysis of individual behavior. To what extent this will in turn affect the general thinking of sociologists is very difficult to predict. In order even to see the situation clearly, it will be advisable to proceed in reverse order for the present section. I shall first discuss some concrete research findings and then try to show what bearing they have on more enduring trends in sociological writings.

The studies I have in mind contain empirical propositions about properties of collectives. Tank platoons composed of friends perform better in maneuvers than platoons composed of soldiers randomly selected. Similarly teams of workers in a factory produce more if they are composed of friends. In play-groups with an authoritarian leader more fights develop among the children than if the leader takes a permissive attitude. The larger a discussion group the more difficult it is to get agreement on issues under debate. Occasionally this kind of proposition is found in studies of larger units. Certain indicators of "goodness of life" like a low crime rate, large per capita contributions to community chests, use of the public library, are positively correlated in American cities of more than 100,000 population. Primitive tribes, if migratory, are less likely to form political alliances than do tribes who have settled in villages: the settled tribes are also more likely to have a more complicated internal social structure.[30]

All these findings have the same formal character that we are used to from innumerable studies on individuals, inter-relating properties like IQ. income, vote, etc. The well-known "scatter diagrams" could be drawn up; only now each point would correspond to a collective like a boy scout group, or a city or one of the several hundred tribes included in the Yale crosscultural survey.

It is therefore not surprising that other elements of quantitative research have also been applied to "populations," the elements of which are themselves collectives. Students have developed dimensions according to which collectives can be classified. This leads naturally to the notion of profiles. For example, a military department and a committee within a large university would be compared. They have about the same degree of "flexibility" and "permeability" but "control"

---

[30] For a review and discussion of these and other studies, see Daniel M. Goodacre, III, George P. Murdock and Max Bavelas, "Interrelationship of Group Properties," in Paul F. Lazarsfeld and Morris Rosenberg (eds.), *The Language of Social Research* (Glencoe: The Free Press, 1955). Section IV B.

and "stratification" is much higher in the governmental unit, while "hedonic tone" and "stability" is superior in the academic group.[31] Finally indices have been developed to combine various properties: indices of integration for cities, standard of living indices for countries, etc.

Yet very rarely does one find any discussion of these empirical data in terms which are so familiar to psychologists. There is no talk of underlying concepts, no parallel to the notion of the intervening variable, no discussion of diagnostic procedures, although there is certainly no lack of the object itself. Sociological theorists deal continuously with the cohesion of groups, the stratification of societies, the intimacy of interpersonal relations. These are, in formal terms, *traits of collectives*. One would therefore expect that they could be subject to the same kind of analysis which has been reported in our preceding discussion.

One reason for the lack of interest in this parallel is certainly a confusion of its formal and its substantive elements. Recently a social psychologist has made the point that social scientists should be more interested in "phenomenology" with arguments which come very near to the notion of diagnostic procedures in sociology. A crucial and typical statement of his deserves closer attention.

> Are there characteristics of groups, of a psychological order, which can be studied as such without any necessary reference to the characteristics of any particular member of the group? This, I submit, is a reasonable question for research, and I do not think that the answer is obviously in the negative. In our twentieth-century sophistication we tend to reject the word "mind" because it smacks so much of something that rats do not have and which is therefore not scientific. But we do like the word "attitude"; we feel quite at home with words like "characteristics," "tendencies," traditions," and "customs," and we grow positively smug when we can work in an expression like "pattern of culture" or "social norm." All these terms can be as readily applied to groups as to individuals, often much more readily . . . We have, then, identifiable processes and relationships which are properly regarded as group characteristics and

---

[31] Hemphill and Westie: "The Measurement of Group Dimensions," reprinted in Lazarsfeld and Rosenberg, *The Language of Social Research*. The original source: *Journal of Psychology*, XXXIX (1950), pp. 325–341.

which without too much strain on our part can be regarded as mental or psychological.[32]

In the last sentence the intertwining of two separate ideas is especially marked. The main position seems to me correct: individual traits as well as national characteristics are underlying concepts; the one is predicated on an individual the other on a collective; both have to be inferred from observable data by procedures which I try to clarify in this study. But why call such properties "mental or psychological?" A more neutral term like "inferential" would undoubtedly make the sociologist more willing to participate in the study of the common problem, the study of diagnostic procedure. For it is not long ago that a major concern of sociologists was to prove that sociology had a subject matter and a method of its own. As a result what is common to all the social, or behavioral sciences got rather scant attention. A general scientific policy orientation made some of the classics bypass or blur an important methodological problem. I shall trace this in two cases.

DURKHEIM AND WEBER

In 1895 Durkheim tried to write for the new science of sociology a Magna Charta. In his *Rules of Sociological Methods*[33] the central and reiterated proposition was that "social facts are to be treated as things." The first of his six chapters is entitled: "What is a Social Fact?" And when in the Introduction to the second edition he wanted to clarify his ideas against his critics he tried to sharpen his definition. We read there statements like these:

> Things include all objects of knowledge that cannot be conceived by purely mental activity, those that require for their conception data from outside the mind, from observations and experiments, those which are *built up from the more external and immediately accessible characteristics to the less visible and more profound.*[34]

[32] R. B. MacLeod, "The Place of Phenomenological Analysis in Social Psychological Theory," in John H. Rohrer and Muzafer Sherif (eds.), *Social Psychology at the Crossroads* (New York: Harper and Brothers, 1951), p. 217.

[33] Emile Durkheim, *Rules of Sociological Methods* (University of Chicago Press, 1938). Quotations refer to the American edition by George E. G. Catlin.

[34] Durkheim, *op. cit.*, p. xiii.

From the many examples Durkheim gives for these social objects it becomes clear that one of his aims was to establish on a large scale propositions of the kind reported in preceding pages. He speaks of a "comparative method" when he mentions observations like the following one:

> . . . when one comes in contact with social phenomena, one is . . . surprised by the astonishing regularity with which they occur under the same circumstances. Even the most minute and the most trivial practices recur with the most astonishing uniformity. A certain nuptial ceremony, purely symbolical in appearance, such as the carrying off of the betrothed, is found to be exactly the same wherever a certain family type exists; and again this family type itself is linked to a whole social organization.[35]

These are statistical statements the units of which are collectives.

One might therefore expect that Durkheim would be much concerned with the question of how a variety of indicators have to be combined so that one can really distinguish various family types, social organizations, etc. But this problem he nowhere discusses. As a pioneer of a self-sufficient discipline of sociology his interest concentrated on the mere existence of persistent relations between properties of collectives, for then they deserved a study of their own, different from the psychological study of individuals. At one point Durkheim argues that indicators for such properties are really easier to come by than indicators of an individual's attitude. For the latter "an effort of abstraction is necessary."

> Social facts, on the contrary, qualify far more naturally and immediately as things. Law is embodied in codes; the currents of daily life are recorded in statistical figures and historical monuments; fashions are preserved in costumes; and taste in works of art. By their very nature they tend toward an independent existence outside the individual consciousness, which they dominate.[36]

The last three words are, clearly, gratuitous. The formal nature of such indicators, their "independent existence outside the individual

[35] *Ibid.*, p. 94.
[36] *Ibid.*, p. 30.

consciousness" have nothing to do with the question, whether "they dominate" the individual. But Durkheim was so eager to score a policy point that he did not go on to study more carefully how one would go about actually developing what today are often called structural variables. It is worthwhile noticing incidentally that when MacLeod, the psychologist, and Durkheim, the sociologist, agree that individuals as well as collectives have properties from which we can infer "underlying characteristics" they cannot help claiming in the same breath the superiority of the material with which they each are professionally concerned.

But Durkheim in addition to this professional bias, seems to have held a logical conviction which practically cut him off from the problem we are concerned with in this review. One of the "corollaries" to his first rule reads as follows:

> The subject matter of every sociological study should comprise a group of phenomena defined in advance by certain common external characteristics, and all phenomena so defined should be included within this group.[37]

From the context in which this is enunciated one can infer Durkheim's imagery. A "social milieu" would be characterized by certain indicators and *all* of them seemed to him necessary to establish its existence. In his time the detailed comparative work of the Yale cross-cultural survey type was not yet conceived. As a result Durkheim never faced the problem of what he would do if only *some* of the required indicators were present. Working with selected and rather vaguely described examples, he probably greatly overrated the likelihood that he would ever find many cases where all the "common external characteristics defined in advance" would be present. We found a similar situation when we discussed the transition from the pragmatists to the beginning of detailed personality research. Once the general program was applied to concrete investigations the probability character of indicators came sharply to the foreground. And indeed Max Weber, who was much closer to social research in the modern, or if you please, American sense, had a clearer sense of the problem of inferential concepts. While he did not see all its implication he felt one had to cope with it even on the level of broad scale social theory.

[37] *Ibid.*, p. 35.

At the time prior to the First World War discussions on the notion of probability began which by now have lead to quite revolutionary developments in the philosophy of all sciences. Weber followed these developments with great interest and gave much thought to their bearing upon sociological theory. Sometimes he used them quite explicitly to clarify methodological problems, like the nature of interpretation in the writings of historians.[38] At other times they provided him with an opportunity to develop a telling figure of speech. Then he used probability notions more to indicate a problem without following it up in detail. This happened just in the context which interests us here: the explication of sociological concepts. One frequently finds in his writings passages like the following one:

> . . . it is only the existence of the probability that a certain type of action will take place which constitutes the "existence" of friendship. Thus that a *friendship exists* or has existed *means this and only this:* that we, the observers, judge that there is or has been a probability that on the basis of known subjective attitudes of certain individuals there will result in the average sense a certain specific type of action.[39]

Weber specifically stresses that only in such probabilistic terms can the meaning of social relationships be caught. They cease to exist, he says "whenever there is no longer a probability that certain kinds of meaningful oriented social action will take place."[40] In other contexts[41] he defines Power and related concepts as the *probability* that a person is "in a position to carry out his own will despite resistance" or that a command will be obeyed "by a given group of people."

Here Weber is well aware that if he deals with intended classifications of interpersonal relations or social structures he has to look for appropriate indicators. And they are linked to the inferential concept not by rigid functional relations—as Tolman thought—nor by necessary definitions—as Durkheim required—but by probability relations. Their precise nature he did not, however, specify. As a result he over-

---

[38] Max Weber, *The Methodology of the Social Sciences* (Glencoe: The Free Press, 1949), pp. 180–188.

[39] Max Weber, *The Theory of Social and Economic Organization*, T. Parsons, editor (New York: Oxford University Press, 1947), p. 119.

[40] *Ibid.*, p. 118.

[41] Ibid. p. 152.

looked a problem the importance of which I have intimated before. What if a variety of indicators don't behave in the same way? For instance, mutual support in emergencies might be more "essential" for friendship than similar tastes in food. "Certain command" can apply to a variety of topics: some of them, if not obeyed, might show that "imperative control" is not present; others might be flaunted with various degrees of frequency without undermining the control structure. And what is more serious: if we have data on such a set of indicators, how do we combine them—if combining be desirable—into one index which would permit us to order classes of friendships and to distinguish degrees of authority?

Weber overlooked this problem probably because he too wanted to stress the peculiar aspect of the social sciences. In his case the notion of the "ideal type" served this purpose and kept him from putting his thinking into the terms of research procedures with which he was well acquainted. This becomes especially evident at a point where he was inevitably confronted with a multiplicity of indicators. He defined a bureaucratic organization by a set of criteria;[42] among them were the requirements of hierarchy, of separation of professional and personal obligation, separation of the members from ownership of the tools of work, etc. He defined as "ideal-type" those organizations which satisfied all the criteria. But how about those which satisfied only a proportion of them?

Carl J. Friedrich, in a critique, correctly pointed out that omitting an answer to this question precluded any empirical study of concrete organization.[43] He wanted to compare bureaucracies in various countries. Then he had to use the Weber criteria—or similar ones—as "measuring rods for determining the degree of bureaucratization"; he needed "the judgment of more or less." Because Friedrich compared only five countries, his ranking could still be made in somewhat impressionistic terms. But suppose he had wanted to study scores of organizations. He would have been in the same position as a psychologist who wants to order people according to their level of extroversion. And his problem would have been to combine the absence or presence of a set of indicators into one or a few indices of bureau-

[42] Weber, "The Essentials of Bureaucratic Organization," reprinted in *Reader in Bureaucracy*, Robert Merton, editor (Glencoe, Illinois: Free Press), p. 18 ff.

[43] "Some Observations on Weber's Analysis of Bureaucracy," *ibid.*, p. 27.

cratization. Thus the closer the social theorist comes to empirical work, the more clearly is he confronted with the research problem which is unfolding in these pages. It is not surprising then, that we come nearest to its explicit discussion with authors who have actually focused on the comparative study of communities or on the comparative status of people within a community.

SOME RECENT DEVELOPMENTS

Most social theorists have been concerned with a distinction for which Toennies has coined the two terms *Gemeinschaft* and *Gesellschaft*. The next notable application of his ideas were Redfield's studies on the folk society. His idea was to take a number of Mexican villages and rank them according to the degree of content they had with modern urban centers. His hypothesis was that the more isolated they were, the more would they have preserved the character of intimate *Gemeinschaft*. A folk society he characterized as follows:

> Such a society is small, isolated, nonliterate, and homogeneous, with a strong sense of group solidarity. The ways of living are conventionalized into that coherent system which we call a "culture." Behavior is traditional, spontaneous, uncritical and personal; there is no legislation or habit of experiment and reflection for intellectual ends. Kinship, its relationships and institutions, are the type categories of experience and the familial group is the unit of action. The sacred prevails over the secular; the economy is one of status rather than of the market.[44]

Here collectives are clearly characterized by a number of properties: traditional behavior, no legislation, prevalence of the sacred, etc. And the basic hypothesis requires a ranking of communities according to the way these properties combined into patterns. Thus, inevitably the question had to come up: if communities qualify on some of the criteria, but each on different ones, how far are they on the imputed continuum going from folk to the urban society?

Quite a number of studies out of the Redfield tradition are now

---

[44] Robert Redfield, "The Folk Society," *The American Journal of Sociology*, 52, (January 1947), p. 293.

available, and recently Horace Miner published a systematic review.[45] The author reports many controversies and notes that they are likely to confuse two problems: whether communities can be ordered along the postulated continuum; and whether this order is related to the degree of contact with the outside world. The latter is a substantive problem, the former a classificatory one. Miner shows that some writers are discussing the merits of the indicators selected for study; others worry more about ways of combining them. He himself feels that "no adequate methodological techniques exist for operationalizing and quantifying the characteristics themselves."[46] In spite of a careful reading of the article we cannot tell whether the author is quite clearly aware of the ordering problem involved. But his discussion comes certainly as near to a fruitful formulation as any sociologist has provided so far.

One other point in Miner's paper deserves notice.[47] As a community moves over time away from the folk society pattern, it is not to be expected that "the traits change at the same rate or that they are all independent in the same way in all circumstances." This is indeed a serious problem. Whenever we deal with change over time the probability relation between the inferred classification and the indicators might change itself. If then a unit under study changes its observable property, this can be due to one or both of the following alternatives: that the unit has changed its position in the "underlying structure"; or that the diagnostic role of some of the indicators has changed.

In the folk society discussion we see then writers who have an interesting theoretical idea and are groping for a sharper formal statement of their difficulties. There has come up recently a reverse episode: a writer who took an existing formalism and applied it to a sociological problem involving the properties of collectives.

Cattell introduced the term "syntality" of a collective to indicate his program of developing its "traits." This is meant to show the formal parallel with his work on personality traits.

> The term syntality has been used throughout these studies
> to refer to that in a group which corresponds to personality in

[45] Horace Miner, "The Folk-Urban Continuum," *American Sociological Review*, XVII (1952), 529–537.

[46] *Ibid.*, p. 531.

[47] *Ibid.*, p. 533.

the individual. Thus if *personality* is that formula which enables one *to predict the behavior of an individual in defined circumstances,* so syntality is that which enables one to estimate the behavior of the group as a whole in certain defined material and intergroup (international) stimulus situation.[48]

This procedure consists of collecting large numbers of data on small groups or countries. In the former case his material would come from experiments, where groups are given collective tasks to perform and are then observed in many aspects of their procedure; included are averages of the members' abilities and attitudes. In the case of countries, he would collect all available demographic data, would add information on the intellectual and economic production of the countries and supplement all this by ratings of experts on such cultural matters as the sanctity of the family. This data he would submit to factor analysis and then interpret his findings in terms of such underlying characteristics as "Conservative patriarchal solidarity" or "Bourgeois Philistinism." He stresses that some of these characteristics coincide with traditional sociological concepts, others Cattell considers new creations and still others he himself presents as very tentative. Following his own tradition, he tries to concentrate on factors which have repeatedly appeared in different studies, using different material.

Cattell writes with considerable clarity about one important point which can easily be missed by a casual reader of his papers.[49] The relation between the data he uses and the inferential group characteristics he derives is a formal one— it is provided by a mathematical model. This is quite different from the substantive relations to which his findings might point. Suppose that there exists something like a "Bourgeois Philistinism" which is different in different countries; it might be due to the history of the countries or to the racial constitution of its citizens; it might be located in their attitude or in the economic structure of the country; as a matter of fact, all these factors might play a role. There the substantive problem arises how this characteristic expresses itself in terms of a "tendency to save money from earnings," or a "low percentage of eminent men in art" or any of the other indicators, from which this trait is inferred by techniques of factor analysis. The em-

[48] Raymond B. Cattell and Marvin Adelson, "The Dimensions of Social Change in the U.S.A. as Determined by the P-Technique," *Social Forces,* XXX (1952), No. 2, p. 191.

[49] R. Cattell, "Concepts and methods in the measurement of group syntality." *Psychol. Review,* 55 (Jan. 1948).

pirical study of such "dynamic relations" is imperative. The formal analysis of the empirical data points to their importance and research procedures have to be looked for which would make such studies possible. But the formal versus the substantive aspect of the problem should not be confused.

It will have been noted that Cattell's logical position is very similar to that of MacLeod and it is therefore not surprising to find that he, too, pleads for a reconsideration of McDougall's work in modern revision. Cattell also quotes an early Austrian sociologist, Gumplowicz, as one who "outdistanced most of the psychologists of a generation later by conceiving that laws can be formed about the behavior of groups." But the convergence of thinking in this field is still further enhanced by Cattell's emphasis on different ways in which factor analysis can lead to inferential concepts. In two of his papers he uses data not from different countries, but from the same countries collected at different periods over approximately the last 100 years. According to his interpretation the same underlying characteristics are applicable. However, this might be the same problem which confronted the folk society students. There too, as we mentioned, they noticed the difference between two problems: whether at a given time a number of communities can be ranked on a continuum; and whether with increasing "urbanization" communities develop along the same continuum.

THE LOGICIANS' CONTRIBUTION

I now turn to two topics which have been treated not by social scientists, but by philosophers of science. The first is most closely related to the main point toward which this whole review has aimed. In very recent writings of a few logicians we find a discussion of "disposition concepts," a term practically identical with my own notion of "inferential concepts." The only reason I preferred the latter term is an editorial one: it focuses more on the diagnostic procedures, on the way in which inferences are made from actual observation to intended classification. Secondly, I take up and develop the notion of "property space." While it is now mainly used—explicitly or implicitly—by social scientists, it too has its origin in the work of logicians. The notion permits of more precise formulation of the problem of how to combine a variety of indicators, a topic which we have so often encountered in the preceding pages.

THE DISPOSITION CONCEPT

In recent writings of logicians, frequent discussions can be found of "disposition terms" which refer not to a directly observable characteristic, but rather to a disposition on the part of some physical objects to display specific reactions under specifiable circumstances. The definition of such terms seems to create considerable difficulties. A famous paper by Carnap on "Testability and Meaning"[50] has convinced most of his fellow philosophers that for the introduction of such a term a somewhat different kind of logical operation is needed, which he calls partial definition or *reduction*. Following Hempel's simpler presentation, the correct way to "define" the disposition term "magnetic" would be as follows:[51]

> If a small iron object is close to X at time T, then X is magnetic at time T, if and only if that object moves toward X at time T.

This definition is partial for one obvious reason. If there is no way to approach X with small iron objects, if, say, X is at the bottom of a lake, we could not determine whether it is magnetic or not.

> The [area of] indeterminacy in the meaning of a term introduced by a reduction sentence may be decreased by laying down additional reduction sentences for it which [concern the same term, but] refer to different test conditions. Thus, e.g., if the concept of electrical current had been introduced previously . . . [the first partial definition] might be supplemented by the additional reduction sentence: If x moves through a closed wire hoop at [time] I, then x is magnetic at T if and only if an electric current flows in the loop at T.[52]

[50] Rudolf Carnap, "Testability and Meaning," *Philosophy of Science*, III (1936), 419–471 and IV (1937), 2–40.

[51] Carl G. Hempel, "Fundamentals of Concept Formation in Empirical Science," *International Encyclopedia of Unified Science* (Chicago: Univ. of Chicago Press, 1952), Vol. II, No. 7, p. 26.

[52] *Ibid.*, p. 27.

Continuing this trend of thought, we find to our pleasant surprise that the modern logician is disclosing a practice of the natural sciences, which was considered to be an embarrassing practice by many social scientists. That is, they define important concepts as "intervening variables" or underlying constructs which must be inferred from a list of test situations, which may have to be used simultaneously.

A historian of science might one day try to prove that this discovery of the logical nature of disposition concepts results from the growing importance of the behavioral sciences. It is not without interest that the psychological term "disposition" is here introduced into the epistemology of the natural sciences. The connection with the problem of introspection, which was the starting point in my present review, is explicitly referred to in Carnap's paper. During an autobiographical remark on how he developed his notion of reduction he says:

> . . . The members of our (Viennese) Circle did not wish in former times to include into our scientific language a sentence corresponding to the English sentence S: "This stone is not thinking about Vienna." But at present I should prefer to construct the scientific language in such a way that it contains a sentence corresponding to S.[53]

The formal analysis of the procedure is, of course, independent of its history and its terminology. The question is whether it really covers the research procedure with which we are concerned here. To decide this I must add two more elements in Hempel's exposition. First is his distinction between the empirical and the theoretical import of concept formation.

> . . . science needs terms which not only are suited for the description of particular occurrences, but which also permit the formulation of general laws and theories. The first of these two desiderata for scientific terms calls for empirical import; the second requires, in addition, theoretical fruitfulness or theoretical import . . .
>
> In the theoretically advanced stages of science, these two aspects of scientific concept formation are inseparably connected; for as we saw, the assignment of an interpretation to a system of theoretical constructs presupposes a theoretical network of

[53] Carnap, *op. cit.*, p. 5.

general statements in which these constructs occur. *In the pre-theoretical stages of research, however, which are characterized by the prevalence of description and low-level generalization, it is possible to separate the questions of empirical and of theoretical import; and to do so explicitly may be helpful for a clarification of some rather important methodological issues.* (Emphasis supplied.)[54]

This has immediate bearing on the enterprise in which we are engaged here. Indeed I am trying to clarify how we create "underlying" concepts like traits, attitudes, group characteristics, etc., from a set of empirical observations. I shall pay little attention to the theoretical propositions and systems into which these concepts, measures and classifications enter. No one can seriously deny that most of the social sciences are in what Hempel refers to here as the "pre-theoretical stage of research." On this point, then, the Carnap explication of disposition concepts is fully transferable to our problem area.

On another point, however, we must look for an additional development. Hempel points out what is implied when we use a variety of reduction sentences. Let us go back to the example of magnetism, where attracting metal and inducing currents are used as two test situations.

But since these two test conditions are not mutually exclusive, i.e., may be jointly satisfied by a physical body, the two reduction sentences together entail the assertion that whenever this is the case, the two corresponding reactions will occur jointly, too; more specifically, (the two definitions) together imply a statement to the effect that any physical body which is near some small iron object and moves through a closed wire loop will generate a current in the loop if and only if it attracts the iron object. But this statement surely is not just a stipulation concerning the use of a new term—in fact, it does not contain the new term, 'magnetic,' at all. Hence, while a single reduction sentence may be viewed simply as a notational convention for the use of the term it introduces, this is no longer generally true of a set of two or more reduction sentences for the same term, for such a set implies, as a rule, certain consequences which have the character of empirical laws.[55]

54 Hempel, *op. cit.*, pp. 45–46.
55 *Ibid.*, pp. 27–28.

The reader, who has followed the examples in the previous sections will have noticed that there the reduction sentences are different in one respect. A "magnetic personality" is one that is *likely* to attract other people, which is *likely* to induce in them currents of enthusiasm. As I have repeatedly pointed out, the items of observations are linked to the concepts to be defined by probability relations. One other logician has seen this point very clearly.

In a short paper on "Definition and Specification of Meaning" A. Kaplan moves on from Carnap's partial definition.[56] He recapitulates the position in the following words:

> Whenever a term is introduced into a context of inquiry . . . situations . . . are described in which the term may be applied. Any such description may be called an indicator for the term. But . . . indicators assign to the application of the term under the described conditions, not a logical certainty but only a specified weight. Thus failure to interbreed is an indicator for distinctness of species; but that two animals do in fact interbreed does not logically entail that they belong to the same species but only adds some weight to the assumption.[57]

Kaplan draws his examples from biology, and occasionally from one of the social sciences. The importance of his analysis lies in his clear recognition that the relation between the "indicators" and the concept to be specified does not need to have the rigid relationship implied in the original Carnap formulation. In short, says Kaplan, "What is suggested here is that indicators be formulated in terms of some type of probable implication." He is also aware of an important consequence of this more general approach to our problem. Now if we have two test situations it is not necessary that their outcome be related by a rigid law. To turn once more to the example of magnetism, it is now sufficient to say that attracting iron objects and inducing electric current are correlated, that they frequently occur together but not necessarily always. This is precisely the notion of covariance, which we previously found to be ultimately connected with another dis-

[56] A. Kaplan, "Definition and Specification of Meaning," *Journal of Philosophy*, XLIII (1946) No. 11, p. 283; reprinted in Lazarsfeld and Rosenberg (eds.), *The Language of Social Research, op. cit.*, p. 527.
[57] *Ibid.*

position concept, the personality trait. Covariances can be of different degree, and we are free to decide what amount of covariance entitles indicators to be included in the list which serves as the basis for the specification of meaning. And what is more important, the list of specifying items need not be final, but can change as a result of improved inquiries.

While Hempel stressed that such concept formations are characteristic of an early stage of a science, Kaplan stresses the fact that they facilitate flexibility of thinking and therefore leave the road open for new developments. In Kaplan's formulation.

> This specification at any stage is a provisional one . . . We begin with indicators in terms of which the initial application of context can be confirmed. As the context of application grows, the specified meaning grows—and changes—with it. The stipulation of new indicators effects the weight of the old ones, while they in turn limit the range of choice in the stipulation. The adequacy of a particular indicator is not judged by its accordance with a predetermined concept; the new and old indicators are appraised conjointly.[58]

Thus, something that seemed to be an embarrassing shortcoming of social science concepts, such as I.Q., or introversion or cohesion, becomes the common property of a large group of concept formations in all sciences. In all such cases we have to decide what items should be included in the base of observations from which intervening variables of any kind are inferred. Kaplan adds the important point, that this choice need not be final at any point in time: the progress of theoretical thinking and empirical work might lead to changes and improvements in the selection of indicators, items of observation, basis for reduction, or whatever term is used for this part of the whole scheme.

And yet this explication of the disposition concept is too general for our purpose because it is directed toward so many applications. Today's social science concepts don't form part of a tight logical system. Their role is to summarize a variety of observations and to store them, one might say, for systematic use in a "theory" which we hope will one day develop. In our case the specification of meaning

[58] *Ibid.*, pp. 286–287.

consists mainly in making explicit what kind of observations are to be combined and for what general purposes the "variables" we form are intended. This more specific operation requires the introduction of an additional notion. Our central theme was the characterization of objects—be it people or groups—by a variety of indicators. Now this can be put in a terminology which at the first moment sounds strange but which will turn out to have considerable advantage: the objects are located in a property space.

THE PROPERTY SPACE

The term "space" has had an interesting biography. Originally it was used to connote the direct experience people had when they located things in their surroundings. Then it was seen that the points in a space could be described in algebraic terms. Now everyone is acquainted with the notion of "coordinates." Starting, say, with the corner of a room, any other location in this room can be indicated by saying how high up it is from the floor and how far it is from the two walls which meet at the original corner. To each point corresponds a triplet of distances. This leads to the extension of the notion of dimension. While the points in the room require three data for their location, on a blackboard we can work with only two coordinates—which is identical with saying that the face of the blackboard, or any other plans, has two dimensions. Correspondingly four-dimensional sets become easy to grasp. The best known is the space-time continuum. A bug in a room can be characterized by the point at which it rests and the amount of time it has been there.

There developed finally an inversion of terminology. Whenever a set of objects is characterized by a multiple of data one would talk of them in terms of points in a space. This space would have as many dimensions as the data needed to characterize each of the objects under consideration. The advantage of this terminology is that it brings out formal similarities between materials which would be overlooked because we habitually give them different representation. Take as an example two students who were given three tests, one in each language (L), social science (S), and natural science (N). Assume their test profiles look as follows:

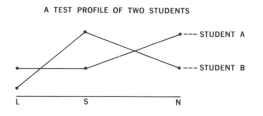

Now the test scores are three groups of data and therefore can be considered coordinates in a three-dimensional space. To each test corresponds an axis and the two students now become two points.

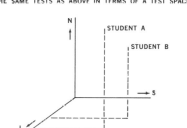

Returning to the two profiles, it is a reasonable question to ask how they can be compared. If a series of such profiles were given, could we order them according to their similarity to each other? "Similarity" is, of course, a vague term and can be "measured" in a variety of ways. But the space representation of the preceding illustration suggests that the distance between the two points A and B would be an appropriate index.[59] Suppose further that a large number

---

[59] This has been explored in detail by Lee J. Cronebach and G. C. Gleser "Assessing Similarities Between Profiles," *Psychological Bulletin* (1953), L, pp. 456–473.

of profiles are studied and we find their corresponding "points" in the test space bunched in several parts of the space while the other parts are fairly "empty:" This would lend to a definition of "types," which would be applicable to a large variety of materials.[60]

So far our examples have all still assumed that the basic data which characterize our objects are in some way quantified. But this is not necessary and with this last step the most general notion of property space is reached. The dimensions may, for example, be rank numbers of merely positions in a preestablished list. All people with Christian, middle, and family names can be put into a three-dimensional "initial space" in which each dimension has 26 "classes," the letters of the alphabet. Therefore, a man with the parameters (4, 1, 3) would have the initials D.A.C., and David Arthur Chester and Donald Avery Casey would belong in the same "point" in this set of objects. In other cases, the properties might well be dichotomies, i.e., attributes which take on two values only. Suppose, for example, people are classified according to whether they are male or female; native or foreign born; above or below 35 years of age; residing in a city below 100,000 population or above. This would provide a space of four dimensions but on each of them, objects could only have two distinguishable positions; or to put it still another way, each of the four coordinates could take on two values only. The whole "space" would therefore consist of $2 \times 2 \times 2 \times 2 = 16$ "points."[61] This space will be of basic importance for our final discussion.

It is important to acquire a certain facility in adapting a variety of subject matters to a property space representation. Suppose, e.g., that the administrator of a housing project is concerned with the "state of occupancy" for the ten buildings of the project. This term might correspond to a one-dimensional space if the administrator thinks of the total number of apartments rented. It might be ten-dimensional if the vacancies in each building are to be distinguished; then each building is one dimension and the number of occupied apartments in each building is one of the ten properties by which the "state of occupancy" is characterized. A manufacturer might wish to compare the state of

[60] *See* Carl G. Hempel and Paul Oppenheim, *Der Typusbegriff im Lichte der neuen Logik* (Leiden: A W. Sythoff Publishers, 1936).

[61] Paul F. Lazarsfeld, "The Algebra of Dichotomous Systems," in Herbert Solomon (ed.), *Studies in Item Analysis and Prediction* (Stanford: Stanford University press, 1961). [Footnote added for this collection.]

satisfaction existing in a number of shops through the use of a three-dimensional space; total number of complaints expressed in each shop, number of topics on which complaints are expressed, and proportion of workers in each shop who express complaints. The number of properties and selection of indicators to be used to represent a vague term like "satisfaction" is a substantive problem. The notion of property space, however, applies to whatever decision is made, even when the decision is not explicitly stated.[62]

THE RELATION OF MANIFEST TO LATENT PROPERTY SPACE

Many of the authors reviewed seemed to ask: What is friendship, prudence, cohesion or satisfaction? Actually these writers visualize themselves as being confronted with concrete cases of "friendship" or "prudence" and want to know how to recognize them, how to relate them to each other, and so on. If I could ask these writers some further questions, they would say something like this: They want to distinguish "types of friendship," or "degrees of prudence," or they want to distinguish between "friendship" and "love," or between "prudence" and "distrust." From a research point of view, these are all problems of classification, although of a special kind. "Measurement" is also a special case of classification; it is irrelevant at this point to distinguish "measurement" from "ordering" and other classification devices.

The reader should have no difficulty in seeing in the many preceding examples that the terms mentioned, such as "traits," "social facts," "disposition concepts," etc., are really special cases of classificatory characteristics. They have one thing in common: they are *intended* characteristics; that is, they are ways in which we *want* to organize a set of objects under investigation. This locating of "objects" (individuals, groups, social relationships) cannot be done directly in the cases we have discussed. We are dealing with *latent characteristics*, in the sense that their parameters must somehow be derived from

[62] For further examples of such property spaces and their applications to social research problems, see Allen H. Barton, "The Concept of Property Space in Social Research," in Lazarsfeld and Rosenberg (eds.), *The Language of Social Research* (Glencoe: Free Press, 1955), p. 40 ff.

manifest observations. The terms manifest and latent have no other connotation here beyond the distinction between data directly accessible to the investigator (manifest), and parameters (latent) which in some way must be inferred from the manifest data.

The matter can be reformulated in the following way: Empirical observations locate our objects in a manifest property space. But this is not what we are really interested in. We want to know their location in a latent property space. Our problem is to infer this latent space from the manifest data, and this inference is identical with what before was described as the diagnostic procedure. The advantage of this reformulation lies in the fact that we can now raise the following question: why do we give preference to latent property space? There are three reasons for this.

a) Consider the kind of manifest observations the social scientist usually works with. They are qualitative data: answers to questionnaires, existence of certain things (does a city have an opera house, has a person voted or not, etc.). But we would like to work with more continuous variables so that objects can be ordered and differences, if possible measured. We would like to talk about the cultural level of a city or the degree of political interest in an individual. It will turn out that the dimensions of a latent property space have indeed this character of continuity which the data of the manifest space usually don't have.

b) Our manifest observations are likely to have very many dimensions: a questionnaire contains numerous questions; the usual way to assess the purchasing power of an area requires the consideration of numerous data like taxes paid, number of registered cars and telephones, volume of retail trade, etc. But all these data are collected for the final purpose of classifying objects within very few dimensions. Most often we try to achieve one-dimensional schemes, especially in attitude research; or we try to reduce the social and economic world of a person to two dimensions like power and prestige. Again it turns out that latent property spaces are likely to have only a few dimensions as compared to the high dimensionality of manifest observations.

c) In any empirical classification guided by conceptual considerations we try to overcome the accidental elements inherent in the use of indicators. Suppose we want to order people according to how they feel about the role of government in economic affairs. We might ask them a series of questions as to public ownership of railroads, mines, banks, etc. It is reasonable to assume that the more someone favors laissez faire the fewer of these items he will answer in an assertive way (for public ownership). Still we know that many individual idiosyncrasies will creep into the answers. A strong laissez faire person has just read about a mine accident and under this impact he gives an assertive answer to the mine item; a strong interventionist happens to know a very fine bank president and therefore excludes the bank item from his list of assertive responses. In the manifest property space we are at the mercy of these vagaries. But in the latent space, as we shall see, we can take them into account and thus achieve a more "purified" classification.

Actually these three points are interrelated. We achieve continuity in the latent space by reducing the number of dimensions from the manifest space. We buy, so to say, continuity and pay with dimensions. We correct for accidental elements by assigning a mediating role to the latent positions. They are derived from the totality of all manifest data and therefore permit adjustments in any part of the manifest space. Obviously this is not the place to follow up all these ideas into their mathematical formulation. For my concluding remarks it is enough if the reader gets a feeling of the way we have now formulated the basic problem and the direction of any answer:

The purpose of many concepts is to locate people or social objects into an intended system of classification. This system is called a latent space. But what we actually observe is a multidimensional classification of the same objects by a large number of indicators which form a manifest space. The reader of this essay is asked to take one thing on faith: it is possible to infer from an object's position in the manifest indicators space its position in the conceptual latent space. This transformation is designated as "latent structure analysis."[63] This being accepted, the claim is made that many problems of "measurement" and operational translation of concepts can be classified and organized by this basic idea of manifest and latent spaces and the connection beween them.

Finally the limitations of this whole trend of thought needs to be acknowledged. My general concern is how are "variables" in the social

---

[63] The pertinent techniques are now available in a publication by Paul F. Lazarsfeld and Neil W. Henry, *Latent Structure Analysis* (Boston, Mass.: Houghton Mifflin Company, 1968). [Footnote added for this collection.]

sciences formed today? What do authors mean when they talk about the cohesion of a group, the anxiety of a person? How can their conceptual intentions be translated into adequate research procedures? We have *not* discussed how a better developed social science of the future might one day develop and use these concepts.

The limitations I have imposed on my topic are best seen if I consider for a moment the problem of prediction, which if I didn't mention it would be brought in by every critic. Obviously even in what Hempel calls the "pre-scientific" stage of our work, we use concepts in order to arrive at generalizations and, therefore, implicitly in order to predict. Many decades hence some of our concepts will have fallen by the wayside and others will have stood up under the ultimate criterion: did they contribute to, and will they fit into, a large body of laws and theories. Today we are still far from this goal. We are experimenting with concepts for their own sake; we are testing which, of many imbedded in our humanistic tradition, permit a transfer into more precise language. We want to know what gains and losses ensue from such translations. Occasionally, as in the case of Durkheim's suicide study, the desire to interpret leads us to introduce new concepts for which we then need, if possible, more direct "measurements." One can question whether this is a necessary and productive stage in the development of the social sciences, but no one can deny—and this review has shown it—that it is of dominant concern in the intellectual scene of today. Its clarification is bound to be helpful.

A very important question, but a different one, is whether these concepts, if translated into "variables" of some kind, help to predict other variables. Obviously no one would waste time on concepts to which he doesn't impute, at least tacitly, some predictive merit. The correctness of his assumption then becomes a matter of research different from the intrinsic analysis of his concept and its relations to the set of its indicators. A concrete example might help to sharpen the distinction. In marriage studies, length of engagement has been investigated as a predictor of happiness. Here we want to predict happiness and therefore we need to classify actual marriages by some criterion of success. Such a criterion will usually be a composite of various indicators, as, for example, how the two married people feel, how often they quarrel, how much time they spend together, and so on. The way this criterion is built has to be decided by logical, psychological and statistical considerations that can be the topic of much controversy; but we certainly cannot regress to still another criterion which marital happiness is in turn supposed to predict.[64]

The question is sometimes raised as to whether such a procedure does improve the validity of a concept. If by that is meant that we shall know more about its predictive usefulness, the answer is no. Only by relating a variable to *other* variables can this question be answered. Latent structure analysis—as even the name indicates—deals with the intrinsic nature of a concept and not with its relation to other concepts. On the other hand one can raise the question of the value of such formal analysis in the total picture of scientific progress. To answer the question in general is the business of the professional logician. But it is easy to give concrete cases to show that our formulations dispel some fuzziness which marred earlier statements of the problem.

One well-known study showed that people with authoritarian personalities are likely to discriminate against ethnic minorities. To single out authoritarian personalities a series of questions were used to see how punitive the respondent felt in a variety of areas. Obviously, it would have been possible to include aggression against ethnic minorities as part of the indicator set for an authoritarian personality rather than consider it a separate concept and variable. The decision on such matters has to be guided mainly by substantive and theoretical considerations. But one auxiliary criterion might come from latent structure analysis. By putting both sets of indicators together the latent space could turn out to be very complex. Each set kept separate might be unidimensional, which has many advantages. Still, there are situations in which multidimensional latent spaces, such as latent typologies, are justifiable; therefore, the formal analysis cannot completely guide the research decision. A second example may be taken from Lloyd Warner's division of American communities into six classes. He uses a variety of indicators to allocate people into these classes. Now, a special kind of latent structure analysis permits a decision as to whether to a given set of indicators there corresponds a latent space with the population located as six discrete points. But if the test contradicts Warner's assumption, one of two things can be done; 1) either

---

[64] The difference between intrinsic analysis of variables and their use for predictive purposes has been clearly stressed in Louis Guttman, "The Quantification of a Class of Attributes: A Theory and Method for Scale Construction," in P. Horst, *et al.*, *The Prediction of Personal Adjustment* (New York: Social Science Research Council, 1941), pp. 319–348.

abandon the six class theory or, 2) look for other indicators which keep the theory intact and permit the actual allocation of people to the six classes. Once again the formal analysis cannot decide the issue but it can clarify the relation between conceptualization and empirical research.

It was the purpose of these concluding remarks not only to warn the reader against undue expectations as to substantive results, but also to forestall unjustified skepticism toward the role of formalization in the total scheme of scientific inquiry. I wanted to make a contribution to a methodological problem, and not to the substantive store of the social sciences. I hope the historical introduction has shown how the problem has been with us for a long time, and that review was sorely needed.

CHAPTER 2

HISTORICAL NOTES ON THE EMPIRICAL STUDY OF ACTION: AN INTELLECTUAL ODYSSEY

It has often been said that each generation rewrites history in the light of its own contemporary problems. In the same way, one might say that each generation of psychologists has rewritten "theories of action." At some periods and in some contexts, the study of action has been considered the very center of psychological analysis; at other times and in other contexts it has received no attention at all.

One very good indication of varying interests in the study of action can be found in the psychology textbooks of different periods. Invariably, American textbooks written during the 1920's included a chapter on the "psychology of action." Such a section usually contained a graph in which a line from left to right represented the passage of time. This line would be divided into a number of sectors denoting different phases of the "activity in progress" (*M. Bentley, 1925; R. Woodworth, 1923*). Although different authors distinguished different numbers of phases, there were always at least three: one indicated the beginning of the action—a task is taken on, or an intention is acquired; the middle phase dealt with elements which push the intention forward; and the final phase referred to the resolution or consummation of the act. Usually, also, the relative importance of various factors at different phases of the activity were considered and discussed—the motives of the actor, outside influences impinging on him, and his information about the world around him. It was taken for granted that

Unpublished manuscript completed in 1958 and circulated in mimeographed form.

one or two examples would make clear what the word "acting" referred to: the man going to town to mail a letter, the child exploring a toy, the bird flying to a rock. By the middle of the century (with the exception of Woodworth's textbook on which we will comment later), the examples, the topic, let alone sections devoted to it, completely disappeared. The term "action" does not seem to appear in the recent textbook of H. Garrett (*1950*), or Hilgard (*1953*). It may be that we have up to now looked into the wrong textbooks and that the social psychologists have maintained interest in this problem. But this, again, is not the case. If we look at Krech and Crutchfield (*1948*), Sherif (*1948*), and T. Newcomb (*1950*), nowhere do we find an explicit treatment of human action or a mention of the term in the index.

This is a puzzling situation, and it raises the question of what has happened to the study of action. One answer might derive from the nature of the problem and the intellectual mood of psychologists in the period between the two World Wars. Anyone who has tried to define action has had reference to its goal-directed character. Whichever writer discusses action, it is defined as a behavior sequence deriving from a purpose of the actor which he or at least the investigator understands as meaningful. Even Warren's *Dictionary of Psychology* (*1934*), which attempts to do justice to all possible theoretical positions, defines action as "a general term for all movements or patterns of movements with which certain conscious patterns are or have been correlated." If the notion of action requires some reference to consciousness, then it is not surprising that in the decades which saw the intellectual dominance of behaviorism there were not many scholars in the United States willing to approach such an apparently unrewarding subject matter.

Correlative with the general character of this trend was a more specific one. When Karl Bühler commented (*1927*) on the ambivalent attitudes of social scientists to the problem of action, he noted:

> Action is a historical, or more precisely a biographical concept. . . . Every human action has its history (Aktgeschichte)—sometimes a long and rich, sometimes a short and poor one. Raskolnikov needed weeks from the first emergence of the idea to the final (consummatory) act. (In other cases) the theoretical psychologist has to consider seconds and fractions of seconds, if he wants to analyze a quick decision, which immediately turns into execution.[1]

[1] Karl Bühler, *Die Krise der Psychologie* (Jena, 1927), p. 52.

Again during a period of stress on an oversimplified image of operational definitions, aversion against such a seemingly amorphous concept should not surprise anyone.

The situation would be very simple if it were all a matter of intellectual fashion. Now that most of us concede that introspection in one form or another is here to stay (*E. Boring, 1953*), and that "partial definitions" are alleviating our logical conscience (*A. Kaplan, 1946*) we would expect that the study of action will slowly be resumed. And, indeed, a president of the American Psychology Association, in his presidential address of 1951, placed the matter on the top of the agenda for the profession. Robert Sears (*1951*) states his conviction in not uncertain terms

> . . . What is needed at present is a single behavior science, with theoretical structure that will account for the *actions* and the changes of *potentiality for actions* both of individuals and of groups . . . action is clearly more significant than perception or traits . . . actions are the events of most importance, and actions are most available to observation and measurement . . . there is no virtue in a descriptive statement that a person or a class of persons possesses such-and-such a trait or need unless that statement is part of a larger one that concludes with a specification of a kind of action to be performed.[2]

And clearly Sears' concerns are with just the kinds of situations which interest us here. What he wants is a theory of action to deal, for example, with "whether a marriage will terminate in divorce or whether citizens will buy bonds or vote for a Congressman" etc. He stresses that "even those changes commonly interpreted as perceptual, such as art and music appreciation, are evidence in the form of choices as to where to go, what to look at, what to listen to."

In this connection, I advisedly speak of a concern, and not of a problem. The topic of how people make choices between available alternatives is such a broad one, having the character of a general intellectual program, that we cannot derive from it directly what might be the appropriate ways of empirical study and theory formation. This raises a second and more important question: what can really be meant by a theory of action? Perhaps no one can answer this question at the moment. But we certainly cannot overlook the fact that the need for

---

[2] Robert R. Sears, "A Theoretical Framework for Personality and Social Behavior," *American Psychologist*, (1951), pp. 467 ff. (Presidential address).

an answer was once very paramount and has somehow been thwarted. Now that we seem to have a second chance, we might easily be in for another disappointment if the lessons of the past are not taken to heart. Indeed, as I shall try to show, there seems to have been a set of additional difficulties beyond the academic temper of the times, which have stood in the way of successful and continuous development. These have been partly accidental in nature, connected with the disruption of two World Wars and the transfer of the center of gravity from European to American locations of research. In addition, however, an interesting intellectual difficulty has appeared.

After an initial frontal attack on the study of human action, the main students concerned each selected a different aspect of the total concern, and the work of each has developed without any careful effort at integration. It is true that in learning theory, as well, there are various schools and controversies, but these controversies themselves show the existence of a common core of interest and an effort to reconcile available facts and methods. This has not been the case in the empirical study of action. Therefore, as I follow these different trends, I shall organize our attention roughly around *three questions:* 1) Which elements in the general concern with human action have been selected by an author or school as a specific problem? 2) What contributions were they able to make? 3) What prevented them from integrating their work with that of others into a more general whole? Because this review covers the turbulent times of the last few decades, we will find that the difficulties that were met were partly intellectual in nature and partly social. The slowdown of academic work in Europe and the shift of general emphasis to the American scene will turn out to be important in various forms. I shall, therefore, give more space to writings which are not available in English translation and treat with more brevity literature which is easily available here and which has become part of American textbooks.

THE WÜRZBURG SCHOOL AS AN EARLY MATRIX FOR THE STUDY OF HUMAN ACTION

The empirical study of action began very vigorously at the start of this century when a group of German psychologists, known later as the Würzburg school, went about finding out, "what happens when people do something." This was part of a general tendency to transcend the tradition of Wundt and to submit the "higher mental processes," especially thought and will, to experimental investigations. The accepted method was still the sharply controlled laboratory experiment. The stimuli, however, were intended to elicit complex reactions and free rein was given to detailed introspective reports of the subjects and interpretation of these reports by the experimenters.

The basic pattern of the experiments was as follows:

1) The subjects were informed of the task they were to perform.
2) A 'ready' signal was given, indicating to the subject that the experiment was about to proceed.
3) One or a few seconds after the 'ready' signal, a stimulus was given to the subject and he had to carry out the task which had been agreed upon in advance.

The stimuli to which the subjects were exposed were of various kinds. In the early experiments the subjects were instructed only to add two simple figures which would appear before them or to find a rhyme to a nonsense syllable. Later the number of stimuli, and the possible responses, were increased and varying combinations of uncertainties between stimulus and action were introduced. The whole field was so new at this time that any finding was of interest. The reaction-time was found to be clearly related to the complexity of the task. If letters were to be substituted in nonsense syllables, some group of letters seemed to have greater propinquity than others. However, most of the attention of these investigators was given to analyzing the reports of the subjects. It turned out, for instance, that the intention to solve the problem was most clearly experienced in the "before period" between the 'ready' signal and the actual exposure to the stimulus (step 2). Once the stimulus was exposed, the reaction followed automatically without the intention being experienced again. From this derived the famous doctrine of the determining tendencies, which is so closely related to the subsequent history of the concept of attitudes (*G. Allport, 1935*). It is not easy today to reconstruct what the members of the Würzburg school would have considered the main purpose of their work. The transfer of experimental procedures to higher processes was certainly one main motive, as mentioned before. There were also involved discussions around the question of what are the basic elements of mental experiences and we would not be too interested in these discussions today. Very characteristic and fruitful for our present discussion, however, was the intense interest of the Würzburg group in the sequences of concrete acts and the laws by which their course is regulated. It is this broad approach which made the Würzburg school the matrix for a number of the specific developments which we are about to describe. And it is this unity of approach which has regained significance.

Because of the important historical position of the Würzburg school, it is regrettable that its work is accessible to the American reader only in fragmentary form. Boring (*1950*) has given a very insightful, brief description of their work. There he makes the important statement as to how "it became clear that the problems of thought and action are essentially the same . . . the key to thought as well as to action is to be found in the preparation of the subject." However, this dual interest of the Würzburg school in thought and in action has led to a singular difficulty in most other secondary reports of their work. They can almost be considered projective tests reflecting the interests of the reporter. For example, we have the first textual translation of some of the original writings by Ach and Bühler in an annotated reader on *Organization and Pathology of Thought* (*D. Rapaport, 1952*). Since the editor's interest is centered on thinking, he apologizes for one of his authors, pointing out that although his "discussion is couched in terms of action peculiarly, the appearance in consciousness and the effects of thoughts are the subject matter of this discussion." On the other hand, the American reader might turn to Lindworsky's textbook on *Experimental Psychology* (*1930*); it is the only translated text which was written in the spirit of the Würzburg experiments, even if the author did not quite belong to this tradition. Lindworsky's own work was mainly in the field of will, and therefore he includes the Würzburg school in the section of his book dealing with "volitional life."[3] He, too, apologizes, indicating that the reader can hope "to gain a better understanding of the experiences of attention, since the most important of these experiences may be explained only as expressions of

[3] Johannes Lindworsky, *Experimental Psychology*, translated by Harry R. De Selva (New York, 1930), pp. 303–338.

volition." As far as thinking is concerned, the most detailed secondary source at this moment, as far as I know, is Humphrey (*1951*). The most thorough review of the volitional aspect of the whole tradition is available only in German. N. Ach (*1935*) published a 200-page review of the experimental work on the psychology of will, carried on during the first third of this century. I shall repeatedly refer to this comprehensive text.

Beginning about 1910 the Würzburg school tradition was developed essentially in three directions, carried on partly by the members of the group itself, their students, and those who were indirectly influenced, and partly by scholars who wrote in opposition and yet were clearly marked by the Würzburg stamp.

The main three trends can be easily understood if the original experimental scheme is meaningfully enlarged. The first step, the reader will remember, consisted in the subject being given a task by the experimenter. If we now substitute for the experimenter other sources of goals—society, the past experience of an individual—this branches out into what is usually referred to today as the problem of motivation. In this the main attention of the student is directed toward the question of the nature and origin of goals. The second step was initiated by the 'ready' signal of the investigator. At this point, the intention to act was set up in the subject, and the determining role of this intention all through the rest of the act was one of the main topics of the Würzburg school. A considerable amount of subsequent work remained concentrated on studying what happens with intentions, once they are set up, whatever the broader motivation behind them might be. In the third step, the final reaction of the subject was released through exposure to the stimulus. This is easily broadened in the study of the influences and occasions which transform an intention into a final consummatory phase of an action. The three trends, then, which we shall now exemplify, are characterized by their emphasis either on the general problem of *goals* (motivation) or on the successive transformation of *intentions*, or, finally, on the *influences* which seem to push the act forward to its final conclusion. The three case studies which seem to illustrate best these three points are Karl and Charlotte Bühler, for the first; Kurt Lewin, especially in his relation to Ach, for the second; and, for the third, a type of research which is not easily identified but which will become apparent when examples are cited.

ACCENT ON GOAL/ KARL AND CHARLOTTE BÜHLER

Among the members of the Würzburg group Karl Bühler's early
work *(1913)* went furthest in the effort to study complex thought
processes. In the course of this work, however, he became the one who
maintained and strengthened most the interrelation between the psychology of thought, on the one hand, and of will and action, on the
other hand. In retrospect, he formulated the situation as follows:

> In a complex arithmetical expression we have numbers, on the
> one hand, and operational signs, like addition and multiplica-
> tion, on the other hand; in the same way, when we observe an
> artist or a craftsman, we notice that he works with material
> but that he performs certain techniques and manipulations on it.
> This is essentially what has slowly been brought out: in think-
> ing, as well as in any other activities, *we need a certain number
> of operations and these are the ones which are the crucial ele-
> ments for a systematic analysis.* (Emphasis supplied.)[4]

The interrelation between materials and operations has probably
remained one of Bühler's central themes. It first led him into his major
contributions on the perception of color and form. In both studies the
emphasis was on the fact that perception depends not only upon what
is presented to the subject but also what he does with it; these ideas
led through the experiments of Brunswik and his students directly to
the modern interest in motivated *and directed* perception, a topic that
cannot properly be pursued here. But parallel to this work, Karl Bühler
also turned to child psychology to a rather far-reaching development
in our field of interest (1930). The first paragraph of his book contains
a sentence which is revealing in many ways. Bühler describes as his purpose the study of how the child becomes a human being (Menschwerd-
ung). The word Mensch in German has the connotation of man, with
special emphasis on the spiritual and creative elements which distinguish
him from nonhuman beings. Bühler was obviously not satisfied with
merely describing the motivational elements in perception. Through
the study of the child he wanted to find out how the capacity to form
and reform the outside world came about. The book accordingly ends
with a chapter entitled, "Elements of a General Theory of Mental Development." Here, again, we must remember that the word "geistig,"

---

[4] Bühler, *op. cit.;* a free and condensed translation of page 13.

translated here as mental, has a very broad connotation in German, implying everything which is characteristic of the mature human being.[5]

The scene was thus set about as follows. The mature human being is characterized by creative activity on physical and social objects. The main task of psychology is to study the origin and development of this faculty. A theory of action is therefore needed, the center of which would be the proper understanding of goals: the main empirical source for such a task ought to be developmental and comparative psychology. Bühler's theory of mental development was at that time a variation around the theme of three consecutive steps through which the springs of action progressed. They might be translated as satiation, play and achievement. First the child is interested only in the intake of food, it craves satiation; then the exercise of its developing faculties provides "functioning-pleasure"; finally, work on objects becomes an additional source of enjoyment. Three levels of activities, in the narrowest sense, correspond to these three basic relationships: mere reflex action, learning by trial and error, and finally, creative intelligence.

Ten years after Karl Bühler's book appeared, his wife and close collaborator, Charlotte Bühler, published her book *Childhood and Adolescence* (1927). In this, the idea of phases of development had become dominant, and the central theme deals with how the ability for mature human action (Handlung) slowly grows out of the first primitive, and mainly physiological, actions of the newborn infant. Again, there is development from mere receptive gratifications to the enjoyment of one's own functioning, and, finally, the goal-directed organized performance is in the center of the analysis. The theme is systematically enlarged by a distinction between the three main object areas toward which these activities can be directed: things, people, and what we would today term "culture," that is, ideas, norms and institutions. Charlotte Bühler thus distinguishes "phases" which are construed from an interweaving of these steps toward maturity with these three sectors of the world. In an early phase, for example, the typical child would have maturity in dealing with inanimate things, but would be on the level of mere functioning in talking about his future occupation.

---

[5] Linguists tell us that the root of the German word Mensch can also be found in the English word mind, the German word Meinung, and even in Minne, which is an older German term for love. It is important to remember that the German terminology has to some degree retained this consonance of meaning.

In a next phase (around 8 to 13 years), the child reaches a certain maturity in his personal relationships with people, in beginning to integrate himself into groups in the role of member. But it still "plays" at responsibilities which the later citizen has in his community. Finally, in adolescence, maturation begins to cover cultural and institutional subject matters.

Five years later this basic idea was further extended in Charlotte Bühler's book on *The Course of Human Life as a Psychological Problem (1933)*. Her central problem was as follows. The adolescent has the first glimpses of the notion of devoting his life to an objective, transcending his own individual existence. What was the further development of this goal striving? Charlotte Bühler introduces the concept of "self-determination" meaning the striving toward a selected goal, implying the individual's intent to dedicate himself and his feeling that he is meant to accomplish certain specific things, a feeling which in the case of some people assumes even the conviction of being destined to a certain role or development.

This "self-determination" toward an end in life begins as a prepatory, experimental and preliminary one in what is called life's second phase (about 15 to 25 years); this is followed by a definite self-determination in the third phase of life (25 to 45 (50) years) in which the individual usually settles down with a definite occupation, family, home; in the fourth phase (45 (50) to 60 (65) years), the individual evaluates the success, results, products of his striving and often experiences the so-called "climacteric" self-reproaches about his failures which made him fall short of his own expectations and goals. This self-evaluation may lead on to increased feverish endeavors to bring in the harvest as envisaged in years before or it may lead on to resignation, despair, actual breakdown if it seems "too late" to change the unfavorable course of events. The final fifth phase of a contemplative retrospection on life, paralleling the initial first phase before self-determination to goals sets in, occurs in this harrassed time and civilization only with those who voluntarily or by necessity will disengage themselves in their late years from the struggle of goal-striving to live in retirement from life.

This development of the individual's self-determination through life is, in Charlotte Bühler's theoretical system, shown in relationship with a psychobiological process of maturation. Based on the biological facts of growth, reproduction and decline, she defines phases of expansive, stabilized and restrictive growth and reproduction processes which represent the underlying psychosomatic tendencies to the self-determination changes.

As far as the empirical study of action is concerned then, the work of Karl and Charlotte Bühler led to a system of categories by which goals of human action could be systematically described. Before turning to the implication of this, a digression is necessary into the source and variety of data with which they and their students worked.

DATA AND CATEGORIES FOR ANALYZING HUMAN GOALS   By the end of the first World War Karl Bühler had reached the conviction that the analysis of human action would be the focal topic of a modern psychology. But while at first it seemed to grow naturally out of the Würzburg effort to study "higher mental processes," two intellectual developments had come about in the meantime which made the program appear more complicated. This is what Karl Bühler describes, as the contemporary constructive "crisis of psychology" (1927). On the one side there now were the behaviorists who made it increasingly difficult to speak of perceptions, intentions, or any of the other concepts of goal-directedness which were indispensable for the definition of an act. While most German psychologists were immediately hostile to behaviorism, on philosophical grounds, Bühler from the beginning hailed the contributions which might be expected from the "Americans," a term he used synonymously with behaviorists. There was still another attack, however, against classical German tradition, coming from a movement of which Bühler himself says, "No one talks about it except the Germans, and even among them it is still very controversial."

At the end of the 19th century, Dilthey had become very impatient with experimental psychology, as developed by Wundt and his students. He was one of those who wanted to see the complex problems of mental life investigated, but he wanted it done quickly, as opposed to the Würzburg scholars who were willing to slowly extend the scope of experimental work. Basically, Dilthey's suggestion was to take human products, such as art or philosophical writings, and to analyze their structure in order to derive from it psychological knowledge about those who created these works. In principle, this is the idea which, in more modest form, underlies the use of projective methods in psychology today. It seems justified, therefore, to refer to this whole

movement as projective psychology, although at the time it was called
"geisteswissenschaftliche" psychology. Dilthey mainly wrote of intellectual and artistic products, while later on, institutions and physical objects in cultural use were included as desirable sources.[6] Bühler's
position was as follows: There are three aspects under which human
action can be seen. The aspect of the private experience of the actor,
to wit introspection; the aspect of his observable behavior in a concrete situation, which meant, of course, behaviorism; and the aspect
of the product brought about by the act, projective-psychology. His
effort in the *Crisis* was to show that all three aspects are indispensable
for a study of human action, and that all forces should concentrate on
clarifying the relation between these three aspects and the corresponding sources of data.[7]

This general approach led to a very catholic use of a broad range
of data. Continuous observations were carried out, with the help of
Rockefeller funds, at a central home maintained by the municipality
of Vienna for families unable to take care of their children. The study
of adolescents was facilitated by a large collection of diaries which,
incidentally, are kept by young people in Europe much more than in
this country. Biographies of adults were amply available in the literature for upper-class and professional groups. They were supplemented
by elaborate case studies collected in old age homes. Questionnaires for
adolescents were somewhat in the Stanley Hall tradition, collected with
the official cooperation of schools and of labor unions. Students were
trained to keep day-long records of the interactions and conversations
within families in the course of their normal routine. The material thus
collected was analyzed in terms of categories that formed what might
be called today "biographical functionalism." In his early writings Karl
Bühler had already begun to stress how the child's play seemed to train
him for performances needed in later life. In a recent summary, Charlotte Bühler (1951) stressed that "a need at any given moment is not

---

[6]   We shall return to this point in a later context.

[7]   It would be highly desirable if Bühler's *Crisis* were translated into English,
for two reasons. This book reflects excellently the very perceptive reaction of
one who saw the clash of three intellectual traditions, and his analysis of the situation would ensure against the possibility of historical provincialism on the part
of modern students. The book also contains some very important ideas on the
logic of projective psychology (especially pages 137–165).

only related to that moment but also to the future . . . it implies in its complex tension pattern a dynamic relationship to a partially fore-shadowed future."[8]

Only a few of the basic categories can be mentioned here. I have already referred to the distinction between actions performed in response to outside stimuli and expansive actions, in which the initiative comes from the acting subject—the distinction, as it were, between satiation and self-realization. Another distinction is between those goals which are essentially taken over from the environment and those which grow out of the maturation process of the subject. Here, it will be remembered, the notion of maturation was so conceived that it could be applied throughout the life span. Actions were distinguished according to whether they grew out of the need of the moment or whether they had a conscious anticipatory character, taking into account future situations.

Where do we locate the contributions which the Bühlers made to the empirical study of action, conceived as a broad programmatic concern? The answer can be attempted in three ways. First, looking at the matter in their own terms, the emphasis is on broad, almost philosophical implications. When Karl Bühler, in the first edition of his book on child psychology, write his chapter on "The First Act of Wills," he implied the hope that such studies would in the long run contribute something to the "foundation for a moral or legal evaluation of human activities." In the introduction to the third edition, he stated apologetically that new editions were needed so rapidly that he was still unable to add a summarizing chapter on how his analysis is related to the crucial problems of norms and values in modern society. From the biographical work of Charlotte Bühler it is fairly clear, however, where such a development would lead. We are all acquainted with efforts of social psychologists to develop tables of basic needs, close to the biological foundations of the human being. It could be said that the work of the Bühlers was partly directed toward *developing a table of ultimate needs characteristic for the mature human being.* Empirical studies of values have recently moved toward the center of interest for social scientists. In this country they have mainly been patterned along the

[8] Charlotte Bühler, "Maturation and Motivation," *Personality,* 1 (1951), p. 206 ff.

lines of statistical attitude studies or along the lines of generalization from anthropological and historical material. The emphasis on the developmental and biographical approach to the empirical study of values adds an additional technical dimension which deserves careful attention.[9]

We can look next at the empirical studies that were done at the Vienna Psychological Institute. When the Bühlers left Vienna in 1938, a considerable number of biographical studies were under way. Some of their findings were ably summarized by Else Frenkel (*1936*) who was Charlotte Bühler's main assistant in the supervision of these investigations. Special attention should be given to the studies cited there on the appearance of the notion of duty in the diaries of adolescents, and on the statistical shift from the notion of needs to the notion of fulfillment in the correspondence of adults. A study based on interviews with unsuccessful suicides has since appeared in an English edition. The investigator used the list of ultimate needs developed under Charlotte Bühler's direction, which, for this specific purpose, were divided into those that belonged in the personal sphere of life; such as friendship, love, home, reputation, and so forth; and those that belonged into what she called the material spheres of life, including income, health, occupational success, and so forth. Her conclusion was that if losses to the individual occurred in such combinations that adequate compensations become impossible, then "the individual's living space suffers a maximum restriction and then may lead to catastrophe. Suicides usually happen when such difficulties occur in at least one subjective personal sphere and at least one objective practical one."[10] Cross-analyzed against this typology of human needs was biographical information. The various difficulties were likely to show up at characteristic phases of the life cycle, and their effect could very well be a latent one, coming into play at a later period when conjoined with added difficulties. A series of similar investigations of occupational choice was recently reviewed and further developed by Eli Ginzberg (*1952*). This is probably one of the main American investigations that consciously

---

[9] It is interesting to note that Charlotte Bühler turned to psychotherapy in this country. But even when she summarized her work in this context, her culminating section is called "The Problem of the Aim of Life." (Unpublished manuscript.)

[10] Margarette Andicz, *Suicide and the Meaning of Life* (London, 1947), p. 158, English edition.

carried forward the work of the Viennese school applied to a specific decision area, and therefore it deserves special attention by the student interested in the continuity of social research.

Now it is characteristic for all these studies that they refine the understanding of goals but do not deal with what might be called "implementation": the way goals are transformed into specific intentions and finally, under the influence of concrete situations, into ultimate specific decision. And in this third form the question of the Bühlers' place in the history of the empirical analysis of action cannot yet be answered.[11] We shall meet this situation several times again. The political catastrophes in Europe have interrupted a number of intellectual developments which have not yet been taken up in this country. There are many indications that the continuity is about to be resumed—as a matter of fact, the present historical notes are an effort to help bridge the gap. But as of this moment, the accent on goals, most richly represented by Karl and Charlotte Bühler, has remained only one section of a broader program. We now turn to a second one.

ACCENT ON INTENTION/ KURT LEWIN

Early in the Würzburg period Ach developed a technique by which he attempted to bring out more clearly the course of intended activities. He introduced obstacles: he had subjects learn pairs of syllables; he then offered the first syllable in the pair, with the instruction that the subject respond not with the syllable already learned but rather with another one. This led to more explicit efforts to perform the task which, in turn, made it easier for the subject to report his experiences and for the experimenter to analyze his materials.[12] This so-called combination technique was picked up just before the first World War by a Berlin student, Kurt Lewin. He reported results which were at variance with Ach's finding, and out of these followed a great deal of discussion on the theory of associations, in which we have no direct

[11] It has to be kept in mind that I am referring here only to their study of human goals. Presently we shall trace two other lines: Karl Bühler's insistence on phenomenological description, which greatly affected his students' work in applied psychology; and his ideas on interaction (Steuerung).

[12] For e.g., *see* Lindworsky, *op. cit.,* p. 193.

interest here (*Lewin, 1917*). What is relevant in our context is that Lewin spent the next fifteen years elaborating the basic idea of Ach and developing a series of influential experiments.

There were two basic changes that Lewin made in contrast to Ach. One was that his subjects did not work with meaningless materials, but performed tasks much more "close to life." Secondly, the obstructive forces were not perseverations resulting from past training; they consisted in the interruption of tasks by the experimenter through giving subjects problems which were impossible to solve, or making them work to a point where "satiation" led to discontinuation, and so on. The basic idea, however, remains the same. An intention was set up in the subjects and an obstacle was added, the experiments having the purpose of analyzing the conditions under which the intention was not carried out. As Lewin put it himself:

> The problem is: how does the act of intending bring about the subsequent action, particularly in those cases in which the consummatory action does *not* follow the act of intending?[13]

Lewin's experiments have become so well known in this country that they do not require summary here. However, since we shall be interested in the role they play in the general context of our problem, and especially in the course of Lewin's own development, some comments are necessary on the way they are so far available to the American public. Seventeen of these studies were published between 1927 and 1934 in the *Psychologische Forschung*, then the journal of the Berlin Gestalt psychologists. They are introduced by two general programmatic papers by Lewin, published there in 1926. The second, and much more important one was called "Intention, Will and Need." It is only since 1951 that this paper has become available in English translation through its inclusion in Rapaport's collection (*1951*). Rapaport correctly remarks that more than any later writings of Lewin this paper gives the best understanding of Lewin's concept of dynamics, "which still bears its freshness and the earmarks of its origin."[14] The papers on the experiments themselves are all of considerable length, each averaging about 100 pages, but the only place in which even an inventory is

[13] Kurt Lewin, "Intention, Will and Need," (1926), translated in D. Rapaport, *Organization and Pathology of Thought*, 1951.

[14] David Rapaport, *Organization and Pathology of Thought* (Columbia University Press: 1951), p. 95.

available to the American reader is a curious one. In 1935, when Lewin
had come to this country for the first time, a collection of his earlier
papers was published under the title, *A Dynamic Theory of Personality*. Lewin includes there, as an appendix, a classified summary of the
main context and purposes of these German studies, and he stated there
that his purpose was to investigate "the structure and dynamics of personality and of the psychological environment." This, however, was
by no means indicated in the title of the series which, throughout the
whole course of Lewin's work in Germany, was called "Investigation
on the *Psychology of Action* and of Affectivity" (italics ours).

In this shift of terminology there is symbolized quite an important
segment of the problem history which I am trying to trace. It is
quite simple, to begin with, to show what aspect of the total program
of a theory of action Lewin selected for himself. He singled out the
second step, the intention, and followed it through its course. In his
programmatic paper he was still very much interested in the relation
of this to the other two main elements of the original scheme, to wit,
goals and occasions for consummation. He spoke of intentions as quasi-
needs, because he wanted to compare them with more permanent motivational needs, out of which specific intentions grow. He was also
aware that in the original experiments by Ach the intention was carried
out at one specific moment, when the experimenter exposed the material on which the subject had to perform the task. But Lewin stressed
that "not in every act of intending are occasion and consummatory
action so specifically defined." A variety of occasions can turn an intention toward its consummatory end, and inversely, if no such occasion occurs, substitute intentions might develop or the intention might
die out. Yet this integration of goal, intention and occasion, stressed in
Lewin's original program, was not maintained in his concrete studies.
The accent moved to the study of the intention alone, and, furthermore, the experiments favored those situations in which nothing had to
be done or could be done by the "actor." In retrospect we now can
state it succinctly: the Lewinian experiments on action have laid the
groundwork for a powerful theory of frustration in the broadest sense;
they have nowhere led to a theory of choice or decision.

One of two reasons might explain this situation. It might either
be that the interruption of Lewin's European work, as in the case of
Bühler, led to a social discontinuity in research. Or, perhaps, the accent
on intention led to a point where its re-integration into a general approach turned out to be intellectually more difficult than was antici-

pated. The former element certainly played a role. When Lewin came to this country, the behavioristic trend was still very strong and the interest in learning theory was at its peak. It is quite possible that Lewin felt that it was a hopeless task to get American students interested in a theory of action, which had been deeply rooted in a European tradition. But there are also strong indications that Lewin became aware of the intrinsic difficulty of the intellectual situation and shifted to another subject matter. The following reconstruction suggests further scrutiny of Lewin's German action studies for confirmation. It it is correct, then it highlights a salient problem for any future efforts in action theory.

Every psychologist is acquainted with the very helpful graphic symbols by which Lewin's German students were taught to illustrate the experimental findings and their conceptual interpretations. An intention was a tension system, symbolized by a closed curve on the printed page. The system could have strong or weak borderlines; it could be homogeneous or subdivided; it could be connected in various ways with other such systems. With these symbols a number of basic ideas could be represented, such as the strength of an intention, its connections with other dynamic psychological elements, its stability, and so forth. Through a small number of such concepts Lewin was able to organize a surprisingly large array of interesting empirical findings; and even more, such a representation used in one study gave very concrete leads to further experiments. As Lewin himself said in retrospect, it slowly occurred to him "that the figures on the blackboard . . . which were to illustrate some problems . . . might, after all, be not merely illustrations but representations of real concepts."[15] Out of this grew his book on *Principles of Topological Psychology*. This book develops, in a systematic and coherent way, his general idea of how psychological relationships could be represented by a symbolism borrowed from topology, the mathematics of non-metric geometry. It is now perfectly clear that this representation had nothing to do with topology in the mathematical sense.[16] But the analogical use of some of these symbols certainly proved stimulating.

[15] Kurt Lewin, *Principles of Topological Psychology* (New York, 1936), p. vii.

[16] The mathematically untrained reader who would like to get an idea of the background from which Lewin drew his concepts will find easily understandable a short introduction in Courant and Robbins, *What is Mathematics* (Chapter V, pages 235–272).

Lewin took the matter up again and published his Duke University monograph on the "Conceptual Representation and the Measurement of Psychological Forces." There are two differences between the 1936 and 1938 publications. One is unimportant in our context: in 1938 we find a heavier use of mathematical symbols; what is important for us is that we now find an intensive treatment of the notion of *valence* which was hardly mentioned in the 1936 book. What might be the background of this striking difference? In the seventeen German inquiries into the theory of action the word valence (Aufforderungscharakter) had appeared more and more frequently. It referred to the relationship between needs and intentions, on the one hand, and the objects—the outer world—on the other. If a man is very hungry, then he will eat food which he usually would refuse. But also, the sight of a piece of juicy fruit might suddenly whet his appetite. If we have forgotten that we intended to mail a letter in our pocket, the sight of a mailbox might remind us of it. Objects have valence in the sense that they can strengthen our intentions, bring forgotten ones to mind, and, most of all, turn intentions into consummatory acts. Especially in the latter sense the valences correspond to the occasions of the general scheme of action. An analysis of the interrelationship between valences and intentions would probably be the crucial step in the development of an integrated theory of action.

Now, if I am not mistaken in my interpretation, it is at this point that Lewin found himself defeated. In the German experiments on action the notion of valence, however often the term appeared descriptively, never played any real role in the systematic analysis. This is, of course, a statement which would need careful checking in the text.[17] We surmise that Lewin was in the midst of a very serious intellectual conflict here. On the one hand, he was very aware that the interplay over time between "need" and "occasion" might well be the central problem of any theory of action. In his programmatic paper he had already included pages of vivid examples taken partly from the studies of his students which were then in progress, and partly from everyday life experiences. He created the word valence, which, in its German

---

[17] It will be necessary at some time to make a collection of the places at which the sequence of studies in the *Psychologische Forschung* used the word valence, to determine whether they could really be dispensed with; a recent re-reading of most of the papers has greatly stressed the conviction of this writer, although documentary proof is clearly needed.

form, was a linguistic achievement well worth being classified with such other portentous neologisms as "inferiority complex" or "primary group." But at the same time he obviously realized that tagging and describing a phenomenon does not make it a manageable object of scientific inquiry. As he wrote in his programmatic paper:

> The proposition that 'such-and-such a need exists' is *to a certain extent equivalent to the proposition that 'such-and-such a region of structures has a valence for such-and-such actions.'*[18]

The crux, of course, lies in the apologetic words, "to a certain extent." Inasmuch as valence is equivalent with needs, it does not even help conceptually to analyze further how needs affect the perception of objects and how, in turn, physical objects can affect intentions. If, however, there is an intellectual surplus value in the notion of valence, then to elicit what it consists of would be the decisive problem. In his *Principles* (1936), Lewin obviously took the position that he could do without the concept of valence. He includes there only a short discussion on the relation between the physical and the psychological world (Chapter 8), in which he does not do more than to reiterate some of his descriptive material. Even the terminology avoids the term valence; he only distinguishes between physical objects which are alien in the sense that they intrude upon a person's world—such as disturbances from the outside—and other objects which have already been embedded in the psychological and biological stream of a person's life. It must have occurred to Lewin, however, that by temporarily excluding the "valence" from his system he could not really develop a "theory of action" in which the mutual interplay between desires and the characteristics of choice objects would be a crucial concern. In his next effort, therefore, he gave the notion of valence practically top billing. His programmatic statement now read as follows:

> Instead of linking the need directly to the motoric, the need is linked with certain properties of the environment. The environment then determines the motoric.[19]

[18]   Kurt Lewin, *op. cit.*, p. 122.

[19]   Kurt Lewin, "The Conceptual Representation and the Measurement of Psychological Forces," in *Contributions to Psychological Theory*, 1 (1938), p. 108.

The earlier effort of systematization, then, sees action as controlled from within; objects in the physical world are either psychologized or they are treated as random interferences. The new effort treats action as controlled from without. People are visualized as acting like bodies in a field of forces. Only by adding something which would presumably be the residual of past biography would the effect of the outside objects be different from one person to another. The measurement of the valences of the outside objects therefore become as crucial now as they were negligible before. In both efforts, however, Lewin, who is so vividly aware of the problem does not see a way to really clarify the relation between needs and occasions.

Later he turned to group dynamics, greatly enriching the recent developments in social psychology. Our indebtedness for these contributions should not blind us to the fact which is so significant in the present context: Lewin's program for the analysis of actions of individuals came to a rather sudden stop; his accent on intention, like the accent on goals, awaits integration into a more comprehensive approach. Still, we have to ask what specific contribution Lewin's ideas on action psychology can make to the study of specific decision.

THE MORPHOLOGY OF ACTION   Lewin does not state any specific propositions in this whole area of decisions and choice and, as far as we know, he never made any systematic effort to develop this program further after coming to this country. There are two isolated efforts by early students of Lewin. One is a study by Wright (*1937*), which had a very pertinent topic—whether barriers increase desires—but the findings were inconclusive. Another series of studies showed that the more similar to us two objects are, between which one has to choose, the more time it takes to make up one's mind. These studies are only replications of early studies by Ach, and might have contributed to Lewin's feeling of how little progress had been made in four years on this crucial problem of choice. Two other writers, who were not personal students of Lewin, have applied his concepts to the description of buying activities. J. Clawson (*1950*) and W. G. Bilkey (*1951*) wrote for a market research audience and therefore had to give most of their space to the mere exposition of the merchant and advertiser who wanted to find out "what makes a customer tick." Clawson mainly makes the point that a careful analysis of the process of buying, in psychological terms, would be helpful but it is not clear whether strictly Lewinian terms would be more useful than any other. Bilkey tries, at least in principle, to make a concrete application to the problem of budgeting. He carries out an example in which the valences of various commodities are assumed to be known and where the reorganization of the budget, under the assumptions of income and price changes, is followed through. This, of course, is so close to the use of the concept of utility in traditional economics that the question can be raised whether it is a well known approach with simply a change in terminology.

At this point, an insertion might be appropriate on the interesting role which Lewin's terminology and graphic symbolism has played over the last twenty or thirty years. No one can deny their original suggestive character; but no one has made a serious effort to pinpoint what this suggestiveness consists of. The problem would nevertheless be very important, because it is quite likely that in a new field of research a productive terminology might be very important, even if it does not immediately lead to coherent systems of propositions. There exists an interesting possibility that a contribution can be made to this problem, in connection with Lewin's work, by turning the strange duet performed by Lewin and Ach for a number of decades. Lewin has, throughout his German period, felt that he had to fight against associationism. His programmatic paper, as well as the work of his German students up to the end, is full of explicit or implicit references to the progress they have made beyond Ach's early efforts. Inversely, Ach has obviously followed Lewin's work with great ego involvement. When in 1935 he published his massive review of the psychology of will, which he considered an appraisal of his own life work, he commented in very great detail on practically every study included in Lewin's theory on the psychology of action. Of a few of them, especially those related to satiation and to level of aspiration, he was highly complimentary. But of most of them he was highly critical on three points. First, quite contrary to Lewin, he felt that making experiments close to life, clouds their psychological implications. He therefore had his Ph.D. candidates in Göttingen repeat most of Lewin's studies, especially those collected on interruption and forgetfulness; but in his studies the materials were always meaningless syllables on which, rather ingeniously, the same operations were repeated which Lewin's students carried out on meaningful tasks. By and large, Ach found most of

Lewin's empirical results corroborated, so that at this point a test cannot be made.

On a second point, however, the long distance dialogues between the two scholars would be very revealing. Ach translated all experimental findings into a very simple terminology, making them ever more specific "laws of determination." He claimed that Lewin's elaborate terminology and symbolism obscured the meaning of the results and made it more difficult to systematize them. For the purpose of the present paper it was not possible to analyze carefully whether Ach's position has merit. But it is probably the only time in the history of action analysis that the same set of experiments are available with very different kinds of materials and in very different terminology. One impression can be reported, as a result even of a preliminary comparison. It is quite likely that the choice of specific problems and the experimental ideas were definitely due to Lewin's richer imagery; after all, it is not likely to be a coincidence that the Göttingen group only repeated the studies but did not think of them. On the other hand, it is not unlikely that the cataloging and interrelating of the findings could be more economically done in terms of Ach's simpler schemata.

However this may be, an accent on intention is likely to stress the various ways in which a course of action can develop through time. This is meant when we speak of the morphology of action. Lewin has not developed a system of pertinent categories as the Bühlers have done in regard to goals. But especially in his early writing stimulating suggestions can be found. Thus in his programmatic paper, Lewin suggested an interesting classification of actions according to whether they were controlled and uncontrolled, on the one hand, and intended or not, on the other hand.[20] An uncontrolled action is one in which a person behaves like a body tossed through a field of forces; there are uncontrolled, intended actions—a child who decides to pass by a dangerous dog, and then runs for his life. Inversely, there are controlled actions that are not preceded by a phase of intending, such as conversation or certain (nonautomatized) occupational activities. It is easy to think of the other two combinations: intended and controlled is exemplified by the carrying out of a plan; unintended and uncontrolled is what we normally refer to as an impulsive act. "To establish the ac-

[20]   Rapaport, *op. cit.*, p. 144 *ff.*

tion type to which a psychological event belongs" is a program which Lewin sketches in these few pages and which is still waiting to be carried out. Anyone who has done empirical studies knows how crucial certain of these morphological distinctions are. Voting for example has to be done on a specific day, while the decision to buy a car can be postponed. Action with prescribed and with free terminal date must thus be distinguished. Whether or not we bought a good meal, we know as soon as we taste it; whether or not we bought a good suit takes many months to determine; whether or not we voted for the right candidate, we may never know. The testability of an action is another category which plays a great role in empirical research. Here is a juncture of theory and field work which deserves careful attention.

We have now followed two directions in which an original concern with "why people act the way they do" became specialized. Both the accents on goals and on intentions were prepared in the early Würzburg experiments and their subsequent generalization. A third element has still to be traced: the occasion which brings the intention to consummation, or in generalized form the "influences."

ACCENT ON INFLUENCES/ THE EMPIRICAL STUDY OF PROPAGANDA, ADVERTISING AND OTHER MANIPULATIVE EFFORTS

In the Würzburg experiments the interviewing of the subjects who had performed his simple task played a very important role. Often an hour-long "protocol" was held regarding a decision which might have been reached in one or two seconds. These interviews were made the object of a savage attack by W. Wundt (1907), and, as a consequence, a considerable amount of attention has been given to their methodology over the years. Karl Bühler (1908) wrote the first systematic defense of the method of "Ausfrage"—a term which Wundt created as derogatory one, but which was accepted as appropriate by its proponent. Ach (1935) wrote a very useful summary of the literature which ensued. The main aspects of the technique used were the following:

    a)   It was definitely a matter of retrospection, not introspection; the subject reported his experiences after the completion of the act and did not try to observe himself while he performed the task.

b)   The interviewer made maximum use of the time sequence character of the experience. Occasionally, the method of "fractionization" was used; this meant that in a series of interviews the interrogator singled out varying phases for emphasis, according to where clarification was needed.

c)   An idea which we might call synthetic structure played a considerable role. It turned out that the experiences of a number of subjects would differ in detail but that certain broad features were common to all. The purpose of the interview, therefore, was a two-fold one; on the one hand, to bring out the broad common structure by cumulation from one interview to the next; on the other hand, to facilitate the discovery and reporting of specific individual reactions to be accounted for later by the interpretation of the analyst.

d)   As the studies went on, the purpose of the interviews was not to serve as a catch-all for whatever the subject might have experienced. Rather, the role and location of specific elements in the course of the experience was the main purpose, for example, to see at which point the determination through the task did and did not play a role.[21]

A reading of these old discussions, including careful scrutiny of the original protocols, would still be worthwhile today. For this methodological heritage of the Würzburg school is in several ways related to another development in the study of action for which it is difficult to find an existing text. Perhaps the best way to proceed is with a reminder of a well-known type of research problem.

In the area of modern manipulation, such as propaganda and advertising, we are often confronted with a peculiar situation. A political party or a major manufacturer might have invested a large amount of money on a campaign, making use of some specific medium such as speeches over television, or a series of ads placed in a few magazines. The manipulator knows that social and applied psychology are not yet in a position to tell him in advance whether the campaign will be successful or not. But at least he would like to know at the end of the campaign whether his extensive effort helped him to reach his goal—

[21] Narciss Ach, *Analyse des Willens* (Berlin: Urban and Schwarzenberg, 1935), pp. 40–59.

an increased number of voters or of consumers. Even this post hoc information, however, is not easily collected. In certain specific situations, in mail order campaigns for example, success may be measured fairly easily. Still most of the time the contingencies and ramifications of a campaign are so diversified that measurement of effectiveness is, to say the least, very blurred.

Outsiders often feel that traditional laboratory experiments should be helpful. But this is by no means always the case. In an experimental situation, for example, it will always turn out that an educational radio or television program will affect the attitudes of those who are exposed to it. In real life situations, however, the people who are most likely to be influenced are those who do not expose themselves to educational programs. Due to this self-selection of the audience, the actual effect might be zero, in spite of the results found in the laboratory.

The following trend of thought suggests itself in the foregoing situation. The difference, after all, between human beings and animals is that human beings are aware of some of the influences that are exerted upon them and should be willing to give retrospective accounts of what led them to perform a certain action. Why, therefore, should it not be possible to check the effectiveness of campaigns by interviewing the people who were reached, and who might or might not have acted as a result of them? Whether the testing of propaganda effects by direct interviews will, in the end, be feasible is still a matter of considerable debate. But it is quite clear that a necessary, although perhaps not a sufficient, condition is very systematic insight into the kind of interviews which would be necessary for such a purpose. Thus we can understand easily that one branch in the development of the empirical study of action led to the problem of tracing influences by retrospective interviews. For a number of obvious reasons—multiplicity of situations and availability of research funds, among others—most of the pertinent writing has been done in the commercial field of market research.

The whole situation is best exemplified in a monograph entitled "The Technique of Market Research from the Standpoint of the Psychologist" (*A. Kornhauser and P. F. Lazarsfeld, 1937*). The authors pointed out that specific research techniques could be better understood, better integrated and better carried out if there were a "master technique" from which particular procedures could be derived. And, in their view, "psychological analysis of action is a master technique in market research." In their monograph they attempted to clarify the meaning of action analysis, and then to exemplify specific applications. They pointed out that the situation in which an individual found himself at any given moment determined the next stage of his action. For example, a person with an interest acquired in the past talks with a friend; he is changed by that conversation, and moves, so to speak, to a new stage; this newly oriented person is then confronted with a new situation, for example, an advertisement; from this new situation he takes a new step toward the final action. The relevance of this scheme to market research can be seen in the following quotation:

> This longitudinal analysis of action may begin at stages near to or remote from the final purchase. . . . Whatever the starting point, a complex background already exists in the makeup of the person himself, a summary of preceding experiences. It is necessary, in consequence, to begin at the point chosen with whatever then existing understanding of the individual one may possess and to proceed by tracing the most significant steps leading from that point to final buying habits. . . . Beginning with the psychological background, the problem is to analyze the steps by which people move to the attitudes and buying responses in which the interest of the particular investigation centers. . . . Of course in a specific investigation one cannot ask all the hundred questions which are required by some scheme. But this is not necessary. Only in general the explorer must know far more of the structure of the action than what he is actually then asking about. You may survey tentatively scores of points that might be inquired into, and you may end with an interview schedule of five questions. But these five questions will be vastly different from the ordinary ones. You will have explored and decided the best spots at which to pitch your interrogation. By analyzing the whole act, one sees what part is significant for a given purpose.[22]

The authors then go on to indicate the technical implications of this general analysis. If people are asked why they use a particular brand of merchandise, for example, only 2 or 3 percent will mention that they were influenced by advertising. In terms of a general action analysis, however, it is clear that individuals who say that they

---

[22] A. Kornhauser and Paul F. Lazarsfeld, "The Techniques of Market Research from the Standpoint of a Psychologist," *Institute of Management Series*, 5 (1935).

switched to a new brand because of its good quality—and this is maintained by some 60 percent of the respondents usually—really condense their experience in retrospect. Obviously, before using the product they could not have known about its quality from their own experience. It is therefore appropriate to ask them how they learned about these features of the product. Experiments have shown that, when such specifying questions are used, there will be a marked increase (about 20 percent) in the number of respondents saying that advertising was an effective source of knowledge guiding their behavior.

If one wanted to go further, one could use the method of fractionalization, and employ a variety of such specifying questions. One could ask purchasers how they first learned about the product; whether they looked for information, and if so, where; what were the crucial episodes that finally made them buy, and so forth. Again, it has been shown that the additional efforts to locate the role of advertising at different phases of the purchase make it easier for subjects to give relevant retrospective reports.

There is no space here to develop in detail the general code of research techniques into which this approach has evolved over the years. But the propinquity to the Würzburg ideas about method of "Ausfrage" should be obvious even after this short description. A direct link was established by a division of applied psychology which was established in the Bühler Institute at the University of Vienna under the direction of this writer. A systematic summary of the ensuing studies was published for American readers under the title, "Psychological Aspects of Market Research" (*1934*). The approach is, of course, by no means restricted to marketing studies. Influences on voting, on migration, on committing of crimes can be studied in this way. The notion of "accounting scheme" is central to the efforts of tracing influences by retrospective interviews. Prior to any such study we have to decide what group of factors are to be considered. In a study of migration, for example, a respondent should tell at least what "pushed" him away from his former place, what determined the specific time of the migration, what "pull" did the new place exercise, and how did he know about this attraction before migrating. This should provide an accounting scheme consisting of four "categories," and for each category a specific piece of information has to be collected. This makes for a much richer inventory of influences than if we ask the respondent only "why did you migrate." And inversely such an accounting scheme permits a more systematic statistical treatment as compared with a loose "case study." Many logical aspects of this accounting scheme procedure still await clarification.[23]

How should we assess this development as it grew out of the general matrix of an integral study of human action? Much of the relevant impetus came, undoubtedly, from the desire to manipulate people—propaganda and advertising. But in its application to criminology, for example, it was the reverse side of the coin and took a remedial turn. What is common to all of these studies is that their findings were most likely to be useful for institutional purposes. If they are successful, they can lead to improvements in crime prevention, to better organization of occupational counseling services—and, for better or worse—more successful propaganda.

> [COMMENT, 1970:   The whole procedure has become known as "reason analysis," a somewhat unfortunate term. An entry under this term in the new *International Encyclopedia of the Social Sciences* by Charles Kaduschien gives a picture of more recent developments. Chapters 8 and 9 in Zeisels *Say it With Figures* (Fifth Edition 1968) gives a large number of concrete examples. The present volume includes a paper on the "Art of Asking Why (*1934*), which was the first presentation to an American audience.]

The shortcoming of this approach should not be overlooked. Skillful retrospective interviewing can isolate the role of outside influences; but it cannot easily connect them with the dispositions and sentiments that prevailed at the time of the act. It is unlikely that a respondent can remember, or even know, that he followed a neighbor's advice because he reminded him of a person whom he trusted when he was a child. Thus the retrospective reconstruction of an activity in progress is likely to be fairly complete on the side of the "stimulus"—and this is enough for many practical purposes; but it will miss much of the "inner" elements of the process—which are needed for a more

---

[23]   There exists a very interesting parallel between these accounting schemes and a schematization by Tolman (*1951*) in which he coordinated the Lewinian pictorial devices with his own theoretical concepts. Characteristically enough, the main example which Tolman carries through his paper is that of a man who goes to a restaurant for a meal and whose choice of eating place is to be explained.

systematic analysis. Only a repeated set of observations, made at the time of the event can get this full picture—an idea to which I shall return at the end of our review.

Let me now return to my starting point. The full course of human action extends from a broad set of motivating goals, out of which specific intentions emerge. These, in turn, evolve through a variety of situations, one of which will provide the occasion for a final consummation of the act. I have followed the development of three major trends in research, which I have dubbed, respectively, the accent of goals, intentions and influences. I have lamented the fact that these developments have not only been unintegrated, but that, due to a series of external circumstances, and perhaps to the intrinsic difficulty of any program of integrated action research, they have moved more and more away from each other. I could at this point close my historical note. But the term *action* (Handlung) played a very great role with another group of German writers. Their concern was very different from that of the laboratory workers. In recent American writings a lack of distinction between the two traditions has created confusion. This justifies some additional browsing in the past.

THE "ACTION-LANGUAGE" IN THE GERMAN TRADITION OF "HUMAN STUDIES"

There exists a body of inquiry that the French call "sciences morales" and the Germans "Geisteswissenschaften." An English writer suggested the name "human studies" (*Hodges, 1952*). I shall adopt this term for brevity, and the reader should keep in mind that in its origin it covered mainly jurisprudence, economics and history, with occasional inclusion of linguistics and analysis of art. In Germany the foundations of these human studies were made the topic of special analysis. Since the time of Kant, the question "How is natural science possible?" had remained a central theme for all philosophers. Toward the middle of the century a similar question became paramount for those studies that dealt with the major social institutions, their interrelationships and their development. The object of these studies also acquired a standard term "Objectiver Geist." We might translate it as "autonomized projection," conjoining two terms which other authors

have introduced. Kardiner speaks of projective systems, when he studies the psychological roots of primitive beliefs. But the German tradition of "human studies" included technology and artistic products,
and it stressed that they had all taken on functional autonomy in
G. Allport's sense—they had intrinsic characteristics which could be
deduced by looking at them as complex extensions of a basic notion of
"human action." But it was not an empirical study of action which was
under consideration, as it was with the psychologists. The idea was
rather that the notion of *Handlung* properly conceived would be a
kind of systematic frame of reference within which available knowledge and prevailing procedures could be located. It is not simple, but it
is rather important for our purpose, to get a feeling for this use of *action
schemes as an ordering device*. It so happens that a young jurist, who,
twenty years later was to become Minister of Justice in the first
Weimar Republic, provides us with a very good example. He wrote a
review and reanalysis of all the available literature (more than fifty
references) on *The Concept of Action in Its Importance for Legal
Systematics* (*Radbruch, 1903*). He was very explicit in stating that the
problem was not to study empirically "what happened when people
did something" but to construe a concept so that the salient legal distinctions could be taken account of.

> The concept of action has to be the solid structure upon which
> the doctrine of crime is to be based.[24]

It appears that the legal philosophers were confronted with problems
of the following kind: On the one hand, a punishable crime was an act;
on the other hand, you could also be punished for negligence (for *failing* to do something), or for an intended crime, even if it had not led
to the final consummation. The task of a theory of action was to give
it all those characteristics, and not any more, which were necessary to
subsume under it everything for which the law provided punishment.
Correspondingly, the starting point of Radbruch's analysis is an inventory (this would be referred to as content analysis today) of all the
places where the penal code uses the term "action."[25] And therefrom he

---

[24] Gustav Radbruch, *The Concept of Action in Its Importance for Legal
Systematics* (Berlin: 1903), p. 96.
[25] *Ibid.*, p. 26.

went on to construe "a concept of action which would satisfy the requirements of a legal systematics."[26]

This writer does not know whether the problem is still important in contemporary German jurisprudence or whether it ever played a similar role in the Anglo-Saxon tradition. But it certainly makes fascinating reading to learn about what Radbruch calls the doctrinal history ("Dogmengeschichte") of the concept of action,[27] the way it was discussed and redefined over and over again to adapt it to changing ideas about legal responsibility and criminal guilt. Radbruch for his own solution takes into account some introspective observations suggested by what he calls "psychological jurisprudence."[28] But he never has any doubt that action as the central concept of criminal law has to be analyzed in the light of classificatory needs, and not as a result of empirical observations.

The specificity of the legal problem and the clarity of Radbruch's presentation is not paralleled by more ambitious efforts to derive general categories for the human sciences from a formal notion of action. Dilthey was most specific as to his goal. The life of an individual was action on the largest scale; history was a system of such lives. The analysis of action would therefore provide a "critique of historical reason" (*Vernunft*); it would answer the question, "How is history possible" in a way similar to what Kant tried for the natural sciences in his *Critique of Pure Reason*. A perceptive British philosopher has traced Dilthey's ideas on this matter through the many volumes of his collected works. (*Hodges* (*1952*), especially Chapter IX). A latter attempt, but belonging to the same tradition, has been made by Fryer (*1933*). He distinguishes five major types of autonomized projections, difficult to understand and impossible to translate. They are characterized according to different elements of an action scheme: one, exemplified by art (Gebilde) corresponds to the expressive function of action; another, exemplified by tools (Geräte), to its instrumental aspect. In addition the very nature of all "objectiver Geist" is "derived" in several steps from the action of concrete individuals to the permanent traces they result in: from a man pointing the way, to the road sign and finally to, say, the system of musical notation.

The Germans who wrote in this tradition seem to have taken it

---

[26] *Ibid.*, p. 75.
[27] *Ibid.*, p. 78, p. 131.
[28] *Ibid.*, p. 112 ff.

for granted that some kind of "action-language" is mandatory for a discussion of the human sciences. The origin of this tradition goes at least back to Fichte, as one can gather from occasional references. It is like the case of a modern theoretical physicist who as a matter of course writes in mathematical terms. Actually these efforts can well be considered the precursor of the modern mathematical models in the social sciences—which so far are essentially a device for organizing concepts and assumptions.

The compulsion of using action language, without justifying its merits, becomes especially clear in a paper by Max Weber (1913) on some basic categories of sociology.[29] Its main purpose is to define a number of concepts, which might—or might not, as Weber himself stresses—turn out useful for a systematic sociology. The task at hand is to take notions from every-day language and to make them more precise by showing in what respect they represent "the course of human action of a special kind." He states what today one would call a strictly reductionist program. Concepts like state, feudalism, etc., should "without exception be reduced (reduziert) to the actions of the single individuals involved." The paper was written for a philosophical journal (M. Weber, *1913*) and contains many digressions and inconsistencies within its fifty pages. Its central distinctions refer to three types of actions. In one type people act together but are controlled only by the requirement of a concrete situation: the example he gives is a group of streetcar passengers trying jointly to help a fellow passenger who is suddenly stricken by illness. Another type consists of those actions in which the conduct of the actor and other people is prescribed by definite rules: the most extreme example would be an army. In between there is the type of action in which the interplay is governed by some kind of informal understanding which is less binding than the rules relevant to the latter type above but more stable and probably more explicit than the haphazard "orientations" of the first type.[30]

---

[29] This paper has to our knowledge never been translated. It is in many respects quite different from the introduction to his great posthumous work, which forms the first chapter in the Parsons-Henderson translation of *Theory of Social and Economic Organization*.

[30] The three terms could be translated "joint action," (Type I) "agreed action" (Type II), and "organized action" (Type III). The last two seem sometimes subdivisions of the first and sometimes coordinate with it; in any case, Weber stresses repeatedly the "fluid transitions" existing between the major types.

A variety of social phenomena like market, associations, organizations and of "social relations" like competition, domination are analyzed in terms of these types of action. At first glance the circular character of this "casuistic" (Weber himself uses this legal expression) is surprising. The types of action are described in terms of the social situation in which they occur; in turn these "configurations" are defined in terms of action types. Thus the action language seems to force one to say everything twice. This is, however, not a cogent objection. It could well be that through this procedure one could arrive at the minimum of elements, the combination of which would permit organizing a large number of concrete phenomena. Whether Weber could have achieved this we shall never know, because he did not pursue this plan in its original form.[31]

What is important for our present purpose is Weber's awareness and insistence that he is not concerned with an empirical study of human social action. His purpose is to develop an action scheme through which sociological concepts can be organized. He is aware of the parallel to Radbruch's efforts; he refers to him in the introduction to this paper as well as at other points of his methodological writings. Empirical action studies he explicitly considers a different task assigned to the psychologist. For seven pages he dwells on this distinction, and the following quotation is most characteristic.

> From the notion of a mystic-contemplative religiosity one can *deduce logically* a lack of concern with the well-being of others. And yet *psychologically* it may happen that this type of religiosity leads to a kind of Euphoria, which is experienced as a peculiar feeling of love for everyone. (Emphasis supplied.)[32]

Here psychology is opposed to logic. From the context it is clear that by logical deduction he means the kind of systematization he tried in this paper. Weber is not stopped by any doubt whether logic can derive one sentiment (Unbekümmertheit) from another one (Religiosität). For this is exactly the conviction he has: from the elements of

---

[31] In his subsequent work along this line (M. Weber, *1920*), he did not try a coherent systematization but was satisfied with defining only a specific list of concepts.

[32] Max Weber, condensed translation, "Methodische Grundlagen der Soziologie," in *Gesammelte Aufsätze zur Wissenschaftslehre* (Tübingen, 1922), p. 412.

an action-schema one should be able to build up concepts which permit derivations of this kind. Or, to put it differently and more appropriately: this is the intellectual ritual through which he felt obliged to go when he reflected on the methodological foundations of his creative work.

It is clear that even for such a formal program "action of the individual" is by no means the only formal scheme conceivable to serve as a starting point. Other efforts are well known in sociology: Wiese's reduction to a basic number of social relations, like cooperation and antagonism; W. I. Thomas' emphasis on a set of basic attitudes, like his four wishes. But Weber was trained as a jurist, had worked on economic problems and was well acquainted with the general concern regarding the foundations of the human sciences. If his new preoccupation with sociology was to have status, it too had to be linked up with the notion of *Handlung*.[33] This would have been all right if Weber had not deeply felt and dimly known that the use of this formal action language needed reconciliation with the empirical study of concretely preformed actions. From the writings available in English it would seem as if he had brushed the problem aside by casual references to an imaginary psychologist who will take care of it. But from untranslated sources it becomes clear that Weber was, several times, very close to such empirical work and that it caused him considerable anguish. Thereby hangs a tale which deserves a special place in our historical sketch.

AN AMBIVALENCE IN MAX WEBER'S WRITINGS ON ACTION

Weber repeatedly emphasized the difference between formal action models which were the business of the social sciences and empiri-

---

[33] How much Weber is influenced by his legal background can be seen by his definition of action (*M. Weber, 1913*):

> Action (including willful neglect and acquiescence) is defined as an understandable . . . behavior toward objects.

The clause in parenthesis echoes almost automatically the kind of writing by Radbruch that I have alluded to.

cal studies of action which belonged to the psychologist. One of his untranslated methodological papers deals with the relation between the economic doctrine of marginal utility and the Weber-Fechner law (*M. Weber, 1908*). A colleague, Brentano, had pointed to the geometric similarity between the law that a constant increase of the stimulus makes for a relatively decreasing increment in sensation, on the one hand, and the law that a constant increase in the supply of the same good makes for a relatively small increase in its utility, on the other hand. Max Weber stressed that the two things should never have any relation to each other. Theoretical economics is not concerned with how people behave but with how to draw up an action scheme from which the idea of marginal utility and other economic concepts could be derived.[34]

But he was far from deprecating empirical psychological studies. In Germany since 1872 there existed an "Association for social policy." (Thereafter referred to as the Association.) Its core was formed by a group of university professors who were worried about the growing antagonism of the German workers, organized in socialist unions, toward the German state. They wanted on the one hand to impress upon industrialists the need for social reforms and on the other hand remove the workers from the influence of Marxist thinking. Their procedure was to organize studies of social problems, like cost of living, taxes, tariff; and they discussed the findings at yearly meetings. Representatives of union, industry, and government were invited to participate. Their hope was that studies and discussion would lead to legislation and what today we would call improved labor-management relations.

In 1908 upon the previous suggestion of Alfred Weber, Max's

---

[34] It would be interesting to trace the role of the action language tradition in economics. No one can escape a feeling of pleasure if he reads the detailed introspections of a leading economist of the Austrian school who attempted to use his experience as a mountaineer when he discussed "The Motivation of Present Economic Action Through Future Needs" (*E. von Böhm-Bawerk, 1907*). How was this translated into the "wirtschaftliche Handlung" of the economic man? And how has this schematization finally been replaced by indifference curves and mathematical formulae? Several authors have stressed the sociological elements in the writings of economists, e.g., Marshall (Parsons, *1932*) or Keynes (*Lekatchman, 1957*). We are raising here the reverse question. The economists at the turn of the century started with vivid psychological descriptions and from them abstracted schemata to explain why capital bore interest and similar matters. What is precisely this procedure, which moves, as Weber put it, "from trivial but uncontestable facts of the daily experiences by many people to theoretical conceptions?"

brother, it was decided to start a series of studies on "selection and adjustment (occupational choice and experience)" of workers in large industries. The parenthesis is part of the official title. The investigations were to be based on data available in the offices of selected factories and on direct interviews with their officials. It was to be a collective enterprise of collaborating university institutes, represented by their heads in the association. To guarantee a unity of purpose, three documents were made available. The first is a "methodological introduction" written by Max Weber and only subsequently published in his collected papers on sociology and social policy. He formulates the two problems implied in the title of the program as follows:

a) What is the effect of big industry on the personal characteristics, the occupational destiny and the private style of life of its workers; what physical and psychological qualities do they develop; and what role do they play in the course of the worker's life?

b) To what extent is the potential and actual development of large industries determined by characteristics of the labor force rooted in its ethnic, social and cultural origin, its traditions and living conditions?[35]

The second document is a working plan of about 2,000 words, probably developed by Max Weber in collaboration with the committee of three professors (Herkner, Schmoller and Alfred Weber) who were to coordinate the various studies.[36] It instructed the collaborators along the following line. They should first describe the technological features of the factories under study. Then they should analyze the composition, geographic origin and work history of the labor force, required qualifications and difficulties to satisfy them. Special emphasis should be put on recent changes. The third and largest block of problem units is devoted to the activities of the worker in the factory:

[35] "Methodologische Einleitung für die Erhebung des Vereins für Sozialpolitik," in *Gesammelte Aufsätze zur Soziologie und Sozialpolitik* (Tübingen, 1924).

[36] Herkner was the leading labor economist of the period; Schmoller was the great old man among the social scientists, the middle-of-the-roader who, from the beginning, had been president of the association, his main field being economic history; Alfred Weber was Max's younger brother and later became, like him, a sociologist.

chances for advancement and for satisfaction of special work interests; experience with various wage systems; mobility; training facilities; effect of aging, etc. A final block is clearly meant to refer to sociological problems: social distinctions among types of workers, degree of cohesion, features of daily life different from other population groups with similar income, aspirations for their children, etc.

Much of this information is to be gotten from experts or by participant observation. But attached to the general plan is a formal questionnaire of 27 questions to be answered by the workers in personal interviews. The questions pertain either to topics on which statistics are desired (like occupation of parents and leisure time activities), or to topics on which, supposedly, only direct interrogation can provide information, such as reasons for their occupational choice and goal in life. Altogether most of the sixteen studies finally published are organized along the outline and give numerical results derived from the questionnaires.[37]

The greatest attention was given by everyone to a third document prepared by Max Weber. He obviously attached much importance to it. Its 200 pages were published at once; and on a later occasion, he described how hard he had worked on it; he made endless computations himself "because only during the continuous and personal analysis of figures will the investigator hit upon those ideas which he needs to interpret his findings and to develop new problems." (*Association, Vol. 138, 1911*) The title of the paper is "Regarding the Psycho-Physical Aspects of Industrial Work." Its starting point is the following problem. Differential qualifications of various types of workers are obviously of interest to the social scientist. Can they be measured? Does contemporary work in experimental psychology give some leads for ways of doing so? What other procedures could be used to answer, in the frame of the Association's Enquete, such questions as: are there innate abilities to work? Do they differ among various races? How are they affected by sex and age of the workers, their social origin, etc.? (M. Weber, 1924e–1909.)

The first hundred pages of the paper (Sections 1–5) are devoted to a detailed review of the existing literature with special emphasis upon the work of Weber's colleague, Kraepelin. He had published five volumes of papers, which reported laboratory experiments dealing with concepts which today still form the foundation of industrial psychol-

---

[37] The whole enterprise will hereafter be referred to as "Enquete."

ogy: learning curves, fatigue, monotony, effect of interruptions, etc.[38]

In a sixth section on "methodological problems," Weber raises the question, whether the results of laboratory studies based mainly on pencil and paper tests, can be applied to the much more complex factory situation. He is doubtful and wishes that experiments on real working machines could be carried out. This he considers financially impossible, because such experiments would cost at least twenty dollars a day. (*Sic!* p. 119.) So the next best thing to do is to look at records of piece-rate earnings and of production records as they are kept in the natural course of industrial production. The next 120 pages are devoted to a secondary analysis of such data, which Weber got from the textile factory of his wife's family.

There is no space to describe here the brilliance of his procedure. He begins by looking for variations during the day, in the course of the week and over longer periods. The findings are partly interpreted with the help of Kraepelin's psychological categories. However, when it comes to discussing individual variations, he introduces the workers' desire to influence the piece rate, the role of the rate booster, the attitude of organized workers and of pietistic women (Section 9). In analyzing the role of marriage as a stabilizing influence, the similarity to Durkheim's interpretation of suicide rates is striking, although the latter is not mentioned (Section 10). At one point he analyzes the behavior of a few workers who attend simultaneously two weaving machines which differ in regard to difficulty and to piece rate. He shows that after a period of trial and error the worker finds an optimum balance between effort and earning; his data and discussion could be directly translated today into a mathematical learning model. (Max Weber, 1924e–1909, pp. 209–217.)[39]

[38] This writer is not aware of any material which would permit tracing the relation between the contemporary work of Kraepelin and the Würzburg school. In Weber's writings and letters one finds frequent reference to publications by contemporary psychologists; we could not find a reference to the Würzburg group, who by all expert agreement turned out to be the most important one.

[39] Weber at that time was obviously very much interested in the use of statistical methods in the study of more complex social phenomena. A series of books had appeared on the world of manual workers, written by Levenstein and based on questionnaires and letters. Weber wrote a ten page review hailing the idea but criticizing the impressionistic procedures of the author. He gives detailed advice about what kind of tables should have been run and explains the use of correlation coefficients, which were practically unknown in the Germany of that time. He expresses the hope that the problem of class consciousness could be approached in this way. From the review one gathers that he had spent some time inspecting the original material (*M. Weber, 1909*).

The monograph anticipates in every respect the approach which today would be taken for an analysis of voting, radio listening, buying or any other action performed by large numbers of people under comparable circumstances. Careful statistical analysis is used to deduce as many generalizations from the data as possible and to interpret them in the light of the appropriate conceptualization, either available already or newly advanced for the purpose at hand. The paper was much admired by everyone who was connected with the Enquete. At the 1911 meeting of the Association for Social Policy, when Herkner reviewed the whole Enquete, a special report was given by an assistant of Weber who had collected some additional data, using his approach and corroborating his findings.[40] What influence did it have on Weber himself? How did he link this whole experience to his and his contemporaries' concern with "Handlung"? The answer is surprising and significant for the development we are tracing in this paper.

Max Weber, after having thrown himself so vigorously into this whole effort, completely deserted it after a while, and as far as we know, never connected it with any of his sociological writings.[41] As a matter of fact, beyond his original directions, he seems not even to have remained in contact with the actual studies. None of them refer to his personal sponsorship. At the general discussion of 1911 he was not listed among the discussants whom the chairman announced in advance. But in the end he did intervene at length. The leading German statistician, Bortkiewich, criticized politely but incisively various shortcoming in the studies.[42] Thereupon, Max Weber got up, acknowledged some mistakes in the statistical procedures, and defended others in considerable detail. True to his great interest in probability literature, he was especially reverent to Bortkiewich, an early leader in the applica-

---

[40]   Association Report, Vol. 138, p. 139 *ff.*

[41]   There is one cross-reference to the paper on human work in a later edition of the Protestantic Ethic and inversely in Section 9 of the paper, a reference to "the larger context in which I have tried to analyze these things elsewhere" (p. 162).

[42]   In discussing the occupational choice of women, Bortkiewich pointed out that really two questions are in order: why do they work at all? Why in a specific occupation? Only during the present review did the present writer become aware of Bortkiewich's priority in the art of asking why. It is surprising that Weber overlooked the significance of Bortkiewich's remarks, as he himself made very astute remarks on questionnaire construction in his discussion of Levenstein, cited above.

tion of mathematics of social data. Only at one point was he flippant. Bortkiewich had very aptly criticized the naive categories that the studies used when they classified the reasons for occupational choice. Of the eight pages in the stenographic report given to Weber's remarks the following lines cover his reaction to one of the basic problems in the empirical study of action,

> I agree that [these data] have no value for the question: why have these people really chosen their occupation? Possibly the answers are quite useless. I consider it possible, however, that they are worthwhile under another aspect: what do people answer to such a—if you please—stupid question? (great hilarity)
>
> Sometimes stupid questions provide quite valuable answers.[43] (great hilarity)

The ambivalence of this comment is characteristic for his whole attitude during the discussion. All other participants reiterated their admiration for the great importance of the Enquete. Weber, while defending many of its details, stressed that in his opinion nothing much came of the whole affair, at best a few hypotheses and the "high probability that with the help of future material after a long, long while valuable and crucial results might ensue."[44]

Having pointed to a strange reaction of Weber, we might as well go a step further and venture a more general interpretation. Why did Weber so emphasize the separation of empirical psychology from his own sociological work? There is indirect evidence that real resistance was at work. Let us look at a sequence in his life, as reported by his wife. He was deeply devoted to his mother, from whom he acquired his interest in social amelioration, developed in sharp contrast to the political conservatism of his father, a member of the German parliament. At 29 he married after having been greatly worried whether he would ever be able to "satisfy a woman."[45] When he was 33 there was an open and violent break with his father over the question whether his mother would be permitted to visit him alone each year for a

---

[43]   Association for Social Policy (Report of 1911 meeting), p. 193.

[44]   *Ibid.*, p. 190.

[45]   Marianne Weber, *Max Weber, Ein Lebensbild* (Heidelberg, 1950) p. 171 and p. 195.

month. The quarrel led to a separation of his parents; the father went alone on a trip and died two months after the scene without a reconciliation with his son Max. Two more months later the latter had his famous nervous breakdown, which for almost five years made all intellectual work impossible. Sketching the course of events in four pages, Marianne Weber refers to the sense of tragedy everyone felt at the funeral of Weber senior, and adds:

> But the oldest son (Max) has no feeling of guilt; the quarrel of seven weeks before was clearly inevitable.[46]

Even for the layman this does not appear to be a very insightful statement. Given the intellectual closeness of Weber and his wife, we may assume that this resistance to psychological interpretation was common to both. One bit of corroboration comes from a brief reference to Freud (M. Weber, 1924e, 1909): "These theories are becoming increasingly outmoded." It is greatly to Weber's credit that he knew at all about Freud in 1908; but the diagnosis as to Freud's chances for intellectual survival is surprisingly wrong for a man who, in connection with other innovations of the time—the role of probability, e.g.—was so farsighted.[47]

There is another aspect to this almost compulsory tendency to keep the reality of human action separated from the constructs of the human sciences. In the papers connected with the Enquete, Weber uses terminology which does not appear in his historical writings. The

---

[46] *Ibid.*

[47] *See* Max Weber, 1924e, 1909.

Had Max Weber been a poet or a prime minister some psychoanalyst would undoubtedly have written his biography. (The older Pitt, Lord Chatham, was a victim of similar cycles of powerful activities and paralyzing depressions; several biographies of him exist.) Such an analyst certainly would point to the way Marianne reacted to her husband's illness:

> Weber's supreme self-sufficiency had often raised, for her, the question whether he really needed her. [Mrs. Weber always refers to herself in the third person.] Now she doesn't need to doubt any more. Out of the dark abyss, which his illness creates, great happiness emanates for her: the strong man needs her continuous care and presence; she is permitted to serve him (*Ibid.*, p. 249).

The question could be raised, incidentally, why the two students of politics who were so proud of their realistic approach—Machiavelli and Weber—were both so defeated in their desire to obtain a major public office.

workers in the textile factory have moods, dispositions and, most of all, attitudes. The latter term appears literally about a dozen times (Attituede).[48] Now none of this, as far as we can see, ever appears in his historical writings. We have selected Parsons' translation of the Protestant Ethics as a test. The term "attitude" appears about 40 times in the translation, and the context makes its appearance seem quite natural. Still, in none of these places did Weber himself use the word in the German text. He has a plethora of nouns instead: Anschauung, Gesamtstimmung, Gesinnung, Art des Empfindens, etc. He obviously felt that action of historical persons or groups, which were reconstructed from letters, recorded customs, etc., should be described in a terminology different from one which the "psychologist" uses if he studies real human beings. There is, indeed, an important methodological problem here. But Weber did not solve it and, as a matter of fact, never even formulated it.

He was, as we just saw, acquainted with, and for a while strongly attracted by, the empirical study of action which had started at the beginning of the twentieth century. And yet he strained to link the new science of sociology exclusively to the formal action language of the traditional German human sciences. Why? We suggest that an unconscious resistance to an alternative solution was partly responsible; he felt personally endangered by material which came too close to the reality of human action without historical distance or pseudo-logical terminology to shield him.[49] The matter has been well formulated by Paul Keczkemeti. Handlung stands in the center of Weber's methodological writings, only tangential to his thinking, and played no role at all in his substantive work (personal communication).

All this would only have historical interest if it were not for a young American traveller who came to Heidelberg a few years after

[48] It also appears in his general discussion of the use of questionnaires in social research, mentioned above.

[49] In this connection one should take into account the difference in style, which is so striking in Weber's writings. Repeatedly it has been remarked that his methodological writings are unnecessarily involved as compared to his substantive work, and even more to his verbal presentation (Marianne Weber, p. 322) and her report (p. 683), that Weber had to drop a course on sociological categories, because students could not understand him. His most turgid writing occurs undoubtedly in the above mentioned paper, where sociological concepts are defined in terms of action language. In contrast, the empirical paper on human work is written with lucid simplicity. We have no explanation for this contrast.

Weber's death. Everyone there was still living under the impact of this intellectual giant. His historical writings were the pride of German sociology. His work for the Association probably was rarely mentioned—maybe partly because he had there engaged in many very ill-tempered fights (including court trials) with colleagues and *de mortuis nil nisi bene*. If one wanted to know the methodological foundations of his work, where could one better turn than to his own declarations. There one met something of highest prestige in Germany—Handlung. And it sounded like something which in the American scene had been badly neglected.

The visitor did not need to know that a formal "action-language" had become traditional within the human studies and had a very different purpose than the empirical study of human action. So Weber came to this country in terms of a "theory of action" which—whatever positive contribution it made—blocked American sociologists from serious concern with human action as a topic of empirical inquiry.

PARSONS' REVIVAL OF
MAX WEBER'S ACTION-LANGUAGE

It is well known how T. Parsons tried to build up the notion of "social sytem" from a set of "unit acts" and their interconnections over collectives and over time. He was aware of, and pointed out, the many contradictions and obscurities in Weber's methodological writing; nevertheless, he was convinced, and stated so explicitly, that Weber's concept of action is substantially the one he himself wanted to make the basis for a modern program of sociology.[50]

Parsons' general contributions are not under discussion here. What matters to us is the role the "Harvard Movement" plays in the history of scientific concern with human action. We have by now seen that it has two traditions: one is the empirical approach, dominant among pre-behavioristic psychologists. The other is a formal one characteristic for the German human studies and well exemplified by some of Weber's methodological papers. In order to locate Parsons properly, his

---

[50] Talcott Parsons, *The Structure of Social Action* (New York: 1937), p. 642.

relation to Weber needs to be clearly understood. He distinguishes four elements of the "unit act": the actor, the goal, the situation (means), and the normative orientation. He introduces these distinctions with the sentence: "An act involves *logically* the following (elements)."[51] Now we saw above that Weber, too, used "logical" in such contexts. The distinctions are logical in the sense that they are made for a definite purpose: to focus attention on the roles of norms and expectations. It would be as logical to make other distinctions: e.g., actor, goal, means and influences that help the actor select the means appropriate for his goal. This scheme would focus attention on technical and social problems of manipulation, characterize social system by the prevailing type of communication, and so on. An action-scheme proposed for classificatory purposes is necessarily suited to the main substantive interest of the proponent. Parsons has never denied the classificatory character of his system and the discussion in the literature has followed his lead (*Swanson, 1953; Ramsoy, 1957*).[52]

But Parsons has added and utilized one important methodological advance which has been made in recent years. Weber, as we saw, distinguished types of action and related to each a corresponding sociological concept. Parson, however, proceeds in two steps. He first "deduces" from an action scheme his pattern variables and then combines those to characterize various types of social configurations. The notion of variables and the understanding of types as combinations therefrom, Weber probably missed because in his comparative sociology he was restricted to a few cases and scarce historical material. Suppose he could have visualized the Yale cross-cultural files or UNESCO's comparative attitude surveys and thus conceived the application of variables to the description of collectives. Could it be that then the methodological contradictions between the clarity of his statistical insights and his ritual use of the German action language would somehow have been resolved? The possibilities can be seen in an instructive revue by Peter Blau (*1957*) of the procedures available to

[51] *Ibid.,* p. 44.

[52] Just as the legal philosopher desires to organize and relate the various punishable acts, so Parsons himself says explicitly "the discrimination of various possible modes of normative orientation is one of the most important questions with which this study will be confronted" (*Ibid.,* p. 47). In the end this leads to the derivation of the notion of "culture" more elaborate but in principle similar to the derivation of the German "objektiver Geist" from an appropriate notion of "Handlung."

study comparatively a large number of organizations. He mentions in passing that Weber's notion of "Verstehen" in sociological research can be seen as the use of intervening variables in a statistical analysis, the units of which are collectives.

It may be, however, that for Parsons the reverse question can be raised: Given that he himself says that his pattern variables are his main contribution (*Parsons, 1953*), why do they have to be "derived" from an action scheme, the only justification of which is that it helps to develop various classifications for the pattern variables? The question is welcome to remain rhetorical, because our task is to point to the consequences of Parsons' move, whatever it merits.

And here one is struck by the paradoxical convergence of two trends moving in opposite directions. In Germany the tradition of action schemes in the human sciences impeded the incorporation of empirical studies of action into the body of legitimate sociological endeavor. In the United States, empirical studies of social actions might have been the relief for latent intellectual tensions: protest against primitive behaviorism, desire to overcome the static side of early community surveys, opposition to irrelevant minutiae. The mere term "action" was bound to start a crusade in the USA, and hardly anyone knew or noticed that here were two brothers with the same name and maybe the wrong one was anointed.

At this point a linguistic element enters which should not be underrated: the ambiguity of the English term "interaction." Let us construct an extremely simple scheme which can bring out the main idea. We have three persons, A, B, and C, who each pursue a goal in

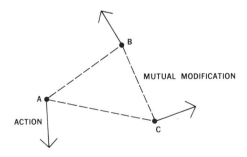

an area of activity, say politics or occupational advancement. We indicate this goal by a solid arrow attached to the name of each person, and one might think of this arrow going into the third dimension outside the paper. The three have some social relations with each other, and these are indicated by broken lines. The lines may symbolize a large variety of things: the expectations A, B, and C have of each other; the extent to which they depend upon each other's approval; the practical help or difficulties they do or may provide for the pursuit of the three group members.

The German language would provide two very different terms for the arrows and the broken lines, even on the highest level of generalization. The goal pursuing activities are, of course, our old friend Handlung. For the various ways in which people modify each other's action there is no equally standardized word. But there was much acceptance of a term which Karl Bühler proposed: *gegenseitige Steuerung*. One possible translation would be "mutual control," if the term control is taken in its weakest connotation, just indicating that people somehow modify each other's pursuits. The word was taken from the then newly developing field of electronics. If we use a public address system, then the main source of electric energy comes somewhere from a central power house; our voice, when we speak into the microphone, only modifies this energy by moving light pieces of steel back and forth in the electric field. Maybe, for the present purpose, the best term to use is "mutual modification." It, together with the individual actions themselves, describes the social system in its most primitive form. (Be it remembered that we include under mutual modification what goes on in the mind of A as he takes into account the expectations of B, even if B is not aware of his own role in A's stream of activity; influence is a special case of modification.)

The distinction between action and mutual modification is, of course, a schematic one; and there are continuous interrelations which come about over time. From moment to moment the actions of a group of individuals are changed by mutual modification; in turn, the modifications shift as the goal pursuing activities change in their character. But this is a well known situation which occurs whenever we deal with a number of factors, and in its most precise form can be represented by a system of simultaneous difference equations. This of course is not the line to be pursued here. What matters is the way in which the English language comes into the picture.

There is a great temptation to call the arrows in the above scheme actions and the broken line interactions. The danger with this terminology is that the basic difference between the two conceptual ideas gets lost because of the linguistic similarity of the two terms. In German the word interaction does not exist. Max Weber used the term "social action" to indicate the combined phenomenon, the action of individuals *and* the mutual modifications they bring to bear upon each other. I submit that the following happened. The English terminology of action and interaction made many people forget the very different conceptual purposes that the two terms were supposed to serve. It is quite understandable that sociologists are more interested in mutual modification of individual actions than in the study of those actions themselves. But it is going too far to make the "theory of action" become tantamount with the theory of mutual modification and thus crowd out the other half of the whole problem. A kind of conceptualization is needed that looks at the human being as a goal pursuing entity whose activities are modified by his socii. It is probably too late to reclaim the term "actor" for this other purpose, but one should at least be aware that a terminological gap has been created which can very easily become an intellectual pitfall.

Terminologies always have a bearing upon the course of scientific endeavors. Parsons took as his coat of arms a term that he really needs only for classificatory purposes and that is now sorely missed by those who want to continue another tradition: the empirical study of Handlung—be it in terms of activities which similar people perform under various circumstances or in terms of the conditions that make for joint efforts. Earlier or later some sociologists will have to speak for the system of concrete actors, the ones who in all spheres of social life have to choose between alternatives, are object and relayers of advice and who, when their collective experiences clash with their expectations, move on to new goals. Out of such studies new knowledge will flow into the theory of action which so far is still unfinished business.

POSTSCRIPT 1972   Since this was written in 1958 and privately circulated, Roscoe Hinkle has traced the treatment of "action" among early American sociologists. If I read him correctly he concludes these authors had even in their theoretical writings a more concrete imagery, not affected by the formal German action-language and much closer to the tradition reviewed in this essay. The Germans have remained true to their terminological ancestry. Hans Thomae (1965) edited a Reader which combined classical German papers with translations from Allport, McClelland and the Kinsey Report; of course the collection is entitled: "die Motivation des menschlichen Handelns." A most interesting coincidence is a biography by Arthur Mitzman (1970). He uses as centerpiece exactly the material I quoted in the section on Weber's ambivalence. (See especially footnote 47.) I know that the author was not aware of my paper and so we have here another case of simultaneous discovery. May I be permitted to refer to two of my own publications which try to be examples of empirical studies of action—one in the field of political sociology (Berelson *et al.*, Chapter 13) and one in the sociology of business (Lazarsfeld, 1959).

BIBLIOGRAPHY

Ach, Narciss, *Analyse des Willens* (Berlin, Wien: Urban and Schwarzenberg, 1935).

Allport, Gordon, W., "Attitudes," in *Handbook of Social Psychology,* Carl Murchinson (ed.), (Clark University Press, 1935), pp. 798–844.

Andicz, Margarette, *Suicide and the Meaning of Life* (London, 1947).

Bentley, Madison, *The New Field of Psychology* (New York: D. Appleton-Century-Crofts, 1924, 1934), Chapter VI, "Acting," pp. 209–31.

Berelson, Bernard, R., Lazarsfeld, Paul F., and McPhee, William N., *Voting.* (The University of Chicago Press, Chicago, Ill. 1954).

Bilkey, W. J., "The Vector Hypotheses of Consumer Behavior," *Journal of Marketing,* (1951).

Blau, Peter M., "Formal Organizations," *American Journal of Sociology,* (1957).

Boring, Edwin G., *A History of Experimental Psychology:* Würzburg School, (New York: D. Appleton-Century-Crofts, 1929), pp. 401–10.

Bühler, Charlotte, *From Birth to Maturity* (London: Paul, 1935).

——, *Die Menschliche Lebenslauf als Psychologisches Problem* (Leipzig: Hirzel, 1933).

——, "Maturation and Motivation," *Personality,* Vol. I, No. 2, (1951).

Bühler, Karl, *Die Krise der Psychologie* (Jena: Fischer, 1927).

——, *Die Axiomatics der Sprachwissenschaften.* Kant Studien, (1933).

——, *The Mental Development of the Child* (New York, 1930). (First German edition, 1921.)

Clawson, Joseph, "Lewin's Vector Psychology and Analysis of Motives in Marketing," in *Theory in Marketing,* Cox and Aldarson (eds.), (Chicago, 1950).

Courant and Robbins, *What is Mathematics* (London: Oxford University Press, 1941).

Frenkel, Else, "Studies in Biographical Psychology," *Character and Personality,* Vol. V, No. 1, (Sept. 1936), pp. 1–34.

Freyer, Hans, *Theorie des objektiven Geistes.* Teubner, Berlin, 1934.

Garrett, Henry E., *Psychology* (New York: American Book Co., 1950).

Ginzberg, Eli *et al.*, *Occupational Choice: An Approach to a General Theory* (New York: Columbia University Press, 1951).

Hilgard, Ernest R., *Introduction to Psychology* (New York: Harcourt, Brace and World, 1953).

Hinkle, Roscoe C., "Antecedents of the Action Orientation in American Sociology before 1935," *American Sociological Review*, Vol. 28, No. 1, (February 1963).

Hodges, H. A., *The Philosophy of Wilhelm Dilthey* (London: Routledge and Kegan Paul, Ltd., 1952).

Humphrey, George, *Thinking* (New York: John Wiley and Sons, 1951).

Kaplan, Abraham, "Definition and Specification of Meaning." *The Journal of Philosophy*, Vol. XLIII, No. 11, (May 23, 1946), pp. 281–288.

Kendall, Patricia L. and Lazarsfeld, Paul F., "Problems of Survey Analysis," in *Continuities in Social Research.* R. K. Merton and P. F. Lazarsfeld (eds.), (Glencoe, Illinois, 1950).

Kornhauser, A. and Lazarsfeld, Paul F., "The Techniques of Market Research from the Standpoint of a Psychologist," *Institute of Management Series, 16* (American Management Assoc., 1935).

Krech, David and Crutchfield, Richard S., *Theory and Problems of Social Psychology* (New York: McGraw-Hill Book Co., 1948).

Lazarsfeld, Paul F., "Reflections on Business," *The American Journal of Sociology*, Vol. LXV, No. 1, (July 1959).

———, "The Use of Panels in Social Research." Proceedings of the American Philosophical Society (November, 1948).

Lazarsfeld, Paul F., and Merton, Robert K., "Friendship as Social Process," in *Freedom and Control.* Berger, *et al.*, (eds.) (Newark: Van Nostrand Co., 1954).

Lazarsfeld and Rosenberg (eds.), *Language of Social Research,* Section V, "The Empirical Study of Action" (Glencoe, Illinois: The Free Press, 1955).

Lewin, Kurt, "The Conceptual Representation and the Measurement of Psychological Forces," in *Contributions to Psychological Theory*, Vol. I (Duke University Press, 1938).

———, *Die psychische Tätigkeit bei der Hemmung von Willens-vorgängen und das Grundgesetz der Association* (Berlin, 1916). Also *German Journal of Psychology*, Vol. 77, pp. 212–247, (1957).

———, *A Dynamic Theory of Personality.* Selected papers, translated by Donald K. Adams and Karl Zener (New York: McGraw-Hill Book Co., 1935).

———, "*Intention, Will and Need*," (1962), translated in D. Rapaport,

Organization and Pathology of Thought (New York: Columbia University Press, 1951).

——, *Principles of Topological Psychology* (New York: Duke University Press, 1936).

Lindworsky, Johannes, *Experimental Psychology*. Translated by Harry R. DeSilva (New York, 1930).

McClelland, David C. *et al.*, *The Achievement Motive* (New York: Appleton-Century-Crofts, 1953).

Mitzman, Arthur, *The Iron Cage* (New York: Alfred Knopf, 1970).

Newcomb, Theodore M., *Social Psychology* (New York: The Dryden Press, 1950).

Oberschall, Anthony, *Empirical Social Research in Germany: 1848–1914*. (Paris, France: Mouton & Co., 1965).

Parsons, Talcott, *The Structure of Social Action* (New York: McGraw-Hill Book Co., 1937).

—— and Shils, E. A. (eds.), *Toward a General Theory of Action* (Cambridge: Harvard University Press, 1951).

——, "Some Comments on the General Theory of Action," *American Sociol. Review* (1953).

Radbruch, Gustav, *Die Handlungsbegriff in seiner Bedeutung für das Strafrechtssystem* (Berlin: J. Guttentag, 1903).

Ramsøy, Odd, "Exploring Connections between Some Concepts in the Theory of Action," *Acta Sociologica* (1957).

Rapaport, David, *Organization and Pathology of Thought* (New York: Columbia University Press, 1951).

Schuetz, Alfred, "Common-sense and Scientific Interpretation of Human Action," *Philos. and Phenomenolog. Research* (1953).

Sears, Robert R., "A Theoretical Framework for Personality and Social Behavior," *American Psychologist* (1951, Presidential address), pp. 476–83.

Sherif, Muzafer, *An Outline of Social Psychology* (New York, 1948).

Swanson, G. E., "The Approach to a General Theory of Action by Parsons and Shils," *American Sociological Review* (1953).

Thomae, Hans, (ed.), *Die Motivation menschlichen Handels* (Kiepenbeuer and Witsch, Köln-Berlin, 1965).

Tolman, Edward, "A Psychological Model," in Parsons and Shils, *Toward a General Theory of Action* (Cambridge: Harvard University Press, 1951).

Warren, Howard C., *Dictionary of Psychology* (Boston: Houghton Mifflin, 1934).

Weber, Marianne, *Max Weber, Ein Lebensbild* (Tübingen, 1926).

Weber, Max, "Die Grenznutzenlehre und das 'psychologische Grundgesetz,'" in *Gesammelte Aufsätze zur Wissenschaftslehre* (Tübingen, 1922).

———, "Methodische Grundlagen der Soziologie," in *Gesammelte Aufsätze zur Wissenschaftslehre* (Tübingen, 1922).

———, "Über einige Kategorien der verstehenden Soziologie," in *Gesammelte Aufsätze zur Wissenschaftslehre* (Tübingen, 1922).

———, "Zur Methodik Sozialpsychologischer Enqueten," *Arch. f. Sozialwissensch.* (1909).

———, "Methodologische Einleitung für die Erhebung des Vereins für Sozialpolitik," in *Gesammelte Aufsätze zur Soziologie und Sozialpolitik* (Tübingen, 1924).

———, "Zur Psychophysik der industriellen Arbeit," in *Gesammelte Aufsätze für Soziologie und Sozialpolitik* (Tübingen, 1924). Originally written 1909. Verein für Socialpolitik. Report on the Congress of 1911.

Wundt, W., "Über das Ausfrage Experiment und die Methoden der Denkpsychologie," *Psychologische Studien*, Vol. 3, 1907, pp. 301–360.

Zeisel, Hans, *Say It With Figures* (New York: Harper and Row, 5th ed., 1968).

CHAPTER *3*

MASS MEDIA OF COMMUNICATION IN MODERN SOCIETY

At first a question came to my mind as to why the topic, the mass media, was included in a conference on freedom in a democracy, along with such basic problems as race relations, and the role of religion. I really do not think, after briefest consideration, that it is too difficult to understand why the mass media are a topic of concern to so many people. In the first place, we see people spending an enormous amount of time on the mass media: reading the newspapers, going to the movies, watching television. Secondly, to many of us comes an urge to reform—a feeling, "If we could only have a hand in newspaper articles we read, or in radio speeches we hear, how we could influence people, and how we could improve this country." We have the conviction that if we could only use these media for the best ends, we could do great things.

There is a third reason why the mass media play such a role in our thinking today. We read the editorials; most of them seem wrong. We listen to radio programs, though they seem so stupid. There is an interesting reason for our constant disagreement with what we read and hear. We pick our friends, by and large, because they agree with us. When you think of it, you rarely associate with anyone who disagrees with you—because the way friendships are formed is around agreement. But the newspapers and the radio intrude upon us with

From Borah Foundation Lectures, University of Idaho (Moscow, Idaho, 1954).

different opinions. As a matter of fact, the only way we occasionally know other people's minds is through the mass media. And as these people seem often very wrong and uninformed, so the mass media seem often wrong and uninformed too.

Now, with your permission, I should like to talk about the mass media in a somewhat more serious and analytical way, concentrating on three major aspects. First, a little historical retrospection is needed, in order that you may see this present concern with the mass media not as something which has flared up in the last ten or fifteen years, but as something which has a real history. Secondly, I would like to tell you a little of what we know about the mass media, for there is in existence a considerable amount of information. Then as a third point —a consequence of my first two—I should like to go back to the problem which is probably foremost in your minds, that is: what can we do about the mass media? But the question of what we can do is better discussed in the light of 1) how has the problem developed? and 2) what do we actually know about it?

HISTORICAL RETROSPECT

To begin with, we might go back to the year 1500, with the notion that a conference is held at the University of Paris, celebrating its three hundredth anniversary. There a professor is asked to give a speech on the great new invention of fifty years before—printing. And his topic: "What will the important new invention of printing do to society?" (This is not too far-fetched. Radio broadcasting, as you know, began in the 1920's, and I remember vividly having given my first speech on "What Radio Will Do to Society," in 1930.) What would the professor have said in 1500 about printing? He would have argued very cogently that it would have no effect at all, because books were so expensive. A printed book was not thought to be much cheaper than one copied out by monks in a monastery, so what difference would it make whether you could print a lot of books or whether you had only a few books? Then, too, religion was the only problem which really mattered in 1500; but the question of religion is for the pulpit, or for the private thought of individuals, and you cannot print books about religion. It is not a topic which can be conveyed in print. And so for all these reasons, it is quite clear that printing would not have any effect; and that settles the matter in 1500.

Let us move now to 1700, and let us imagine another convention going on. Two things have to be reviewed. First, in the 200 years of the Reformation, Protestantism had become dominant in a large part of Europe. And by 1700 there was a feeling that this change had something to do with the invention of printing. Even the translation of the Bible into German would not have had the same effect if printing had not been invented; and a tremendous amount of pamphlet writing had fanned the flames of the Reformation. Finally, the victory of Protestantism in Europe had given people the feeling that perhaps there were various roads to salvation, and that there were other things to worry about than whether they had the one true religion which happened to be prescribed by the Pope. So by this time the relation between reading and the Reformation would have been quite obvious. But another thing would have been noticeable in 1700. By then England had gone through two revolutions, and the whole idea of democratic government, of parliamentary representation, had become a part of the Anglo-Saxon heritage. All that would have been impossible without print. The ideas of general suffrage and general education are very closely related, in the sense that educated people want to have an influence on the government and want a government which has as its goal more education.

Let us move now to 1800 when the relation between democracy and a free press would have been most outspoken and not at all clouded by doubts. Still another conference might be imagined, this time in this country. The buildings might not be as luxurious as the University of Idaho has to offer, but still our 1800 conference can be envisaged in the United States. By this time another quite startling development had come about, and this is the close relationship between the press and politics in public affairs. Another revolution, as you all know, was centered around a number of major writers like Thomas Paine. And by 1800 you have the beginnings of the party system, with the disagreements between Jefferson and Hamilton being mainly fought out in the first national newspapers of the country. And while Jefferson and Hamilton wrote under all sorts of pseudonyms, there were always very close interconnections, in their discussions, between government, politics, and the press. The whole idea of freedom, which so strongly imbued the American Revolution, was closely related to the freedom of the press. Freedom of the individual and freedom of expression of opinion were considered identical with the right to publish a newspaper. And that was not very surprising, for in 1800 publishing a newspaper simply meant the setting up of a little printing press and the printing of a sheet with perhaps 500 circulation, which might go up to 1,000 or 1,500 circulation, and appear once a week or once in two weeks. It was at that time that the interrelations between printing and the mass media and democracy were very outspoken. And that was probably the period when the identification of liberty—as it was then called—with freedom of the press, was most obvious in people's minds.

Then by 1900, when we might have held our conference in any one of hundreds of meeting houses all over the country, the matter had become slightly more complicated. In one respect, people were still very optimistic. Much had changed between 1800 and 1900 in this country. Large cities had developed; the country had become industrialized, and therefore we had lost the Town Hall atmosphere. The small villages where everyone knew everyone else were no longer the main living pattern. But around 1900 everyone was sure that it did not matter, because the newspaper became a substitute for the face-to-face contacts in the Town Hall. Most writers, and the political scientists who began to flourish at the turn of the century, were very optimistic about the role of the newspaper, believing it would make for great mutual understanding. Though the Town Hall meeting was no longer practical nor possible, the newspaper would provide the link between people's ideas, and would be a substitute for the old village and town hall philosophy.

This tone of optimism was slightly dampened not so much by the people concerned with politics as by those concerned with culture and art. This problem, by then obvious and much discussed, was: What would the rapid spread of literacy and rapid spread of newspapers and magazines do to the level of culture? And the problem was quite clear. As long as you have an illiterate people, it would be needful to clamor for schools and for literacy, and to make speeches supporting them. Then you might go home to the few of your friends who really cared for music and for books, and retire to a world where you could read Shakespeare and Wordsworth and Goethe. But people had not noticed in time—and this is one of the first examples of what we like to call unanticipated consequences—that although cultured people went about and provided schools for everyone, the people who came out of these schools did not always want to read Shakespeare. They wanted to read what they found easy and entertaining.

And so, around the third quarter of the nineteenth century, all sorts of things happened which were disturbing to the reformers. For example, the so-called penny press appeared in this country. This had the freedom of the press, provided by cheap printing. The price of the newspaper went down to a sixth of its original price over a few years, and circulation jumped from 1,000 to 10,000 and very quickly to 100,000; but the content of newspapers was very changed. They featured murder and sex stories, and suddenly there was a new kind of use of mass media which no one had anticipated. As a matter of fact, people were quite worried, because not only did a cheap press appear, but even literature changed. Suddenly, people started to clamor for sentimental novels, and writers made money not by writing for a few people but by writing for the masses of the population. There was wide complaint about the lowering of standards of literature. In 1900 there was still optimism as to the political values of newspapers and magazines, but we began to have much discussion and concern as to their cultural implications on the level of taste.

And now let us come back to our conference today. What has happened? First, we note a completely new series of media. The printed media are just one of the three major groups, along with radio broadcasting devices and, more recently, television. Secondly, we have gone through two wars and we have seen the development of modern dictatorship, especially Fascism and Communism. And we have become aware that the modern dictatorships are quite different from those of old tyrants which we used to deplore when we read Greek drama, because the modern dictators make very successful use of mass media. There is very good reason to believe that the Germans by themselves would never have gotten rid of Hitler, and that probably the Russians, in the majority, are not really rebellious against Communism—and that among the main devices by which the dictatorships maintain their power are the mass media.

In our own country most of all, but also in all other Western democracies, a very great change has come about in the mass media themselves. In the 1700's, to go back once more, the governor of the then province of New York set up a special prize for a printer to settle in New York City, as one was needed to print the ordinances of the assembly. When the revolutionaries took over, the printer no longer printed what the governor wanted, but rather what the rebels decreed. Today the *New York Times* does not print just what the government wants it to say, nor is it on the other hand, a rebel against the government. It is in business. And all the mass media—radio, television, and the movies—have become big business enterprises, not concerned, or not *necessarily* concerned with ideas, but with the delivering of something which people want. They are making money in a legitimate way, as General Motors or Chesterfield Cigarettes wants to make money. This situation in this country, where there is no political misuse of mass media by a dictatorship, can be best expressed in the following way. Up to, let us say, the middle of the nineteenth century, there was a two-cornered relationship: the government was on one side and the citizen on the other. The citizen's opinion was expressed through the newspaper, and therefore freedom of the press was identical with freedom of the individual and freedom of thought. And the relation between the government and the citizen was identical with the relation between the government and the press. Today, we have a three-cornered situation; the citizen, the government, and the business of communication. And a variety of alliances are being made. Sometimes the citizenry sides with the government against the communication industry, and we have, for example, the Federal Communications Commission, which enforces regulations in the public interest on the radio industry. In regard to newspapers and the printed media, there is a little more difficulty, as they are heavily protected by the First Amendment. However, you are familiar with the discussions aimed at regulations affecting libel, or at the protection of minority opinion. We could say quite a bit about this if we had time, for just as we have situations in which the citizens and the government sometimes side against the communications industry, we also find that sometimes the industry and the citizens side against the government. There are all types of interesting combinations which come about.

So the whole question of the mass media really has become much more complicated today, and the study of the mass media has newly emerged. Up to about thirty or forty years ago, the whole discussion of the mass media, as I indicated to you in the historical retrospection, was mainly a question of oratory, of opinion, and of philosophy.

Today it has become a legitimate task of the social sciences to carry out what is called communications research as part of sociology and social psychology in many universities. This is a very new development and it is, so to speak, the academic and intellectual shadow of the great changes which have come about in the world.

COMMUNICATIONS RESEARCH TODAY

Communications research, as an academic discipline, has grown up very quickly. At this moment there are several hundred courses being given and about a dozen textbooks are available in an area in which nothing of this kind existed thirty years ago. Usually, the presentation of the material is covered in four steps. We first discuss the whole structure of the industry, and much attention is paid to the trend toward concentration. There are approximately 2,000 newspapers in this country, but there are fewer than 150 places in the entire United States with more than one newspaper. Many observers are concerned about these one-newspaper towns, and others report that diversity of coverage is guaranteed by the fact that radio and television also perform news function. However, the newer media show a similar tendency toward concentration. A few networks control a great part of the important programs. In the movie industry the Supreme Court has recently intervened in this matter of concentration. A large proportion of the movie theaters were owned by the same companies which owned major studios. As a result, independent film producers, even if they could obtain money to produce novel kinds of films, had difficulty in exhibiting them. It was feared that this would result in retarding the development of new production ideas in movies, and so the joint management of production and exhibition is now made much more difficult.

Another interesting aspect of the mass communications structure is the complicated interlocking of various groups with diversified interests. A manufacturer of consumer goods, for example, would have to worry only about whether he pleases his customers and therefore sells his goods. A radio network faces two functions: it must please its customers in the sense that it must get people to listen. At the same time, however, it has to prove to the advertiser that it was successful;

otherwise the advertiser may not give the necessary time to build up the program or may be disappointed in the kind of audience he is getting. This makes more difficult the adherence to a consistent program policy. Even when we speak of an advertiser, we oversimplify the matter, as the manufacturer usually acts through an advertising agency, and considerable difference of opinion, and even of interests, may exist between the two. On the other side, the unions play a peculiar role, especially at the points where the mass media are tied in with show business. Great entertainers and artists are rare, and therefore hold a commanding bargaining position. They are, however, often in the same unions as the broad masses of musicians and actors and, through them, very closely allied to the unions made up of technical personnel. As a result, relatively small unions often have a considerable role through indirect influence on major decisions in the industry. Even outside the entertainment world, in the newspaper field, the influence structure is unusually complicated. Take as an example, the peculiar development of newspaper columnists. They have taken considerable hold on the public, and you will often find that a columnist can express an opinion quite different from that of the owner of the newspaper, because he is valuable as a circulation builder.

After a discussion of the trends and complexities of the management of mass media, a professor or a textbook usually turns to an analysis of the content of mass media. This is such a broad field that it is not possible to give a picture of the many studies which are now available. My colleague, Bernard Berelson, has written a textbook especially devoted to the techniques and findings of content analysis. The main reason for the growth of this work is really the singular difficulty faced by the individual investigator in attempting to gain ideas of what the mass media are doing, as a whole. For example, there are many complaints regarding the amount of cruelty exhibited on children's programs over television. But we have no answers to questions like this: is the trend upward or downward? Is there more cruelty on television than in the fairy tales we tell our children without hesitation? How do radio and television compare in these respects? There are many other examples in which the mere descriptive use of content analysis is useful. There is little doubt, for example, that we have had, in the last decade, an increasing separation of the editorial and the news functions of newspapers. Yet studies have shown that some newspapers will still, in large degree, adapt their news coverage to their editorial policy. As long as this situation remains a matter of vituperation, not much is gained. If, however, the facts are put into cold statistical terms, they often have a considerable effect on the management of newspapers. At the time of the first atomic bomb test on Bikini Island, a major sex crime occurred in Chicago. Some Chicago newspapers gave more and more prominent space to the sex story than to the atomic energy experiment. I recall that when the figures were published, each newspaper tried hard to prove that its performance was really better than the study indicated. I cannot but believe that in the long run impartial and consistent content analyses of this kind will have an effect on the policy of the newspapers.

Content analysis is not restricted to simple statistical descriptions. Sometimes it can move into a more subtle direction, and then raise new and interesting problems. Take as an example the daytime serials, the so-called soap operas, of radio. These programs, to most of us, will be unworthy of attention, although about half of all housewives listen to them with avidity. Still, if these programs are studied systematically, some interesting observations can be made. The plots of the stories tell us, for the most part, how lower middle class families got into trouble and then got out of it. They are likely to have one element in common: the men create all the mischief and the women solve the problems which the men create. Now it is readily understandable why things are presented in this way.

After all, women are the main listeners and the producers want to be sure that the women are pleased. But what is the effect of this policy likely to be? Will it give the women more self-confidence or will it make it more difficult for them to manage their family affairs successfully and to overcome real difficulties? Content analysis does not solve this problem but it points up its importance. And it should not be answered that all of these things are obvious and do not require systematic research. During the war a group of liberal writers asked some of my colleagues at Columbia University to study the treatment of racial minorities in magazine stories. They had a suspicion that Italians were usually characterized as gangsters, that Negroes were never presented in professional jobs, that a greedy banker usually had a Jewish name, and so forth. This, as well as many other interesting related findings, were proved by a content analysis of magazine stories. But the most interesting fact was that some of the liberal writers who had suggested the study were among the worst offenders, without knowing it themselves. After all, a magazine story must be short and must move swiftly. The temptation is very great indeed to use racial stereotypes for the purpose of letting the reader know more quickly what topic the story is about to deal with. Our writers had faced a conflict between their convictions and the expediencies of their craft, which they did not realize themselves before seeing the findings of our study.

Probably the most important contributions of communications research come from a third phase, when the student turns to the study of the audience itself. It is quite surprising how much we can misjudge the reactions of people different from ourselves. I have no doubt, for example, that the majority of you feel that radio commercials are abominable and that everyone hates them. This, however, is due to the fact that you are members of a relatively small stratum of highly educated people. At most, a third of the population, if not less, feels about commercials as you do. Another third does not mind commercials, and the remaining third positively likes them and finds them interesting. The latter would include people whose daily lives provide little stimulation. They experience commercials as some of us enjoy window shopping. They are entertained by the various tricks of voice and sound effects which have been developed. If some of you want to go on the warpath against commercials, you would have to argue on the grounds of general principles; if you think of yourselves as the voice of the people you will discover that you are mistaken—if you mean by people all of them, and not just those who are like yourselves.

Audience studies have unearthed quite a number of findings which are of general interest. The story on the commercials is, for example, only one example of a much more general result. Taste in mass media is tremendously dependent upon education. We do know that rich people vote more Republican than do poor people. But this is slight compared to the class difference we find when we compare the audience vote on serious music. Listening to good music is restricted to a very small sector of an educated upper class. The same is true for so-called educational programs. People who do not have a certain amount of education to begin with are much less likely to expose themselves to serious topics on the radio, even if these topics are presented in sugar-coated forms. This finding can be still further generalized.

People as a whole have a tendency to read about, to look at, and to listen to topics which are close to the environment in which they live. A magazine story whose hero is an older person will find more older readers. If the story is placed in a rural setting, this, too, will be reflected in the composition of its readers. This is a rather unexpected result, as one might expect people to use the mass media for new experiences rather than to have reiterated things they have already experienced. Nevertheless, the latter is the case. Most people look for themselves in the mass media, rather than for the world. Even when we ask people who are their favorite movie performers, women are more likely to mention women and men to pick their favorites from among their own sex.

There is, by now, a rather hackneyed formula which organizes communications research in its major phases: Who talks about what to whom, with what effect? "Who" is the industry; "what" is the content; and "whom" is the audience. The effect, conjectured, or derived from actual studies, has already been implied in many of my examples. This is the point at which communications research is most closely tied in with the main topic of these meetings. You would not be interested in the study of specific effect, which is so important for the propagandist or the advertiser. You are undoubtedly more interested in the effects which the mass media have upon society and on its broad values. From my historical introduction you will probably gather two points. First, the effects come about quite slowly and would be very difficult to trace with certainty. In addition, they become very different as the social and technological context change. I think it would be more fruitful, then, if I end by discussing some of the basic problems which arise at this point.

MASS MEDIA AND SOCIAL VALUES

Offhand, it might be supposed that if we just look at the content of the mass media we can best study what the social effects will be. But as our preceding examples have shown, this is not likely to get us very far. On the one hand, the content of the mass media depends very much on the general structure of their management; this, as we have seen, is very complex indeed. For certainly, if we should want different content, there is not just one agency to which we can turn. On the other hand, even if we should change programs, the audience remains a self-regulating factor, determining what to select out of the complexity of newspaper content and television programs—how to understand them and how to adapt them to their peculiar needs. Short of a persisting regulation of the whole process at every step, we must weigh all of the various consequences which would follow any specific move in this network of interrelated influences. And as we contemplate matters in this way, we will become aware that the essence of the problem is this: the mass media of communications are a juncture at which a number of basic American principles, in which we all believe, come into contradiction with each other. Let us consider a few of these difficulties.

By and large, this country believes in free enterprise as far as its industry is concerned. It also believes that the government, on its various levels, has a responsibility for libraries and similar services. How about the mass media, then? The mass media come under the heading of business enterprises and therefore should have no government interference. On the other hand, they are of primary cultural importance and therefore are certainly in the domain of public responsibility. We have experimented with a variety of solutions. For radio and television the Federal Communications Commission symbolizes a relatively far-flung role of the government. In the movie industry we rely essentially on a strong system of self-regulation. The newspapers are very much on their own. All of these systems have their own advantages and disadvantages, and they have developed in part accidentally and in part for social and technological reasons. There is one thing which we have not done. We have not developed devices by which we can review our experiences and improve our decisions.

Now how about the notion of majority preference in the mass media? If the majority wants a Republican press, then we agree that we should have one. If the majority wants bad radio programs, should we have them also? The creed of giving people what they want comes into conflict at this point with the creed of leadership and advancement of cultural standards. Compulsory inoculation against disease or advanced methods of elementary education are not matters that are decided by majority vote, but are left to experts who are likely to be

well ahead of general public opinion. Where do the mass media belong
in the continuum, the two ends of which are represented by political
choices, on the one side, and decisions of experts, on the other.

A third conflict is the one between complete freedom of expression and the idea that the mores of the community have to be
respected. This, of course, is one of the oldest and best-known di-
lemmas, because it has been so much discussed in the field of sex
mores. Where does legitimate concern with morals turn into dangerous
censorship? No one, in principle, wants to preserve bad comics; but if
a committee of vigilantes is organized against them, there is no telling
what such a committee would mobilize itself to fight next.

How can such basic conflicts of value be resolved? First of all,
they have to be recognized. This recognition is usually rarer than you
would suppose. Some groups will get a bright idea and be quite convinced that they are promoting a basic American ideal. But they
usually do not realize that they are, at the same time, violating another
basic American ideal, one which they would cherish as much if they
happened to meet it in another context. After the problem has been
recognized and clarified, all possible solutions need to be reviewed.
And here again we are usually quite shortsighted. The advocates of
an idea see only the advantages of their plan but do not anticipate the
bad consequences it might have in other areas in the long run. But not
all things can be settled by rational analysis and discussion. In every
society there are basic conflicts of interest which must be reconciled
in the best manner possible. In the mass media field, perhaps the best
example of this is the conflict between business interests and the cultural values of the intellectuals. No one can deny that the mass media,
due to American business enterprise, have made spectacular technological progress. But if the main concern is with the levels of taste and of
intellectual maturity in this country—and most of you in this audience
would share this professional concern—then our interests and the
interests even of the enlightened businessmen are in conflict, however
understanding we, and however enlightened they might be.

We thus face three tasks in this field: a constructive and dis-
passionate formulation of the problem; independent and informed
analysis of implications and consequences; and a willingness and ability
to reconcile legitimate conflicts of interest. Some individuals would
hold that "everything will come out well in the end," as a result of
the much quoted "free discussion in the market-place." But society

has probably become too complex to make this hope a very realistic one. The time has probably come to set up some machinery by which advancement on these three problem areas can be facilitated. Such machinery might profitably be built on at least three levels, and I shall conclude by giving an example of each.

On the local level, you might have a committee of all the groups interested in the mass media, just as there exist the Community Chests, combining all groups active in local charities. Such a local committee would include the managers of the media, parent-teacher associations, and certainly representatives of colleges wherever they exist in local situations. Think of the many mutual interests held by radio and television stations, colleges, and newspapers. The local station usually does not have the facilities to do audience surveys; they often do not even have access to existing knowledge resulting from communications research. Social science departments could provide the stations with facts for which, in turn, the stations would give free time to colleges for various program experiments which English, Speech, or Music departments might want to make. The local newspapers either have no television or radio columns or they have very bad ones, mainly filled with items about Hollywood divorces and engagements. I am confident that many local papers would appreciate a well-written column of program criticism, by members of a college faculty. Undoubtedly, many other examples of collaboration, appropriate to a specific local situation, would come to mind.

On the state level, a recent development in the television field provides a very interesting example. The Federal Communications Commission has reserved 240 channels for educational television. In most areas, state subsidies will be needed to utilize these channels. But there is much justified hesitation at putting these educational stations directly under state management, because of possible political misuse. A solution might be some form of public corporation, pooling the resources of the state government, of private contributors and of cultural agencies, such as libraries, museums and colleges. Something like the British Broadcasting Corporation, or the Port Authority of New York, or the Tennessee Valley Authority might provide the model for a composite institution which would make best use of the available television channels.

On the federal level, still another idea might be pursued. One or several of the large foundations might set up an institution similar to the Committee on Economic Development. Such a center for cultural development of the mass media could perform three major functions. First, it could engage in basic research by pooling present knowledge and making funds available for long-range studies beyond the means of a single research agency. We know virtually nothing about the effect of the mass media upon children or about their actual role in the formation of public opinion; only studies carried on over many years would provide the necessary data. At the same time, the task of review and analysis of the major problems, as we have described them above, waits upon the existence of such a center, the members of which would have public confidence and support, would represent the various interest groups, and would back their judgments by con-tinuous work rather than haphazard enunciations. Finally, a national center could provide the local committees with factual information and technical advice.

I would summarize the situation, then as follows. The mass media have become a justified concern in our democracy, but I do not be-lieve that they have necessarily become a danger. Or we can at least keep them from becoming dangerous by extending our knowledge about them and arranging for systematic discussion and co-operation on the local, state, and national levels. We need to be worried about the mass media only if we fail to make provisions for collective think-ing and collective action. In the end, what the mass media will do to our society will depend upon what we, as citizens, do with the mass media.

Part Two

Critical Sociology

CHAPTER 4

THE ROLE OF CRITICISM IN THE MANAGEMENT OF MASS MEDIA

If there is one institutional disease to which the media of mass communication seem particularly subject, it is a nervous reaction to criticism. As a student of the mass media I have been continually struck and occasionally puzzled by this reaction, for it is the media themselves which so vigorously defend principles guaranteeing the right to criticize.

Manifestations of this nervousness are not difficult to point out. There are traces of it even at this conference. The Commission on Freedom of the Press has been mentioned at least twenty times, for example. And the same nervous reaction crops up at the conclusion of a highly competent 27-page report on economic problems, the final sentence of which states that "We should do research on ways to acquaint the public with the problems of the communications field so that undeserved criticism can be avoided."

The reaction of the radio industry to a review of programs by the Federal Communications Commission was still more extreme. Some of the criticisms contained in the Blue Book were hard to agree with, but all in all the Blue Book was not a particularly severe document and most people agree now that in the long run it did more good than harm. At the time that it appeared, however, the National Association of Broadcasters appealed to the American people to fight for their basic rights; in one communique the heroes of the American Revolution were called upon to rise again and to keep the FCC from checking

Reprinted from *The Journalism Quarterly*, 25:2 (1948), by permission of the publisher.

whether broadcasters were living up to the stipulations of their license.

The reverse side of this picture is that the critic himself becomes nervous. Because he anticipates the kind of reaction which his criticism will elicit, he is somewhat hesitant to make it. This is a rather serious matter. Those of us social scientists who are especially interested in communications research depend upon the industry for much of our data. Actually most publishers and broadcasters have been very generous and cooperative in this recent period during which communications research has developed as a kind of joint enterprise between industries and universities. But we academic people always have a certain sense of tight-rope walking: at what point will the commercial partners find some necessary conclusion too hard to take and at what point will they shut us off from the indispensable sources of funds and data?

Now this is not the occasion to attempt a complete exploration of the roots of this nervousness. But certainly one part of the explanation is that criticism of the mass media is not recognized as a formal and legitimate field of intellectual endeavor. Consequently, the critics are suspect: they are thought of usually either as persons airing a pet peeve or selling a pet scheme. The obvious contrast here, of course, is with the whole field of literary and art criticism. Where there is such a tradition of criticism, and where there are persons who make it their profession to develop and apply standards of judgment, book reviews or criticisms of art exhibitions are greeted with a calm sobriety much like the response to a weather forecast. But for rare instances, they are not the occasion for nervous hysteria or bitter recrimination.

Thus, the problem seems to be one of finding ways to make such criticism more bearable both for those who offer it and for those who receive it. It is my feeling that one very effective way of doing this would be to regularize and formalize the role of criticism in the management of mass media. Not only should the problems of criticism be thoroughly discussed at conferences such as this, but they also should be the subject-matter of systematic courses and training programs. Students and researchers should come to think of criticism as something being systematically studied; they should be persuaded to undertake critical examinations of the mass media and to produce material amenable to criticism. If the whole area were institutionalized in this way, then there would be less emotionalism connected with it.

But what should be included in a program dealing with the role of criticism in the management of mass media? What courses would be relevant? What research should be carried out? I propose to answer these questions by discussing five broad topics. These might be considered sections of a division in an Institute of Communications Research; they might be thought of as courses to be taught; they might be thought of as the subjects for systematic research. But however they are conceived, they seem to cover the major questions with which a division on problems of criticism would be concerned.

I would start with the section which would be most acceptable, both to students and to outsiders—how the mass media, the newspaper and the local radio station, improve conditions in the community through vigilance, through criticism, and through crusades. While we are most concerned with criticism *of* the mass media, this criticism *by* the media is part of the total picture, and therefore must be considered.

While the topic is a familiar one, there seems to be little information available at the present time. Every journalism professor discusses criticism of the community by newspapers, but I have wondered what materials are used. I have tried unsuccessfully to acquire pertinent materials. I have found a book by Radder on the service of the newspaper to the community and another by Bent in which newspaper crusades are described. Frankly I have found little else. And there are some very important questions which remain unanswered so far as I know. For instance, there does not seem to be any information on how many crusades are going on at the present time. Are they increasing or decreasing? Are they more frequent in two-newspaper or in one-newspaper towns? In big cities or in small cities? Are they undertaken more frequently by newspapers with definite political affiliations, or by independent newspapers?

We know very little about the usual outcome or effects of such crusades. The few stories which we have, deal for the most part with successful crusades: through the efforts of a newspaper a corrupt politician has been put out of office, or the innocence of a man proved. But how many crusades have been unsuccessful? There is not the slightest record of that. And, under what conditions are they successful or unsuccessful? Then there is a whole series of questions concerning the effects of such crusades on the newspapers themselves. Do crusades usually result in increased circulation and advertising revenue, or are they dangerous to the financial interests of the publishers? An accurate case book on crusades might show that they are not only acts of heroism and altruism, but also good business. In that event your students could feel freer to undertake crusades and thus to bring about a variety of improvements in the community. In sum, then, while there is a prevalent feeling that newspapers should crusade, many of the important facts are missing.

Criticism of the community by radio stations presents a somewhat more complicated situation. As you know, the Mayflower Decision has been interpreted as prohibiting radio stations from crusading for pure water or better housing. Hearings now under way have split the industry as well as the general public. Some feel that it is the right and the duty of licensees to express their points of view on public affairs. Others feel that the industry would profit financially and that the community would be safeguarded from bias if broadcasters did not participate in public discussions. There are counter arguments on both sides. The radio industry derives its income from the big business firms; therefore, will not the broadcaster always side with big business? Doesn't he anyhow, is the answer; wouldn't it be better to bring his point of view out into the open and insist that he give time to the "opposite side"?

This seems a good solution until one realizes that many questions have more than two sides. Who is to decide how many points of view there are? The matter is made still more complicated by the fact that everyone seems agreed that the broadcaster should not be partisan in straight politics; but where does politics end and government begin? Students should become sensitized to the complexity of this kind of problem. We hope that once they are sensitized they will not just follow whatever party line the industry happens to adopt, but will try to reach some decision of their own.

While newspapers are not only permitted but actually encouraged to criticize social conditions, and while there is great uncertainty as to what critical role the radio should serve, there seems to be a very definite feeling that the slightest degree of social criticism in a movie is something very dangerous. Recall what happened in the recent hearings before the Committee on Un-American Activities. These hearings were designed ostensibly to determine whether or not the movies exercise Communistic influence, but that topic was not mentioned once. All of the questions concerned the political affiliations of the writers: were they Communists? No one examined the films to see whether they contained Communist philosophy or were revolutionary or dangerous. The only piece of evidence on the content of the movies came from one elderly woman who said that in one film a young boy refused to work for a pawnbroker, because his parents were poor people. If that isn't Communism, asked this woman, what is it?

Perhaps it is dangerous for the media to criticize social conditions, but at the present time we have no evidence one way or the other. We don't yet know what such criticism does to the audiences or to the media themselves. We don't even know how frequently the media undertake such criticism.

Here then we find a broad area of research with many facets. It is sociologically interesting to study why we hold such different folk-ways as to the kind of criticism which is appropriate for different media. It will be very useful to describe systematically how much constructive criticism the different media actually exercise; and our whole discussion will be much more fruitful once we know what kind of criticism influences whom and under what conditions.

The psychological advantages of starting your discussion of criticism in this way should be clear. It is easier to encourage open discussions of criticism when the industry is in a position to throw bricks rather than to be hit by them.

Once the students are accustomed to talking about and thinking about criticism quite frankly, then you might turn to the opposite type of criticism: that leveled against the mass media by respected intellectuals and liberals. In order to make this second series of problems more palatable, I would start with an interesting topic which deserves further investigation. Let me describe it in this way. Twenty or thirty years ago liberal organizations were concerned almost exclusively with questions of social betterment—child labor, woman suffrage, economic insecurity, the exploitation of workers, and so on. These same liberal organizations are today almost as exclusively concerned with the danger of radio, the danger of newspapers, and the bad effects of motion pictures. I have no content analysis, but I am quite sure that an examination of the writings and speeches of liberals would show that they have shifted their attention from economic and social problems to the mass media. We might almost say that their concern has become an obsession. I think that I would be looked upon with less suspicion at Columbia University if I proposed a return to a 50-hour work week than if I suggested another 30 seconds of commercial announcements for each 15 minutes of radio time.

We undoubtedly are better off today then we were 30 years ago, but life is still not so wonderful that it might not be worthwhile to concern ourselves with social betterment from time to time. Why is it then that the mass media have become the bête noire of the liberals? This is a question which must be answered for the young student. And, as a matter of fact, it must be answered for the older practitioner as well.

Last year when I raised the same questions at a meeting of the National Association of Broadcasters, and presented data which show that the better educated sectors of the community dislike and distrust radio, my audience found it hard to understand. Broadcasters think of themselves as honest, hard-working, and decent people; why is it, then, that doctors and preachers and teachers dislike them?

I tried to explain it in the following way. The liberals of today feel terribly gypped. For decades they and their intellectual ancestors fought to attain certain basic goals—more leisure time, more education, higher wages. They were motivated by the idealistic hope that when the masses were no longer exploited, when they had time and money and education, they would develop into fine and culturally satisfied human beings. But what happened? After the liberals had fought their battles and won their victories, the people spent their newly acquired time and money on movies, on radio, on newspapers, and on magazines. Instead of listening to Beethoven, they listen to Johnny Mercer; instead of listening to the Chicago Round Table, they listen to Charlie Mc-Carthy; I almost wanted to say that instead of going to Columbia University they go to the Columbia Broadcasting System.

The liberals feel betrayed. They hoped that the increased time and money which they fought for would be channelized in directions and activities which interested them; instead it was drained off by the mass media. The situation of the liberals is much like that of the high school boy who, after weeks of saving, accumulates enough money to buy a bracelet for a girl, and who then learns that the girl has gone out with another boy to show off her nice new trinket. You can very well understand why the liberals are angry, and perhaps you can almost sympathize with them.

One important point to keep in mind is that some of the misunderstandings between liberals and members of communications industries have their historical roots and implications. If you can make this understandable to the young student who will some day be a practitioner in the communications field, then he will recognize that he is not being personally attacked nor is his honesty being impugned; social critique of mass media is nowadays often the form in which broad social issues are discussed.

I don't think that I should try here to enumerate all of the misunderstandings which arise, or to analyze the factors which are involved. Let me mention just one and you will then see how you could spend a leisurely month or two of your criticism course elaborating and documenting each point. For example, consider what has happened to the concept of freedom of the press over the course of American history. At the time of the Revolution, there was a very simple two-sided relationship. On the one side were the citizens; on the other was the government, which interfered as little as possible with the citizenry. In these early days some citizens established small newspapers; and others gave speeches from soap boxes, but they weren't very different. Anyone who had political theories or an interest in political activities was either an actual or potential publisher, so that the publisher shared common interests with other citizens. There was thus a two-sided relationship in which the citizen and the publisher together fought for their freedom to criticize the government.

In the last century, however, the situation has become vastly more complicated. The simple two-sided relationship has been superseded by a complex three-cornered structure. The citizens still represent one corner, the government still represents another, but now there is also the communications industry. Providing facilities for the expression of opinion has become a major business enterprise. It is no longer possible for an individual to present his ideas directly; they must pass through the channels of some medium of mass communication. This new three-cornered relationship between the citizens and the government and the industry leads to complicated and sometimes surprising alliances. Occasionally, the citizen forms an alliance with the industry against the government; occasionally with the government against the industry; occasionally, he finds himself faced with an alliance between the government and industry. Many questions about the mass media can be answered if this development from a two-sided to a three-cornered relationship is kept in mind; confusion results if the historical trend is lost from sight.

There is one final point which I should like to bring out in discussing the criticisms made by the liberals and intellectuals. So far I have assumed, implicitly if not explicitly, that we know exactly what their major objections to the mass media are; that we know the ways in which they consider the media dangerous or harmful. Actually, this is not the case; we have only rather vague impressions and feelings. It is quite important, therefore, to undertake researches on such questions as the following: How much criticism is there actually? Toward what specific aspects or features of the mass media is it directed? How much of it is documented in a way which would lead us to believe that it is justified? Clearly we cannot help the students understand and antici-pate the liberals' criticisms until such basic information is collected and analyzed.

So far we have talked about the criticism of the community by the mass media, and the criticism of the mass media by the intellectuals of the community. But what about the remainder of the community, the 70 or 75 per cent who could pass any FBI loyalty test without difficulty? They must, of course, be brought into the picture. Here the problem ties in somewhat with the previous one, for much of the intellectual's criticism results from the fact that a large part of the community, a vast majority in fact, want the media exactly as they are—only more so. They not only refrain from criticizing the media; they are actually very pleased with what they hear or read or see in a movie theater. This permits the mass media to argue that they produce what is wanted and demanded.

The problem is not as simple as this argument might imply, how-ever, for it involves a conflict between two major tenets of American life. On the one hand we have the belief that part of our strength as a democracy rests on the fact that in the last analysis things are done as the people want them to be done. But this does not mean that we have no school because children dislike going to classes, nor does it mean that we have no vaccinations because people dislike having their arms pricked. This is where the second principle comes in. There are certain crucial matters in which we feel that the welfare of the country as a whole is more important than some individuals' desires or preferences. On such matters we trust that experts in the field will provide the right guidance.

Now which of these two principles should be paramount in the management of mass media? Do we "give the people what they want," or do we believe that there are experts who know the best balance for the total supply which the mass media provide? It is not too difficult to suggest an answer. Obviously, we do not want magazines and radio programs in this country to drive audiences away. But almost no one would propose that the media be based on the lowest common denominator; publishers and broadcasters have a cultural responsibility. Their business is affected by public interest. Thus the best solution would be to have mass media aim just slightly above what would be the simplest level at any time. In this way, we shall have a general acceptance of media content, as well as a slow, systematic intellectual progress to which the media themselves will contribute.

Obviously it is easier to make this recommendation than it is to carry it out. Continuous investigations are necessary in order to find out what the level of acceptance is likely to be; and experiments will tell us how we can offer better programs and better literature without losing our audiences. There is some suspicion that the communications industry underrates the level of American audiences. Why, for instance, are the pocket books in England so much better than the same type of paper-bound mass literature produced in America, where formal literacy is the highest in the world?

But, at the same time, well-meaning reformers have a curious tendency to shy away from the true state of affairs. An interesting example is provided by some experience with radio research. For a variety of reasons, the radio industry is keenly aware of the cultural dilemma which we are discussing here. The advertisers look for big mass audiences and therefore dread experimentation with different types and levels of content. The FCC, on the other hand, exercises at least a certain psychological pressure toward higher standards. Many broadcasters, as individuals, are probably inclined to follow the latter course. Therefore, they want to know how far they can go. As one step in learning the answer the National Association of Broadcasters has started to make periodic surveys to find out how people look at radio. Now, as one would expect, the mass of the people want to be entertained and not educated. They don't dislike commercials and they are not particularly aware of the problems which the communications experts discuss so hotly. These are the facts with which one has to reckon, whether one likes it or not. When the first of these series of surveys appeared, the liberals were sharply critical, saying that the results would be detrimental to their good cause. The final social effects of facts, however, depend upon the use which is made of them by all parties concerned. The results of the survey are not a mandate but a guide for us. It would be most desirable if the printed media and the movies were to follow the example which the radio industry has provided.

In this third area of our general scheme, we have something that resembles criticism in reverse. People who work in the communications industry should be critical of their own audience. We expect them to set their standards higher than mere commercial success would force them to do. In other words, we expect them to be professionals. This brings up the interesting question—under what conditions does a skilled group develop professional standards? Many social scientists have been concerned with this question. The medical profession, the British Civil Service, teachers, and many other occupational groups have been studied from this point of view. It would undoubtedly be advisable to include such studies in the program suggested by this paper.

But at the same time it would be a mistake to consider it only "natural" that the masses of the population do not want the mass media to have more sophisticated standards. We should not resign ourselves by saying that this is a fact of "human nature." Why is the human-interest story, the sensational headline, or the trivial best seller so successful? This is what we must determine. Perhap when we have better answers, the psychological appeal of these successful stories can be preserved but linked up with more worthwhile topics. The comics which started as mere entertainment are now being used as a tool for mass education. The "Professor Quiz" type of radio program is being used more and more by educators and broadcasters to disseminate useful information. The short story, a technological by-product of the mass magazines, has become an art form in its own right. Here again, then, another area of necessary investigation can be opened up.

The problem of standards of media content easily leads into the fourth area of the present discussion. How do the mass media treat each other? Current developments in the mass media make this question an interesting one. The newspapers have always felt that it was their special privilege to advise and regulate the other media. They have, of course, printed book reviews from the very beginning of their publication. But as movies and radio became more established media, newspapers began to include movie reviews and columns of radio criticism. Somehow the newspapers seem always to have known what was good for the other media. But this flow of criticism has become less one-sided in recent months. CBS now has a 15-minute program criticizing the press. The *New Yorker* magazine published Liebling's articles on newspapers. Slowly, then, the newspapers are being made to taste their own medicine. But there is nothing like a balance as yet: the bulk of criticism still flows from the newspapers.

The newspapers, however, base their criticism of mass media on incorrect and inadequate premises. This can best be understood if we look at the problem historically. For the ancient Greeks, art had a very definite purpose: art should make man "a better citizen in his community." There was thus a clear criterion as to whether a specific piece of art was good or bad: did it achieve its purpose? As time went on, broader purposes were conceded to art: it might influence man's moral standards, his intellectual level, and his esthetic sensitivities. However, among the great German critics of the eighteenth century, there was consensus on one point. Each drama or poem had to be judged according to the effect it exercised upon people. With the beginning of the nineteenth century this question became less dominant and a new topic moved into the foreground: the relationship between the artist and his product. This is quite a remarkable shift; not art and the consumer but art and the producer become the main interest of nineteenth century criticism.

Quite a complex of factors can account for this change. With the development of industrial society, audiences became more and more sharply stratified; perhaps the critic realized that different groups might be differently affected by an art product, and perhaps, therefore, he became discouraged at the thought of having to speculate as to possible effects in different groups. The Romantic Era also highlighted interest in the creative personality. Whatever the reason, it had become obvious by the middle of the nineteenth century that the main concern was whether or not an art product was a true expression of a great personality.

Now it is easy to see what had to happen when this type of criticism was applied to products of mass art. A radio program or a movie is produced by a large number of people. How can it be judged solely according to its relationship to the artistic personality?

Undoubtedly, we must revise our standards. We shall have to become accustomed to judging products of mass art according to their effects on the audience. We shall have to return to what the classicists considered an appropriate standard of criticism. But we do this at a time when everyone is extremely aware of social and psychological differences. The task is therefore a complicated one. Let me exemplify the matter by one drastic example.

The radio has created a new art form—the serial drama. We would like to know what it does to the women who listen to it regularly. Does it make them neurotic, uninterested in public affairs, less willing to read? Or does it teach them a lot about life which they would never learn from their own small sphere of experience? Does it help them over many a lonely hour and, therefore, make them happy? Some of these questions we can answer by studying the content of these serial stories. If they give an inaccurate picture of modern life, their effect cannot be good. But to determine whether the effect is bad would require rather complicated empirical studies with listeners. We have only started to carry out such studies, and, obviously, until we have much more information, daytime serials cannot be discussed very reasonably. Certainly the criteria which literary criticism developed during the last century cannot be meaningfully applied to such a different type of art product.

Thus, the entire question of the judgment of mass media is wide open. We don't as yet know how to proceed, but we can at least note the confusion which results if the problem is completely overlooked. Many magazine stories are written by means of a formula. Thus, they are in no way the expression of an artist inspired by his God. But, perhaps, it is a good formula, evoking all sorts of noble sentiments in the reader. Why shouldn't such a story be more desirable than the product which has no effects upon the audiences at all? It is true, of course, that the social psychologist does not as yet have sufficient skill in the study of effects. Therefore, let us try diligently to develop such skills and let us not be deterred by the "Victorian" critic who thinks that he is an esthetic radical when he scorns the use of research in art criticism.

One misunderstanding must be avoided. Audience research does not imply that the audiences' likes or dislikes provide the ultimate standard for mass art. It is the manner in which one is affected by a program or a movie which matters. Liking plays only a partial and mediating role. If a radio network broadcasts a documentary program, the problem is to determine whether or not its message gets across, rather than whether or not it suits public taste. In the long run, obviously, a message cannot reach people if it cannot be understood, or if it creates resistance. The *merit* of the message, i.e., its value, is determined through extensive discussion; the *effectiveness* of the message is determined through empirical research. And in the last analysis, this is true for all kinds of effects, be they spiritual, intellectual, or esthetic.

It may be a long time before audience research can really discharge the very great role it will have to play in the development of standards for mass media. But the students of mass communications should be informed of its procedures and its purposes. While students are being trained in the role and nature of criticism they should read carefully the type of revelations which editors and broadcasters receive from their research divisions. It is very helpful, indeed, to read a criticism of a movie or a radio program when it is framed in terms of what the product did or did not do to the audience, whether they enjoyed it or not, whether they understood it or not, whether it excited them or left them cold, and so on.

Students should parallel their reading of these specific research reports with a careful examination of the average movie or radio review found in daily newspapers or even magazines. You and they will be surprised at how verbose, empty, and hazy these latter reviews seem when compared with research reports. The research man may use lofty language, but his discussion is firmly anchored to what he actually determined about reactions and effects upon the audience.

Columbia University is at present preparing a broad study of the development of criticism and its relation to mass media. I hope that it will not be long before we shall be able to provide you with some material to clarify this old and rather complicated topic.

By now our imaginary student should have considerable flexibility of mind. We initiated him by considering the traditional idea that it is his right and duty to criticize a community. But right there the first stop-look-and-listen sign was posted: he should *study* crusades in addition to feeling strongly about them. Then we wanted him to understand just why the most progressive sector in the community is likely to scan his work with a watchful and somewhat suspicious eye. Perhaps our student felt somewhat smug at this point: why should he worry about the criticism of the minority if he has the majority behind him? As we saw, this position needs some modification: in his profession he is in a way responsible for the cultural standards of the community. Perhaps the student then became somewhat cynical: aren't all standards relative? The answer was, yes and no. Yes, inasmuch as we must decide what goals we want to achieve. But we should really *know* the effects and implied consequences of the things we do. The whole "science of criticism" has led us toward a large variety of possible investigations. Our student should at least know how they are conducted, what kind of results they yield, and how they are related to the problems at hand. But after we have dealt with history, content analysis, attitude surveys, and effect studies, we still won't be quite through. One more aspect of our problem has to be outlined briefly.

There is a story about a young boy who got his first glimpse of anthropology in high school. He learned to his amazement that there was a time when people did not wear shoes. This was quite a shock: he never realized the customs could be so different. The more he thought about it the more puzzling the matter became. If they had no shoes, how were those primitive tribes able to drive their automobiles?

I suspect that a large number of people working in the communications field feel that the way things are now done is the only way to do them. It seems to me that one of our duties as teachers is to make students sensitive and hospitable to social change.

I do not mean that we can or should agree on a specific social platform, but there is a series of problems, the fifth and last area in this outline, in which the relation between the media of mass communication and the social system as a whole is considered. It is strange, for instance, how often one hears that we must maintain free enterprise in this country in order to guarantee freedom of the press. I do not know, of course, whether or not this is true, but it is certainly conceivable that a country could have a free press and a government-regulated automobile industry. Or again, it is now technically possible for listeners to pay directly for whatever program they want to hear so that neither advertisers nor the government need support the broadcasting system. But the necessary inventions were made after we got used to our present radio system, and consequently very little attention is paid such an alternative possibility.

A wide range of subject matter can be used to develop a constructive sense of relativism. At one end of the range we can discuss technical details like the following: Why did so many magazine stories have a sad ending one hundred years ago while today they are proverbial for their happy endings? Why is it that in this country the sex taboos are adhered to most strictly by the radio, somewhat less by the movies, and considerably less by the legitimate stage? Why are so many movie plots developed in an upper-class setting, while most radio stories are played in a lower middle-class background?

On the other end of the range we ourselves should learn and teach others to think in terms of broad historical connections between the communication media and the social system as a whole. To give just one example, what are some of the ways in which the growth of national magazines and broadcasting has affected other cultural habits of the American people? They probably have greatly handicapped the development of the book industry. A point can be made that the art of conversation will never again play the role it had in the European middle class of the 19th century. The exchange of ideas by letters has probably disappeared forever; here the telephone is another factor to be considered. Some writers have pointed out that the movies and the automobile have accustomed us to such rapid shifts of scene that our whole way of looking at the outside world might be in process of considerable change.

Some sociologists go even farther in their analysis. They point out that in their earlier stages the mass media helped towards the development of democracy because they drew the broad masses closer to the discussion of public affairs. But by now the trend might be reversed. If one, for a few cents, can get any kind of opinion ready-made at the corner drug store, why should one go to the trouble of thinking for oneself? Brain-saving devices might endanger democratic developments if they are not paralleled by more active and personal forms of social participation.

Whatever the facts may be, people who have been trained in this kind of analysis will have a much more detached and constructive attitude toward criticism. They will realize that it is sociology in everyday working clothes, or, if you prefer, social science in the making.

Whoever participates in discussions of mass media is always struck by the recurrence of a familiar kind of episode. At one point someone will say that the mass media do this and that, and someone else will hotly deny the contention. Many of these disagreements are not due to differences of judgment but to ignorance of the facts. We actually are not sure as to what the mass media do. The manager of a network is greatly impressed by the amount of money and effort he invests in an outstanding documentary broadcast; the critical listener is equally impressed by the fact that this fine event consumes only one out of perhaps 100 or more of broadcasting hours. The publisher is proud of how much more carefully today's newspaper separates news and editorial opinion as compared to the newspaper of 100 or 50 years ago; the critic points out that he still can distinguish between a Republican and a Democratic newspaper merely by looking at the front page.

Factual information on the content of the media would go a long way to providing a sound basis for discussion and criticism. The best way to conclude this series of comments, therefore, is to urge such documentation. This country is rightfully proud of its many statistical services. We know quite well how many people get divorced and how much pig-iron is produced every year. But our social bookkeeping lags woefully when it comes to cultural matters. Social research is probably not yet ready to give us monthly information on how many people are happy or unhappy. But nothing would be easier than to set up a service based on sound sampling techniques which would periodically report the content of newspapers, magazines, and radio programs. It is just a matter of developing the appropriate motivation and providing the appropriate machinery.

All of us who are interested in the mass media of communication should keep on reiterating the need for such periodic reports. We should perpetually press for any one of the many ways in which such data could be provided. For instance, why shouldn't we have a regional board, let us say, in each Federal Reserve district? The boards might be composed of representatives of broadcasters' and publishers' associations, universities, and interested professional and civic organizations. The boards would raise the necessary funds and lay out the broad policy to be followed. They would commission expert agencies in their regions to do the actual work, coordinate the techniques of the different regions, and supervise the periodic publications of the findings.

Once such data were available, the whole picture would change. The media could use the data for self-improvement as well as for defense against "undeserved" criticism. The critic would be forced to separate clearly fact and judgment. The student would have magnificent material from which he could derive trends, make predictions, highlight areas of deficiency, and relate the content of the media to other pertinent social data.

CHAPTER 5

THE MASS MEDIA AND THE INTELLECTUAL COMMUNITY

The following selection is an edited version of an introduction to a symposium on *Culture for the Millions* sponsored jointly by the Tamiment Institute and *Daedalus*, the journal of the American Academy of Arts and Sciences. The participants were a group of social scientists, creative artists, critics, mass media representatives, historians and philosophers: Hannah Arendt, James Baldwin, Daniel Bell, Arthur Berger, Alan Willard Brown, H. William Fitelson, Charles Frankel, Nathan Glazer, Ernest van den Haag, Oscar Handlin, Patrick Hazard, Sidney Hook, Gerald Holton, H. Stuart Hughes, Stanley Edgar Hyman, Norman Jacobs, Randall Jarrell, Irving Kristol, Paul Lazarsfeld, Leo Lionni, Leo Lowenthal, William Phillips, Bernard Rosenberg, Leo Rosten, Robert Saudek, Arthur Schlesinger, Jr., Gilbert Seldes, Edward Shils, Frank Stanton, James Johnson Sweeney, and Melvin Tumin.

The original introduction contained some highly specific comments about the papers. Although such observations have been deleted, more general references to the participants have been left in the text. It is hoped that these allusions are self-explanatory.

Reprinted from *Culture for the Millions*, Norman Jacobs (Princeton, N.J.: D. Van Nostrand Co., Inc., 1961), by permission of the publisher.

MASS SOCIETY AND MASS CULTURE

We all know from direct experience that tremendous growth of the population, the complexity of urban life, the mechanization of the productive system, and a changed political structure have engendered in many countries a way of life quite different from the one existing, say, a hundred years ago. In the United States we have to add the rapidly rising standard of living and the development of a large entertainment industry. What the essential features of this new type of society are and how they affect human existence is, as we shall see, one of the major topics of this symposium. The main facts are known to everyone and only the term "mass society" might be new to some.[1] Shils describes the culture of this mass society; he distinguishes three levels of culture, which in colloquial terms are often called highbrow, middlebrow, and lowbrow culture. The classification, although vague, is useful and perhaps inevitable. When we talk of highbrow culture, we think of enduring works of art and the contemporary efforts of avant-gardists who deserve respect because of the seriousness of their intentions. We think of the average movie, the family magazine, or the respectable television program when we use the term middlebrow. By lowbrow we mean such things as comics, detective stories, and vaudeville. It is no coincidence that the examples are cultural products offered to people rather than activities in which these people are engaged.

Although little was said at the symposium about lowbrow culture, a distinction between the top two levels is crucial. For in a nutshell one can say that everyone is concerned with two main problems: What happens *to* highbrow culture in mass society? And what does the great

[1] Since this symposium was held, a very instructive summary of the pertinent literature has been published. Kornhauser, in the first part of "The Politics of Mass Society" shows that the idea has two historical roots: fear that traditional standards will be destroyed by the political movements following the French Revolution; and fear that democratic rights will be lost, engendered by the experience of fascistic dictatorships. Instead of trying one unitary definition of "mass society" Kornhauser shows the types of meanings the concept has acquired in varying contexts.

increase in middlebrow culture *do* to people? The focal point at which both these problems could be unraveled appeared to Shils to be the mass media. All through the symposium this emphasis on the mass media is scarcely questioned, and yet I shall try to show that this is not a completely controversial point of view.

Shils also deals with the consumers and the producers of the various forms of cultural products. He briefly summarizes what is known of the social stratification of "audiences." It is useful to learn that a simple classification of the population by education or by some index of social economic status permits reasonably safe predictions of what people will select on their television sets or do with their free time. But Shils adds an observation which has rarely been made. The cultural activities of *young* people at least in this country are much less related to their social status. Here he implies an interesting problem indeed: Will these young people twenty years hence recreate the stratified pattern of their parents or should we expect greater homogeneity of cultural interests in the future?

In the latter part of the keynote paper by Shils, some of the most urgent issues are laid out. There is the question of historical comparison. Certainly many more people participate in "culture" today than took part, say, one hundred years ago; and this has necessarily lowered the level of the average supply. But if we were to look at strata comparable to the upper class and aristocracy of the nineteenth century, would the same be true? Several papers counterpose the desirability of discerning historical trends with the difficulty of doing so.

Handlin, for example, sees a great difference between the folk art of the past and the mass culture of today. But a careful reading of his contribution suggests that folk art, by his definition, could only have played an occasional role in people's lives. What did they do on long winter evenings? Were they desperately bored? Or is boredom itself an experience which has developed in industrial society? From Handlin's personal remarks one gathers that historians know very little about how people used to spend their time, so comparisons become speculations. But Shils correctly raises a second question: Is there an inherent threat to highbrow culture in mass society? Where does this threat come from? Are commercial interests corrupting the public? Or is it that a mediocre audience, which can afford to pay for entertainment, diverts valuable talent from more worthy pursuits? Is there a withering

away of the elites who stimulate cultural innovations? Shils also introduces the notion of "mediocre intelligentsia." These are the men
and women who, while highly trained themselves, produce the middlebrow culture. Both Van den Haag and Arendt felt that he had omitted
one important category. Their argument was that we should not only
look at the nature and content of the cultural supply; we should be
equally concerned with the way it is received. Van den Haag argues
that members of a mass society have lost the ability to take cultural
issues seriously. The whole idea is symbolized in a statement by T. W.
Adorno: "Radio has made of Beethoven's Fifth Symphony a hit tune
which is easy to whistle." The theme of Miss Arendt's contribution is
related; she says popular culture has made of the classics something to
be consumed rather than understood. Handlin, too, treats this theme
when he compares the folk culture of an earlier period with the mass
culture of the industrial age. Folk art was not necessarily better but
it was much closer to people's daily lives and their social traditions; "it
dealt with the complete world intensely familiar to its audience and
permitted a direct rapport between those who created and those who
consumed this culture."

Nathan Glazer suggested that from a combination of the content
level of the cultural product and the way it is received, one should
derive four types of situations. In an oversimplified form, these are:

    a) Serious work seriously received;
    b) Serious work denatured by the attitude of the "consumer"
        —looking at the reproduction of a great painting inserted
        in a picture weekly, listening to a Mozart aria preceded and
        followed by some popular hit in the frame of a television
        set;
    c) Mediocre works received in a serious mood as exemplified
        by a woman who listens to a day-time drama in order to
        understand her family problems better or the Book-of-the-
        Month Club subscriber who honestly wants to improve
        himself;
    d) Finally, there is bad stuff consumed to fill empty time, this
        being the enemy of the people.

Each of these situations might have been discussed in its own terms,
but it would take a long time to explore them systematically. In retro-

spect, I can only urge the readers to consider this notion of functional variation in *reception*.

Attention should be drawn to characteristic differences between various contributions. The social scientist Van den Haag, gives a list of indictments of the deterioration of human relations in mass society: we have lost the taste for privacy and contemplation, we have replaced sincere personal contacts with an empty gregariousness, and so on. Randall Jarrell, the poet, uses a stream of metaphors and impressive aphorisms which he feels communicate more. One other comparison should not be missed. Shils characterizes mass society in terms which show his basic optimism: Social participation has increased, the rights of each individual are more respected, rationality is more widespread. Van den Haag takes up all these points and, so to say, reverses their sign: Social participation is uninformed and vulnerable to slogans, individualism has broken all human bonds, rationality comes about at the expense of deep and sincere experiences. The interchange might give some readers the feeling which Hughes once expressed half facetiously: that whomever he listens to he has to agree with. Perhaps the fact that positive and negative elements are so interwoven in the contemporary scene is one of its most characteristic features.

MASS CULTURE AND MASS MEDIA

The papers in the symposium, while supposed to deal with mass culture in general, devote most of their space to the mass media. In some ways this should not cause surprise. Since the participants are mostly people who make their living from writing, problems of communication are nearest to their hearts. (Chapter 4 in this collection discusses the critical intensity with which topics related to broadcasting and to a lesser degree movies and the printed media are discussed in the United States.)

The position of the spokesmen for the mass media is represented by Rosten and Stanton, who stress that they make considerable contributions to adult education. Of course they are first of all responsible to their stockholders but they plow much of their profits back into public service features. Interestingly enough, a similar attitude is reported as characteristic of the attitude of businessmen even if their own profits are not involved. One contributor to this volume, Mr. Sweeney, at the time Director of the Museum of Modern Art, blames the board members of many museums for overstressing mass appeal when it is not economically necessary. Museums have the double function of serving the trained mind and acting as educational agents for a broader public. It is regrettable that no expert in adult education was included in the symposium. His opinion would have helped to develop further Mr. Sweeney's observations.

The emphasis on the mass media is characteristic of the American scene and obscures certain other aspects of mass culture. This can be somewhat remedied by a short digression on the public attitude in France.

In one respect the French and the American situations are similar. In both countries the social scientist and the man of letters are likely to be politically left of center. But because the French use the labor party as a point of reference, they debate cultural values in terms of their relation to political militancy. The central theme in discussion of mass culture is usually the use of leisure time. Mass media play only a marginal role. The great symbol of the first labor government under Leon Blum in 1936 was the enactment of laws guaranteeing paid vacations and regulating details of week-end arrangements. Equally characteristic are a number of government supported activities like the popular theatre and the youth sport movement. The issue hidden behind the intensive theoretical discussions about leisure time is whether it will lead to an independent labor class culture or whether it will end in assimilation of all workers to the middle-class pattern.

One. gets a good picture of this climate of thinking through an issue of the magazine *Esprit* which appeared in June, 1959, at the same time as the symposium, which led to the present volume. The issue is devoted to "Le Loisir." The theoretical papers are primarily concerned with the relation between leisure time and participation in social movements. Empirical studies analyze how the legally guaranteed vacation period is utilized by various groups of employees. Data on mass media exposure are used to bring out the sociological meaning of various types of work. Thus, for instance, one study compares two groups of white collar people who have about the same income but differ according to the degree their work is mechanized. The group with more interesting work shows a normal distribution of activities like movie attendance or listening to the radio. Those who have monotonous work show bimodal behavior: they either engage in an excessive amount of mass media activities or they retreat into an isolation which takes them either to the saloon or leads to an impoverished family life. It is this retreatism which is considered the main cultural danger by many authors.[2]

Quite a number of other aspects are often closed out of discussions of mass culture among American intellectuals. Only Hazard in this symposium points out that the objects of daily use have an aesthetic aspect which is definitely part of the surrounding culture. He seems to feel, for instance, that by and large the design of home equipment achieves quite high standards. The social scientist might derive an aesthetic classification from the social role of possessions. Some objects which have high social visibility and lend themselves to social competition are often in bad taste—certain types of cars would be a good example. Other more socially neutral objects like refrigerators and dictating equipment are more easily left to the control of the professional designer and often display considerable taste.

[2] They actually play a different role than they do in the United States. The government-owned radio-television system has definite cultural and social assignments which are maintained by advisory councils of artists and other professional groups attached to the broadcasting agency. It is indicative that the French literature has not created special words for mass media but taken over the English words. Especially interesting are papers which deal with education for leisure utilization. To give just one characteristic example, the French beaches are as crowded as ours, but the problem is raised as to what people should do when they find themselves in such a situation. Instead of frantically trying to preserve a square yard of pseudoprivacy, they should think of joint activities and organize equitable use of available facilities.

THE VOICE OF THE ARTIST

While the scope of this symposium is restricted in one direction, it is enlarged in another. Included in the present volume are the statements of three creative artists and the record of the discussion includes the comments of some others.

They all agree that the goal and task of the artist is to interpret human experience. There is some disagreement as to whether he does so mainly by describing other people's lives or by being especially articulate about himself. But they have no doubt that life for everyone would be much harder if art did not help to make sense out of it.

Some idea of a division of labor is implied. Not every human being can, by himself, add this kind of depth to his own experiences. Only the artist is in a position to perform this task because he lends all his efforts to it; but throughout history he has done this at a great sacrifice. Because the artist's social function is intangible and its importance not easily appreciated, he is usually economically insecure and the contact with his audience, if it exists, is precarious and frustrating. Today additional difficulties are added because of the nature of mass society, the role of the mass media, and in the United States also because of some consequences of its economic system. On the first point the main complaint is that the mass man is unreceptive to contemplation; that a complete separation has come about between artistic production on the one hand and occupational and community life on the other; that it has become less and less clear for whom the creative artist is working; and that he is often restricted to addressing himself to just a small group of experts.

The mass media complicate the matter in a variety of ways. By providing endless diversion, they corrode the desire to pay attention to serious thought. The mass media emphasize the fleeting events of the moment and weaken people's connection with the past, as it is expressed in myths and the kind of symbolism which epics or the Bible provide. This has grievous consequences for the artist, for his creativeness consists essentially in providing new variations on eternal themes.

One feature of the American scene might be described as institutional temptation. It is true that artists are not likely to starve as they did a century ago; there are fellowships, foundation grants, and teaching positions at the universities. But they all require the artist to do a great many things that are not essential to him. He is rarely paid for performing his most creative function. Although nothing keeps him from starving as his ancestors did and following his own dreams, I think we all agreed that in an overpowering institutional setting, such individual solutions are hardly possible.[3]

The second target of the artist's complaints—and also pointed out at length by Miss Arendt—is the role of the popularizers. The existence of a large audience wanting some easy information and eager to pay for it creates a new group of technicians who take the original and make it palatable, be it fashioning a movie out of a drama or a magazine article out of a serious piece of analysis. This again increases the sense of despair for the serious artist. In terms of fame and material success, he finds himself pushed into the background as compared to the mass communicator; compared with the past, he suffers less absolute and increasing relative deprivation. This point lends additional complexity to the debate with the defenders of the mass media. Rosten in his paper points out how hard he and his colleagues try to popularize important subject matters. However, the artist can more easily condone the ineptness of a bad writer than the slickness of a popularizer. The grievance, incidentally, does not seem to be restricted to the artist. The physicist Holton mentioned that he and his colleagues resent the image of the scientist portrayed by the mass media.

It was surprisingly difficult to get artists to talk in terms of their own experience. Perhaps in such a symposium the artists resent playing the role of guinea pigs. In this sense then the presence of the creative writers was a noble experiment but not a complete success. The partial failure shows, however, how important it would be to pursue the effort further. What is needed are men and women who are willing to talk

---

[3] I was recently struck by the observation that in countries like Switzerland and Austria mountain climbing is rapidly declining; the number of professional guides, for instance, has greatly decreased. This is due to the fact that more and more cable cars and hard surface automobile roads are being built. Here again the point could be made that no one has to use these technical devices; one could still reach mountain peaks by his own strength. But it is obvious that such pursuits lose their sense if at the end of such a climb one meets all the people who have come up with the help of some technical gadget.

to us social scientists about themselves as artists in the world of mass culture, rather than about the nature of art.

Interestingly enough, it is the musician Arthur Berger who is most specific and articulate. Perhaps it is reading and explanation of musical scores which gave him analytical training. Among his interesting points was the idea that one should not be overjoyed by the extensive performance of classical music over radio, because the unanticipated effect might be a freezing of musical taste. The trend in artistic style has always been toward increasing complexity, and it usually takes a new generation of laymen to accept what was considered revolutionary and unharmonious in their parents' day. Such acceptance might now take much longer because broadcasting puts all its weight behind works which people are accustomed to hearing. Berger singles out quite a number of other impediments built into the technology and social structure of the mass media. New works are difficult to play and require a great deal of rehearsal. But because of union rules and other traditions developed in broadcasting, lengthy rehearsals become almost prohibitive today. Incidentally, magazines, too, develop a distinctive style and television has producers who are believed to know what the medium requires. All this means that in many areas professional techniques interpose themselves between the artist and the public. Whatever the need for or the justification of this trend, the artists do not seem to take it kindly.

Berger suggests concretely that broadcasters should make unconditional grants to modern writers and composers. Their contribution should not be linked to the suitability of a work for television or radio. It should rather be looked on as an additional tax, because a broadcasting license turns over a public property—the airwave—for the benefit of a private businessman. While he did not put it quite this way, the remarks of A. W. Brown went in the same direction. A former president of the Metropolitan Educational Television Association (which provides educational television stations with program material), he pointed out that, because of lack of funds, only about 50 education channels have been put in operation out of 250 available channels. More such stations would give artists a larger number of outlets. If one adheres to the formula that commercial broadcasters should make somewhat less money than their franchises permit in the free market, it is easy to conclude that they should give active financial support to educational television.

I might be permitted to add one remark which is personal in the sense that it concerns only my own professional specialty. The artists in the symposium request effort and respect for difficult modern art. At the same time they are impatient when they are confronted with the corresponding problem in the social sciences. Mr. Jarrell said at one point that he loved anthropologists but hated sociologists. The context made it quite clear that what he dislikes are statistical tables difficult to read and what he is pleased by are essays on cultural subjects more akin to poetry. Two men who took pessimistic positions in the discussion have a similar record. The *Reporter*, of which Mr. Kristol was the Managing Editor, and *Commentary*, of which Mr. Glazer is a frequent contributor on social sciences, have been consistently hostile to all modern trends in the social sciences. As Mr. Hazard put it in an aside, empirical social research might be the counterpart of atonal music. It seems to create the same hostility among modern artists which their work creates among the general public.

And yet there is one type of research which might help on some of the problems which the artists brought up. I mentioned above that the way people receive or "consume" cultural products is of considerable concern to some of the participants. Seldes, for instance, comments on the passivity of modern audiences; Hook, on the other hand, insists that he does not understand what is meant by this frequently used term. Now it so happens that mass communication research has developed sophisticated interviewing techniques which bring out what people feel while they watch a movie or television program, at what points they are involved, where they misunderstand the content, and so on. Such analysis of the listening experience has been used mainly for the purpose of improving the effectiveness of propaganda, commercial or otherwise.[4] There is no reason, however, why it should not be used for more objective ends.

[4] It is not possible to give a complete picture of this procedure without devoting much more space to it. The best examples can be found in the studies that the Army did during the last war on the reaction of soldiers to films designed to give an understanding of the contemporary historical situation. The results are summarized in the third volume of *The American Soldier* (Princeton, N.J.; Princeton University Press, 1949, Ch. 4). A more detailed discussion of the technique I am referring to is given by Merton *et al.*, in *The Focused Interview* (Glencoe, Ill.: The Free Press, 1958), and in Tore Hollonquist and E. A. Suchman, "Listening to the Listener," in P. F. Lazarsfeld and F. N. Stanton (eds.), *Radio Research 1942–43* (New York: Duell, Sloan and Pearce, 1944).

As a matter of fact, such an effort was made once by I. A. Richards, who was one of the pioneers of the "New Criticism" which started in England after the First World War.[5] His Cambridge group was interested in substituting a structural analysis of the work of art for romantic speculation about the author's personality. Richards wanted, in addition, to look at the other side of the coin and to study the structure of the readers' experience. He developed a procedure which seems to be little known and to which more attention should be given.[6]

Richards asked a number of his students to read carefully an array of poems ranging from serious pieces to conventional trash. He then requested them to describe in detail all the reactions, associations and opinions they had. These reports he analyzed and classified carefully. The main product is a detailed description of what today we would call the audience experience. The purpose of Richards' experiment as well as the organization of his book are best described in his own formulation of his three aims:

> First, to introduce a *new kind of documentation* to those who are interested in the contemporary state of culture whether as critics, as philosophers, as teachers, as psychologists or mainly as curious persons. Secondly, to provide a new technique for those who wish to discover for themselves what they think and feel about poetry (and cognate matters) and why they should like or dislike it. Thirdly, to prepare the way for *educational methods* more efficient than those we use now in *developing discrimination* and the power to understand what we hear and read. [Emphasis supplied]

I have never quite understood why Richards' idea has not been pursued. Perhaps it falls in a no-man's land between psychologists and students of literature. Perhaps Richards' rather primitive techniques seem disappointing. But as the studies quoted above show, we now

---

[5] A vivid description of how this movement originated can be found in F. N. W. Tillyard, *The Muse Unchained* (London: Bowes and Bowes, 1958).

[6] I. A. Richards, *Practical Criticism* (London: Kegan, Paul, Trench, Trubner and Co., Ltd., 1929).

know that one can give a very good picture of how a specific type of person understands a work of art, how he is affected by it, and how it fits into the stream of his personal experiences. I would strongly urge a convergence of these research techniques with serious artistic concerns. Obviously, the goal is not to custom tailor creative production to the wishes of the man in the street. But a great many interesting and mostly unpredictable outcomes can result from a systematic confrontation of the artist with his actual and potential audiences. To say the least, the type of controversies which the present symposium exemplifies could be referred to a firmer body of facts.

DILEMMAS OF REFORM

Stuart Hughes in his paper takes the position that one cannot have political without cultural democracy; we are paying for our freedom of opinion by letting the people have the freedom of choice in cultural matters. Phillips in the discussion objects: he does not see any necessary connection. A somewhat different formulation might make the issue more concrete.

The expression "paying for" is indeed vague and perhaps fatalistic. What actually happens is that, in the mass media field, we are confronted with a set of basic values not all of which can be fully realized. Schlesinger, for instance, argues for a stronger role of the government in broadcasting policies. Even if television is accepted as a business, the idea of free enterprise does not preclude some government regulation. He correctly points out that at many points in our economic system we have laws on wages and hours and similar business decisions. In the communications field, however, we run into a conflict with the First Amendment, which specifically precludes government interference in the realm of ideas. Even if this difficulty could be resolved by stating that television, like the movies, conveys primarily entertainment and thus lies outside the First Amendment, a realistic problem remains. American broadcasting is really quite free so far as political controversy goes. It is questionable whether the opposition party would have a fair chance in a government controlled system. One would, therefore, have to seek a form of regulation for cultural but not political matters.

Once this is conceded, another question comes up. In a democracy, is there any justification for imposing elite standards on the whole country? In this connection a distinction which is often overlooked must be made. The realistic issue is not whether the majority should accept what the intellectual minority prefers. The problem is whether *within* the realm of what was referred to as middlebrow culture standards could be developed and should be maintained. The Federal Communications Commission, for instance, receives many complaints about the abundance of violence in television dramas. The question then arises whether one finds less violence there than, for instance, in *Hamlet*. Everyone has an uneasy feeling that this is a specious argument, but it would be difficult to articulate clearly under what conditions an overabundance of violence is regrettable. While there is no answer on this specific problem, there are similar issues on which communication research can provide answers.

What I am trying to say is that even if we accept the legitimacy of middlebrow culture, it is still possible to develop standards which make for improvement on its own terms. The role of the elite, then, would not be that of dictators but of advisers. Concretely this role can take a variety of forms. Hyman describes what he as a college teacher does to influence the standards of his students. On another occasion Robert Hutchins has stressed the importance of periodic reviews. One of the proposals of his Commission on the Freedom of the Press was that the content of mass media be sampled under appropriate categories so they could be subjected to the limelight of public opinion. This was supposed to make for improvement without specific regulation.

Another dilemma which deserves attention is due to a special piece of broadcasting legislation. The Federal Communications Act provides that, in order to avoid collusion on the setting of advertising rates, the anti-trust laws should apply to broadcasting. On this it proved ineffectual. But in present application it also precludes concerted action on program content. Stanton in his paper points with justified pride to the many fine programs in an average week on CBS. Competing networks could make the same claim. But what would be overlooked is the fact that for competitive reasons all of these programs are usually heard at the same time. The value of the existing program supply could be greatly enhanced by a very simple procedure. At present the networks pit against each other programs with mass appeal at one time and programs with elite appeal at another time. Nothing but legal traditionalism prevents an arrangement by which on some days one network has a large audience and another network has a smaller number of connoisseurs: on other evenings the situation would be reversed by agreement. It is not so much the commercial nature of broadcasting but a narrow interpretation of commercial competition which accounts for some of these difficulties.

Since this symposium was held, interest in the problematics of the mass media has extended, at least temporarily, to broader public groups. It is rather characteristic that this interest was not aroused by the cultural critics but by moral indignation over cheating on a television show. This raises the question whether discussions like the one published in this book have any practical utility at all. And here we can once more turn to the teachings of history. The contribution of Leo Lowenthal shows that every technological innovation in the field of communication was experienced by some people as a cultural danger: the less expensive book, the lending library, the magazine and so on. It is really startling how timely the discussions which Lowenthal reports from the 17th and 18th century sound today. Stimulated by his material, I went back to the first recorded discussion of mass communication: Plato's *Phaedrus*, the dialogue concerned with the skills and the social implications of the public orator. Socrates, of course, takes the position which the pessimistic critics in this volume take and he, too, goes back to history. He feels that the misery started with the discovery of writing.[7]

> For this discovery will create forgetfulness in the learners' souls, because they will not use their memories; they will trust to the external written characters and not remember of themselves. . . . They will appear to be omniscient, and will generally know nothing; they will be tiresome company, having the show of wisdom without the reality.

In spite of this dire foreboding, writing, orating, printing and now broadcasting have spread, and society still survives. Matters often look bad, but somehow they always stop short of being disastrous. True, as in other fields, especially in social legislation, it was often the

---

[7] *The Philosophy of Plato* (Jowett translation), New York: Modern Library), p. 323.

accidental event which triggered the improvement. But this would not have happened if a continuous stream of criticism had not kept us prepared to take advantage of such opportunities. It is the tragic story of the cultural crusader in a mass society that he cannot win, but that we would be lost without him.

CHAPTER 6

ADMINISTRATIVE AND CRITICAL COMMUNICATIONS RESEARCH

During the last two decades the media of mass communication, notably radio, print and film, have become some of the best-known and best documented spheres of modern society. Careful studies have revealed the size of the audiences of all major radio programs and the composition of this audience in respect to sex, income, and a few other criteria. The circulations of newspapers and magazines are recorded by specially organized research outfits, and others report currently on which magazine stories and which advertisements are read week by week. Books, radio programs, and movies are tested as to the difficulty of the language they use and as to how adequate they are for the different educational levels of the population. The types of entertainment that different groups of people prefer are being investigated all the time, and many promotional campaigns are tested currently as to their success. A number of important new techniques have been developed in the course of all these research efforts. Modern sampling techniques, for instance, have made great progress because it has been realized that the practical value of a study would be lost if it were conducted among a group of people who are not representative of those sections of the population which the sponsoring agency wants to reach. Interviewing techniques have been greatly refined for similar reasons. The competitive character of much of this work has led to ever better methods of recording facts as to the extent of listening and reading. Where a subject matter doesn't lend itself to simple recording devices, great prog-

Reprinted from *Studies in Philosophy and Social Science*, New York, 1941.

ress has been made in developing indices for complex attitudes and reactions.[1]

Behind the idea of such research is the notion that modern media of communication are tools handled by people or agencies for given purposes. The purpose may be to sell goods, or to raise the intellectual standards of the population, or to secure an understanding of governmental policies; but in all cases, to someone who uses a medium for something, it is the task of research to make the tool better known, and thus to facilitate its use.

As a result, all communications research centers around a standard set of problems. Who are the people exposed to the different media? What are their specific preferences? What are the effects of different methods of presentation? One who uses media of communication is in competition with other agencies whose purposes are different, and thus research must also keep track of what is communicated by others. Finally, communications research has to be aware that the effect of radio, print, or the movie, does not end with the purposive use which is made of it by administrative agencies. If advertisers, for example, feel that radio is an especially powerful selling device, then printed media will receive less money, and research will have to see whether radio brings about a general deterioration of the reading habits of the population.

Studies of this kind are conducted partly by the major publishing organizations and radio networks and partly by academic agencies supported by universities or foundations.[2] Considerable thought has been given during the past years to clarifying the social and political implications of this new branch of social research. Its relationship to the pres-

---

[1] For a general orientation in the field see Douglas Waples, *What Reading Does to People*, University of Chicago Press, 1940 and Paul F. Lazarsfeld, *Radio and the Printed Page*, Duell, Sloan and Pearce, 1940. For more current and specific information the *Public Opinion Quarterly*, published by the Princeton University Press, is the best source of articles and bibliography.

[2] Among the universities, the University of Chicago Library School and the University of Minnesota Journalism School are especially active in the field of communications research. Organizations doing similar work with foundation funds are the Adult Education Association, the American Film Center, the Columbia University Office of Radio Research, the Library of Congress and the Princeton Public Opinion Research Project. In the magazine field, *Life* and *McCall's* are currently publishing valuable information. Material on radio can best be obtained through the research directors of the Columbia Broadcasting System and the National Broadcasting Company.

ent crisis is very interestingly discussed in a new study by Harold Lasswell.[3] One who has not participated in work of this kind can get a good picture of its atmosphere from a "fable" written by participants in the course of a series of discussions which took place during 1939 and 1940. We quote:

> In the interests of concreteness, let us attempt to state the job of research in mass communication in a situation which, though purely hypothetical, serves to illustrate what that job involves.
>
> Let us suppose that government leaders and those responsible for mass communication are in agreement with respect to policy toward alien groups in this country. (The public, they believe, should be made aware of the dangers of subversive activities on the part of aliens, but popular antipathy toward aliens in general should be minimized, and, above all, outbreaks of anti-alien sentiment should be avoided.) The policy that the channels of mass communication must serve, then, becomes one of increasing public awareness of specific dangers of subversive action, while, at the same time, building tolerance toward aliens in general.
>
> Suppose that some popular evening radio program, known to attract a considerable portion of the total listening audience, includes an address dealing with the dangers of subversive activities on the part of aliens. News dispatches of the next day or two, however, bring reports from various parts of the country of outbreaks of feeling against alien groups. Reports of local utterances in connection with these outbreaks carry allusions to the broadcast address of the evening. As a result, there is at least a strong suspicion that some connection exists between them and what was said on the evening broadcast.
>
> Conscientious effort to repair the damage, it is clear, involves learning more of what the damage was. The comment it occasioned in the press makes clear that its effects were felt not through the radio alone, but through reports of the unfortunate address which the newspapers carried, in the local utterances which alluded to it, and even in some widely distributed newsreel reports of the local outbreaks that followed. What people then must be reached if the untoward effects of the broadcast are to be remedied?
>
> Something in what was said evidently combined with the predispositions of the listeners and with the current circum-

[3] Harold Lasswell, *Democracy Through Public Opinion*. George Banta Publishing Co. 1941.

stances—with the force of events, and probably with other widely disseminated communications—to set the stage for what ensued.

Each station is asked to assign the best qualified members of its staff to interviewing listeners to determine as best they can what in the address led to the unanticipated outbreaks. Particularly are they urged to have their interviewers talk with individuals who took an active part in the outbreaks in question.

With the help of specialists in such research, the audience originally affected is redetermined. Types of radio programs, press releases, and newsreel treatments are worked out, calculated on the basis of the best evidence available to get a new hearing for the subject, adequate to counter the effects of the original address. Undoubtedly an explanation would be prepared for delivery by the original speaker, but other speakers would be enlisted whose position and identification in the public mind are likely to make their parts most widely influential. All materials prepared are pre-tested at relatively slight expense— indeed, far less expense, proportionately, than merchandisers ordinarily incur in testing the market for new products. Conscientious effort having taken them so far, those responsible agree in wishing now to have some further test of the actual effects of what they have planned by way of remedy. Accordingly, arrangements are made in advance of their campaign to gauge its progress.

A happy ending to this fable can probably take the form of a series of charts which subsequently ease the conscience of all concerned by showing, as their campaign proceeds, a consistent decline in all indices of overt hostility toward the groups against which outbreaks of feeling were directed.

The original speaker, the sponsors, and the broadcasters are still convinced of their initial innocence. But they are plagued a bit by certain recollections. One of them remembers, for example, suggesting extra publicity for the broadcast on the ground that the address to be included was particularly timely. Another recalls that the topic of the address was suggested by by an acquaintance prominent in an organization which presumably on patriotic grounds had for some time been advocating stricter control of aliens in the country. In the end, their feeling is that however innocent their conscious purposes, they too, as Americans of their time, shared the same predispositions in planning the broadcast, and responded to the force of the same circumstances, as did the listeners to it.

Research of the kind described so far could well be called *administrative research*. It is carried through in the service of some kind of administrative agency of public or private character. Administrative research is subject to objections from two sides. On the one hand, there are the sponsors themselves, some of whom feel that they have not really got their money's worth. One good guess, so the argument goes, is of more practical importance than all the details which might be brought to light by an empirical study. There is, however, a fallacy behind this objection. Although speculation is indispensable for guidance in any kind of empirical work, if honestly carried through it will usually lead to a number of alternative conclusions which cannot all be true at the same time. Which one corresponds to the real situation can be decided only by empirical studies.[4] From another side comes an objection directed against the aims which prevail in the majority of current studies. They solve little problems, generally of a business character, when the same methods could be used to improve the life of the community if only they were applied to forward-looking projects related to the pressing economic and social problems of our time. Robert S. Lynd, in his *Knowledge for What*, has vigorously taken this point of view and has shown many ways whereby research could be made more vital.

Neither of these two arguments doubts that research can and should be done at the service of certain well-defined purposes. But at this point a third argument comes up. The objection is raised that one cannot pursue a single purpose and study the means of its realization isolated from the total historical situation in which such planning and studying goes on. Modern media of communication have become such complex instruments that wherever they are used they do much more to people than those who administer them mean them to do, and they may have a momentum of their own which leaves the administrative agencies much less choice than they believe they have. The idea of *critical research* is posed against the practice of administrative research,

---

[4] There is a rather suggestive way to overcome the argument of the futility of empirical research. One might, for instance, tell such an opponent that according to studies which have been done people who make up their minds during a political campaign as to how to vote are influenced by very different factors than those who have more permanent political affiliations. The opponent will find that immediately understandable and will say that he could have come to this conclusion by using good common sense. It so happens that the opposite is true and that it is possible to predict to a high degree the vote of originally undecided people by means of the same characteristics which describe people with actual party affiliations. There are many other examples by which common sense first can be led to conclusions which then are proved by actual data to be incorrect.

requiring that, prior and in addition to whatever special purpose is to be served, the general role of our media of communication in the present social system should be studied. The rest of these remarks are devoted to a formulation of this conception and to a short appraisal of its possible contributions to current communication research.

The idea of critical research has been developed in many studies by Max Horkheimer.[5] It seems to be distinguished from administrative research in two respects: it develops a theory of the prevailing social trends of our times, general trends which yet require consideration in any concrete research problem; and it seems to imply ideas of basic human values according to which all actual or desired effects should be appraised.

As to prevailing trends, everyone will agree that we live in a period of increasing centralization of ownership. Yet, although large economic organizations plan their production to the minutest detail, the distribution of their products is not planned systematically. Their success depends upon the outcome of a competition among a few large units which must rally sizeable proportions of the population as their customers. Thus promotion in every form becomes one of the main forces in contemporary society. The technique of manipulating large masses of people is developed in the business world and from there permeates our whole culture. In the end everything, be it good or bad, is promoted; we are living more and more in an "advertising culture." This whole trend is accentuated still more by the fact that it has to disguise itself. A salesman who has only one line to sell has to explain to each customer why this line suits just his individual purposes. The radio announcer who serves one national advertiser identifies himself to millions of listeners as "your" announcer.

Such an analysis becomes an element of strong concern and solicitude if it is felt that these trends impair basic values in human life. The idea that our times are engulfed by a multitude of promotional patterns is coupled with the feeling that human beings, as a result, behave more and more like pawns upon a chessboard, losing the spontaneity and dignity which is the basic characteristic of the human personality. In order to understand clearly the idea of critical research, one must real-

---

[5] Cf. especially "Traditional and Critical Theory" in the *Zeitschrift für Sozialforschung*, VI (1937), pp. 245–295; "Philosophy and Critical Theory" pp. 625–631. The examples used here in presenting the idea of critical social research were taken from studies done by Dr. T. W. Adorno.

ize that it is being urged by men who have the idea ever present before them that what we need most is to do and think what we consider true and not to adjust ourselves to the seemingly inescapable.

The theory of a trend toward promotional culture leads to the conclusion that certain tendencies of our time jeopardize basic human values because people are kept from developing their own potentialities to the full. To be fit for the daily competition, we do not spend our leisure time developing a rich range of interests and abilities, but we use it, willingly or unwillingly, to reproduce our working capacity. Thus, not having acquired any criteria of our own, we succumb to and support a system of promotion in all areas of life, which, in turn, puts us in ever-increasing dependence upon such a system; it gives us more and more technical devices and takes away from us any valuable purposes for which they could be used.[6]

Thus the stage is set for the procedures of critical research. A critical student who analyzes modern media of communication will look at radio, motion pictures, the press, and will ask the following kinds of questions: How are these media organized and controlled? How, in their institutional set-up, is the trend toward centralization, standardization and promotional pressure expressed? In what form, however disguised, are they threatening human values? He will feel that the main task of research is to uncover the unintentional (for the most part) and often very subtle ways in which these media contribute to living habits and social attitudes that he considers deplorable.

What are the operations into which critical communication research could be broken down? The answer is not easy and a first attempt might be made by visualizing how a student would be trained to make observations in everyday life and to try to interpret them in terms of their social meaning. You sit in a movie and look at an old newsreel showing fashions of ten years ago. Many people laugh. Why

[6] It might help to clarify these ideas by comparing them briefly with other trends of thought, such as the consumer movement on the one hand and propaganda analysis on the other. The consumer movement is concerned with concrete wrongs in current advertising and might even denounce all advertising as economically wasteful. For the critical approach, business advertisement is only one of the many promotional forms by which present society is maintained and its cultural rather than its economic implications are discussed. A similar difference appears in comparison with propaganda analysis. The problem is not that people are misled in regard to certain isolated facts, but that they have less and less opportunity to develop standards of judgment of their own because wherever they turn they are caught by some kind of promotion.

do those things which we admired just a little while ago seem so ridiculous now? Could it be that we avenge ourselves for having submitted to them under general pressure, and now that the pressure in favor of these particular styles has been lifted, we compensate by deriding the idols of yesteryear? At the same time, we submit to the style-promotion of today only to laugh at it a few years from now. Could it be that by laughing at past submission, we gather strength to submit to the present pressure upon us? Thus, what looks to an ordinary observer like an incident in a movie theater, becomes, from this point of view, a symptom of great social significance.

Or you find that a large brewery advertises its beer by showing a man disgustedly throwing aside a newspaper full of European war horrors while the caption says that in times like these the only place to find peace, strength, and courage is at your own fireside drinking beer. What will be the result if symbols referring to such basic human wants as that for peace become falsified into expressions of private comfort and are rendered habitual to millions of magazine readers as merchandising slogans? Why should people settle their social problems by action and sacrifice if they can serve the same ends by drinking a new brand of beer? To the casual observer the advertisement is nothing but a more or less clever sales trick. From the aspect of a more critical analysis, it becomes a dangerous sign of what a promotional culture might end up with.

A next step in trying to explain this approach could be taken by applying it not only to an observation of daily life, but to problems we meet in textbooks current in the social sciences. A text on the family, for example, would not be likely to contain a detailed analysis showing how one of the functions of the family in our society might be that of maintaining the authoritarian structure necessary for our present economic system, that the predominant position of the father might prepare the child to accept the privations he will suffer as an adult, and to do so without questioning their necessity. Applying this to a study of the family in the depression we might depart from the traditional question of what changes the depression has brought about in family life. Couldn't it be that the family has influenced the depression? Interesting research problems would come up: what was the effect of different family constellations upon people's ability to find out-of-the-way jobs, to use initiative in organizations of unemployed, and so on? Another example could arise from a well-known observation which can be found in every text on social psychology, to the effect that the way we look at the world and react to the problems of the day is determined by our previous experience. The notion of experience is taken as a psychological concept which does not need much further elucidation. But could it not be that what we call "experience" undergoes historical changes? Visualize what experience meant for a man who lived in a rather stable, small community, reading in his newspaper elaborate accounts of events he considered news because they happened a few weeks before, spending many an hour walking through the countryside, experiencing nature as something eternally changeless, and as so rich that years were needed to observe all its details. Today we live in an environment where skyscrapers shoot up and elevateds disappear overnight; where news comes like shock every few hours; where continually new news programs keep us from ever finding out the details of previous news; and where nature is something we drive past in our car, perceiving a few quickly changing flashes which turn the majesty of a mountain range into the impression of a motion picture. Might it not be that we do not build up experiences the way it was possible to do decades ago, and if so wouldn't that have bearing upon all our educational efforts? Studies of smaller American communities have shown that since the turn of the century there has been a steady decrease of efforts in adult education of the old style. Now radio with its Professor Quiz program brings up new forms of mass education which, in their differences from the old reading and discussion circles, show a striking parallel to the development sketched here.[7]

Omitting a number of details and specifications, the "operation" basic to this approach consists of four steps.

    a)   A theory about the prevailing trends toward a "promotional culture" is introduced on the basis of general observations. Although efforts are steadily being made to refine and corroborate this theory it is taken for granted prior to any special study.

    b)   A special study of any phenomenon consists in determining how it expresses these prevailing trends (introduced in (a)) and in turn contributes to reinforcing them.

    c)   The consequences of (b) in stamping human personalities in a modern, industrial society are brought to the fore-

---

   [7] Cf. W. Benjamin's study on Baudelaire in this periodical, Vol. VIII (1939–40), p. 50 ff.

ground and scrutinized from the viewpoint of more or less
explicit ideas of what endangers and what preserves the
dignity, freedom and cultural values of human beings.
   d)   Remedial possibilities, if any, are considered.

Before we turn to the value which such an approach can have for
the specific field of communications research, it is first necessary to
meet an objection to the idea of critical research which may be raised
against it on its own ground, to wit, that so much of its effort is spent
on what might be called "showing up" things, rather than on fact-
finding or constructive suggestions. It must be admitted that being constructive is a rather relative concept, and that the question of what are
relevant facts cannot be decided only according to established procedures. The situation is somewhat similar to the wave of criticism
which started with the reports of the Royal Commission in the British
Parliament and with the English social literature of the Dickens type
in the first half of the last century. Then, the task was to discover and
to denounce the material cruelties of the new industrial system: child
labor, slum conditions, and so on. Not that all these horrors have now
been eliminated, but at least there is enough public consciousness of
them so that whenever a student finds similar conditions, for instance
among migrant workers or sharecroppers, some steps toward improvement are taken. The trend of public opinion and public administration
is toward better social conditions. In cultural matters, a similar development has not yet taken place. The examples given above will be taken
by many readers as rather insignificant in a field which is not of great
practical importance. It might very well be, however, that we are all
so busy finding our place in society according to established standards
of success that nothing is more important at this moment than to remind ourselves of basic cultural values which are violated, just as it
was of decisive historic importance a hundred years ago to remind the
English middle classes that they were overlooking the sacrifices which
the new strata of industrial laborers underwent when the modern industrial world was built. As Waller has pointed out,[8] the moral standards of tomorrow are due to the extreme sensitiveness of a small group
of intellectual leaders of today. A few decades ago the artist who was
destined to be the classic of the succeeding generation was left to starve

---

   [8]   *The Family*, Dryden Press, 1931.

in his own time. Today we are very eager not to overlook any growing talent, and we have fellowships and many other institutions which try to assist the growth of any seed of artistic development. Why should we not learn to be more hospitable to criticism and find forms in which more patience can be exercised to wait and, in the end, to see what is constructive and what is not.[9]

And now for the specific contributions which the idea of critical research can make to the student who is engaged in the administrative research side of the problem. As long as there is so little experience in the actual cooperation of critical and administrative research, it is very difficult to be concrete. One way to put it is to point to the strong intellectual stimulation which derives from such joint efforts. There will be hardly a student in empirical research who does not sometimes feel a certain regret or impatience about the vast distance between problems of sampling and probable errors on the one hand, and the significant social problems of our times on the other. Some have hit upon the solution of making their social interests their private avocation, and keeping that separate from their research procedures, hoping that one day in the future the two will again merge. If it were possible in the terms of critical research to formulate an actual research operation which could be integrated with empirical work, the people involved, the problems treated and, in the end, the actual utility of the work would greatly profit.

Such a vitalization of research might well occur in a variety of forms which can only be exemplified and not stated in a systematic way. Quite likely, for instance, more attention will be given to problems of control. If we study the effects of communication, however fine methods we use, we will be able to study only the effects of radio programs or printed material that is actually being distributed. Critical research will be especially interested in such material as never gets access to the channels of mass communication: What ideas and what forms are killed before they ever reach the general public, whether

---

[9] It is quite possible that the radio industry could lead in releasing some of the pressure which, at this time, keeps much social research in conventional forms and cuts it off from expanding into new fields. Already, in the field of politics, the radio industry has proved itself more neutral and more balanced than any other large business institution. The necessity of keeping in touch with the large masses of the population might also make them more amenable to trying methods of research even if, at first, they seem less innocuous. An honest analysis of program contents and program policies might be the first testing ground.

because they would not be interesting enough for large groups, or because they would not pay sufficient returns on the necessary investment, or because no traditional forms of presentation are available?

Once a program is on the air or a magazine is printed, critical research is likely to look at the content in an original way. A number of examples are available in the field of musical programs.[10] Serious music on the radio is not unconditionally accepted as good. The promotion of special conductors, which exaggerates the existing differences and detracts from attention to more important aspects of music, is pointed to as another intrusion of an advertising mentality into an educational sphere. The ceaseless repetition of a comparatively small number of recognized "master works" is derived from the necessity to keep public service programs more in line with commercial fare of the radio. From such an analysis concrete suggestions evolve as to how music programs on the radio should be conducted to make them really serve a more widespread music appreciation. A discussion of the social significance and the probable effect of popular music, to which almost 50 per cent of all radio time is given, is also available and so far represents the most elaborate analysis of a type of mass communication from the point of view of critical social research.[11] Similar studies of printed matter can be made. For instance, what is the significance of the great vogue of biographies during the last decade? A study of their content shows that they all talk in terms of sweeping laws of society, or mankind or the human soul to which every individual is submitted and at the same time point up the unique greatness and importance of the one hero they are treating.[12] The success of this kind of literature among middle class readers is taken as an indication that many of them have lost their bearings in regard to their social problems. These biographies reflect a feeling that we are swept by waves of events over which the ordinary human being has no control and which call for leadership by people with super-human abilities. By such analysis anti-democratic implications are carved out in a literary phenomenon which otherwise would not attract the attention of the social scientist.

---

[10] See T. W. Adorno, "On a Social Critique of Radio Music," on file at the Office of Radio Research, Columbia University.

[11] See T. W. Adorno, "On Popular Music," in this issue.

[12] Such an analysis has been carried through by L. Lowenthal of the Institute of Social Research and is now being extended to the many biographies which are currently appearing in American magazines with mass circulation.

On the other end, upon studying the actual effects of communications, larger vistas are opened to someone whose observations are influenced by the critical attitude here discussed. To give only one example: We praise the contribution which radio makes by enlarging so greatly the world of each single individual, and undoubtedly the praise is deserved. But is the matter quite so simple? A farmer might be very well equipped to handle all the problems which his environment brings up, able to distinguish what makes sense and what doesn't, what he should look out for and what is unimportant. Now the radio brings in a new world with new problems which don't necessarily grow out of the listener's own life. This world has a character of magic, where things happen and are invisible at the same time; many listeners have no experience of their own which would help them to appraise it. We know that that sometimes has very disturbing effects, as witnessed by the attitude of women listeners to daytime serials,[1] by the attitude of millions of letter writers who try to interfere with the world of radio without really believing that their efforts will make any difference. It certainly should be worthwhile not to stop at such incidental observations but to see whether people's attitudes toward reality are not more profoundly changed by radio than we usually find with more superficial observations of their daily habits.

CHAPTER 7

CRITICAL THEORY AND DIALECTICS

Germany makes its contribution through what has come to be known as critical theory. This has created a schism among German sociologists and has some repercussions abroad. One must distinguish a recent and a more remote history of this trend.

In the mid-1920's the University of Frankfurt created an Institute of Social Research of which Max Horkheimer became director in 1931. Several years before Hitler came to power, the Institute undertook a number of studies, the results of which suggested that the German working class probably would not resist the Hitler movement because the German family fostered submission to authority.[1] In 1932 the Institute began to publish a journal which brought to public attention a number of younger men, all of whom were to make their mark: Theodor Adorno, Walter Benjamin, Erich Fromm, Herbert Marcuse. The introduction to the first issue emphasized that the journal would cover all social sciences because the group was striving for an "understanding" of the total course of history. The titles of the papers in this first issue were somewhat more specific. An economist discussed with approval the Marxian theory of prices, and two other papers dealt with the societal determinants of literature and music respectively.

The "Gesellschaftliche Lage der Musik" by Adorno is an article on music (44 pages long with a second installment of equal length in

Reprinted from "Main Trends of Research in the Social and Human Sciences," (Paris: Mouton, Unesco, 1970), pp. 111–117.

[1] *Studien über Autorität und Familie,* Studien aus dem Institut für Sozialforschung (Paris: Librairie Félix Alcan, 1936).

the next issue), which, in retrospect, set the direction for the program. A translation of the first three sentences will be helpful:

> Whenever music sounds today it reflects the contradiction and crevices which split contemporary society; at the same time the deepest gap separates music from just that society which creates it and its atomization, a society unable to absorb from its music more than its rubble and wreckage. The role of music in its societal setting is exclusively that of merchandise; its value is determined by the market. Music doesn't serve any more immediate needs and use but submits itself like any other merchandise to the constraints of the market.[2]

When Hitler came to power the Institute left Germany for the United States. Because of this interruption it took several years before a programmatic statement was available. It appeared in 1937 in an article by Horkheimer entitled "Traditional and Critical Theory.[3]

The paper has three themes. First, the structure of modern science is described as one element in the rise of the middle class out of the pre-capitalist world. This is a summary of the well known Marxist position. The notion of a pure science following its own course had a liberating effect in the 19th century; today it implies the acceptance of monopoly capitalism.

The second theme concerns the nature of this new world. Here Marxist theory is treated more selectively. Poverty, unemployment and even exploitation are barely mentioned. The emphasis is on alienation, fetishism and false consciousness. People today still believe that they act on the basis of individual decisions, actually, however, their behavior is molded by social mechanisms.[4] Their destiny is determined, not by the competition of independent individuals, but rather by national and international conflicts between ruling cliques in government and the economic system.[5] No one has ideas of his own any longer; so-

[2] Theodor W. Adorno, "Gesellschaftliche Lage der Musik." It is impossible to reproduce in another language the type of German in which this and all subsequent papers by Adorno are written. The length of the sentences, the rhythm of the words, and the piling up of nouns—often the same noun repeated with slightly different meanings—has an hypnotic effect on the reader which might well explain some of the attraction his publications have today for many young German students.

[3] Max Horkheimer, *Zeitschrift für Sozialforschung*, 6 (1937), pp. 245–295.

[4] *Ibid.*, p. 253.

[5] *Ibid.*, p. 259.

called public opinion is a product of the ruling private and public bureaucracies.[6] Human solidarity is more likely to be found in criminal gangs than in established society.[7]

Sociological analysis practiced against this background of necessity becomes critical theory; this is the third and essential theme. As a matter of course, social analysis should point to the elements just mentioned. But it should not look at them as isolated shortcomings but as the consequences of the basic social structure, a system which is based on production for profit. The relation between research regarding what exists and social goals to be strived for is stated as follows:

> To see the course of history as a necessary product of an economic mechanism implies already the protest against the present order and the idea of an autonomy of the human race; this means an order in which social events are not any more the result of a mechanism but grow out of free collective decisions. The insight that what happened so far was necessary implies already the fight for a change from a blind to a meaningful necessity.[8]

On one point this neo-Marxism is quite different from the earlier variety. Marx was convinced that the proletariat was a social force which would provide the leverage for basic social change. Observations of Hitler's Germany, of American labor unions and of the Russian bureaucracy have shaken this conviction. In subsequent publications this "Marxism without proletariat" became ever more pronounced. But it is already clearly implied in the programmatic article by Horkheimer. He assigns to the critical theorist the task of allying himself with "progressive" elements and individuals (presumably from all social classes) who are willing to "tell the truth." This alliance will lead to a dialectical process which will generate "liberating, propelling, disciplined and powerful forces."[9] This is a different position from that taken by former Utopian socialists, because technological changes have made a new organization of society possible. "Critical theory declares things do not have to be as they are now. Mankind can change its existence. The possibilities are now available."[10]

6   *Ibid.*, p. 287.
7   *Ibid.*, p. 291.
8   *Ibid.*, p. 280.
9   *Ibid.*, p. 269.
10   *Ibid.*, p. 279.

In this paper no concrete examples are given nor is the mode of analysis explicated. It was left to two of Horkheimer's associates to fill in the details. Herbert Marcuse provided the historical background in a brilliant review, "The Foundations of the Dialectical Theory of Society";[11] in a later edition of this work he added an instructive preface on dialectics and suggested as slogan: "the power of negative thinking."[12] For Marcuse dialectics and critical theory are the same. His 1960 preface succinctly summarized the 1937 Horkheimer article as follows:

> Dialectic thought starts with the experience that the world is unfree; that is to say man and nature exist in conditions of alienation, exist as other than they are . . . to comprehend reality means to comprehend what things really are and this in turn means rejecting their mere actuality. Rejection is the process of thought as well as of action.[13]

Almost by definition an "outsider" cannot really tell what this critical theory is about, although Marcuse's historical review certainly helps one grasp the main intent.[14]

One must supplement these cues by turning to Adorno who became the contact man with the world of the professional sociologists. Adorno faced two fronts, with very different effects. On the one hand he discussed in principle the relation between theory and empirical research. On the other hand he commented extensively on concrete sociological topics. In this second endeavor, Adorno's analytical observations have generally been drawn from the sphere of culture, and especially from music on which he is an outstanding expert. His general approach here can be fairly easily located. In one sense it resembles

---

[11] Herbert Marcuse, *Reason and Revolution* (Boston: Beacon Press, 1960), pp. 258–323.

[12] For American readers this was an amusing allusion to a popular Protestant theologian who preached the "power of positive thinking."

[13] Marcuse, *op. cit.,* Preface.

[14] In recent years Marcuse has ceased to be an historian of ideas and has become instead a political prophet who has influenced German students directly, and students in other countries indirectly. It is easily understandable that someone who is against injustice, poverty and war would feel comforted and stimulated by the undertow of critical sociology. While Marcuse's recent pamphlet on *One Dimensional Man* has gone through many editions in many languages, it can hardly be included in a survey of sociological trends.

Parsons who applies a number of his basic concepts to a variety of topics such as the medical system, child-rearing, relations between nations, etc. More specifically, Adorno emphasizes latent functions, that is, connections which are not easily recognized by the superficial observer. But he adds as a characteristic ingredient an emphasis on those latent functions which, in his opinion, serve to deceive modern man and to mask from him the nature of a basically bad society. Thus one finds in his writings many statements like the following: "theory wants to point out what secretly keeps the whole machinery working"; empirically observed facts do not reflect the underlying true social relations; they are the veil by which these relations are masked." Adorno keeps reverting to the idea that social reality must be observed and studied, but for purposes of demystification and unmasking.[15] As one illustration one can take his contention that music in our times has become a fetish. We live in a world of promotion, propaganda and advertising which forces upon us the categories in which we perceive the world. We believe in star performers, although few of us could distinguish one good violinist from another. The same is true for fine instruments, and yet we flock to a concert where the performer is scheduled to use a genuine Stradivarius. Of a major symphony we can hear and remember only the main themes; as a matter of fact in "music appreciation" courses we use devices which reinforce this reification;[16] serious, popular, and other types of music are forced upon us by radio schedules, etc. Only detailed study of this kind of analysis can convey its creative element; there is no doubt that it enriches sociological thinking.[17]

But on another front Adorno and his followers have done much harm. The matter is best explained by a brief retrospective account. When, after the war, the majority of the Frankfurt group returned to Germany, they at first tried to convey to their German colleagues the merits of empirical social research which they had observed in the United States. In 1951 they convened a general meeting on the role of empirical social research, chaired by the venerable Leopold von

[15]   At one point he says that empirical social research accepts "was die Welt aus uns gemacht hat fälschlich für die Sache selbst." Such a sentence could not be understood without Marcuse's detailed discussion of what Hegel meant when he said that the dialectic method brings out the true nature of the objects it analyzes.

[16]   "This is the symphony which Master Schubert never finished."

[17]   I have tried to spell out this idea with more details in an article on "Administrative and Critical Communications Research," included in this volume.

Wiese.[18] Adorno presented the main report. Obviously, the older generation of sociologists feared that these new methods would endanger the humanistic traditions of their work. Adorno provided many concrete examples to demonstrate how all aspects of sociology can be enriched by empirical studies.[19] Of course, quantitative findings have to be interpreted, but this is known by all intelligent research workers. He especially wanted to dispel the idea "widely held in Germany that empirical social research consists just in counting the opinions of individuals and overlooks the many problems due to the dynamics of group life . . . In the majority of such studies one combines depth interviews with quantitative findings and compares the reaction of people in isolation and in group situations."[20] Together with some insightful criticisms, this paper could stand today as a most adequate discussion on the contribution of concrete empirical studies to general sociology.

Within a period of five years, however, the situation changed completely. Adorno embarked on an endless series of articles dealing with the theme of theory and empirical research. These became more and more shrill, and the invectives multiplied. Stupid, blind, insensitive, sterile became homeric attributes whenever the empiricist was mentioned. According to Adorno the research worker was only interested in verbalized subjective opinions of individuals in which he had naive confidence. If one examines the paper most frequently quoted as the first major expression of this new line, one can hardly believe that it was written by the same author as that previously quoted.[21] Thereafter one paper followed another, each reiterating the new theme. All have

[18] *Empirische Sozialforschung 1952*, Institut zur Förderung öffentlicher Angelegenheiten, E.V. (Frankfurt am Main).

[19] Theodor W. Adorno, *op. cit.*, pp. 30–33.

[20] *Ibid.*, p. 35 (condensed translation).

[21] Theodor W. Adorno, "Soziologie und empirische Forschung," *Logik der Sozialwissenschaften*, Herausgeber Ernst Topitsch (Berlin: Kiepenhever, 1965; originally published in 1957). It is difficult to interpret the changes in Adorno's position. If one were to apply his technique, one might say that in 1951, it was still profitable to take an "American position," while five years later the garb of the all-encompassing philosophy was more likely to lead to the elite position he now holds. A friendlier interpretation would be that the younger generation of German sociologists became over-impressed by empirical methods and that Adorno felt he had to support the embattled position of serious reflection. Very occasionally, he still overcomes the rigidity of his arguments by a truly dialectic move. The Kinsey report, according to him, is on the one hand a typical outgrowth of a statistical barbarism, but at the same time deserves to be defended against old-fashioned humanists who denounce it for ideological reasons.

two characteristics in common. First, the empiricist is a generalized other—no examples of concrete studies are given. (The 1952 paper contained several interesting examples.) Second, the futility of empirical research is not demonstrated by its products, but derived from the conviction that specific studies cannot make a contribution to the great aim of social theory to grasp society in its totality. Empirical research had become another fetish concealing the true nature of the contemporary social system.

Adorno's position gained increasing attention, and in 1961 the German Sociological Society found it necessary to call a special meeting to debate the issue. The main topic was "logic of the social sciences." The exponent of what one might call the official theory of science was the Austro-English philosopher, Karl R. Popper, and the co-reporter was T. W. Adorno.[22] Since this meeting the so-called positivist-dialectic discussion has become the central theme of German sociology.

Neither of the reports offered any surprises. Adorno stressed the continuity of his position. "Critical sociology, for its concepts to be true, is necessarily at the same time a critique of society, as Horkheimer in his paper on traditional theory has demonstrated." Dahrendorf, in summarizing the discussion, pointed out that both speakers were so polite that it was difficult to really perceive the basic differences. According to him, the only clear distinction was that, for Popper, theory is continually evolving by trial and error, while for Adorno, it is, at least at its core, an eternal verity. Dahrendorf underscored his disappointment in the meeting because there was so little reference to specific sociological problems and to the uses of sociology for concrete social decisions.

Indeed there is a striking contradiction between the continuing excitement over the debate and the paucity of lessons to be learned from it. One almost has the feeling that partisanship depends more on how one feels about the Vietnam war than how one wants to work as a sociologist. In a subsequent article on the Tübingen discussion Habermas gave expression to this difficulty. He is the first and, as far as I can tell, the only commentator who has tried to specify the difference between an "analytical theory of knowledge and dialectics." He discusses the disagreement under four points: 1) how the object of

[22] "Interne Arbeitstagung der Deutschen Gesellschaft für Soziologie, Tübingen," *Kölner Zeitschrift für Soziologie und Sozialpsychologie,* 14 (2), 1962.

sociological analysis is constituted; 2) the relation between theory and factual evidence; 3) the relation between theory and history; 4) the relation between science and praxis.[23]

Habermas' efforts to break down the issue into specific components are certainly helpful but again the sociologist attracted by the atmosphere of critical theory could not learn how to proceed if he wanted to study a specific topic in its spirit.

Each point is highlighted by a quotation from Adorno and additional comments are written in his style. The whole situation becomes aggravated by the position of the "positivists." One of the main German centers of empirical social research is undoubtedly the University of Cologne. Its senior sociologist, at the Stresa international conference, has given apt descriptions of critical theory backed by well-chosen references.[24] He comes to a pessimistic conclusion: one should make a sharp distinction between a "theory of society" and "sociological theory" and beware of the former. The critical theorist deals in speculation "where he uses material data in an uncritical and uncontrolled way and rushes in too hasty a way to its conclusion . . . research has no meaning in itself, e.g. in order to corroborate or reject hypothesis but is just used for sustaining a revolutionary action." By thus divorcing the two areas he in turn forcloses the possibility to utilize perceptive elements in critical theory for the enrichment of the total field. The consequence can be exemplified by the important German text on empirical social research which the Cologne group has published. The section on the philosophic foundations of social research makes no mention whatsoever of critical sociology. Neither does its author find a place for it in his reader on the Foundation of the Social Sciences.[25]

---

[23] Jürgen Habermas, "Analytische Wissenschafts-Theorie und Dialektik," in Topitsch *op. cit.* Habermas plays an interesting role in German sociology. He is a partisan of the Frankfurt persuasion without having belonged to the original group. He did an excellent empirical study on "Students and Politics," but was not successful in relating his findings to his general social analysis. He wrote an enlightening book with much interesting material on historical changes in the notion of public opinion. At the same time, he published a long monograph on the logic of social sciences, which never refers to any historical or empirical investigation.

[24] Renee König, "On Some Recent Developments in the Relation between Theory and Research," in *Transactions of the Fourth World Congress of Sociology,* Vol. II (1959), pp. 275–290.

[25] Hans Albert (ed.), *Theorie und Realität* (Tübingen: Mohn, 1964) and in *Handbuch der empirischen Sozialforschung* (Stuttgart: Euhe, 1967), pp. 38–64. The British sociologist Bottomore in the new *International Encyclopedia of the*

One must go to another country to find the only attempt I am aware of to make dialectics something like a research operation which can be taught and learned. I have in mind the work of a French sociologist who has made a serious effort along this line. Georges Gurvitch in a book on *Dialectique et Sociologie*[26] gives an extensive review of dialectic ideas in the history of philosophy. He then describes his own position which he called operational dialectics and which he considers important as a tool of sociological research. He warns against making dialectics a cure-all. According to him the fetishism of contradiction is dangerous. Rather one should distinguish five specific dialectical procedures which in various combinations are a useful starting point for any sociological work. It is not easy to condense Gurvitch's ideas but the following summary should give a first picture.

A dialectic operation consists of the selection of two elements in a social situation and then to see how they are related. They can complement and interact with each other and might create ambiguities for the participants. It is this relation and the outcome to which it leads that is at the core of the different operations. The substantive content of the elements can vary greatly from one case to another. I am giving the French titles and one brief example for each procedure. A reader of Ango-Saxon literature will at many points find ideas with which he is familiar in a different terminology.

1) *La complémentarité dialectique*. Here the subject matter is the relation between us and the others, between planned and spontaneous activities, and so on. Some of the examples are close to the notion of role conflict.[27]

2) *L'implication dialectique mutuelle*. This covers mutual interaction between social structure and technology, between broad cultural patterns and social interaction on the more microscopic level. In this second procedure of dialectization Gurvitch includes also the way cultural importations to a country are adapted to its own tradition.

3) *L'ambiguïté dialectique*. Many of the examples of mutual interaction are taken up here again but under a new aspect.

Social Sciences has a penetrating and informative entry on Marxist sociology. He too makes the point that the Marxist heritage is split into a philosophical and empirical trend. While he is not very explicit, I have the impression that he believes more in a mutual interpenetration than either Frankfurt or Cologne do.

[26] Georges Gurvitch, *Dialectique et Sociologie* (Paris: Flammarion, 1962).

[27] *Ibid.*, p. 196 ff.

An individual or a group which lives at the intersection of two or more social systems has often considerable difficulty in finding its own social identity. Literature on reference groups might be relevant here.[28]

4) *La polarisation dialectique.* As one would expect there is also always the possibility of an antagonistic development. This is probably the procedure which comes closest to the more conventional notion of dialectics. Obvious examples come from the antagonism between classes, revolution and war.

5) *La mise en réciprocité de perspectives.* This dialectic procedure consists in bringing out the elements which are neither identification nor separation but where the reciprocity has become so intense that it leads to an observable parallelism. His examples are easier understood than the concept itself. Bureaucratic organizations create as well as attract certain personalities. Public opinion is an aggregate of individual opinions at one time but in turn induces change of individual opinions. Inventions are due to individual creation but are more likely to occur under certain historical conditions.

Gurvitch is explicit as to the role which his dialectic procedures are to play in sociological work. "They don't give us an explanation, they lead to the threshhold. Dialectic prepares the frame for explanatory work."[29]

For two reasons it seemed justified to draw attention to Gurvitch's ideas. For one, each effort should be applauded which tries to explicate concretely such vague terms like dialectics.[30] Second, there is salient parallel here between Gurvitch's dialectical operations and Parsons' pattern variables. In both cases the point is being made that a number of basic orientations should be taken into account in any sociological investigation. It is true that Parsons mainly thinks of the orientation of an acting individual or a group while Gurvitch thinks more in terms of the analyzing sociologists. But the two perspectives can be easily translated into each other. Only a more detailed scrutiny could decide

---

[28] *Ibid.,* p. 206.

[29] *Ibid.,* p. 318 ff.

[30] I should here like to cite my article on "Administrative and Critical Communications Research: Studies in Philosophy and Social Sciences," reprinted in this volume.

whether there are additional parallels between the five dimensions which each author develops.

Finally a comparative remark. There is hardly any other idea which leads such a different life in various countries. In the 16 volumes of the New Encyclopedia of the Social Sciences there is no entry for the term dialectic. On the other hand, a simple introductory manual on "Methods of the Social Sciences" written for French students by two professors of law, states as a matter of course that the dialectical method "is the fullest, the richest, and obviously the most advanced method of explanation in sociology."[31] *The Standard American Reader on the Philosophy of Social Science* contains no paper on dialectics.[32] The corresponding German Reader edited by Topitsch which we have repeatedly quoted contains three papers on this topic.

This last discussion has already moved us from Germany to France. We cannot leave this country without at least a brief reference to its most recent interest, a kind of counterpoint to dialectics.

There can be no doubt that in linguistics, anthropology and literary criticism, structuralism is an important term. One could also point to concrete work which would permit trying a reasonable definition. But neither the work of Levi-Strauss nor the movement around Roland Barth belongs in the domain of the present essay. And in sociology I don't find any real traces. Piaget has written a monograph where he argues that structuralism pervades all modern thinking including the social sciences. But when it comes to sociology he hardly gives any concrete examples. If we leave out for the moment the study of small groups, then the only sociological reference Piaget makes is to the way Parsons uses the term "structure."[33] One sometimes has the impression that Piaget thinks that wherever mathematical models are used they are by definition part of the structural movement. But that would hardly contribute much to the clarification of the issue.

In fact the only type of this sociology I could find comes from

[31] Roger Pinto and Madeleine Gravitz, *Méthodes des sciences sociales* (Paris: Librairie Dalloz, 1964), p. 379.

[32] May Broadbeck (ed.), *Readings in the Philosophy of the Social Sciences* (New York: MacMillan, 1968).

[33] Jean Piaget, *Le structuralisme* (Paris: Presses universitaires de France, 1968) p. 86.

sources outside of France. When linguists classify various languages, they often set up general attribute spaces to locate in them the various languages. In doing so, they use implicitly the kind of procedure which has been discussed at the end of our Chapter 1. As a matter of fact one American linguist specifically stresses the parallel.[34]

One other problem which might also belong in a discussion of structuralism: the typology of broad social and economic systems which has recently been revived. The interest probably originates with Marx who was much interested in describing the historical phases of society which precede the origin of full-fledged development of capitalism.[35]

Recent social change in underdeveloped countries has brought the problem very much to the attention of social scientists. Will these countries on their way to modern industrialization develop forms of societies different from any known before? If so, how can they be described without introducing a bias which can come from the experience of Western social scientists. Kula has suggested that something like an anthropology of Western industrial society would be needed written from the point of view of, say, an African social scientist.[36] The most intense work on this kind of social typology has been made by Wittfogel in his work on Asiatic despotic societies. In his main publication he also reviews the history of this typological idea; his information is instructive but probably biased because of his strong stand as a converted anti-communist.[37] It is interesting to note that historians have become interested in this problem as witnessed by a collective work on feudalism which raises the question whether the type abstracted from European history also applies to history of other countries.[38] The book

---

[34]   Joseph Greenberg, "Nature and Use of Linguistic Typologies," *International Journal of American Linguistics*, (April 1957).

[35]   *See* the introduction of E. J. Hobsbawn to a new translation of Marx's *Pre-Capitalist Economic Formation* (New York: International Publishers, 1965).

[36]   Witold Kula, "On the Typology of Economic Systems," in *The Social Sciences: Problems and Orientations* (The Hague and Paris: Mouton, UNESCO, 1968), pp. 108–144.

[37]   Karl A. Wittfogel, *Oriental Despotism: A Comparative Study of Total Power* (New Haven and London: Yale University Press, 1957).

[38]   Rushton Coulborn (ed.), *Feudalism in History* (Princeton, N.J.: Princeton University Press, 1956).

by Eisenstadt on centralized bureaucracies, discussed in our Chapter 3, would also deserve re-analyzing from this typological point of view.[39]

---

[39] The whole topic has been brought to my attention by the Polish Marxist, Professor Sachs, rather late in the writing of this essay. The complex literature mentioned here deserves much more detailed scrutiny than I can give it at this moment.

Part Three
Qualitative Research Techniques

CHAPTER *8*

THE ART OF ASKING *WHY*

THREE PRINCIPLES UNDERLYING THE FORMULATION OF QUESTIONNAIRES

I. ASCERTAINING WHAT A QUESTION MEANS; THE PRINCIPLE OF SPECIFICATION.

Asking for reasons and giving answers are commonplace habits of everyday life. We have all had the experience of acting under certain impulses and certain influences so many times that we are sure that our fellow men have had the same experiences and reasons for their own actions. And we are seldom disappointed if we inquire. Our respondent not only had had reasons for his actions; he usually knows, also, in which reason we might be especially interested, and it is upon this assumption that he bases his answer. If a friend explains why he has come to see me, he does not start to tell me that he was born, and that he moved to this city two years ago, although these, too, are reasons for his being here today. He is aware that most of these reasons are known as well to me as to him, and he picks out the reason which he hopes will contribute especially to a mutual understanding of the present situation.

In market research, the question-and-answer business is not so simple, and the ease of furnishing answers in everyday life may involve

Originally published by Paul F. Lazarsfeld in 1934 in a marketing journal (*The National Marketing Review*), now defunct.

dangerous pitfalls. In social intercourse, it is most likely that what is important for our respondent is important also for us who have made the inquiry. In market research interviews, we cannot rely upon this good fortune. The purpose of our *why* questions is to discover all of those factors which determine the purchases of a certain group of people; or, to put it more exactly in anticipation of a later part of this paper, we want to know all the determinants of a certain sort. Such knowledge should permit us to increase our future efficiency in this field by providing a more complete and accurate basis for anticipating demand factors of the market. We cannot leave it up to the respondents to tell us whatever they are inclined. The average consumer is not trained to survey offhand all the factors which determine his purchases and he usually has a very hazy understanding of the *why* question. On the other hand, the information we want should be exact and precise. This creates the initial problem in the art of asking *why* in market research: how can the gap between these two attitudes be bridged?

We have, in general, three possible purposes in market research in asking people questions:

a) *Influences toward action.*
We may want to know by which media people have been *influenced* to act the way they did, which is the case when we want to evaluate the role of certain advertisements, of advice of friends, etc.; or

b) *Attributes of the product.*
We may want to know if it were the *attributes* of the product itself, and which of them—its taste, its color, or its use —led the customer to buy; or

c) *Impulses of the purchaser.*
We may want to know certain *tendencies* by which the consumer was controlled: Whether he bought for himself, or as a gift; whether he bought under sudden impulse, or after long deliberation; whether it was an habitual or a unique·proceeding, etc.

The consumer, however, is seldom aware of these varying interpretations. For example, take a simple question such as why some one bought a certain brand of coffee. One respondent might answer that he liked the taste, and another that a neighbor had told him about the brand. These two respondents interpreted our question *why* in two different ways. The one thought that we were interested mainly in the attributes of the coffee; the other, that we had in mind the outside influences which affected his choice. The answers, therefore, are not comparable. The neighbor who spoke to the one respondent may very well have mentioned the good taste of the coffee; and the man who told about the good taste may have heard about it from a neighbor in the first place. So the two cases may have had the same sequence of determinants affecting the two respondents, only the interpretation of our question *why* in different ways led to seemingly quite different answers. But it is possible, as we shall see, to ask our question in such a specific way that both of our respondents will tell the whole story.

The importance of the problem involved here becomes still more evident when we turn to the statistical treatment of answers given to a *why* question. The usual table of reasons as we find it in current market research studies would record the result of our coffee question by stating: X respondents bought their particular brand of coffee because of its taste; Y people bought it because of some advice they had received. But these figures are apt to be completely erroneous. What the research man may really discover is: X people understood his question as pertaining to influence, and the influence they had experienced was advice; Y people understood the question as pertaining to attributes, and the decisive attribute for them was taste. This danger is illustrated by the following diagram:

Respondent has been actually determined by:	Respondent understands the question to mean Pertaining to:		
	Influences	Attributes	
Advice	X	N	X + N
Taste	M	Y	M + Y

Advice was the real determining factor for X + N people, and *taste* for M + Y people. But the question, improperly put, made the student lose the true reason of M and N people and his results were, therefore, unsatisfactory. (In practice, the matter would be still more complicated by two-way interpretations of the question; but we need not go into that much detail.)

From these illustrations, we can make the generalization that the innocent question *why* may contain many pitfalls and is actually only the beginning of a research design. If we want to carry out our program skillfully, we must state precisely in which of the infinite number of determinants of an action we are interested. Only when we make it clear to ourselves and to our respondents which groups of determinants are at stake will we get results which permit a sensible statistical treatment, which is, of course, the aim of every field study.

The real task, therefore, which confronts the market student every time he starts out with a *why* program is to be constantly aware of what he really means or seeks to discover by his questionnaire. What special question he will ask depends upon his decision. In the example just discussed, he will be constrained to start with two questions: "What made you buy this brand of coffee?" and "Why do you like it?" There is a probability that the wording of the first question will furnish, chiefly, reports of influences, as answers, such as radio advertising, magazine advertising, grocers' displays. However, many respondents will answer the question, "What made you start to use it?" with such an answer as, "because it is a stronger brand." Then we, as interviewers, will recognize that this answer is based on attributes, and must proceed to look for influences by asking, "How did you know that this coffee is a strong brand?" The respondent will then have to report the media, or say, "I don't know."

In order to make the basic principle of these considerations quite clear, let us take a somewhat different example. We shall assume that our program is to ask a group of individuals, "Why did you change from one brand of cigarettes to another?" Here again, if we put the question this way, the respondent must decide for himself what we mean, and he may either tell why he stopped using his old brand, or report why he chose the new one. If we then try to treat the answer statistically, we lump together the responses to two different questions. Therefore, we should ask the two questions really involved: "Why did you stop using the other brand?" and "Why did you choose this new one?" This last question, as we already know, is to be split again into two questions, one pertaining to *influences* and one to *attributes*.

The reader may be troubled by the fact that, according to the technic developed, the answers to the question *why* will not normally be recorded by one table but by several tables. There is really nothing astonishing in this; very often one word of our everyday speech becomes a group of figures in exact research. For instance, we speak about the position of a point in space and understand every well what we mean. But when it comes to numerical treatment, this position is represented by three figures, the three co-ordinates. In the same way, the reason for an action might well be represented by several indices. The number of indices necessary depends to a great extent upon the complete purpose of the investigation, as we shall soon see.

Before proceeding, let us briefly consider what ought to happen when we are forced for one reason or another to use the general *why* question. We have already excluded one unjustifiable procedure, namely, to construct one table and to record simply every type of answer as often as it has been given. The diagram used above reveals that the figures so obtained will be misleading. Let us take the example regarding the change of cigarette brands. Since by hypothesis, the respondent has been asked only one general question, whereas he should have been asked three, he will answer this question according to his own interpretation. He will report either a *dissatisfaction* with his former brand, an *influence* leading him to the new brand, or some *attribute* of the new brand inducing him to make the change. We should, therefore, segregate these answers and present them in three separate tables. Let us suppose for the sake of simplicity that every respondent reports only one element. According to his own interpretation, the answer of one respondent will be inserted definitely in one of the three tables; if he answered, for instance, that a certain advertisement made him change, his answer will be recorded under "advertisement" in the table of influences. In the two other tables—pertaining to dissatisfaction with the previous brand and attributes of the new brand—he will contribute an entry to the columns *dissatisfaction unknown* and *attribute unknown*. The result will be three tables, each with the column "unknown" heavily loaded. But at least the rest of the entries will yield sensible and comparable results. We would, for instance, be able to say with some truth that, among the influences recorded, advertisement was more important than personal advice, whereas if only one tabulation were made, our conclusions would be unsound.

We might call the handling of the whole set of problems involved herein the *principle of specification*. We have elaborated on it because much of the disrepute in which the statistical treatment of reasons gathered in field studies has fallen, is due to errors connected with this principle. This, however, presents only the negative side of the question. The constructive task is to find the concrete questions which should be substituted for the general *why* program. We have already mentioned that that depends very much upon the purpose of the study. What we want to do is to pick out from the indefinite number of factors which determine a concrete action the ones which are of interest to us. To further illustrate this point, let us take the reasons for book buying. Our *program* is to find out: "Why did you buy this book?" A respondent will give, out of the same concrete experience, quite different answers, according to the particular word stressed: BUY, THIS, and BOOK. If he understood: "Why did you BUY this book?", he might answer, "Because the waiting list in the library was so long that I shouldn't have got it for two months." If he understood: "Why did you buy THIS book?" he might tell what interested him especially in the author. And if he understood: "Why did you buy this BOOK?" he might report that he at first thought of buying a concert ticket with the money but later realized that a book is a much more durable possession than a concert, and such reasoning caused him to decide upon the book. If our study is undertaken as a service to the publishing company which wants to be in a better position to compete with libraries, we will have to specify in our questions the *buying* aspect versus all other methods by which a book may be acquired. If a library wants us to find out in what books people are most interested, it is the characteristics of the book which need more specification in our questions. If the survey in which we are engaged is a leisure-time study, we will have to stress all questions which pertain to *book-reading* in comparison with other means of entertainment. There is actually no element of a concrete purchase experience which cannot be made the object of a *specified why question* for a *general why program*.

We have seen the limitations and pitfalls in the use of one question. Follow-up questions which specify definite motives are one means to correct this difficulty while more careful tabulation of answers to a single question are apt to bring more truthful conclusions. One final point on the *weight* of reasons has been made. Even after we have ascertained attributes *and* influences the question remains: Was the neighbor's authority or the vision of the coffee's taste more important? Without entering into details we mention three possibilities in getting this information. We might use the way our respondent reports immediately as our source of information. He may mention first the neighbor and the taste only upon our second question: What did the neighbor say? Then we might decide that the neighbor had more weight as a factor. Or we might use a special question; interviewing about the movie attendance we might ask: Was the theater or the show *more* important? We shall find an example in our next paragraph.

The third way, to leave the decision to the interviewer, is illustrated as follows. In interviewing about the influence of advertising, for instance, it is sometimes advisable to ask a respondent to report any example in which he bought a certain commodity under the influence of an advertisement. We will get widely varying replies, and the problem is then how to make them statistically comparable. To accomplish this, the *interviewer* must keep in mind what we want to know. We are interested in where the advertisement was seen, in order to know something about the successful medium; what the advertisement said, in order to check up on the effectiveness of the presentation; what point in the advertisements led to the purchase, in order to know what were the successful appeals. While the actual question in which we are interested is not answered directly by this method, the interviewer has an elaborate supply of facts upon which to make a decision. So we leave it to him to decide in which of the following three main classifications the respondent's answer should be placed. Has the advertisement actually aroused a *new wish?* For instance, on a hot day, a picture of an iced drink makes us enter a drugstore and ask for it. Or has it been used as a source of information about a *need of which he was already aware?* For instance, did he look in the newspaper today to see where a stocking sale is to be found? Or did the respondent see the advertisement before and did it become effective only when the corresponding *need was aroused by some other circumstances?* It is surprising to what extent these three possibilities cover, for practical purpose, the dynamic aspect of all reports regarding purchases executed under the influence of advertising. However, the problem of the weight of different determinant factors involves quite a few complicated aspects, which we cannot elaborate here. Instead, the examples cited are offered as a contribution to the *principle of specification.*

II. ENABLING THE INTERVIEWEE TO ANSWER: THE PRINCIPLE OF DIVISION.

We have not yet applied our principle to the discussion of a concrete questionnaire and for a very good reason. What we have stated so far is not sufficient to lead to practical applications. Imagine, for instance, that we want to know the influences and the attributes which determined a certain purchase, and we straightway ask the housewife for them. We certainly should not get very satisfactory results. After ascertaining what we want to know, we must enable our respondent to give us the right answers. Here we touch upon the field of the psychology of interviewing, which has received much attention in this country. Bingham and Moore[1] have gathered much valuable material about the right way of keeping the respondent's attention, of avoiding leading questions, of creating an attitude of trustworthiness, and so forth. We do not intend to repeat here material which has been successfully dealt with elsewhere. But there is one point, related to what we have said above, which needs our special attention—the *technic of fitting our questions to the experience of the respondent*. In specifying our general *why* program, we might be forced to *specify it in a different way for different types* of purchase experiences undergone by different individuals. Suppose, for instance, that we want to know why certain people prefer silk to rayon. There may be respondents who have given much thought to this topic; this one will be well able to give us her reasons directly, while another one may never have earnestly thought about the subject, and, therefore, will be unable to give immediately the reasons for her preference. After having selected the people who prefer silk to rayon, we must ask them first: "Have you any special reasons for your preference?" The one who has some may be asked directely what they are; the one who has none will have to be questioned differently. We will probably have to ask her about her general experiences with fabrics and will have to infer from her report the reason for her partiality.

Such a procedure was followed by a company which manufactured electric motors. It wanted to ascertain from individuals by means of a questionnaire the reasons *why* they bought only of that company. In the first trial questionnaire, it appeared that some respondents were able to give very definite reasons, whereas other answers were completely evasive, or stereotyped, or otherwise of no value. Therefore, the subsequent questionnaire elaborated upon the inquiry. The first question was: "Had you any special reason in this instance to buy from our company?" If the answer was "yes," the re-

---

[1] Walter V. Bingham and Bruce V. Moore, *How to Interview*, 2nd edition, Harpers, 1934.

spondent was asked about the process of his deliberations and efforts which led to the purchase; and, as he was selected in this way, he was able to give satisfactory answers. The other individuals, mainly clients who habitually purchased from this company, were given another series of questions which tried to trace the origin of their habits as to influences and tendencies.

Another questionnaire which was used in a study of movie attendance will help to summarize our whole approach to the problems of specified *why* questions. The study was made to determine "Why people attend movies?" The determinants in which we were interested were: the situation which gave rise to attendance at the movie; the part played in the decision by the persons accompanying the respondent; the sources from which information was gathered; and the decisive features of the show and the theater. There was no question inserted as to how our respondent came to the movie, although a taxicab company might have been most interested in this aspect. Possibly some reader may not at once realize how the vehicle used for conveyance to the movie can possibly be the answer to a specified *why* question. But let him consider the following case: "Why did Mary, but not John, come in time to my party yesterday?" Answer: There was a bad snowstorm. Mary came on the subway. But John used his car and got stuck. He therefore came too late *because he drove his car*. The movie attendance questionnaire follows:

Did you go primarily (I) just to go to a movie, or (II) because of a certain picture?

I——— II——— Both———

If I or Both:
1) When did you decide to go to a movie?
2) Why and under what circumstances did you decide?
3) (If not yet inserted) When and how was your company chosen?
4) As to the special theater or show. (Check.)
   a) Was it proposed by someone in the company?
   b) Did you have it in mind yourself?
   c) Did you look for or get special advice or information?
   If (b), how did you know about it?
   If (c), where did you look for advice or information?

5) How many pictures were taken into consideration?

6) Which was more inducive, (A) the theater——; (B) the picture——; (C) does not know—— (Check.)
Remarks for Interviewers: If B or C, ask question 7 first. If A, ask question 8 first. But ask both questions in any case.

7) What interested you in the picture? (Please try to remember all the details.)

8) What made the theater suitable to your choice?

If II.

1a) When did you learn about this picture?

2a) How did you learn about it?

3a) What interested you in it when you heard about it? (Please try to remember all the details.)

4a) (If not yet inserted) When and how was your company chosen?

In All Cases:

1b) (If not yet inserted) When and under what circumstances was the final decision made? Why did you go at this particular time?

2b) What other uses of the time and money spent in seeing the movie were considered?

This questionnaire contains several examples of what we called the technic of fitting the question to the experience of the respondent. Take for example, the question on the media of information. If a respondent went to the movie because of a certain picture, he is very likely to remember offhand how he learned about this picture; it was the first reason which started his whole movie attendance. On the other hand, if he just went to the movie because he wanted some relaxation, he will not remember so well why he selected the special show. Therefore, in order to fit our questions to his experience, we have to proceed this way: First, we will ascertain if he went for the sake of a certain picture or not. In the former case, we might at once ask him "How did you learn about this picture?" In the latter case, an additional question has to be inserted first. We will ask him: "When and under what circumstances did you decide to go to the movie?" This question should lead his memory back to the concrete situation in which he decided to go and then he will be more likely to remember what information he looked for in order to pick out a special picture. In a second question, we will find him prepared to give us all necessary information about influences. Another example is the way we ask about the respondent's companions in this questionnaire. If our respondent were invited to go to the movie, he will have mentioned his companion in the first question as a reason for his decision. If he were the inviting party, a special question will be necessary to find how he chose his companion. The questionnaire has to be flexible enough to cover both cases in such a way that the respondent feels at his ease in remembering the whole process of decision.

The reader is undoubtedly aware that this technic of fitting questions to the experience of the respondent is in conflict with usual procedure. Traditional opinion is that a question should be so worded as always to insure the same reaction on the part of all those interviewed. We advocate a rather loose and liberal handling of a questionnaire by an interviewer. It seems to us much more important that the question be fixed in its *meaning*, than in its *wording*. This new emphasis places the responsibility on the interviewer for knowing exactly what he is trying to discover and permits him to vary the wording in accordance with the experience of the respondent. The resulting margin of error would be much greater if a standardized question were to be interpreted in very different ways by different respondents who have their own different experiences in mind. If we get the respondent to report to us the determinants of his experience to his best knowledge and recollection, our results will be much more homogeneous than in a case where we have inflexible words but have not taken any care for ascertaining the meaning placed upon those words by our respondent.

This whole technic may be described as *"The principle of division."* It consists in adapting the pattern of our questionnaire to the structural pattern of the experience of the respondent from whom we are seeking our information. By this method, we find much easier access to the motives controlling his actions than if we try to compel the respondent to conform to a stereotyped questionnaire, which he may not understand in the way we intend. Our method, moreover, is supported by the most eminent authority. Plato, in his *Phaedrus*, speaks about the *principle of division* and points out the *wisdom of separating on the basis of the natural subdivision, as does the skillful carver, who seeks the joint rather than break the bone.*

III. ASCERTAINING WHAT THE ANSWER MEANS: THE PRINCIPLE OF TACIT ASSUMPTION.

We have briefly discussed the necessity of specifying the meaning of the *why* question, and that of adapting the question to the experience of the respondent. There is a third point which deserves our consideration. Suppose we ask a man what pleased him most in the coat he bought. Why doesn't he answer that he was most pleased by the fact that the coat had just two sleeves? He would certainly never have bought it with 3 sleeves, however pleasing to him other of the attributes might have been. The reason is clear: There is a tacit assumption between interviewer and respondent that coats have only two sleeves and therefore that fact will not be mentioned in spite of its predominant importance.

Very often, however, the particular consequences of this principle of tacit assumption are omitted. Let us suppose we want to know what attributes are important in the consumption of tea. If we ask: "*Why* do you drink tea for breakfast?" we immediately get answers pertaining to the use and effect of tea: It is quickly made; it keeps one awake; it doesn't burden one's stomach in the morning; and so on. If we ask: "Why do you drink X brand tea?" we get much more specific answers concerning the tea itself; because of its nice color; because it requires less sugar; because it is economical to use; and so on. But the former group of attributes is almost completely omitted. Of course, the two series of responses are by no means contradictory; in the first group the merits of tea were judged in comparison with those of other beverages, coffee, cocoa, milk; whereas, in the second group the general qualities of tea were taken for granted in a tacit assumption, and secondary distinctions between different brands were discussed. The best results are obtained by asking both ways and interpreting the differences in the two series of answers.

Such tacit assumptions are not always easy to realize. In a study of candies, three brands of different price and quality were at stake. It was the medium brand which met most frequently the objection of being ordinary. The best brand was of high quality and nicely wrapped; the medium was also wrapped, but was of a lower quality; the cheapest brand was unwrapped. People apparently felt that the best brand and the cheapest gave just what they promised, whereas the medium brand made promises in its appearance which were not kept by its quality. Therefore, the objections of low quality were more frequent with the medium than with the cheapest brand.

The role of tacit assumptions shows up everywhere where questions are involved. Therefore, it might be worth while to quote a remark from one of Chesterton's detective stories, which brings it out in a very amusing way:

> Have you ever noticed this: That people never answer what you say? They answer what you mean, or what they think you mean. Suppose one lady says to another in a country house: 'Is anybody staying with you?' The lady does not answer: 'Yes, the butler, the three footmen, the parlor maid, and so on,' though the parlor maid may be in the room, or the butler behind her chair. She says: 'There is nobody staying with us,' meaning nobody of the sort you mean. But suppose a doctor inquiring into an epidemic asks, 'Who is staying in the house?' then the lady will remember the butler, the parlor maid, and the rest. All language is used like that; *you never get a question answered literally, even when yet get it answered truly.*[2]

The whole matter has, of course, immediate bearing upon the formulation of questionnaires. I quote the following questions from a questionnaire concerning shoe buying: "What is most important to you in buying shoes: color, price, durability, style, quality, fit?" Such a question and the resulting statistical tabulation have been used over and over again, with quite contradictory results. In Germany, much discussion centered about the problem of whether customers lay more stress upon quality, or upon style, because different investigations following such procedure had brought out different results. Now, price and color and style are items which can be easily ascertained at the time of the purchase. Quality and durability, on the other hand, are attributes which we can test only by wearing the shoes. While the purchase is being made, we must judge them by indirect criteria. One person might judge the quality by the style; another, by the price; still another by some feature of the leather. Therefore, the people who state that they bought according to quality have made varying assumptions as to how quality can be ascertained at the moment of purchase. Con-

[2]   G. K. Chesterton, *The Invisible Man.* "Innocence of Father Brown."

sequently, this whole group should be recorded according to the concrete criteria used, and not according to a word which implies a tacit assumption unknown to the interviewer. This can be easily done by adding another question about this ill-defined attributes: "In buying, how do you recognize quality and how do you recognize durability?"

The reader, who may recall similar cases, will readily see the benefit to be derived from a previous careful analysis by market research men of terms which they use, in order to describe attributes. They would not only obtain more reliable results; they would be more prepared to refute objections which originate from misunderstandings. Professor Donald Laird,[3] of Colgate, conducted an experiment to show of what little use it is to ask a woman about attributes of commodities and their importance to her. He took identical pairs of stockings and perfumed them slightly with different scents. Then he asked certain women to select the pair which seemed to them to be of the best quality. The women definitely preferred a certain perfume, and Laird made the point that these women thought they judged quality, whereas they actually judged scent. But what about this word *quality?* No definition is given or presupposed. As a result, the women first exhausted the more usual criteria of quality, perhaps texture, or body of the weave, and as these did not give any clue, they finally relied upon scent as a criterion of quality, inasmuch as a definition of quality was left entirely to their own interpretation. The only thing which Laird's clever experiment shows is that scent can be used in tacit assumption as the definition of quality. No intrinsic difficulty in this kind of research is shown except that the basic problems have to be brought to light more clearly.

There is a similarity between this principle of tacit assumption and our principle of specification: Everything depends upon the purpose of the study. If we want material for writing advertising copy, then the word *quality* used by our respondent is satisfactory for us, since we intend to approach him with words anyhow. But if we want to use our interviews for guidance in shoe manufacturing, we want to know exactly what the word *quality* connotes to the consumer. It is, therefore, advisable to formulate questionnaires in such a way that the returns can be used for both copy writing and production guid-

[3] *Journal of Applied Psychology,* June, 1932.

ance. We cite by way of example a question on book buying. The respondent was asked: "How did you learn about this book?" The problem was to ascertain: "What interested you in it?" The typical answer was: the title, or the author, or the subject matter, but in order to get more definite information, the following check list was used, which proved to be successful.[4] The respondent was first required to give his general answer, then was asked by the interviewer to specify this reply according to the following possibilities:

What interested you in it?

Title. . . . ; previous work of author . . . . ; fame of author . . . .
Subject matter which I understood from source above (the information) . . . . ; from glancing at the book . . . . ; from
the jacket . . . . ; from the title . . . .
Nothing in the book itself, but its reputation . . . . ; the authority of the recommendation . . . . ; reading was professionally required . . . .
External features of the book (color, size, binding, etc.)
Specify . . .
Other reasons.

The tabulation of the results will depend upon the use which is to be made of the data. If the answers are to be used for writing advertising copy, a table according to the main groups will be most useful. If a jacket design or a store display of books is at stake, the sub-items become of chief importance. Very often in current market research, we would find that the subject matter of a book was a reason for buying. Our example shows that subject matter can mean at least four different things, and just what it means in a special case has clearly to be ascertained by the provisions of the questionnaire.

The problem of tacit assumption constitutes such a strong limitation upon the use of questionnaires alone, that it is sometimes necessary to resort to a combination of experiment and interview. In many instances, it is not possible to ascertain positively what tacit assumptions the respondent is holding in mind, and an experiment is helpful in bringing out the real facts of the situation. A product experiment in

---

[4] No attempt is here made to discuss the problem of the checklist vs. free answer. Professor J. G. Jenkins at Cornell is now working on conclusive experiments in this field.

market research is, from a theoretical point of view, a tool for eliminating the respondent's tacit assumption by variations of stimulus. We cannot discuss the field of experiment here, but we want to give as a final example, an experience which is just on the line between interview and experiment.

Donald Cowen offered a few hundred women two brands of the same food product: the one was the leading brand in the market, the other a new brand of his company. The subjects divided about 50–50 for the two brands. Then he added the question: "Do you prefer the product you just selected to the product you have at home?" Here the adherents of the leading product responded in general: "Not especially." The adherents of Cowen's product definitely preferred it to the brand they had at home. The inference was clear; the two products were in taste about equally popular; but the one, the leading brand, had a flavor or taste similar to that of the product already in use, whereas the Cowen product had a radically new taste. This very important difference would not have been brought to light either through the mere choice experiment or by a question: "Why do you like it?" It was a happy combination of experiment and interview which broke down a tacit assumption. It is the conviction of this writer that such a combination will prove more and more successful in the field of product improvement.[5]

IV.   SUMMARY AND THEORETICAL BACKGROUND.

The assumption of this paper was that the consumer we have in front of us had carried through a concrete purchase. Our problem was to record all the factors which had determined his purchase; or, better, all the factors which were important for our investigation. We have assumed that this consumer is perfectly willing to answer our questions. The main point was to formulate our questions in such a way that the different determinants really came to light. We have seen that three principles must be observed: the *principle of specification, of division,* and of *tacit assumption.* It is evident that our problem is a very restricted one and by no means covers the whole field of psychology in market research. It is, therefore, very important to end

[5] I refer especially to the interesting efforts of Alexis Sommaripa in connection with the Psychological Corporation.

this paper with a short theoretical consideration which will enable us to show the connections between our problem and some others not discussed here.

Psychologists who have analyzed the structure of action, as, notably, Carl Buehler and Madison Bentley have done, agree that the determinants of an action fall into three groups: biological determinants, biographical determinants, and what we might call instantaneous or actual determinants of the first degree. These differences are easy to demonstrate in a purchase which is, of course, just a special case of action. Some one buys a book. He wants to read on the train, therefore he selects a detective story. He is especially fond of a certain author. He is in a cheerful mood, and therefore he spends more money on it than he intended. These are all determinants of the first degree. We could go on in our investigation: Why doesn't he like to read historical novels on the train? Why is he fond of this special author? What gave him his cheerful mood? The answers to these questions would be biographical determinants. They might lead us, more or less, far back into the biography of our respondents. The biological determinants are so obvious that we need not bother with them in an interview. Why does he read the book instead of eat it? Goats like to eat paper, but the biological composition of our respondent makes paper-eating uncomfortable for him.

If one wants to define explicitly the determinants of the first degree, he might put it this way: The circumstances under which the decision for purchase has been made, the purpose of the purchase, and all the factors which carry this decision on until it has actually been executed, represent the actual determinants of the first degree. It is evident that the number of different determinants can vary greatly from one purchase to another. If we buy some foods under the immediate influence of how nice they look, the number of determinants of the first degree is much smaller than if we shop around for days in order to find a certain object. That does not mean, by the way, that the number of biographical determinants is smaller in the former case. It might well be that we are led far back when we want to find out why these foods appeal so much to our respondent, whereas the shopping for the other object might have a short history as to its biographical determinants.

It is probably clear to the reader that, in this paper, we have been dealing with the techniques of ascertaining the determinants of the first degree which motivate a purchase. Here let us introduce a new term: *The complete motivational set-up of the first degree.* By this, we shall understand all the determinants of the first degree which are of significance for our study. This concept is of practical importance because it gives us a certain check as to the value of our questionnaire. A questionnaire is satisfactory when, and only when, it actually secures the *total* motivational set-up of the first degree. Let us suppose, for instance, that a woman gives as her reason for a purchase in a certain store that she has a charge account there. This reason is acceptable as long as she maintains a charge account only at this store. As soon as she has charge accounts in other stores also, we must demand additional reason for her selection of this store. Or, let us suppose that in a leisure-time study, reasons for time-spending are asked. Some one tells us: "I was bored, and, therefore, visited a friend." This is acceptable only if we have reason to suppose, or if the respondent tells us, that he always visits this friend when he is bored. If that is not true, we must seek an additional reason for his going to see this friend, rather than taking a walk, for instance. On the other hand, if there is only one shoe store in town, or only one which is socially "possible," we don't need to ask, in every case, why this store has been selected.

Every concrete topic of research offers new problems for getting the complete motivational set-up of the first degree. The movie questionnaire, discussed earlier in this paper, gives many examples of this sort, and the reader is asked to go back once more to it and consider it in the light of this new concept, which, in the preparation of a good questionnaire, must be taken into consideration. Further, this concept becomes a useful tool in training interviewers. In a characteristic way, even good interviewers, in the beginning, will turn in incomplete motivational set-ups. They will, for instance, report that their respondent wanted to see a certain picture and therefore, went to see it on Tuesday night. The picture, however, has been shown three consecutive days, and the respondent's interest in this picture does not explain why he went Tuesday. Such a report indicates that some determinants have escaped our interviewer. We have to train him in such a way that he realizes, on the spot, that the motivational set-up he secured was incomplete. If he understands it, he will have a very good criterion as to whether or not his interview was satisfactory. I believe that, in such training, quickest progress can be made by utilizing this concept.

The necessity for getting a complete motivational set-up may compel us to use additional tools of research beyond the mere asking why. Take for instance, the problem of ascertaining the reason why certain people did not vote in an election. It would be completely erroneous to tabulate in one straight table their reasons for not voting. Two men might report in a hasty interview that their reasons for not voting were that they were out of town. Our principle of specification quickly teaches us that not voting involves two items: amount of political interest, and the sort of hindrance that kept them away from the polls. One man might be eager to vote, but a dying relative may make it imperative for him to leave town. Another man might care so little for politics that he goes on a fishing party on election day. So if we want a complete motivational set-up, we need two sets of data, and in order to get the one we have to ascertain the amount of political interest of these two respondents. That might lead us to quite new technical problems, which we cannot discuss here. Probably an attitude scale or some other tool for measuring the amount of interest of our respondent will have been used to this end.[6] But still it will leave us in the realm of a set-up of first degree, because an interest which makes us do something is a typical example of an actual determinant of first degree.

So much for the importance of the word *complete* in our concept; now to the restrictions implied in the words *first degree*. Suppose we have ascertained that a certain color appealed especially to our respondent, or that he is especially interested in one author, and so on. Do we not miss just what is essential for our study if we fail to go back to the biographical determinants and ascertain why he likes this color, or why he is interested in this author? We will not answer the question here. It would lead us not only to new technics of ascertaining biographical determinants, but it would make us face an altogether new problem: the technics of interpretation. These technics of interpretation are of enormous importance and as great a contribution of psychology to market research as the art of asking why.[7] We can only touch on this subject in this paper, in one connection, the technic of ascertaining a motivational set-up of first degree, where it impinges closely upon the content of this article. We might, for instance, find

[6] *See* R. Lichert, "The Technique of Attitude Measurement," *Psychological Archives*, 1932.

[7] *See* "The Psychological Approach to Market Research," *Harvard Business Review*, October 1934.

that, in a particular study, many respondents, asked why they disliked a certain commodity, might answer, "I don't know" or "I just dislike it." This answer is completely legitimate and an actual determinant of the first degree. What such a great amount of emotional dislike means is a completely different question. For example, I happened to read a market survey regarding the use of a canned beverage. A third of the respondents approved the idea because it would be inexpensive and convenient. Another third said merely that they disliked the idea, but could give no definite reason for this dislike. The research man made the point that this latter group could easily be convinced because they themselves admitted the weakness of their point. Such a statement is, of course, preposterous. The mere fact that these respondents had an emotional dislike for this canned beverage showed that there were strong biographical roots still to be discovered. The only thing which we can do with such information is to point out that we have detected a sore spot. That is in itself a strong point. We ought not to weaken our position by going beyond our own means. We have to keep the problems of interpretation constantly in mind in order not to leave the field where the technics we discussed in this paper are located. But, on the other hand, we will not depreciate the importance of an adequate technic of asking *why* by the fact that there are other equally important things to do. It is the part of wisdom in any field, and it is consistent with the progress of methodology to develop the method step by step with the ultimate aim of integration of all of the elements into the larger pattern of methodology for the entire field. It would be indefensible to hold back simply because one step is all that could be taken at one time.

The reader who has followed our deliberations and matched them with his own experience will probably disagree with some of our statements and will feel that we overestimate the importance of others. But that is always true of discussions in a field which, at the present stage of its development, requires chiefly careful, logical, and psychological analysis. Whenever the writer of this paper has found something in his field which he believed new, he met a Mr. Smith who had already done the same thing. On the other hand, he always found scores of Mr. Joneses who did not know what Smith and he had attempted. So this paper was written for Messrs. Jones, with an apology to Smith.

CHAPTER 9

PROGRESS AND FAD IN MOTIVATION RESEARCH

A review of the topics discussed in recent meetings on business research would undoubtedly reveal that the word "motivation" occurred with unusual frequency. The explanation for this is not difficult to find. In the early days of business research, the intellectual climate was such that great emphasis was given to what was then called objectivity. The study of sales figures, the analysis of media circulation, the search for good indices of purchasing power—these were at the center of attention. But, in the course of carrying out these studies, we became increasingly sensitive to the irregularity and unpredictability of the behavior which we were investigating. More and more, interest turned to the individual consumer, and the question as to why he acted as he did.

On this level of generality, however, the question makes little sense. If a member of an audience were asked why he is present, he could, of course, answer, "Because I was born." If this event had not taken place, he obviously could not have come. Still, one cannot consider this a useful answer. We are usually interested in very specific "causes," those which seem relevant in view of some practical problem of merchandising or advertising. An initial classification of such causes may prove helpful. The determinants of choice and action, especially as far as buying is concerned, fall into three broad groups. The first might be called *influences:* the advertisements we read, the people who

"Proceedings of the Third Annual Seminar on Social Science for Industry-Motivation," arranged by Stanford Research Institute, March 23, 1955.

influence us, the situations which lead to a specific buying decision. The second might be called *attributes* of the products: the design of a car, the package in which cigarettes are sold, the taste of a beverage, the contents of a film. Finally, there are the individual's attitudes and purposes, often described by the word *predispositions*. Every salesman knows that he must gauge whether a prospective customer is uncertain of himself, or whether he has strong convictions and prejudices; and an advertiser words his message differently for negroes and for whites; the airlines try to determine whether people are more eager to get speedy transportation, or are more concerned with the danger of accidents. If we want to influence consumer purchases, we must choose the proper channel of influence, and we must stress those attributes which fit in best with the consumers' predispositions. An appropriate blending of these three factors is the aim of all market research that claims it takes human motivation into account. Only if we start with such a systematic definition of the problem can we reach an adequate appraisal of the various research techniques which have developed over the last two decades.

Before proceeding further, one additional restriction seems advisable. Many problems properly falling under the heading of "motivation" can be dealt with through traditional statistical procedures. For example, in magazine research we can ask readers two sets of questions: which specific magazine stories they have read, and what their age, sex, occupation, and birthplace are. No "why" is involved here. And yet if we cross-tabulate the contents of a story with the characteristics of its readers, we obtain a finding very much in line with the main topic of this paper. We find that readers have a tendency to select stories which mirror their own lives. Women prefer to read about women; people raised in small towns prefer stories which have a small town setting; older people prefer to read about older heroes. This finding is easily interpreted in terms of motivation. People read stories not so much to learn about those aspects of life with which they are not well acquainted; rather, they read in order to gain additional insights into the kind of world in which they themselves live. But I propose to by-pass research studies of this kind, which make use of psychological notions only to interpret objective statistical data. It seems more appropriate to concentrate on techniques which delve directly into the factors which make people act as they do.

THE STUDY OF INFLUENCE

Every business creates its own laboratory, often on a gigantic scale. Through advertising, sales forces, counter displays and many other devices, the consumer is persuaded to buy a certain product. The problem is how to profit from past experience to improve future sales efforts. The most obvious idea is to ask past consumers why they bought the product, and to derive from their answers general rules as to which inducements are successful and which are not. This idea is often met with the objection that people don't know why they buy. But such pessimism is based on a misunderstanding. In order to answer the question which we have raised, we do not need to determine the infinite number of factors which enter into a concrete purchase. Our interest should be a much more limited one: we want to know whether a specific advertisement or a specific piece of advice played a role in an individual's decision to buy. And this we can find out if we use appropriate interviewing techniques. Let me illustrate this point with the results of a concrete experiment.

Some years ago a large sample of housewives was asked why they bought Maxwell House coffee; only a very small percentage said that they were influenced by advertising. In view of the objective success of advertising, this seemed to indicate that these women did not want to admit having been affected by what they had heard or read. And indeed, some did say that they bought the coffee because it was "good to the last drop," thus pointing to a hidden effect of the famous advertising slogan. Actually, however, the misleading findings were the result of inadequate interviewing. A second question was asked of all women who had mentioned an advantage of this brand of coffee as the reason for their purchase. They were asked, for example, "How did you know that it would be good to the last drop if you hadn't tried it before?" As a result of this specifying question, the number of women who told of advertising influences increased ten-fold.

To put the matter more generally: in order to study the effectiveness of an influence, one has to be certain that one's questions are fitted into the actual experience of the consumer. Suppose, for instance, that an individual reports that he bought a radio set on the advice of the salesman who waited on him. We know that a purchasing situation is usually rather complicated, so we ask a follow-up question: "Did the salesman show you only one make of radio?" The answer to this might very well be: "Oh, no. He showed me another brand too, but I had never heard of it, while the one I finally bought I had seen advertised, so I had more confidence in it." By using a variety of such devices we can obtain a pretty clear picture as to whether or not a certain campaign influenced people. This is not the appropriate occasion to give you a lecture on the art of asking why. But a recently published book contains a collection of studies exactly along these lines: if you want to pursue the point further you will find a large number of examples elsewhere.[1]

By proper interviewing procedures one can often obtain results of a rather general nature. Another study was designed to compare the effectiveness of advertising with the effectiveness of personal advice which individuals receive in the course of their buying activities. The inquiry dealt mainly with small consumer goods like breakfast foods, soaps, cigarettes, and so on. The following four results might interest you:

1) The subjects in the study reported more incidents of personal advice than of exposure to advertising.

2) The proportion of personal influences which were actually effective was greater than the proportion of ads which actually played a role in affecting final purchases.

3) The persons who exerted influence, and those whom they influenced, generally came from approximately the same walks of life. This is of considerable practical importance. One often hears that influence percolates down from the top of the social ladder. If you can get the banker or the minister to do or buy something, then, after some time, everyone will follow suit. But this study indicated that such vertical opinion leadership, while it undoubtedly exists, is not as dominant as is sometimes assumed. There is also a great deal of horizontal leadership: people in the same social stratum influencing each other. This finding has obvious implications for the choice of proper advertising media.

4) Often, however, these opinion leaders are themselves channels for advertising efforts. People who are more likely to

[1] *The Language of Social Research* (eds., Paul F. Lazarsfeld and Morris Rosenberg. Glencoe, Ill.: The Free Press, 1955), Part V, "The Empirical Study of Action."

influence others in their purchases are, in turn, more likely to be affected by all sorts of advertising. The idea of a two-step flow of the media of mass communications thus emerged. Often, advertising is first effective with the opinion leaders who exist in all walks of life; then, by personal influence, it is transmitted to the rest of the population.

One will draw different conclusions from such findings according to the kind of product one has to sell.[2] My main objective was to direct your attention to the kind of motivation research which is especially concerned with tracing and evaluating outside influences. I shall describe one practical application of this whole approach. Around 1930, while I was still an instructor at the University of Vienna, I was contacted by a new steam laundry. It was the first of its kind in the city and was having unexpected difficulty in finding customers. We agreed to conduct a study to find out why Austrian women did not want to send out their laundry and what could be done to overcome their resistance. The first part of the question is not pertinent here, and the result is only of tangential interest: it seems that the housewives of that time felt that sending out their laundry would deprive them of some of their prerogatives as mistresses of their households. But there were instances in which a housewife became a customer of the new laundry, and in those cases we could investigate, by the techniques just described, what influences brought this about. Typically, it was neither advertising nor personal advice, but, instead, a very characteristic type of situation. When an emergency arose—when the children were sick or unexpected house guests came to visit—then a housewife was more likely to send out her laundry. She had the idea that she would do this only as long as the emergency lasted, and then would resume her habitual home washing once more. But in some of these cases the feeling of relief from drudgery was so great that a permanent change in habit came about.

This was as far as the psychologist could go in his analysis. The promotion manager of the laundry, however, read the report in the right spirit. He asked himself whether he could not single out occasions when such emergencies would be especially likely to lead to new customers. He therefore arranged to get a daily list from the City

[2] The details of these findings can be found in E. Katz and P. F. Lazarsfeld, *Personal Influence* (Glencoe, Ill.: The Free Press, 1964).

Hall of the names of women who had just died. He then wrote a letter to each family, saying that the deceased had put all her love into the washing of laundry, but now that she had gone something had to be done about it, and didn't they wish to use the services of his company? This man had properly transferred the general meaning of our finding to a new situation. It might amuse you to hear—and, incidentally, it is quite characteristic—that this procedure permitted further variation. Soon after I came to this country I gave a speech on psychological aspects of market research, and reported this study and its application in some detail. A few months later a member of the audience, by co-incidence also connected with a laundry company, wrote me a letter of acknowledgment. He had begun to speculate whether he could think of other emergencies of a rather general nature. So his company started a discreet campaign intimating that, every four weeks, women find it especially difficult to perform the hard work which a house-hold requires, and suggesting that sending out laundry at such times would provide considerable relief. As a result of this campaign, he reported, his laundry showed an appreciable increase in its patronage.

THE STUDY OF EFFECTIVE ATTRIBUTES/ IMPACT ANALYSIS

Perhaps the best way to introduce the second type of study is to discuss specific techniques. For example, a device known as a "program analyzer" was developed for use in radio research; it has since been applied to other media, like motion pictures, television, and, in an adapted form, to printed material. It consists of the following procedure. A radio program is played to a group of people, usually from a platter. Each member of the group holds in his hands a green and a red button, and each is instructed to press the green button whenever he likes the program especially well, and the red one whenever he dislikes it. Each button is connected electrically with a pen which writes on a moving tape when the button is pressed; and the tape, in turn, is synchronized with the program. Thus, each participant records his immediate reactions to the different parts of the program as he hears them, and this record is available to the investigator as soon as the program is completed.

In a second step, the respondents are interviewed. The portions

of the program to which they reacted one way or another are played
back to them, and they are asked to recall what accounted for their
positive or negative attitudes. The psychological trick behind this procedure is quite obvious. If we were to interview the listeners during
the program we would destroy the continuity of their experience. If
we interviewed them only after the program they would have forgotten many of their reactions. The purpose of the program analyzer
is to fix the points at which the participants felt strongly without in-
terrupting the flow of their attention. Afterwards, then, they are asked
to relate their reactions to the specific content of the program. The
type of interviewing which is required in this type of study is quite
interesting. Not only does the interviewer have to know the details
of the program very well; in addition, on the basis of preliminary experiments he must be able to make pretty good guesses as to what
reactions each part of the program is likely to provoke. For it is one
of his tasks to assist the respondents, even when they are inarticulate,
in their reports of what it was about a particular sequence which they
particularly liked or disliked; and this he can do only if he is prepared
to pick up the slightest clues offered by the persons whom he is interviewing.[3]

What is this technique getting at? We want to know, in considerable detail, what it is about a specific performance which affects
people positively or negatively. In other words, this kind of media
research is very closely related to what is otherwise known as product
research. There are many examples of such research. For instance, the
flavor of a toothpaste may be varied slightly to find out which one
representative consumers like best; or the packaging of cigarettes may
be experimented with to determine which type gives the customer the
strongest feeling of reliability.

The difference between this kind of study and that discussed in
the previous section is fairly clear-cut. In the earlier instance, we wanted
to know what mediates between the product and the consumer—we
called it influences. In the studies which we are considering here, we
want to find out what it is about the product itself which affects
people. There might be some value in labelling the present group of
studies *impact analysis*. Because I have personally had more experience

[3] Many examples of this procedure are reported in a paper on the "focused
interview" by R. K. Merton and P. L. Kendall, portions of which are reprinted in
The Language of Social Research, op. cit.

studying the impact of mass media than of products, I shall choose my examples from the field of communications. One major study of relevance in this connection was designed to compare the impact of radio commercials and newspaper advertising. We selected a number of products which were nationally advertised in both media, and we then asked our experimental subjects to listen to a commercial and read a printed ad pertaining to each product. (Of course, the usual precautions of sampling and varying the order of presentation were observed.) As is so often the case, one can hardly cover all aspects of the act of purchasing in a single study. And so this inquiry did not purport to evaluate the ultimate effects of the two media on purchasers. Instead, we were concerned with the way in which our subjects reacted to the message at the time of reception. Here are a few examples of what was found. So far as ability to repeat the content of the message was concerned, the respondents remembered more details from printed ads than from radio commercials. The subjects were asked to describe what ideas went through their minds; of what the message reminded them; how vividly they visualized the product and its use; and so forth. Here again the printed ad created a broader imagery. When it came to liking or disliking the advertisement, reaction to the printed ads was fairly neutral. Radio commercials, on the other hand, were either very much liked or disliked. For good measure, the respondents were also asked to describe messages they remembered from their previous experience. In answer to this request, many more radio commercials than printed ads were recalled. Taking all of this material together, the difference in the impact of the two media could be summarized as follows: the emotional reaction to radio was much stronger and longer lasting than the reaction to print; what might be called the cognitive impact was in favor of print. This gives some leads as to the kinds of products which would be better served by one or the other of the two media; further research along this line would be pertinent.

A more obvious practical application can be derived from another type of result. When you study the impact of various messages in the way which we have been describing here, you are often struck by what has been called the "boomerang effect." Frequently the impression which a message makes is quite different from what was intended. We once studied a radio program which had been produced by a medical association. The main theme of the program was to warn prospective patients about quacks, and to urge them to seek help from legitimate doctors only. The writers of the program selected x-rays as a case in point. If you went to a quack he could burn you or give you cancer or harm you in some other horrible way; only an M.D. knows how to use x-rays competently. When we analyzed the impact of this program, we found that many listeners now felt that they would never submit to any kind of x-ray treatment. The distinction between the quack and the certified physician was lost because the possible dangers of x-rays had been so overemphasized. At another time we studied a film entitled "The Battle of Britain." Produced by the Army, it was shown to soldiers during World War II in order to make them appreciate the great contributions which our British allies were making to the war effort. It dealt with the defense of London during the first blitz. One sequence of the film showed British dockworkers toiling at their jobs so that the necessary supplies might be sent to London; in this scene, one or two of the crates which they were unloading were marked "USA." This was enough to create the following reaction in many American soldiers: without American materiel, the Britishers couldn't have done anything, so they really don't deserve too much credit. With many soldiers, the film had an effect opposite to that intended; as a matter of fact, all of them thought in terms of Lend-Lease, although at the time of the blitz, Lend-Lease did not yet exist.

There is no doubt that such boomerang effects occur very frequently. Anyone who has a commercial message should make every effort to pre-test it in advance, so that such unintended effects can be detected before the message is given wide circulation. Very often this does not require complicated research machinery. Through a rather small number of focused interviews, one can discover elements in a pamphlet or a film or a radio program which are likely to derail the audience. At the same time, these derailments themselves give valuable leads as to the kinds of predispositions with which one always has to reckon. This leads us to our third type of study.

THE STUDY OF DISPOSITIONS/ STYLE OF 1935

The topic to which I now turn is undoubtedly the one which interests you most. As I mentioned before, the phrase "motivation research" has become very fashionable in recent years, though it has been used in a very restrictive way. The general problem of why people act as they do legitimately includes the inquiry into influences and into effective attributes, or impact analysis. It is true that more recently motivation research has been confined to the study of dispositions. But I have purposely discussed the other two elements first, so that we can now look at the whole matter in a more balanced way.

To improve this balance still further, I also want to change my technique of presentation. I am not only concerned about an imbalanced approach to the why-problem; I am also apprehensive lest the historical perspective on the matter be lost. It is sometimes assumed that motivation research—even in a restricted sense—is a brand new development. Actually it is part of a long trend, and its contributions can be properly appraised only if they are viewed in a long-term context.

It was during the early 1930's that market research became a fairly well-structured profession. At about that time, a professional organization—the American Marketing Association—was formed. It continues to dominate the field, and now has thousands of members recruited from universities as well as from commercial organizations. In those early days, there was no textbook describing this new field of endeavor. So the American Marketing Association appointed a committee to write such a text; it was published by McGraw-Hill in 1935. Among its scores of chapters only one, of 13 pages (Chapter XV), describes the techniques which are pertinent to today's deliberations. Twenty years later, in 1955, the same publishing house put out a book on *Motivation Research in Advertising and Marketing*, sponsored this time by the Advertising Research Foundation, which, as you know, is the agency of a number of associations concerned with commercial research.

I propose to compare these two publications, appearing as they did twenty years apart. Such a comparison will serve two purposes. On the one hand, it will put today's developments in a reasonable perspective. It should warn against fadism; it should show you that all research progress is slow and that any productive development is built on achievements of the past. On the other hand, this comparison should also demonstrate that progress is actually being made and that we have greater understanding and better techniques today than we did 20 years ago. We might describe our present-day situation as follows.

Two decades ago, we were well aware what the problem was all about, and we set the compass in the right direction; as a consequence, our research today moves on a much broader front. At the same time, however, we are in danger of overrating the progress of the last few years and of believing that we are further along than we actually are.

In 1935 what is now called motivation research was termed the "psychological approach" and was considered a kind of pioneer adventure. I want to give you a picture of how the problem and the available knowledge were then described. The organization of Chapter XV of the marketing book I will keep intact but, while there were originally several examples given for each point, I will give only the minimum number necessary for illustration. I have also eliminated the numerous statistical tables in order to save space. The present reader will notice that these reminiscences end at the next subtitle.[4]

Psychology, as a science, is only in its infancy and so little is known that there is no single general system on which one can draw for interpretation in market research. What can be done is to group roughly the different procedures of psychological research and give a few examples for each as to its importance for the market research student. The following brief outline has no claim whatever to comprehensiveness or finality.

As a matter of expediency in classifying different procedures of interpretation, the following two approaches are to be considered:

1) Hypothetical Approach. Here the student is concerned with determining the general structure of human personality. He looks for the basic instincts; makes hypotheses about the mechanism through which the adult personality develops from native equipment; examines and classifies the traits which combine steadily with some fundamental types—and so on. Close relation to psychiatry is frequent.

2) Descriptive Approach. This is an approach which is culti-

---

⁴ This reporter was a member of the committee of the American Marketing Association which wrote the book entitled *Techniques of Marketing Research*. Among the chapters entrusted to him was the one from which the following sections are taken. For this reason, and to increase readability, they are not put in quotation marks. A word of excuse might be appropriate so that this whole discussion doesn't sound too egotistical. Some of the main exponents of what is today called motivation research in the more restricted sense were students of this reporter's at the University of Vienna: notably, Ernest Dichter and Herta Herzog of McCann-Erickson. He thinks that they are still his friends, even if he views their great personal success as only one element in a broader picture.

vated much more in Europe than in America. In this approach the student is mainly interested in a careful analysis of complex psychological phenomena. Introspection plays a great role. How do we experience our emotions? How do we carry through our purposes? What are the decisive features in the objects which we like or dislike? Introspection, however, is not the only medium. One might, for instance, try to construct different "worlds," such as the world of the adolescent or the world of the primitive mind—as these "worlds" are revealed through careful analysis of the achievements, preferences and forms of conduct among adolescents or among primitive tribes. The main weight with the descriptive approach lies in a careful analysis of a phenomenon, as a basis for further experimental or theoretical consequences. In this approach other social sciences are frequently involved. Here now are the details:

1) The one psychological topic which, above all others, has permeated books relating to market research is the identification of the so-called lists of instincts. The idea is that it might be possible to find in every human being a basic equipment of desires to which sales efforts can successfully be directed. An approach of this sort has theoretically very definite shortcomings: So many different lists of instincts are possible that they can contribute little toward a definite understanding of human activities. From a practical point of view they may be useful sometimes in reminding the market research man of possibilities which he might otherwise overlook. A famous sales promotion man once found in such a list the "desire for being alone." He was delighted—it never having occurred to him that people might want to be alone—and, at once, he drew up a brilliant advertisement connecting his product with this newly identified desire.

The difficulties connected with arbitrary lists of instincts are avoided by those theoretical approaches which reduce all human activities to one fundamental instinct, or drive, or desire. All of the schools working in this direction are more or less derivatives of Freud's psychoanalysis. An outstanding example is Adler's theory of *inferiority complex*. His idea is that the basic human desire is one for personal security. In order to be secure, people strive for dominance of others; and, as long as they are not secure, they have a feeling of inferiority which accounts for a great many things that they do. Whether this theory is acceptable as a whole or not, a great many experiences in everyday social life can actually be accounted for by means of Adler's system. Here is an example of its value in the interpretation of a market research.

In a study of shoe-buying habits, one woman complains that she usually feels inhibited and uncomfortable when buying shoes. She is obliged to sit in her stocking feet, which leaves her helpless and at the mercy of the salesman. She also fears that she may have a hole in her stocking and so hesitates to expose her feet—which, also, may be neglected or deformed. It is impossible to get up and leave, for she must first regain possession of her old shoe. Briefly, this lady reported a definite inferiority complex when buying shoes. This is, of course, the kind of statement which only a very sophisticated consumer is apt to make. But after the investigator's attention had been called to this feeling, he went back to other interviews and found there various distinct traces of this inferiority complex. He found that respondents, speaking of their experience with shoe salespeople, often gave a tone of resentment to their report which he did not find in interviews concerning other commodities. For example: "He always looked at my mother instead of me"—"He seemed to question my purchasing power"—"He glanced disrespectfully at my feet."

Evidently, it is important to know that such a feeling of inferiority plays a great part in the buying of shoes. This accounts partially for the heavy turnover of customers in shoe stores, it suggests a special training for salesmen in this field and it might even lead to important innovations in the arrangement of shoe stores.

It is one of the features of the hypothetical approach connected with Freud that not only is a basic instinct ascribed to all human beings, but definite hypotheses are made as to how our everyday activities are linked with that basic drive. One of the mechanisms brought to discussion by Freud is a *mechanism of repression.* Freud assumes that some of our desires are not socially acceptable; that in the course of our growing up we repress them more and more; but that a keener psychological observation would still find traces of these repressed desires. One of the traces might be seen in the little mistakes which people make. A man might leave a lady declaring that he would never see her again; but if he should leave his gloves in her home, the psychoanalyst would interpret this instance of forgetfulness as an evidence of a repressed desire to go back.

A Freudist would go rather far with this concept of repression. In a restaurant, for instance, some people dislike to have the meals for their partners and themselves served from the same dish. If both have ordered French fried potatoes, such a person feels uneasy if the orders are not served on two dishes. The psychoanalyst would say that such a man has a desire to get for himself everything which is served and to leave nothing for the other person; but, socially, he disapproves of such an attitude and so it becomes repressed. Still, it exists and, in a situation which might bring it back to the surface, the man feels uneasy. He tries to keep on the safe side by preferring two dishes instead of one.

It is characteristic of all the interpretations discussed in this section that they assume some very general rules to be existent in the field of psychology. By linking actual results with concepts such as inferiority complex, repression, extroversion, the interpreters draw their conclusions from all of the implications of their concepts. That is justified scientific procedure. But, so far, few such concepts have been definitely established, and for the majority of current problems one has to draw on more modest knowledge, which does not try to cover the whole realm of human behavior. Such are the interpretations now to be considered.

2) Close, quick, and sure observation of details and a readiness in recognizing their significance are generally characteristic of the psychological attitude. The way a man enters a room, the speed or hesitation with which he makes a remark, the books he looks at first when he approaches a shelf—all of these, to the psychologist, offer indices of a man's aims, problems, and habits. This is just the technique the psychologist uses in the descriptive approach in market research. In any marketing study he will observe the widest possible range of details; taking no result at its face value, he will try to find out what psychological meaning each item has; and he will look at each result not alone in its isolation, but in combination with as many others as possible. It is along these three steps of descriptive approach that some examples will now be given without attempting any general statements.

Why should anyone be better equipped to know the details of a business than the owner—the businessman himself? This is an argument frequently advanced against any professional market research. There seems to be, however, something like a specific blindness of the expert in his own field. He is so set toward a certain trend of activity that he overlooks important items. Some time ago, for example, experiments were made by psychologists regarding the "feel" of rayon.

It turned out that the modern rayons are so soft to the touch that blindfolded subjects could not distinguish them from costly silks and, in tests, frequently gave rayon an emphatic preference. About the same time that these tests were being made, a large rayon company held an exhibition of dresses in a fashionable New York center. Each dress bore a conspicuous tag—"Don't touch." Here, out of a traditional thriftiness, the manufacturer was depriving himself of his best selling point—the soft touch of his fabrics. It would probably have been much more profitable to that manufacturer to have replaced every dress soiled by touch rather than to have deprived all the prospective buyers of the delight of feeling the softness of the fabric.

Whatever we are told or observe has to be subject to *psychological generalizations*. In the laundry study mentioned above we had tabulated situations which induced housewives to send their laundry out. We could tell how often it occurred because of loss of a maid, sickness of a baby, etc. But the really useful approach was to see in all this *situations of emergency* so that the promotion people could then think up additional applications.

Another example involves a study of tea. On the European continent tea consumption is small. A survey recorded the different situations in which tea drinkers had started to use it. Instead of a simple listing of the different items, the *common psychological denominator* was sought. It was found then that at *special turning points* of their lives people seemed most likely to change their drinking habits: after leaving college, when they made their first trip, after getting married—at such moments they seemed most susceptible to suggestions pertaining to new beverages. Here, again, the practical consequences are evident.

The general advice to be deduced from such studies is that when one has a special result it is well to always ask "What does this mean psychologically?" Sometimes it is not possible to give the meaning in one or two words but it is there nevertheless and it is important to be aware of that fact. In one study the attitude of people toward the food value of milk was obtained by asking them which they felt to be more nourishing—milk or one of four other foods considered in physiologically equivalent amounts. The result of this question showed that people estimated the food value of milk to be higher than the physiologically equivalent amount of string beans and potatoes; but they underestimated the value of milk as compared with eggs, and, most heavily, as compared with beefsteak. Psychologically, what does this mean? Evidently there is a tendency to feel that milk is a *weak* food. It seems to compare favorably with vegetables but, when it comes to meat, the traditional token of strength, milk is taken much less seriously than it deserves. Here, there is no such convenient word as "emergency" or "turning point," but a good research man could point out clearly the practical consequences of the psychological interpretation implied in this result.

Underlying all interpretations is a sort of assumption to the effect that behind every result there is something more important than the result itself. Or, to put it more professionally, the interpreter *generalizes the special* items in order to get at their psychological meaning. This procedure presupposes that what a single individual or a whole group does in buying a commodity is an outgrowth of a more deeply rooted psychological attitude. This more general attitude will also be exhibited in other items than the special one under discussion. If, for instance, there really is a feeling of inferiority that accounts for people's attitude toward shoe salesmen, signs of it should be found in other phases of the shoe purchase also. And, of course, they are. They are found, for example, when observing customers as their shoes are taken off by the salesmen. The first movement is usually a characteristic withdrawal of the foot beneath the chair on which the customer is sitting; only after some hesitation is the foot put back on the footstool.

In this same way it could be shown, in all of the other interpretations, that when a good inference has been made as to an underlying psychological situation, it is always corroborated in other parts of the study. At this point the consideration can be reversed to arrive at the following rule: if a good interpretation is desired *coordinate as many results as possible*. This, because the larger the basis of data from which the interpreter proceeds, the more likely is his psychological analysis to be correct and productive.

This point is made clearer by a rather elaborate example drawn from a study of the men's ready-made clothing market. Among others, the three following questions were asked:

1) What factors are important in a good suit?
2) What factors played a part in the actual selection of the last suit bought?
3) What difficulties developed during the wearing of the suit?

The statistical results showed that, as a general requirement, the matter of quality is of relatively great importance; but, during the course of the purchase, one is not in a position to pass judgment on the quality and hence falls back upon more superficial characteristics, such as a pleasing pattern or color—only, subsequently, in disappointment, to experience the difficulty in wearing which concerns the problem of "quality" all over again. Here interpretation is already involved. But more data are available.

In conversations with respondents about the clothing salesmen, it was found that they want the salesman to be, above everything else, dependable in his statements, earnest and consistent. This is very different from the "keep-smiling" qualification required in the selling of some other commodities.

Finally, when asked their reasons for the choice of the store, almost half of the respondents replied—"recommended by others." This, again, far surpasses the importance of such a group of answers in other market surveys.

Now, all these points can be combined in the following statement: in buying ready-made clothes, there is a special difficulty involved in recognizing the quality of a fabric, although much importance is attached to it. So, the whole purchase becomes a problem of confidence—the dependable store, the dependable salesman. The attitude of the group of men questioned about clothes buying, therefore, was determined by the wish to solve the problem of confidence involved in that type of transaction.[5]

Every study confronts the student with a new problem. He has to think over the matter in each case anew. In all cases, however, he will find how helpful it is to use this rule: try as hard as possible to find several sections of the results which permit a *joint* psychological interpretation. The student may be sure then that he is nearest those features of the whole problem which are psychologically most important.

[5] The interpretation of these data in an actual case led to an immediate consequence. The manufacturer was advised to introduce a series of devices in his stores which would transform them from the ordinary tailoring shop into a sort of laboratory for clothing engineering. This he did by displaying pictures which showed how the materials had been woven, small machines which tested the material's resistance to wear and various other demonstrations; and his enterprise achieved considerable success.

1955/ THE STUDY OF DISPOSITIONS BECOMES "MOTIVATION RESEARCH"

Now let us look at George Horsley Smith's 1955 monograph on motivation research and see what progress it signifies. It begins with a 30-page section on "The Psychological Frame of Reference." This is a very competent summary of what can be called, in the broadest sense of the term, basic psychological concepts. Twenty years ago only two terms were mentioned, and those in a gingerly fashion— "mechanism of repression" and "inferiority complex." Obviously, the hospitality of businessmen to such ideas has greatly increased. Smith doesn't hesitate to talk about identification, projection, displacement, reaction formation, and so on. I can only urge you to read his instructive presentation of these ideas. A second section of some 40 pages deals with methods of interviewing. If I am not greatly mistaken, no basically new ideas have emerged in recent years. The 1935 publication covers about the same ground and gives similar examples. But in the third section, entitled "Indirect Questioning," great technical progress is reflected.

In recent years we have become acquainted with the new *projective techniques*. In essence these enable subjects to give us information without their being aware that they are doing so. Perhaps the best example is the so-called thematic apperception test. Suppose that you want to know whether a person has an anxious disposition. Obviously you cannot ask him head-on whether he is anxious. But you can show him a picture. This picture would have a certain vagueness: for example, it may show a man running, in a fairly unidentifiable background. You ask the respondent to invent a story as to why he thinks the man is running. One subject tells you that the man is taking physical exercise on a beach. Another thinks that the man is a convict who just broke out of jail and is running away from his guards. It is a fairly convincing argument that the second respondent is more filled with apprehensions than the first.

Probably the most frequently quoted application of projective techniques to a business problem is the study, by Hare, of attitudes toward instant coffee. He gave his subjects two shopping lists which were identical in every respect except that one listed instant coffee and the other regular coffee. He then asked the respondents to describe the housewives who had made up the two lists. This hypothetical woman who had instant coffee on her marketing list was likely to be described as sloppy and not really concerned with her duties as a housewife.

I cannot possibly reproduce here the many pages of instructive examples which Mr. Smith gives in his review of the various techniques by which modern psychologists have learned to tap the inarticulate needs, fears, hopes and biases of the persons whom they study. I can only urge you to study this section of the monograph carefully.

There is a third element of progress which deserves to be mentioned even though it was not given as much attention as it perhaps merits in this publication of the Advertising Research Foundation. Scholars have broadened the notion of motivation. In this modern research, people are no longer considered isolated individuals. It has been recognized that many of their dispositions are determined by the role which they play in the whole social fabric. This has been brought out especially clearly in the work of Burleigh B. Gardner and his associates. He would say, for instance, that the motivation of an average middle-class person is different from that of either the upper or lower classes. The real upper class man feels rather secure and does not care too much what other people think of him. The lower class person sees little hope for his future and therefore is primarily concerned with immediate and quick gratifications. It is the middle-class man who shows the most complex motivation structure. He is not on top of the social heap, but he has hopes that he can get there. His actions are therefore controlled by a strong status drive, and he is willing to defer many immediate gratifications for the sake of future advancement.

You can get a good idea of this whole mode of thinking if you look at a study of daytime serial listeners carried out by Gardner's teacher, Lloyd Warner. (This study is summarized in the Smith monograph on pp. 133–138.) He arrived at the following conclusion: *Lower middle-class women who listen to these programs are rigidly conventional. They carry out their functions as wives and mothers in a circumscribed and routine world with a well-worked-out system of rights and wrongs. . . .* A small contrasting group of upper-middle-class career women showed strikingly different psychological tendencies from the middle majority members. They had less stereotyped thinking, felt themselves less at the mercy of impersonal outside forces, saw more positive and amicable interpersonal relationships and placed women and men on a more equal and independent footing.

I also want to draw your attention to Appendix II of Smith's monograph. It is entitled "Some Motivation Findings," and reports a number of stimulating examples from studies done by various research organizations. I think it is justified to say that, in these studies, the number of areas to which psychological interpretations have been applied is greatly increased; but they are no different, in principle, from the few examples which were available when the American Marketing Association published its book.

Now that we have stressed the gains made in the last 20 years some attention must be paid to the losses. I want to single out two points: one where neglect blocked progress and one where expediency led to a deterioration. Even from the few examples I gave of older studies, you will notice a serious effort toward clarification. What does really happen when we observe or interview people and than make inferences as to their underlying motives and dispositions? How do we know that need for security is important for one product and concern with masculinity for another? No one really has the answer yet. Only by tracing carefully all steps in our research will we slowly learn to distinguish dazzling guesses from sober conclusions.

Unfortunately recent motivation research discussions have been infused with an element of bravado; if you just turn to the right organization you will get results and it doesn't matter how these results have been obtained. This is not the way an applied science makes progress. Of course in every field bright people do better work than dumb ones but the field as a whole progresses only if the work of the leaders is submitted to detailed scrutiny. In the whole 250 pages of the monograph sponsored by the Advertising Research Foundation you will not find one word on the crucial problem of how conclusions are reached once the field material is collected. Not even the simplest distinctions are made. Some projective tests can be scored and the results obtained by different investigators can then be compared. Observations and personal interviews on the other hand are much more open to the investigator's personal biases. Those of you who have time or who have a competent assistant should study a piece of analysis like Gardner Lindzey's discussion on "Interpretative Assumptions" in the use of projective picture tests.[6] I am sorry that time forbids me to give you a

6   *Psychological Bulletin*, 1952.

better feeling of what careful self-criticism of research methods can contribute. Still I can at least make some of you curious enough to go into it further.

My second caveat is easier to convey. Often the impression is given that some specific kinds of motivation research can dispense with statistical safeguards. If you interview a few people and that leads you to a good idea the job seems to be done. This may be true in a few specific situations. The copywriter of an advertising agency is in continuous need of new themes so as to turn out fresh copy month after month. He doesn't care very much whether the suggestions he gets from the research man are really sound so long as they are new and plausible. Over the years he thinks he will find out what works and what doesn't work and feels less endangered by a wrong lead than by none at all. But from the point of view of progress in knowledge we need devices for finding out whether a motivational idea is working, to which group of the population it applies, what unanticipated consequences it has and to what extent it is of general validity or linked to a specific product. Only detailed and statistical tests can decide such questions. It is to be hoped that the present use of quickies will not lead to disappointment. A constructive development would be for the work done by the proponents of the new look to be slowly merged with other more conventional types of inquiry into a united front.

OUTLOOK

This is, then, the position I submit for your consideration. What is today called motivation research, in a restricted sense of the word, is very much worth your careful attention, and, if possible, a practical tryout. It is, however, only part of the more general problem of why people buy. It deals mainly with the dispositions which people bring with them to the market situation. It needs to be supplemented by at least two other equally important approaches: the study of influences, through careful retrospective analysis of buying decisions; and impact analysis which studies the way in which the attributes of a product or a message affect the consumer's mind. One remaining question is whether these three avenues of research must remain separated, or whether they can be combined into a single, more general design.

No one, of course, knows the complete answer. But, before closing

I should like to draw your attention to one procedure in which I my-self have great confidence. In the last 15 years or so, so-called panel techniques have been developed. They have their origin in the study of political motivation, and since 1940 quite a few investigations have been carried out during political campaigns. They proceeded as fol-lows. In the spring before an election, field workers would move into a community, and ask a representative sample of respondents how they intended to vote. Then every month or so, until election day, the same people would be reinterviewed. Special attention would be given to those who had changed their vote intentions: efforts would be made to find out what influences they had been subjected to, and what aspects of the political situation, including the shifting images of the candi-dates, had made a particular impression on them. All through the study, efforts would be made to assess each respondent's psychological predisposition. Out of such studies has come a considerable body of knowledge as to why people vote the way they do.[7]

There is no reason why a more integrated approach of this kind should not also be applied to buying decisions. As a matter of fact, Elmo Roper and Associates has carried out exactly such a study within the last few years. A nationwide sample was kept under observation for nine months. In the beginning, each respondent was asked whether he intended to buy certain durable goods, like an automobile or a tele-vision set; they were then reinterviewed, at intervals, to ascertain whether they had actually bought or whether their intentions had been modified. An effort was made to discern all the external and in-ternal factors which would account for observed changes. This study is still the property of its sponsoring corporations. But in the not too distant future the main findings will become available to the public. It may turn out then that the panel approach is one way in which the several aspects of motivation research can be related. In that event, the elements of progress in each of the specialized approaches will be integrated, and the tinge of fadism which often goes with new ideas will disappear.

[7] For a summary of the main findings, see Berelson, Lazarsfeld and McPhee, *Voting* (Chicago: Univ. of Chicago Press, 1954), especially the summary chapters, Chapters 13 and 14.

CHAPTER 10

SOME PRINCIPLES OF CLASSIFICATION IN SOCIAL RESEARCH

Before we can investigate the presence or absence of some attribute in a person or a social situation, or before we can rank objects or measure them in terms of some variable, we must form the concept of that variable. Looking at the material before us in all its richness of sense-data, we must decide what attributes of the concrete items we wish to observe and measure: do we want to study "this-ness" or "that-ness," or some other "-ness"? The precise origin of our notion of this-ness or that-ness may be extremely varied, but it usually seems to involve combining many particular experiences into a category which promises greater understanding and control of events.

In this way we put together a great many behavior items and come up with concepts such as adjustment, authoritarian leadership, prestige, or bureaucracy. When we have formed some such category, we may then break it down into component elements upon which to base research instruments—instructions to coders, ranking scales, indicators; these in turn may be recombined in multi-dimensional patterns, typologies, or over-all indices. We are concerned with the question:

Written with Allen H. Barton. Reprinted in part from "Qualitative Measurement in The Social Sciences: Classification, Typologies, and Indices," pp. 155–165, in *The Policy Sciences*, edited by Daniel Lerner and Harold D. Lasswell, by permission of the authors, the editors, and the publishers, Stanford University Press. (Copyright, 1951, by the Board of Trustees of Leland Stanford Junior University. One of the Hoover Institute Studies made possible by a Carnegie Corporation grant.)

How does one go about forming such categories in the first place? Why pick out certain elements of the situation and not others? Why combine them in just these categories?

It can properly be argued that one cannot lay down a set of handy instructions for the categorization of social phenomena: such instructions would be nothing less than a general program for the development of social theory. One cannot write a handbook on "how to form fruitful theoretical concepts" in the same way that one writes handbooks on how to sample or how to construct questionnaires.

The purpose of this section is not that ambitious. It happens that research does not always begin with general theoretical categories and theoretically prescribed relations among them. At the present stage of the social sciences a great deal of research must be of an *exploratory* nature, aiming at qualitative answers to such questions as the following: What goes on in a certain situation? What do young people do when making up their minds about choosing a career? What kinds of reactions do people have to unemployment? What are the channels of information about public issues in an American community?

Where research contains exploratory elements, the researcher will be faced by an array of raw data for which ready-made theoretical categories will not exist. He must formulate categories before he can do anything else. Probably the best way to start is with fairly concrete categories—the sort of categories which experienced policy-makers or participants in the situation use, worked out in as clear and logical a form as possible. The job of figuring out what theoretical categories are applicable to the given field of behavior will be a long one, and will involve switching back and forth between concrete categories closely adapted to the data themselves and general categories able to tie in with other fields of experience, until both concrete applicability and generality are obtained. The immediate problem is to get the raw data classified in some reasonable preliminary way, so that it can be communicated, cross-tabulated, and thought about.

We will therefore try to codify the procedure used by experienced researchers in forming such preliminary, concrete category systems for the raw materials turned up by exploratory research. Some of the rules are entirely general and formal, derived from textbooks of logic; others have grown out of practical experience. Most of the examples will be drawn from the classification of responses to open-ended questions, but it is hoped that the discussion will also be relevant to the analysis of communications content, of personal documents, and of systematic observations.

The requirements of a good classification system for free responses may be summed up in four points:

1) *Articulation:* The classification should proceed in steps from the general to the specific, so that the material can be examined either in terms of detailed categories or of broad groupings, whichever are more appropriate for a given purpose.

2) *Logical correctness:* In an articulated set of categories those on each step must be exhaustive and mutually exclusive. When an object is classified at the same time from more than one aspect, each aspect must have its own separate set of categories.

3) *Adaptation to the structure of the situation:* The classification should be based on a comprehensive outline of the situation as a whole—an outline containing the main elements and processes in the situation which it is important to distinguish for purposes of understanding, predicting, or policy-making.

4) *Adaptation to the respondent's frame of reference:* The classification should present as clearly as possible the respondent's own definition of the situation—his focus of attention, his categories of thought.

ARTICULATION

The basic purpose of classification is to simplify the handling of a great number of individual items by putting them into a smaller number of groups, each group consisting of items which act more or less alike in relation to the problem being studied. This raises the following problem: if the classification is kept very simple, with only a few broad groupings, it will combine many elements which are not very similar. Important distinctions of a more detailed sort will be lost completely. On the other hand, if the classification preserves all distinctions which may be of any significance, it will contain too many groups to be surveyed and handled conveniently.

The solution of this dilemma is to use an "articulate" classification: a classification with several steps, starting with a few broad categories and breaking them down into many more detailed categories. In this way one can eat one's cake and have it too: when a few broad categories are sufficient, only the simple first step need be used; when a more detailed study is required, the finer distinctions can be found preserved in the later, finer steps of the classification system.

An example will make clear the advantages of articulation. In a study of young people which was made in New Jersey during the 1930's, two thousand boys were asked the question, "What can the community do for its youth?" The replies were so numerous and diversified that a classification in several steps was needed for their analysis. The categories used, with their percentages of response, are shown in Table 1.

Results presented in this form are much easier to read—they "make more sense" than a long list of detailed categories presented in a completely unstructured way. Furthermore they can be handled statistically in ways which would otherwise be impossible. If the sample were divided into small sub-groups in terms of other variables, for instance age and income, the results for the many detailed categories might become statistically unreliable. However, the few broad categories of the first step could still be used with statistical confidence.

It is not always easy to fit detailed categories together to form an articulated system. Where, in the system given above, should one put the response, "better library facilities?" Is it "education" or "recreation"? The trouble here is that the concrete categories in which the data were gathered were not adapted to the final classification scheme. The scheme is set up in terms of "functions"; the answer, "library facilities," is in terms of a concrete institution with several functions. If the answers are to be classified in the present scheme, the right questions must be asked in the first place. When someone suggests a concrete institution with multiple functions, a further question must be asked to discover which of these functions the respondent had in mind.

It should also be kept clearly in mind that there are usually several alternate ways in which a classification can be formed. The responses to the youth survey might have been classified in terms of the distinction between activities aiming at economic advancement, at gratification of cultural wants, and at physical recreation. Some education activities would then fall into the "economic advancement" category, while the remainder, along with some of the recreation items, would fall into the "cultural gratification" category.

Table 1 (IN PERCENTAGES)

Employment			24.5
More		18.7	
Better conditions		5.8	
Education			16.4
High school		3.9	
Free college		3.8	
Free vocational schools		2.0	
Free adult education		4.6	
Education in general		2.1	
Recreation			29.6
Community centers		9.8	
Outdoor activities		14.9	
Parks and playgrounds	6.2		
Swimming pools	5.3		
Other outdoor facilities	3.4		
Clubs		4.9	
Other suggestions			5.4
No suggestions given			24.1
Total			100.0

LOGICAL CORRECTNESS

A classification meets the requirements of logic if it provides exhaustive and mutually exclusive categories at each step of the classification.

An example of lack of exhaustiveness would be the classification of persons influencing voters as "family," "friends," "fellow workers," and "neighbors." This would leave no place for contacts with party workers or with casually encountered strangers. Of course, any classification can be made exhaustive by including an "other" category. This meets the purely logical requirement, but it defeats the purpose of the classification which is to distinguish elements which behave differently in terms of the problem under study.

Mutual exclusiveness means that there should be one and only one place to put an item within a given classification system. There are two sources of violations of this rule: 1) the use of categories on one step of the classification which are wholly included in others; and 2) the mixing of different aspects of objects in a single-dimensioned classification scheme.

An illustration of the first error would be the classification of sources of information as "mass media," "personal contacts," and "newspapers." Newspapers are obviously a subclass of mass media. We should either revise the first category to read, "mass media" (excluding newspapers), or else relegate "newspapers" to a second step in the classification under "mass media," perhaps along with "radio," "magazines," "television," and so on.

Lack of mutual exclusiveness due to mixing different aspects can be illustrated by the following classification of the output of a radio station: "musical programs," "dramatic programs," "serious programs," "recorded programs," etc. These categories belong to various dimensions and they must not be lumped together. If one is interested in classifying programs in terms of all these aspects simultaneously, a multi-dimensional classification must be set up. The categories of such a system are all possible combinations of the varieties on each dimension, for instance: "popular recorded music," "serious recorded music," "popular live music," and so on. Each program will then appear in only one category. If one is not really interested in combining the different aspects, each should be set up as a separate classification system.

ADAPTATION TO THE STRUCTURE OF THE SITUATION

The codification of practices that make for good classification has been easy so far, since it has dealt with matters of form. But now one comes to the heart of the matter: how to set up those particular categories which will be best adapted to the material and the problem being studied? The purpose of categories is to organize a great many concrete items into a small number of classes, so that the situation studied can be more easily understood. In the long run this must involve relating the categories used in any particular situation to more general systems of concepts which cover wide areas of human behavior, so that social theories can be developed which will make each particular situation easier to understand and control.

In many cases the researcher simply uses the customary terms of everyday life. Channels of political influence easily divide themselves into "mass media" and "personal contacts." "Mass media" again subdivide into "radio," "newspapers," "magazines," etc., on the basis of obvious physical and organizational distinctions. In other cases the researcher may take culturally given categories. For example, political values might be categorized as "liberty," "equality," and "fraternity," following the French Revolutionary slogan, and perhaps "security" would have to be added to adapt the system to current materials. Organizations are self-classified as "educational," "recreational," "religious," and so on.

In most exploratory research, however, the investigator will have to develop his own categories. It is naturally not possible to give completely general rules for forming categories which will be best adapted to *any* problem under study. But there is one frequently occurring type of situation for which fairly clear procedures can be laid down. This arises when one is trying to classify "reasons" for certain kinds of action: why people vote for a certain candidate, why soldiers stand up or break down under fire, why people migrate from place to place, or why pogroms, lynchings, or revolutions break out. This case, where the researcher must set up a classification of factors influencing a certain kind of action, will be discussed in detail here.

One starts with a collection of observations of people in those situations, reports about their behavior, or interview material in which the participants themselves are asked to explain their behavior. It is usually not possible to arrive at a satisfactory classification system simply by grouping items which seem similar in content. Rather it is necessary to build up a concrete picture or model of the whole situation to which the reports refer, and then locate the particular report within this "structural scheme." This involves an interacting process.

First it is necessary to visualize the concrete processes and activities implied by the responses, through introspection and an imaginative qualitative analysis of the data, to get a preliminary scheme. Then one tries to apply this scheme systematically to the data, returns to the structural scheme for refinement, reapplies the revised scheme to the data, and so on. One may thereby end up with a classification rather different from that which one started.

We will give two examples of this procedure of formulating a structural scheme for the classification of interview material; one is drawn from market research, the other from *The American Soldier*.[1]

Suppose we want to classify the reasons why women buy a certain kind of cosmetics. Women have a great many comments on their reasons which are hard to group if one takes them at face value. But visualize a woman buying and using cosmetics. She gets advice from people she knows, from advertising, and from articles in mass media; in addition she has her own past experiences to go on. She has her own motives and requirements: she uses cosmetics in order to achieve various appearance values so as to impress others—one might even find out whom—and perhaps to impress herself. The cosmetics have various technical qualities which relate to these desired results. She may also worry about possible bad effects on health or appearance. There are the problems of applying the cosmetics. And finally there is the expense. All of the women's comments might be related to the following scheme: "channels of information," "desired appearance values," "prospective 'audience,' " "bad consequences," "technical qualities," "application problems," and "cost." The reason the comments would fit is that the scheme of classification matches the actual processes involved in buying and using cosmetics. These are the processes from which the respondent herself has derived her comments; the classification, so to speak, puts the comments back where they came from.

Suppose we are studying soldiers' behavior in combat. We ask certain general questions about their behavior, and get a great many responses which are hard to group. But let us, in the words of *The American Soldier*, "analyze the typical and general determinants of behavior in the immediate combat situation. A tired, cold, muddy rifleman goes forward with the bitter dryness of fear in his mouth into

---

[1] Samuel A. Stouffer *et al.*, *The American Soldier* (Princeton: Princeton University Press, 1949).

the mortar burst and machine-gun fire of a determined enemy." What exactly is he up against? The authors list:

1) Threats to life and limb and health
2) Physical discomfort
3) Deprivation of sexual and concomitant social satisfactions
4) Isolation from accustomed sources of affectional assurance
5) Loss of comrades, and sight and sound of wounded and dying men
6) Restriction of personal movement
7) Continual uncertainty, and lack of adequate cognitive orientation
8) Conflicts of values:
   a) Military duty vs. safety and comfort
   b) Military duty vs. family obligations
   c) Military duty vs. informal group loyalties
9) Being treated as a means rather than as an end in oneself
10) Lack of privacy
11) Long periods of enforced boredom, mingled with anxiety
12) Lack of terminal *individual* goals (short of end of war)

On the other hand there are factors which help to offset the stresses:

1) Coercive formal authority
2) Leadership practices—example, encouragement
3) Informal group:
   a) Affectional support
   b) Code of behavior
   c) Provision of realistic security and power
4) Convictions about the war and the enemy
5) Desires to complete the job by winning war, to go home
6) Prayer and personal philosophies

With such an initial visualization of the situation, we can begin to classify free responses in interviews, statements in personal documents, in the mass media of communication, or reports by observers; and we can also reclassify the answers to a great many poll-type questions. Where the analyst has such intimate familiarity with the concrete material as well as the guidance of a certain amount of social theory, the set of categories which he creates is very likely to be useful for understanding the situation.

One brief example may be given of the role of social theory in improving the classification system. The authors of *The American Soldier* note that in many types of organization coercive formal sanctions are not as effective in themselves as they are through the informal group sanctions and the internal sanctions (guilt) which they call up. It would therefore be advisable to get additional information from those respondents who mention formal sanctions as a factor in the combat situation, so that they can be further classified to show whether it is these sanctions *per se* or their effect *through informal and internal sanctions* which are actually affecting the respondent's behavior.

Conversely the authors warn that the mentioning only of informal and internal sanctions by no means implies that formal sanctions play no role. The formal sanctions may play an important part in establishing the norms of the informal group and of the individual conscience, which thereafter will direct the individual's activities along lines laid down by the formal authority. Of course there will exist some informal group and individual norms which run contrary to those derived from the formal authority. A more complete structural scheme on which we might thus base a classification of men's behavior in combat (or of statements relating to it) is given in Table 2.

Table 2 HOW NORMS BEAR ON INDIVIDUAL BEHAVIOR IN COMBAT

Underlying Source of Norms	*Channels*
Norms of formal authorities	*Direct:* a) Formal sanctions b) Internal sanctions *Via group norms:* c) Informal group sanctions d) Internal sanctions
Norms of informal group	e) Informal group sanctions f) Internal sanctions
Individual norms	g) Internal sanctions

Examples of each of the categories in Table 2 would be:

a) I fight because I'll be punished if I quit.
b) I fight because it's my duty to my country, the Army, the government; it would be wrong for me to quit.
c) I fight because I'll lose the respect of my buddies if I quit.
d) I fight because it would be wrong to let my buddies down.
e) You have to look out for your buddies even if it means violating orders, or they won't look out for you.
f) You have to look out for your buddies even if it means violating orders because it would be wrong to leave them behind.
g) I am fighting because I believe in democracy and hate fascism.

One could go on to include other formal and informal groups outside the immediate army situation: churches, family, political groups, and so on, which are sources of norms important to behavior in battle.

To formulate once more the general procedure: the situation or process is visualized which serves as a frame of reference for the whole list of comments or behavior items to be classified, as required by the study. This situation or process is then divided into its different "natural parts" on the basis of experienced personal judgment or general theoretical directives. The thought moves in two directions, building up from the list of comments an organized model of the situation and concurrently dividing this whole into parts. Finally, the two tendencies will have to meet. To put it another way: the line of progress is not directly from the single concrete piece of data to the group into which it might fit; it proceeds rather from the concrete answers to the overall structure which seems to be involved; from this structure the thought turns to the component parts, and here are found the adequate groups for the classification. In this process both intimate knowledge of the concrete situation and the guidance of social theory are needed, both to formulate the initial structural scheme and to refine it as one goes on trying to fit the concrete material into it.

Besides true theoretical models there are certain types of fairly standard structural schemes which have been developed in applied research for use in standard situations. These are discussed in some detail in Zeisel's *Say It With Figures* (1947).[2] We shall only list them here:

[2] Hans Zeisel, *Say It With Figures* (New York: Harper's, 1947).

1) *The push-pull scheme*, used in studies of reasons for migration from place A to place B, or for shifting one's preference from any item X to any other item Y. The elements in this scheme are: the attributes of X and the attributes of Y.

2) *The attributes-motives-influences scheme*, used in classification of reasons for choosing a given item X. The elements of this scheme are: the attributes of X, the motives of the respondent, the channels of influences concerning his choice.

3) *The technical-properties—resulting-gratification scheme* for studying "what is it about X" that the respondent likes. The elements of this scheme are: technical properties of X, resulting gratifications from X to the respondent. (For instance: I like X beer because it's made with more malt, and more malt means better flavor; I like X because he is honest, and an honest mayor means lower taxes; I like the New Deal because it uses Keynesian economic techniques, and that eliminates mass unemployment.

4) *The where-is-it, what-barrier-keeps-it-there, who-is-to-blame scheme* for studying respondent's explanation of shortages of anything. (For instance: sugar is short because it comes from Java, and Java is occupied by the Japanese—so it's the Japs' fault. Or: there's plenty of sugar in the country; the government is keeping it back to create a war psychology, so the government—or the enemy who makes such action necessary to the government—is to blame.)

5) *The underlying-reasons—precipitating-cause scheme*, used in classifying answers to the questions "why did you do so and so?" and "why did you do it *just then?*" This just adds one or several stages to *any* of the elements in the attributes-motives-influences scheme. (For instance: I wanted a car, and when they came out with such nice models I went out and bought one; or, I wanted a car, but when I met my girl friend I just had to have one so I bought one; or, I wanted a car, and when the salesman came around and talked to me about it I bought one.)

ADAPTATION TO THE RESPONDENT'S FRAME OF REFERENCE

One of the first things one notices in applying a structural scheme to the analysis of interview material is that the responses of any given individual may be seriously incomplete in terms of the whole scheme. If this is simply the result of poor interviewing—for instance, of failing to follow up "why" questions with proper detailed probes—the ultimate remedy is good interviewing. But if the incompleteness and vaguenesss are inherent in the respondent's definition of the situation, they cannot be eliminated and one may not want to eliminate them.

For example, a survey of the Norwegian public asked about their explanations for the bad postwar living conditions and their ideas of what should be done about them. The whole array of answers could be classified only in terms of an outline of all major elements of the Norwegian economy. Most individual answers, however, covered only a small part of that structure. Some people wanted less taxes, but did not know what expenses should be cut; others wanted more imports without explaining where the foreign exchange would come from; some people had specific proposals about particular industries, while others had only general suggestions for "more freedom" or "fairer distribution." This was natural, since the respondents who had not followed professional discussions of the economic situation could hardly obtain from their own experience a coherent picture of the whole economic structure.

However, the object of the survey was not to study the Norwegian economy itself, but rather to find out what the public's perceptions and attitudes regarding the economic situation were, and how these related to the respondents' socioeconomic position and political behavior. Therefore, the economic structural scheme was used only as a basis for a much looser and more "psychological" set of categories. Respondents were classified in terms of whether they focused on the production or the income-distribution side of the economy, what goals they seemed to look toward, and which policy measures they advocated. The result was not to find out what the respondent thought about all economic questions, but to find out what economic questions he thought about, and what his opinions were with regard to *those* questions. To classify the many respondents who gave partial or vague answers, special categories had to be introduced at each level of the classification scheme. A highly simplified version of the classification scheme is given in Table 3 to make clear what is involved in adapting a set of categories not only to the objective situation but also to the respondent's frame of reference.

The classification might not tell much about the state of the Nor-

Table 3 CLASSIFICATION OF RESPONSES TO QUESTIONS ON WHAT
SHOULD BE DONE ABOUT ECONOMIC SITUATION

1. Answer in terms of changing the income distribution:

Goal	*Means*
	a) Taxes and controls
	b) Social welfare services
1) More equality	c) Measures against private capital
	d) No means specified
	a) Less taxes and controls
2) Less equality	b) Less welfare services
3) Vague: "Better," "Fairer," etc.	a) Vague or no answers

2. Answer in terms of improving production:

	a) Raise wages
	b) Labor participation in management
1) Raise physical production	c) Less controls and taxes
	d) "Everyone work harder"
	e) No means specified
2) More rational production	a) Better central planning
	b) Less controls and taxes

3. Economic sector and goal not clearly specified:

    a) More controls (purpose unspecified)
    b) Less taxes and controls (reason unspecified)
    c) Unspecified changes in tax system
    d) "Continue government's policies" (unspecified)
    e) Other suggestions of unspecified purpose

wegian economy, but it would tell a great deal about the state of mind of the Norwegian people. Of those giving relatively definite answers, we would know how many thought mainly of altering the income distribution and how many thought in terms of improving production. We would know how many desire change in each of various directions, and how many have unclear notions about what kind of change they want. We would know how many choose each of several major alternative policies as means to their goals, and we know how many have no idea how to achieve their desired goal. Among the remainder, Group 3, we see the interesting phenomenon of those who have policies to suggest, but who cannot say exactly what they are supposed to accomplish.

It is not implied that the responses classified above should be taken at face value. If it turned out that most businessmen wanted lower taxes and less controls "in order to encourage production," while workers wanted higher wages and more participation in management, also "to encourage production," one might suspect that in many cases self-interest was being rationalized. It is an interesting fact that the actual results found many poor people demanding greater equality, but practically no rich people overtly demanding greater inequality. It might be possible by intensive interviewing to obtain material for a classification in terms of "deeper" feelings and beliefs. A trained psychologist handling intensive interviews or case histories might be able to classify respondents in terms of hidden or unconscious motives, using cues and indicators which he is specially trained to notice and interpret.

Something of this kind was done by W. J. Dickson and F. J. Roethlisberger in their study of workers' complaints in the Western Electric Plant. A complaint was considered "not only in relation to its alleged object, but also in relation to the personal situation of the complainant. Only in this way is the richer significance of the complaint realized. The significance of B's grouch about piece rates is better grasped in relation to the increased financial obligations incurred by his wife's illness; C's attitude toward his boss is greatly illuminated by the experience he relates in connection with his father; D's complaint about smoke and fumes is more readily understood in relation to his fear of contracting pneumonia.[3]

Another way in which classification was adapted to the respondent's frame of reference was to distinguish two types of items in the work situation:

> "1) topics which in general the worker takes for granted unless something goes wrong; 2) topics which he does not take for granted even if they are favorable. . . . Subjects such as tools, machines, lockers, washrooms . . . are not talked about unless there is some complaint to be made. This is particularly

[3] W. J. Dickson and F. J. Roethlisberger, *Counseling in an Organization: A Sequel to the Hawthorne Researches* (Cambridge: Harvard Business School, 1966).

true of most items relating to plant conditions; therefore, topics with a high index of dissatisfaction in this area do not necessarily indicate poor working conditions."

Still another such distinction was made when three categories of objects of complaint were distinguished: those referring to objectively ascertainable facts ("the doorknob is broken"); those referring to more subjective sense experience ("the work is dirty" or "the room is hot"); and those referring to social facts ("ability doesn't count") or to social norms ("unfairness") which are not sensory elements at all.

It should be noted that the kind of classification scheme given in the Norwegian example above can also serve a quite different purpose: the tabulation of incomplete data resulting from unsatisfactory data-gathering techniques. This problem arises when one must analyze superficially carried out open-ended questions, unsystematically gathered case materials, or documents originally written for other purposes. The meaning of the categories is rather different in this case: the "vague" and "unspecified" categories do not necessarily constitute real categories of people; they may largely measure deficiencies in the data-gathering procedure. By separating out the incomplete answers, one may observe the distribution of the remaining complete answers. However, one should always realize that if the people with incomplete data could be properly classified, they might upset the proportions observed. The type of classification suggested clarifies the situation as much as possible, but it also indicates the margin of possible error involved in basing one's conclusions only on the portion of respondents about whom full data is available.

CHAPTER 11

A TYPOLOGY OF DISPOSITION CONCEPTS

Before going further, the role of dispositions in empirical action analysis has to be clarified. I have already referred to the distinction between motive as a causally assessed disposition and the merely descriptive use of terms like "needs" or "goals," which are often summarized under the catchall heading of "motivation." No general classification of disposition concepts exists. An author is usually interested in one of them; he tries to define it carefully and then gives a list of comparisons with "related concepts." Thus Allport concentrates on attitudes and discusses how they differ from values, interests, opinions, etc.[1] Kluckhohn focuses on values and tries to differentiate them from attitudes, needs, goals, beliefs, etc.[2] The literature along this line is practically endless.

But, by starting from shifting linguistic usages, one misses just those distinctions which lead to essential variations in research procedures and in interpretations. It is more fruitful to bring out the dimensions along which distinctions have been proposed so that the intent of various authors becomes more comparable and the terminology loses its importance. A scrutiny of various texts shows that three dimensions dominate the discussion. One is generality and specificity (e.g., a personality trait that can be exhibited in many substantive spheres versus

Reprinted from *The American Journal of Sociology*, 65:1 (1959), by permission of the publisher. Copyright © 1959 by the University of Chicago Press.

[1] Gorden W. Allport, "Attitudes," in Carl Murchison (ed.), *Handbook of Social Psychology*, pp. 798–844 (Worcester: Clark University, 1935).

[2] Clyde Kluckhohn, "Values and Value Orientation in the Theory of Action," in Parsons-Shils (eds.), *Toward a General Theory of Action*, pp. 388–433 (Cambridge: Harvard University Press, 1951).

an interest usually directed toward a limited object). Another may be described as degree of directiveness (e.g., an attitude toward versus a desire for something, the former being more of the passive, the second more of the driving kind). A third dimension relates to the time perspective (e.g., a plan or an expectation spans the future; an urge or a perceptual bias focuses on the present). If we dichotomize these three dimensions of substantive scope, dynamics, and time range, we get eight combinations which can serve classificatory purposes and at the same time show what other aspects are involved in the linguistic tradition of these disposition concepts (see illustration). (In a more detailed discussion the three dimensions would be treated as continuous, so that finer distinctions could be made.)

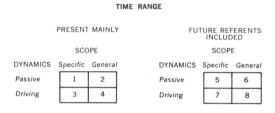

Most terms have been used differently by various authors, and most readers will attach their own private associations to them. This should be remembered in reading a few examples that illustrate the relatively simple three-dimensional scheme, which for our purpose seems useful.

1) *Preferences* as for specific foods and *opinions* on specific issues are specific, passive, and current.

2) *Traits* like broad-mindedness, more general *attitudes* like economic liberalism, as well as such "frames of reference" as looking at issues from a "businessman's point of view" are general, passive, and current.

3) What are usually called *wants* or needs, like being hungry or looking for a new car to replace a worn-out one, are specific, driving, and current.

4) *More directional traits* like vitality and energy or aggressiveness may be described as general, driving, and current.

5) *Expectations* as to future prices and customer demands that are important in modern economic analysis are typical examples of the specific, passive, future-oriented dispositions.

6) *Tendencies* to consider longer chains of possible consequences and *inclinations* like optimism come to mind as examples of the more general, passive, and future-oriented dispositions.

7) Investment *intentions*, occupational *plans*, and schemes for getting promoted to an impending executive vacancy may be described as specific, driving, and future-oriented.

8) The ubiquitous term "motivation" should become less ambiguous here. In the present paper I shall restrict the term "motivation" to a disposition of rather *general scope* and with the implication that it *directs* its bearer toward activities that bridge the present and the *future*.

Type 8 is the one most relevant for general purposes, but, as a by-product, a number of worthwhile distinctions can be tried out. Types 2, 4, and 6 are usually lumped together as traits. We can assume that businessmen are more conservative (Type 2) than, say, university professors and more energetic (Type 4). Whether the businessmen are more optimistic as to future events (Type 6) than professors is hard to guess and might change according to circumstances. The specific (odd numbered) dispositions are pertinent in a variety of contexts. Types 5 and 7, expectations and plans, have acquired importance in recent econometric studies of business intentions. They can both be introduced as variables in time-series studies. There the double role of time becomes especially clear: for any expectation we have to know at what time it is held and to what future period it refers. The relation between the "passive" expectation and the "driving" plan is complex. While plans lead to action, expectations affect plans; we know from voting studies that intentions often color expectations.[3] Type 3, wants or needs, are traditional in consumer studies. Types 5 and 7 often seem more accessible to simple interviews than Type 3; the latter were the entering wedge for projective techniques. Type 1 includes the typical objects of polls.

Thus we see that even this simple classification of dispositions leads to differences in problems and research techniques which can be

[3]   Bernard R. Berelson *et al.*, *Voting* (Chicago: University of Chicago Press, 1954).

derived from the position of the types in the dimensional scheme. Additional variations can be handled more casually because they do not seem to be of much consequence for our subject matter; this holds for the means-end relation, for instance, and the separation of a state (angry) from a trait (irascible). The distinction between physiological and culturally induced wants will become relevant in some studies. But one other complication has to be introduced. It came about when anthropologists and sociologists began to scan these concepts of disposition. A goal may be pursued or a selection made with or without the feeling that doing so is morally desirable or will be socially rewarded. This leads to the notion of norm or value. All the categories listed above can take on a normative element, although some may do so more easily than others. Intentions (Type 7) and wants (Type 3) seem to be more often "affected by public interest" than expectations (Type 5) and frames of reference (Type 2). For most purposes it is enough to refer to the normative element when needed, without doubling the terminology.

CHAPTER 12

ON BECOMING AN IMMIGRANT

INTRODUCTION

Autobiographies deserve to be written under any one of three conditions: if the author is a man of great achievement (Einstein, Churchill); if, due to his position, he has been in contact with many important people or important events (a foreign correspondent); or if by external circumstances he can be considered a "case" representing a situation or development of interest.

In this last sense biographies have long been a tool of social research. Critical situations, like extreme poverty, culture conflicts, and concentration camps, have been studied through the medium of personal documents. In general the source of the material and the analyst who tries to draw conclusions from them are separate: the witness and the expert play distinct roles. The present essay is an effort to combine their two functions. I define myself as an expert witness.

But witness of what? I suppose I am included in this volume because I have been involved in two developments: the expansion of social research institutes in American universities and the development of a research style which prevails in many of them. Both of these elements have their roots in my previous European experience. My task in this paper becomes therefore to analyze as clearly as possible the steps, the social and psychological mechanisms, by which the European

Reprinted from *Perspectives in American History*, 2 (1968). Published by the Charles Warren Center for Studies in American History, Harvard University. Copyright © 1968 by the President and Fellows of Harvard College.

part of my professional biography came into play after I moved to this country, thirty-six years ago.

The general theme of this essay is rather easily stated. When my academic career began, the social sciences in Europe were dominated by philosophical and speculative minds. But interest in more concrete work was visible—symbolized, for instance, by the fact that Ferdinand Tönnies, the permanent president of the German Sociological Society, instituted in that organization a section on sociography. Without any formal alignment my research interests developed in this empirical direction. At the same time in the United States behaviorism and operationalism dominated the intellectual climate; and yet here too a minority interest began to make itself felt, exemplified, for example, in the publication by the Social Science Research Council of a monograph on the use of personal documents, and the intense interest in intervening variables and attitudes.

In this situation I became a connecting cog. A European "positivist" was a curiosity welcomed by men aware of the subtler trends in the American social sciences. While in Europe the development of social science was arrested with the coming of Hitler, in America the evolving trends broadened, became diversified and refined, and required new institutional forms. My experiences and interests permitted me to play a role in this development. Obviously most of the things I did would have come about anyhow. Still, intellectual transportation needs carriers, and it was my good luck that I was one of them.

The present essay tries to account for my experiences by a procedure applicable, I believe, to any descriptive material, personal or collective. I have included documentary material to enable the reader to form his own judgment of certain questions and to illustrate the available historical sources. At the same time I have tried to organize such material around a number of general ideas—integrating constructs —which puts the weight on the mode of analysis.

CALENDAR OF EXTERNAL EVENTS

In the general character of life in Vienna after the First World War, three elements proved to be decisive for the story that follows: the political climate, interest in what was then called "psychology," and concern with what today is described as efforts at "explication."

I was active in the Socialist Student Movement, which was increasingly on the defensive before the growing nationalistic wave. We were concerned with why our propaganda was unsuccessful, and wanted to conduct psychological studies to explain it. I remember a formula I created at the time: a fighting revolution requires economics (Marx); a victorious revolution requires engineers (Russia); a defeated revolution calls for psychology (Vienna).

No sociology was taught at the University except for some lectures by a social philosopher, Othmar Spann. My social reference group was the movement around Alfred Adler whose opposition to Freud had a strong sociological tinge. He had a considerable following among teachers, and was influential in the educational reform movement sponsored by the socialist municipality of Vienna.

Education in a broad sense was of great concern. As a schoolboy— well before entering the university at the age of eighteen—I tried to combine the ideas of the German youth movement with socialist propaganda among my colleagues. Once I became a student I adhered to the rules of the earlier years: now I was "too old" to be a *revolté* and so I became an amateur "educator." I took jobs as counselor in socialist children's camps and as a tutor in high schools for working-class youngsters. All this was part of an effort to promote the spirit of socialism.

Intellectually, the main influence was a group of writers famous in science and the philosophy of science: Ernst Mach, Henri Poincaré, and Einstein. I was impressed by the idea that mere "clarification" was a road to discovery. Euclid's theorem on parallels was not truth but an axiom; it made no sense to say that an event on the moon and another on earth occurred simultaneously. All the ideas which later became known as "explications" held a great fascination for me, and this interest often merged into the conviction that "knowing how things are done" was an educational goal of high priority. When, as a student, I worked in the field of labor education, I often lectured on "how to read a newspaper": what is a news service, how does one take into account the sources of news, what should one watch for in different countries? One of Alfred Adler's main collaborators edited a series of small pamphlets applying his ideas to various substantive areas; I wrote my contribution under the title "behind the schools' backdrops." The main idea was that much anxiety could be avoided if families understood how schools are organized, how report cards come about, how teachers differ from each other in their perceptions of their students, etc. At that time I had virtually no contact with the "Wiener Kreis" although its main leaders had already settled in Vienna. The obvious similarity of what I have just described with their teachings is probably more due to a common background than to direct influence.

Attending the university was a matter of course in a middle-class family, even one of limited means. The natural field of study for someone actively participating in political events was a doctorate in *Staatswissenschaft,* a modified law degree with a strong admixture of economics and political theory. But for me mathematics was a second pole of attraction, and for several years I took courses in both fields. It was almost accidental that I ended with a doctorate in applied mathematics. Immediately after the degree, I began teaching mathematics and physics in a *Gymnasium.*

While I was still a student, my interest in social science took a new turn with the arrival of two famous psychologists at the University of Vienna. There had been no real psychology there until Charlotte and Karl Bühler were appointed in 1923 to build up a new department. Karl Bühler was a leading academic figure who, as a younger man, had contributed to a major revolution in experimental psychology through his work on the psychology of thinking. His wife, Charlotte, considerably younger than he, was made associate professor, and was, in fact, the administrator of the department. (I will hereafter use the correct European term, Institute.) I participated in their early seminars and, after a while, was asked to give a course in statistics.

Slowly, my work as assistant at the university expanded, and I also taught courses in social and applied psychology. I received a small remuneration, by no means sufficient to give up my position in the *Gymnasium.* Still, my desire to shift entirely to the Psychological Institute increased, and around 1927 I got the idea that I would create a division of social psychology at the Institute. This would permit work on paid contracts, and from such sources I would get a small but adequate salary, in keeping with the generally low standard of living. The idea was realized in the form of an independent Research Center (*Wirtschaftspsychologische Forschungsstelle,* a term connoting broadly the application of psychology to social and economic problems), of which Karl Bühler was the president. From then on, I directed the applied studies of this Center, and at the same time gave my courses at the University Institute and supervised dissertations. A number of students worked at the Research Center, and quite a few dissertations were based on data collected there.

Charlotte Bühler divided her work between child and adolescent psychology. My own activities were closely connected with hers in the latter field. She had organized a series of monographs on adolescent psychology, and I was commissioned to write one on youth and occupation. The volume, *Jugend und Beruf*, appeared in 1931. It contained a number of papers by other members of the Institute as well as some of my own. A large part of the book was devoted to a ninety-page monograph in which I summarized all the literature then available on occupational choices among young people. At the same time, I published papers on statistical topics, and—in various magazines of the Socialist Party—on topics in industrial and political sociology. My statistical lectures were published as a "Manual for Teachers and Psychologists." It was probably the first European textbook on educational statistics, and was used widely in various universities.

Around 1930, I began to organize a study of Marienthal, a village south of Vienna whose population was almost entirely unemployed. My two main collaborators were Hans Zeisel, now professor at the University of Chicago, and Marie Jahoda, now professor at Sussex University in England. (The latter subsequently did important reports on unemployed youth for the League of Nations and the International Labor Office.) The Marienthal study brought me to the attention of the Paris representative of the Rockefeller Foundation, and in 1932 I obtained a traveling fellowship to the United States, where I arrived in September 1933.

ATLANTIC TRANSFER/ DIRECTIONAL CUES

The impact of European intellectuals on the United States can be studied in a variety of ways. One approach is to examine a certain field before and after the arrival of specific individuals. Another is to trace the contacts which the immigrant had and the references that Americans made to him either in their own publications or in communications solicited especially for that purpose. A third approach to the transfer phenomenon is to examine how the immigrant himself saw the situation. What was his strategy and experience? Since most of the men with whom this volume deals are no longer living, it seems incumbent upon the few survivors to provide some information on how such a sequence of events looks from within.

The idea of an "expert witness" described in the Introduction is especially useful in this third approach. He reports his concrete experiences and at the same time tries to conceptualize them, to discuss episodes within coherent patterns. But the reader should be reminded that in this case the other participants may be considered expert witnesses too. Historians could unearth additional documents, interview the other participants, and come to conclusions quite different from mine. There are no final verdicts here, only an interpretation of what might be called "strategy": the moves which the actor made more or less consciously and intentionally; the general motivations that guided his reactions and choices; and the character of the total situation, even if the actor was not aware of what this was at the time. Perhaps the term "latent strategy" will serve best.

The beginning of such analysis is found in what might be called *directional cues*. What did the person know about the country to which he came before his arrival? Where did he turn first? What antecedent experience guided his first moves?

I can summarize my experience along three lines, which at first were quite distinct but which ultimately converged: the continuation of my interest in research on unemployment; my interest in finding out more about American research techniques; and my desire to help the Vienna Research Center by establishing contacts for it with relevant organizations in this country.

The Marienthal study had received some attention in the United States through two channels. A visiting American psychologist had seen some of the material in Vienna and, on his return, wrote an article in the *Nation* called "When Man Eats Dog." At the International Psychological Congress in 1932, held in Germany, Mrs. Bühler arranged for me to be on the program; I reported on the first findings, and a number of prominent Americans, including Gordon Allport, Otto Klineberg, and Goodwin Watson, visited me to obtain more details. These were also some of the first people I saw when I came to the States.

At the time my fellowship began, the Federal Emergency Relief Administration (FERA) had just established its first research unit. The Rockefeller Foundation arranged for me to work there as a volunteer. To do so, I moved to Washington and while there met several sociologists working as government consultants. They belonged to the then insurgent group of empiricists who soon thereafter created the Sociological Research Association as a spearhead for their position in the American Sociological Society. These men worked mainly with broad census-type data. Because of the following episode, I acquired something of a reputation in this group as a different kind of technician. The FERA was about to publish a monograph showing a marked correlation between unemployment and education. I suggested that the result might be the spurious effect of age, an idea which today would be commonplace. A cross-tabulation was made and indeed it turned out that the role of age was more important: poorly educated people were older and had a higher unemployment rate. This impressed the FERA research staff. When I spent some time in Chicago in the spring of 1934, they established a small tabulating unit for me so that I could help there on the multivariate analysis of their unemployment surveys.

During this early period I spent time at the few places in which empirical social research was taught. I went to the University of Rochester to become acquainted with Luther Fry, who had written the first book on techniques of social research. I took over one of his classes for several weeks and organized a study of how people decide which movies to attend.[1]

At this time I did not think of myself at all as a sociologist. I went to no national or regional conventions of sociologists, although my fellowship would have provided the necessary funds. As a matter of fact I had only a vague notion of the state of sociology in the United States. I visited Chicago for a few weeks, but primarily to work with Arthur Kornhauser, a prominent applied psychologist. I have no recollection of any memorable meetings there, except for a respectful lunch with L. L. Thurstone. I am sure that I did not meet Samuel Stouffer during the first year. My strongest memory of the visit is an investigation of the University of Chicago faculty that the state legislature held at the time; and I recall being much impressed by Robert Hutchins.

My main sociological contact at this time was with Robert S. Lynd. Because of *Middletown* he was one of the first people I looked up. He was extremely generous with his time and advice. The important role he played in the first ten years of my professional life in the

---

[1] Later the questionnaire served as the model for the Decatur study that resulted in Elihu Katz and Paul F. Lazarsfeld, *Personal Influence* (Glencoe, Ill., 1955).

United States will become abundantly clear in the remainder of this essay.

Throughout this period, my main concern was with the Research Center in Vienna. I had left it in precarious financial condition. The situation deteriorated after the putsch of the Dollfuss government which considered the Center's activities and personnel subversive, probably with reason. My great hope was to get American research organizations or commercial firms interested in subsidizing some of the work in Vienna. I therefore spent a good part of my time with people who worked in the field of market research. I never succeeded in mobilizing help for Vienna, but my efforts had important consequences for me personally. It all began when some of the psychologists I met told me that I would be especially interested in a new development.

Around 1930, a group of prominent American psychologists, including E. L. Thorndike and J. M. Cattell, created a non-profit organization called the Psychological Corporation (PSC). Their plan was, on the one hand, to promote the use of applied psychology among businessmen and, on the other hand, to provide academic psychologists with research opportunities and, I suppose, additional income. When I heard about this I immediately got in touch with the research director of the PSC and volunteered my time.

At the time, American market research was based mainly on rather simple nose-counting. Nonetheless, I expected the PSC, because of the academic status of its founders, to take about the same research position as our Viennese group. But in fact I did not find this to be the case. The PSC had to fight for its existence, and its research activities consisted of simple consumer surveys, in competition with other commercial agencies. I considered it almost a misson to help the PSC do pioneering rather than routine work. Toward this end I proposed a number of projects, always along the line of why people did this or that, but nothing came of these efforts. The PSC's director, who combined radical behaviorism with the desire to have the organization make money, objected that my questionnaires were too long. Understandably, after a while my relations with the Psychological Corporation diminished to the vanishing point.[2]

---

[2] This might be a good place to recall an anecdote characteristic of misinterpretations of norms and roles, which obviously do not happen only to Polish peasants. When I came to offer my collaboration to the director of the PSC, he asked me whether I knew how to use a slide rule. Upon a positive answer, he as-

Such were the main directional cues which guided my first activities. They were accompanied by a number of personal contacts, which were an important part of the process of transfer I am trying to describe. These can only be understood in terms of mutual interaction. Indeed, it will be necessary to shift back and forth between what I think were prevailing tendencies in this country and certain patterns of conduct I had brought with me.

ATLANTIC TRANSFER/—LATENT STRATEGIES

A number of younger psychologists were consultants to the Psychological Corporation, and together we formed a sort of Young Turk movement. The member of this group I saw most often at that time was Rensis Likert, then an assistant professor at New York University. He became interested in the Viennese type of complex market studies, and I cherish an English translation of a tea study which Likert made for his students. Finally, Likert became an ardent advocate of the exclusive use of unstructured interviews, which we in Vienna combined with statistical data.[3]

Another encounter was with an applied psychologist from Cornell,

---

signed me to computing percentages on his main study, called the Brand Barometer. It consisted of reports of what food brands American housewives used based on a national sample. Understandably, I found it boring to compute percentages for days on end. But I thoroughly "understood" the situation: American culture requires that everyone works his way up from the bottom; I was being put to the test before being admitted to true professional work. After a few days, I timidly asked the director whether I had sufficiently proved my endurance. Only then did he understand what a European Rockefeller Fellow is. He had just taken my work as labor for which he did not have to pay, and probably classified me as being supported by WPA. Similarly, on quite a number of my first trips I traveled by coach, even overnight. One day a Rockefeller accountant asked me why I did not use Pullman, to which I was entitled. I had not realized that Pullman cars existed; I had learned in Europe that in the democratic U.S.A. there is nothing like the European distinction between different classes of railroad cars.

[3] A paradoxical situation developed during World War II: Likert was then research director of the Development of Agriculture which conducted morale studies among farmers. I was a consultant to the OWI, which did corresponding studies in urban areas. The research director of OWI was Elmo Wilson, who favored highly structured interviews. Rather heated battles developed between the OWI and the Likert group. I was asked to study the matter and write a report; it was later published in condensed form under the title "The Controversy Over Detailed Interviews—An Offer for Negotiation," *Public Opinion Quarterly*, 8 (1944).

John Jenkins. He became interested in the complex kinds of cross-tabulations we incorporated in our studies. In Vienna I had worked up a mimeographed manual for my students, under the title "How to Get Along with Figures" (*Umgang mit Zahlen;*[4] the title was taken from a famous eighteenth-century book by Adolf von Knigge: *Über den Umgang mit Menschen*). Jenkins made an English translation for his students. I spent the summer of 1934 with him in Ithaca, and we discussed the idea of a "new look" in applied psychology. He later created a department specializing in this field at the University of Maryland.

Simultaneously, the small fraternity of commercial market research experts got interested in my work. Largely through the efforts of Percival White, who wrote an early textbook on market research, I was invited to talk at meetings and to participate in committees of the recently created American Marketing Association. The Association was about to publish an official textbook, *The Techniques of Marketing Research,* and commissioned me to write four chapters. One of these, on interpretation, contained references to depth psychology and is generally considered the beginning of "motivation research." The book was widely used in business schools and helped me later on when I needed cooperation for our radio research work.

It was at that time that the first political questions were included in commercial market studies. Around 1935 polling had become an independent commercial activity, with results of interest to sociologists as well as to psychologists. While the former were quite hospitable, the latter were not, because the enterprise partook too much of the low academic status held by "applied psychology." My sociological acquaintances listened with interest to my adventures in the market research world.

By the end of my first fellowship year, I had developed a network of personal and institutional contacts woven around a rather narrow range of professional activities. It had grown from an effort to help the Vienna Center, to which I intended to return. But the political events

---

[4] When Hans Zeisel came to the United States in 1938, I suggested that he enlarge this text, and the Columbia Bureau arranged for the first publication. I wanted very much to find a good American title. One day in a flower shop I saw a promotion slogan then much in vogue: "Say It With Flowers." I immediately decided that the title of the book should be *Say It with Figures,* and under that title it appeared in 1947. In social theory, this is called functional equivalence. Zeisel has meantime greatly enlarged the scope of the book; it has been translated into several languages, and is now in its fifth U.S. edition.

in Austria slowly nurtured the idea that I remain in the United States. I began to look at people with a view to possibilities of work here in the fall of 1937. Only a position connected with a university was conceivable. But the fact that I had a foot in both the commercial and the academic camps made for a certain amount of maneuverability, of which the following is a typical example.

At the University of Pittsburgh there was a research center which had been created by a man well-known in educational research: W. W. Charters. I spent two months at this Retail Research Institute which, by the time of my visit, was under the direction of David Craig. With him, I organized a number of studies on topics such as "How Pittsburgh Women Decide Where to Buy Their Dresses," or "How Pittsburgh Drivers Choose Their Gasoline." (The first study once made me a house guest of a local Pittsburgh tycoon, Edgar Kaufman, and the second brought me into repeated contact with Paul Mellon.) At that time a large trade association of the major retail stores was established in Washington; its president consulted me as to who should be research director, and appointed Craig upon my suggestion. Toward the end of my fellowship, Craig resigned from Pittsburgh and moved to Washington. Before leaving, he arranged for me to get a temporary appointment at his Institute. The necessary meeting of the trustees had not yet taken place, but Craig wrote me a letter on official stationery, which was sufficient for me to obtain an immigration visa from the American consul in Vienna.

I subsume all these mechanisms of the transfer process under the broad notion of *latent strategy*. It would obviously be wrong to restrict it to a conscious manipulation. All of it has, rather, the character of an underlying vigilance which connects accidental situations to a latent goal. But not even this is enough of an explanation. One has to add a kind of "libidinal" element which makes all these things pleasurable within their own right. I was almost obsessed with the idea that I wanted to be connected with as many studies as possible, and used every occasion to add another one. So I soon obtained funds to study the adjustment of our immediate group, the nine European Rockefeller fellows; the questionnaires I used on that occasion thirty years ago are still available, and might be of some historical interest.[5]

[5]   In retrospect, I am aware of the costs involved in my style of life. All during the two years I saw hardly anything of the country except for research of-

Latent strategies and directional cues involve the interactions that always prevail between dispositions and situations. Latent strategies lead to selective perception of the environment, and they also become crystallized, more precise, more self-conscious as they meet success in an extending sequence of episodes. But what makes for a relatively high proportion of successes? Here I must take recourse to a term like *structural fit*. Both the environment and the life style of the immigrant are patterned in a certain way. The elements of these two patterns may complement each other, and to some degree they did in my case. Thus, in the Introduction I gave examples of my quantitative interests, controlled by strong conceptual training, fitting well into some nascent trends in the American community. Let me give two more examples of such structural fit. The first shows the protective role of a personal idiosyncrasy; the second shows the usefulness of a tangential approach to conventional rewards.

In a letter to Vienna, of which I happen to have a copy, I reported during my first fellowship year that "I find it more interesting to meet with what you might call second-string people; whenever I come to a new place, I pay a respect visit to the big shots and then stay with the people who accept me and make me feel comfortable."[6] Without my knowing it, that helped me escape a certain uneasiness regarding foreigners, which, in my opinion, was quite prevalent at the time; foreigners were rare, and it is understandable that people had ambivalent feelings about them. In 1935, when Lynd began to help me look for a job, he seems to have written one correspondent that I do not look very Jewish; I have the answer from the other man, who writes Lynd that he has heard nice things about me, but he wants to correct Lynd on one point: "Lazarsfeld shows clearly the marks of his race." In 1936, Hadley Cantril wrote Lynd that they were looking for a research director who would have my kind of training but not be so peculiarly "scattered." That the word reflected an image of foreignness would appear from his praise, somewhat later, of the first radio issue of the

---

fices, and I also formed few personal social contacts. At that time, there was not much research going on in the West Coast, and I am probably the only one of the nine foreign fellows who came here at that time who did not exercise his right to a trip to California.

   6   In writing this, I realize that this habit has carried over to the last twenty years, during which I have stayed for considerable time in a variety of European countries. My serious contacts on these occasions are definitely not with my age and status peers, but with younger people.

Journal of Applied Psychology:[7] "The two I especially liked," he wrote, "were those of Herr Director himself for they beautifully illustrate the trends one can discover if statistics are intelligently used." So, even at the moment when he approved of what I wanted to do, the notion of foreignness crept in.

When I appointed T. W. Adorno, newly arrived from Germany, to the radio project I repeatedly had to explain that he did not yet know his way around. I have a memorandum of March 7, 1938, addressed to Cantril and Frank Stanton, the two associate directors of the project, in which I report on my first week of experience with Adorno. I wrote:

> He looks exactly as you would imagine a very absent-minded German professor, and he behaves so foreign that I feel a member of the Mayflower Society. When you start to talk with him, however, he has an enormous amount of interesting ideas. As every newcomer, he tries to reform everything, but if you listen to him, most of what he says makes sense.

As late as 1941, when I was appointed to Columbia, Samuel Stouffer had to fight this ghost. He wrote, in a letter to the appointment committee that is one of the most thoughtful documents of support I have read in twenty-eight years on the receiving end of such mail, that

> In spite of the fact that he has lived in this country for seven years or more, he has a distinctly foreign appearance and speaks with a strong accent. This prejudices some people against him, and I think some are further prejudiced because they feel that there is occasional arrogance in his manner. Actually, Paul is one of the most modest of men, but he does have a rather heavy Germanic way of presenting a topic which tends to make some people feel that there is not as much in the topic as the difficulty in following him would suggest. I think such critics would be occasionally right, but I can testify from experience that there is plenty of pure gold in them thar hills.

Obviously Stouffer felt uneasy about bringing up the topic, and so at the end caricatures himself as a kind of hillbilly.

I offer these examples as a way of characterizing the atmosphere of the period, an atmosphere notably different from the present in

[7] Volume 23 (1939).

which foreign-born intellectuals are a dime a dozen in academic and professional life. But, even so, I was not seriously hampered, because it never occurred to me to aspire to a major university job. I took it for granted that I would have to make some move similar to the creation of the Vienna Research Center if I wanted to find a place for myself in the United States.

This leads to the second illustration of the notion of structural fit. At about the time I arrived in the United States, the problem of how to introduce empirical social research into the university structure had become visible. It was obvious that a new type of research center was necessary, though none had successfully developed. One reason for this was the lack of people whose experience and career needs equipped them to create and direct such centers. Missing from the scene, in other words, were *institution men*.

I have always been interested in the type of men who played major roles in academic innovations. At various times I have tried to show that such innovations can often be traced to people who belong to two worlds but who were not safe in either of them. The best historical examples are Wilhelm von Humboldt who, as a hanger-on at Weimar, belonged to the lower Prussian aristocracy and created the University of Berlin in 1807. Another is Guillaume Budé, who was a hanger-on among the French humanists but who had access to the Court of Francis I and spent his life developing the Collège de France in opposition to the anti-humanistic Sorbonne (1515 to 1550).

The institution man is a special case of a well-known sociological notion: the marginal man who is part of two different cultures. He lives under cross pressures that move him in a number of directions. According to his gifts and external circumstances he may become a revolutionary, a surrealist, a criminal. In some cases his marginality may become the driving force for institutional efforts; the institution he creates shelters him and at the same time helps him crystallize his own identity. In my case there was a general convergence toward institutional innovation. Under the adverse economic circumstances in Austria and the strong current of incipient anti-Semitism, a regular academic career would have been almost impossible. When I came to the United States, I was neither individually known, like some of the immigrant physicists, nor connected with a visible movement, like the psychoanalysts and Gestalt psychologists. (The status of a Rockefeller fellow helped in the beginning; but after a while I did experience the proverbial transition from a distinguished foreigner to an undesirable alien.) On the positive side I did belong, marginally, to a number of areas between which bridges were bound to be built; social science and mathematics, academic and applied interests, European and American outlooks. It seems plausible that such a configuration would lead to a career detoured through an institutional innovation rather than routed directly toward individual mobility.

The form this took was the role of a bureau director. In this role, it is necessary to take reasonable risks, to try deviant innovations without coming into too much conflict with prevailing norms. And in this connection it seems fitting to end this section with the note of the risk I took in coming here. It will be remembered that I went to Vienna to apply for an immigration visa based on the promise of an appointment at the Retail Research Institute at the University of Pittsburgh. The day after I got my visa I received a cable from Craig telling me that he was leaving Pittsburgh because he had taken the job of research director of the Retail Federation; my appointment would have to be delayed until a successor could confirm it. In some way, then, my visa was of dubious legality, and, more important, I had no job waiting for me in the States.

I had intended to inform the Rockefeller Foundation of my decision to move to Pittsburgh. Their regulations required return to the home base at the completion of the fellowship, but in view of the Austrian situation I could rather safely count on their understanding. Now having no guaranteed job, however, I doubted very much that an American foundation would also cooperate on a move which went against government regulations. Either a job or an affidavit of support by an American citizen was required.

I remember, of course, every detail of the few days and nights during which I had to make up my mind. I still had one month of fellowship money left; traditionally, the European fellows spent their last month traveling in Europe, as a kind of decompression procedure. I finally decided not to inform anyone, and used this last $150 to buy a third-class ticket on a slow American boat. I thus arrived in New York as the classic immigrant, penniless. A few weeks later, I began the work which led to the establishment of the University of Newark Research Center.

Part Four

Exchange with Neighbors

CHAPTER 13

PHILOSOPHY OF SCIENCE AND EMPIRICAL SOCIAL RESEARCH

It has been said of German professors at the turn of the 17th century that they wrote all their professional papers in Latin; when they wanted to be very condescending, they used French. In the same way, I feel that modern philosophers of science are only concerned with the natural sciences; when occasionally they turn to the social sciences, they talk of Herbert Spencer or some other scholar who concerned himself with the development of all societies from beginning to end. Philosophers of science do not pay attention to the empirical work in social research which is actually going on today.

In a way, this is easily understood. In the correct sense of the term, as yet there is no systematic theory in the social sciences, only research procedures and a number of low-level generalizations. This would force the philosopher to become acquainted with technical details and results which are often rather boring and would put him at a disadvantage vis-à-vis a colleague who can speculate on the meaning of such basic ideas as the uncertainty principle or the notion of relativity. The reading of empirical social research, which often lacks the big sweep of the more developed natural sciences is not only personally unrewarding but also does not confer much prestige. Understandably the general reader is more curious about the philosophical implications of the natural sciences which have so greatly affected our daily lives.

Reprinted from *Logic, Methodology and Philosophy of Science*, edited by Ernest Nagel, Patrick Suppes, and Alfred Tarski, with the permission of the publishers, Stanford University Press. Copyright © 1962 by the Board of Trustees of the Leland Stanford Junior University.

My central theme, then, is "philosophers of science unfair to empirical social research." But I am not out of sympathy with the members of this congress, and I am doing my picketing not in the mood of accusation, but in an effort to obtain more cooperation. I will make my point by analyzing briefly two papers, each written by men whose good intentions toward us are beyond any doubt. Both authors want to make a contribution to the working men among the social scientists, and if, as I think, they fail in the examples chosen, it is against their will and, in effect, they are the victims of the general intellectual climate which I shall try to characterize.

My first example comes from Carl Hempel and has an ironic implication which I want to point out first. Hempel, probably without knowing it, has had a considerable and highly salutary effect on empirical social research. Almost thirty years ago, he and Paul Oppenheim wrote a paper on the notion of types in the light of modern logic [7]. They showed that when we describe a person or a group in the course of an empirical investigation, we unavoidably use a fixed number of properties. In a formal sense these are all variates but they can be of considerable diversity: quantitative variables such as age, ranks such as position in a competitive examination, dichotomies such as sex, or even unordered classes such as country of birth. These variates form a property space, and their combinations are what today we would call a Cartesian product. Typologies, Hempel and Oppenheim pointed out, are selected sectors of this property space which come about by a variety of procedures which they called "reduction." In their original paper, the authors were able to show how many research procedures can be described and clarified by looking at them as various kinds of reductions. Since then, many investigators have used this idea. A collection of pertinent examples has been published by my collaborator, Allen Barton [1].

I was therefore very anxious to see how Hempel's own thinking on this matter had developed, and the present meeting gave me an opportunity to look at a symposium organized by the American Philosophical Association under the promising title, "Problems of Concept and Theory Formation in the Social Sciences." There Hempel again chose the problem of typologies as his theme [6]. But in the period of twenty years between the two papers, he obviously had succumbed to the occupational hazards of the philosopher of science isloated from the empirical social scientist. Already, the introductory pages are ominous. The only author referred to in the beginning is Max Weber and his notion of "ideal type." And Hempel's statement of what he intends to do contains the following sentence: "Our explicatory efforts will repeatedly invite comparative examples of concept formation in the natural sciences." As a matter of fact, he hopes that he will perform his major service by "a comparative examination of certain aspects of the methodology of natural and social science."

I call this beginning ominous because it implies the two main dangers which I tried to signal in the opening paragraphs of my paper. For one, what we really need is an *intrinsic* analysis of social science procedures. Anyone whose main interest is to compare these procedures with the natural sciences will have one or both of two effects. Either he will tell us that our achievements lag behind those in the natural sciences, which we know only too well, or he will make a dogmatic assertion on the unity of science, which I think is as useful as my doctor's admonishing me to lose weight without his helping me to attain this highly desirable goal. My second uneasiness comes from the invocation of the name of Max Weber, because he is probably the greatest symbol of what I might call "the old methodology," which has proved so wasteful.

Max Weber did spectacular work in historical sociology, a field badly neglected in recent years. But he also wrote a few pages on what he thought he did, calling his procedure the construction of ideal types. These self-declaratory statements contradict each other at many points; they have no visible relation to the actual content of his studies, and they have led to endless and confused literature which is concerned mostly with terminology and, as far as I can see, has resulted in no new investigations. No one has explicated what he did in his actual studies, which has contributed to the difficulty of emulating his skill.

After these first two introductory pages (pp. 66 and 67), Hempel devotes three-and-a-half pages to distinguishing a number of ways in which the term "type" has been used (classificatory types, extreme types); then, on pages 71, he comes to his main topic, "Ideal Types and Explanations in the Social Sciences." At this point, there is still hope, partly because here a new name appears, Howard Becker. Now Becker was indeed the exponent of what he called "constructive typology in the social sciences." This is a modern version of Max Weber's ideas, but more easily accessible to explication. Becker was more concerned with the relation of his work to modern quantitative procedures, and therefore what he writes about his own methodology is easier to analyze than Max Weber's methodological pages, which have as their frame of reference the whole history of German legal and cultural philosophy. In addition, in his descriptive work, Becker dealt with a rather restricted number of types, especially with the definition of sacred and secular societal forms [2]. Finally, Becker directed a number of studies undertaken by his students; the analysis of these would permit us to obtain a fairly good picture of what he really had in mind [12]. For a harassed philosopher who wants to find out how the beleaguered minority of "ideal typologists" thinks and works today, Becker would indeed be a very good topic of analysis. And those of us who do not belong to this tradition would have been very grateful for an explication of Becker's work: it is quite likely that he had something important to say, and he is neglected by the majority of his colleagues mainly because it is so hard to find out what he had in mind.

This is, however, not the way Hempel proceeds. After he has mentioned Becker's name, he returns to Max Weber and for two pages quotes what Max Weber said about ideal types—quotations, incidentally, which are only too well known to every social scientist who tried to forget them when he wanted to know what Weber really did. We still can think that Hempel considered this brief inventory necessary for the instruction of philosophers. It is Hempel's contention that "ideal types represent not concepts properly speaking, but rather theories." No one can quarrel with this position, because no one can tell what a practitioner of ideal types does as long as he has not analyzed actual investigations. But this is by no means what Hempel now does. As a matter of fact, he states his program quite bluntly:

> The idea naturally suggests itself that if those theories are to serve their purpose, *they must have a character quite similar to that of the theory of ideal gases, say.* To elaborate and substantiate this conception, I will first try to show that the alleged differences between the explanatory use of ideal types and the method of explanation in a natural science are spurious; then (in section 5) I will attempt a brief comparative analysis of the status of idealized concepts, and the corresponding theories, in natural and social science. (P. 73; emphasis mine.)

For the next seven pages Hempel gives a brilliant analysis of what in the natural sciences might be called an ideal-type analysis. He points out that in explaining an eclipse of the sun, the scientist only explains major features and not irrelevant details (p. 74). He has very interesting things to say about experiments-in-imagination in the physical sciences. His examples range from levers and pendula to the theory of relativity (pp. 76 f). Having thus defined what in his opinion ideal types are in the natural sciences, he discusses their relation to general laws; his most telling example is a discussion of the theory of ideal gases (p. 80). Having been myself a natural scientist in my better days, I read Hempel's material with great interest. Not for a long time had I been so vividly reminded of Maxwell Boyle, and other heroes of my student days. But I certainly was startled when I found the following conclusion on page 80: "The preceding analysis suggests the following observations on the 'ideal' and the empirical aspects of ideal type concepts in the *social sciences*." (Emphasis mine.)

This of course can only mean that the concluding pages of Hempel's paper would advise social scientists what to do if they wanted to do the same things which, according to Hempel, natural scientists did. Now this might be very good advice, but I always thought that the philosopher of social science would make an intrinsic analysis of what we practitioners actually do, and Hempel's paper has not yet dwelt on this point. Actually, I was willing to waive this objection because any advice from Hempel might be useful; so let us look. Of his four concluding pages, two again summarize what the natural scientist does and only two (pp. 82 and 83) give a concrete example of what all this might have to do with the social sciences. But even this happy ending is slightly marred, because the example he chooses is one which "approximates most closely the status of idealizations in natural science: the concepts of perfectly free competition."

In my opinion, it would have been more enlightening to take examples which are *least* comparable to the natural sciences, such as those with which Weber, Becker, and other men in this tradition were concerned: bureaucracy, folk society, etc. All this talk about ideal types, which never dies and still does not lead anywhere, might be indicative of a genuine problem of social research. The only way to find out is for a philosopher of science to analyze empirical studies and not the manifestos of the representatives of the tradition. I understand that Einstein once summarized his view on the appropriate mathematics for the problems of theoretical physics by saying that in his opinion God does not play with dice. It would hardly occur to Hempel that the issue could be settled by discussing what kind of dice Einstein thought of or how many players he had in mind. But when it comes to the social sciences, that is what he does in the paper which I picked as an example—an unfair one, I confess, as far as Hempel is concerned, but, I think, quite characteristic of the general state of affairs.

It would now be tempting for me to say that space does not permit me to give my own explication of what actually goes on when writers try to discuss historical data or contemporary field observations under the heading of ideal or constructed typologies. However, this happens to be one of the topics I meant for a long time to investigate, but never got around to, certainly, in part, because I knew it would be difficult, time consuming, and perhaps not too rewarding. This might also explain why I was so disappointed when I thought that Hempel had done the work, while actually he followed the tradition of philosophers of science in telling social scientists what he knew about the natural sciences. I will be somewhat better off with my second example because it deals with a topic on which I have written extensively myself.

A large part of our work requires us to translate concepts into operational instruments which permit us to classify people or groups. Such instruments are often loosely called "measurements" but I do not want to enter into the justification of this terminology; what matters here is the practice. The notions we translate sometimes come from everyday language, as in instances when we classify people according to their intelligence or their happiness. Sometimes the concept is newly created by sensitive analysts: the extraverted person or the cohesive group. In recent years, many empirical social scientists have analyzed such procedures and I will describe them only very briefly, referring the interested reader to typical publications [4, 9, 18]. Take, for example, the notion of cohesiveness. The investigator starts with a kind of vague imagery. In the cohesive group, people feel friendly toward each other, they like to be with the group, they would make sacrifices to maintain the existence of the group against outside attack, their self-respect is enhanced by the approval of other group members, and so on. A long list of such properties can be culled from the literature, and anyone who joins in the spirit of the game can add additional "indicators": the members like to meet or at least want to keep in communication with each other; there is a similarity of tastes and goals, agreement as to what is right and wrong, not too much fighting for individual advantages, and so on.

Suppose now a social research project is established to develop an instrument by which a number of specific groups should be ordered according to their degree of cohesiveness. The investigator will proceed in three steps. He will first make a list of all the indicators which have been proposed, often dividing them into subsets; these are called dimensions because they seem to represent various major aspects of the original image. Then, he will select a smaller number of this "universe of items" and combine them into a manageable "test."

Having thus constructed his instrument, he will collect statistical data along the following lines: he will observe a large number of groups and describe each in terms of the various indicators. He knows that rarely will any group be positive or negative on all the test items. There are groups in which people like each other very much but have little opportunity for communication; there are other groups in which everyone is imbued with the group goal although they do not feel very friendly to many of the other members. Each group will thus be characterized by a profile or response pattern. Using an appropriate statistical technique, the investigator will then compute the covariations between all the indicators taken over all the groups he is studying. His basic numerical material will be one or more matrices, the entries of which indicate how well pairs and perhaps triplets and quadruplets of indicators agree with each other in concrete situations.

Finally, he will submit these matrices to mathematical analysis. This can follow a variety of models, but each is explicitly or implicitly guided by the following considerations. The investigator wants to end up with an ordering which does not exist in advance, but is an *intended* classification. It is to be derived from the statistical behavior of the indicators, but, at the same time, it permits us to establish the diagnostic value of each of them. It may turn out, for instance, that mutual friendliness discriminates very well between more or less cohesive groups, while the amount of communication is less decisive. Whatever the empirical outcome, we know that there is only a probalistic relation between the intended classification and the indicators. Even in the groups which are most cohesive according to the final ordering, no indicator has a probablity of +1 of being observed; and even in the most disorganized groups, each of our test items has a more or less small opportunity to be observed.

There are quite a number of conflicting models which can be used for this analysis. But they all have two features in common. They do not use an outside criterion. No one tells us in advance which groups should be considered more cohesive than others; we do not calibrate indicators against superior knowledge. The ordering is derived from a mathematical analysis of the empirical covariation of these indicators. And as I mentioned before, the whole procedure implies a probabilistic mathematics. We pull ourselves up, so to say, by our own bootstraps. We end up by finding two things simultaneously: given that a group belongs at a certain point on the underlying continuum of cohesiveness, we can tell the probability with which it will manifest each indicator; and, given the profile or response pattern of the group, we can say with what probability the group belongs at various points along the intended classification. (For the sake of brevity, I omit here the possibility that the intended classification has more than one dimension, because this does not create any new logical problems and only requires additional computations.)

While we have by now some clarity on these matters and know quite well how the various mathematical models used in the third step are related to each other, there still are quite a number of problems which require further investigation. The matter is of great urgency for us and so it seems very appropriate to choose as my second example a paper by Max Black called "Definition, Presupposition, and Assertion" [3]. A reading of the introductory paragraphs shows how pertinent it could be to our topic. He begins by saying that definition "per genus et differentiam" is by no means the only or even the most frequent way by which we introduce a term into actual discourse. This is undoubtedly true for the type of procedures I have just sketched; as a matter of fact, Black mentions that what he has to say would apply to the notion of happiness (p. 48), which is certainly the type of concept with which we would be concerned. But a more careful reading of the paper again leaves us, I am sorry to say, in the lurch. Black has purposely avoided the kind of difficulty created by Hempel's paper; he makes no references to the natural sciences. But he joins Hempel in the second difficulty. He does not refer to any of the hundreds of concrete studies provided by empirical social research. His main example is the definition of a dachshund. I realize that there are more dog lovers in the world than social researchers and I am willing to accept Black's editorial policy as long as I can apply his examples to my problems. But here exactly is the rub—we have come from Scylla to Charybdis. Somehow between the austerity of Hempel's ideal gasses and the folksiness of Black's dachshund, social research is again squeezed out. I will now try to show briefly why we are frustrated by Black's analysis.

The dachshund becomes a legitimate member of the logician's circle by an initiation which Black describes (p. 41) as follows:

> This dog and that one and that one are clear cases of a dachshund. This one is very nearly a clear case, but has such and such a deviation. This other one is still further removed from being a perfectly clear case. And this one is a borderline specimen and could be called a dachshund or a basset indifferently. The specimens by means of which the meaning of the label "dachshund" is explained are presented in an order, determined by the degree of deviation from one or more specimens that are introduced as typical or "clear cases."

The author stresses that one would use criteria which are "very numerous, admit of variation in the degree to which they are met and no simple conjunctive or disjunctive combination of them is both necessary and sufficient." This is indeed very reminiscent of, say, an intelligence test. And I agree with him that this is "demanded by the complexity and variability of the phenomena to be described." But now let us look more closely at his summary statement:

> According to the account I have been giving, "range definition" as I propose to call it, *requires the exhibition or delineation of one or more typical, or "clear" cases*. Such cases I propose to call "paradigms." The traits or features or properties that vary from instance to instance, and are described in what I have been calling the "criteria," for application of the term, I shall call "constitutive factors." I have already proposed that the things to which the term is applied be called a "range"; it will be convenient to say that a word whose *instances* constitute a range is a "range word." (P. 43; emphasis mine.)

The difficulty here lies in emphasis on the phrase "exhibition or delineation of one or more clear cases". In the social sciences, we can rarely trot out clear cases. This is partly due to the nature of our beasts. But more often, there is not even the implication that such clear cases exist in social research. The actual procedure *moves in a direction opposite to the one Black describes*. He starts out by showing true dachshunds and then exhibits sorts of transitional specimens. He mentions that as he inspects the less clear cases, not all constitutive factors will be present, but implies that they will be statistically related as a consequence of his ordering (p. 46). The social scientist who develops an instrument of measurement *begins* with this covariation and then uses mathematical models to derive ways by which his specimens can be ordered according to their purity. This also precludes the imagery of the "range." We agree with Black that the traditional notion of class usually disappears. But it is substituted by the idea of order in which it is not even possible to distinguish "central ranges" without further assumptions. And Black nowhere introduces the *probabilistic relation between the intended classification and the indicators* (constitutive factors). If I am not mistaken, the word probability does not appear anywhere in Black's essay. One cannot say two sentences about classificatory procedures in the social sciences without introducing probability notions.

I am aware that in drawing on Black's paper, I am open to one objection. Hempel claims that he talks about the social sciences and therefore I can legitimately complain when he concentrates on theoretical physics. But why is it not Black's privilege to write about dog shows? I am afraid the matter cannot be settled without a full reading of his original text. I am confident that what Black really wanted to do is to explicate what we social scientists do when we develop our measurement instruments; there are enough asides in his paper to justify my imputation. But he does not take as his main example one of the numerous and I confess usually tedious papers in which such instruments are developed. By choosing the more attractive dachshund example, he probably retains more readers, but he misses what I think is the crucial point. And at the same time he deprives us of the help the philosopher can give us. I have in a recent paper listed a large number of philosophical problems related to our "measurements," which in my opinion are still unresolved [10].

This brings me back to the main message of my paper. Philosophers of science are not interested in and do not know what the work-a-day empirical research man does. This has two consequences: either we have to become our own methodologists or we have to muddle along without benefit of the explicating clergy. In certain areas, I suppose the simpler ones, we have done our own explications. In my opinion, they are not without merit and I want to bring a few of them to the attention of this audience. There exists something called "projective tests"—the idea is that you show people unstructured material such as ink blots, for instance, and ask them to tell you what they see. Some individuals will see flowers or dancing children; to others, the same ink blot will remind them of witches and skeletons. It is plausible to conclude that the latter person is more anxious than the former. A careful analysis of the procedures involved and the results obtained by a large variety of tests has shown the great complexity of such inferences. The interpretation of the subject may depend upon his mood at the moment rather than upon a more enduring trait; or he may unconsciously repress certain associations just because they would increase his anxieties. A careful collection of these and other possibilities makes it possible to show which kinds of unstructured materials are likely to be more useful and gives leads to better interpretation. Gardner Lindzey, a clinical psychologist, has provided this type of analysis, which in a better division of labor we should expect from a philosopher [11].

My other example is somewhat more complex and still leaves work to be done by volunteers from the philosophical camp. About two or three decades ago a great change came about in social research. The development of sampling and interviewing techniques temporarily shifted the trend of research in the direction of attitude surveys. Some sociologists have viewed this development with alarm: it is atomistic and it endangers insight into the role of the larger collective —be it the small informal group or the larger formal organization. Such "holistic" objections appear in many fields and they always leave one rather uneasy. They probably make a good point, but it is usually not quite clear precisely what point they are making. Now, in empirical research, owing to the increasing availability of funds and of computing devices, a new kind of material is available. We can study people in a large variety of comparable organizations: 200 schools, 150 hospitals, 100 locals of the same union. This permits a statistical analysis of behavior and attitudes within as well as between larger units. These larger units are not vague totalities but are themselves characterized by specified variables. A number of sociologists have recently begun to clarify the nature of this "contextual analysis" and an interesting review can be found in a paper by James Davis [5]. While we then know pretty well what we are doing and where we are going, it is not yet clear which part of the long-drawn-out holistic discussion is caught up by these procedures and what problems are still unresolved or even unexplicated. Here the philosopher with his wider knowledge of the non-empirical literature can be of great help if he were willing to look at these recent empirical developments.

I do not want to claim that we have received no help at all from the philosophers of science. Ernest Nagel has analyzed a paper by Robert Merton on functional analysis which testifies to a close reading of the original text and as a result makes a fine contribution to Merton's effort [14]. And I myself am certainly grateful to the way he has integrated some of my own work on survey analysis into a more general treatise on the philosophy of the social sciences [15]. But there is still a large amount of work to be done. Let me give just a few examples.

Take, for instance, the notion of social process. Every textbook on social change will deal with it in a more or less vague way. For the strict empiricist, a process consists of repeated observations of the same people or groups. Mathematically it can be represented by a system of simultaneous difference equations. What is the relation between these three approaches? What if the data are not only behavioral but include attitudes, plans, and expectations? What is added if the recurrent observations are characteristics of people as well as global characteristics of the collective to which they belong? What meaningful problems are left in the verbal literature after all those more tangible topics are taken care of? Or take the problem of diagnosis. Is what the medical doctor does the same as what we do when we notice that university professors in France do not have their telephone numbers listed in the directory, and when we take this as a sign of their aloofness from students? What is the logical difference between the latter example and the tendency of the clinical psychologist to make inferences from a patient's tone of voice? Philosophers have written much about signs and signals. How much of it applies to our empirical studies, and what new problems in our field do these writings pose? One more example may be taken from the Oxford group of analytical philosophers and their emphasis on careful linguistic distinctions. We must do the same when we translate concepts into indices. Should we think of the integration of a society as a single notion, should we distinguish value integration and social integration, or should we make even finer distinctions before we develop classificatory devices? What is the relation between this type of preliminary linguistic analysis and the one which is usually the end product of the analytical philosopher's work?

Some additional problems can be suggested to colleagues who are also interested in the history of science, which, incidentally, has been equally negligent of the social sciences. Fifty years ago, the French psychologist, Gabriel Tarde, made the notion of imitation a central concept. For several decades, he was forgotten or, if not, ridiculed. In the last ten years, we have a rapidly growing literature on what is called reference group analysis: the fact that people are greatly influenced by the groups they either belong to or want to belong to [13]. Do we face here a cycle in fashions or has something really new been added? And if the latter, why is there this discontinuity between Tarde and modern reference group thinking? To take one more historical example: from time to time, systems of basic categories are proposed and they acquire wide acceptance. At the turn of the century, the French school of Le Playistes had a basic "nomenclature," according to which they wrote hundreds of descriptive monographs [8]. In the 1930's, the Chicago school of Park and Burgess had a set of basic categories which provided the guidelines for numerous studies of specific groups such as juvenile gangs, residents of the ghetto, and others [16]. Today we have Talcott Parsons' pattern variables [17]. What is the relation between these categorical systems, what functions do they serve, and what accounts for their appearance and disappearance?

I do not expect that one short speech will suddenly make the philosophers of science rush to the rescue of people in empirical social research. What is needed to improve the situation are joint seminars at various universities, symposia which do not deal with generalities but discuss concrete studies from both sides, and fellowships which enable humanists to work for a while in a research bureau. Let me, however, stress once more the need to focus on the specific procedures of the social scientist. I obviously want to deny the unity of science as little as I would speak out for sin. But just as I believe that basically scientific work has a unifying rationality, I am also convinced that each subject matter has its own problems which need special attention. We should be guided by the inversion of a French proverb: the more it is the same, the more it is different. In my opinion, at this moment, the detailed explication of the *differential* aspects of empirical social research badly needs the attention of the philosopher of science.

BIBLIOGRAPHY

[1] Barton, Allen, "The Concept of Property-Space in Social Research," in *The Language of Social Research*, Paul Lazarsfeld and Morris Rosenberg (eds.). Glencoe, Ill., The Free Press, 1955.

[2] Becker, Howard, *Through Values to Social Interpretation*. Durham, N.C., Duke University Press, 1950.

[3] Black, Max, "Definition, Presupposition and Assertion," in *American Philosophers at Work*, Sidney Hook (ed.). New York, Criterion Books, 1956.

[4] Cattell, Raymond, "Personality Theory Flowing from Multivariate Quantitative Research." *Psychology*, Vol. 111, S. Koch (ed.), New York, McGraw-Hill, 1959.

[5] Davis, James, Joe L. Spaeth, and Carolyn Hudson, "Analyzing Effects of Group Composition." *American Sociological Review*, Vol. 26 (1961).

[6] Hempel, Carl, *Science, Language, and Human Rights*. Philadelphia, University of Pennsylvania Press, 1952.

[7] Hempel, Carl, and Paul Oppenheim, *Der Typusbegriff im Lichte der neuen Logik*. Leiden, 1936.

[8] Lazarsfeld, Paul, "Notes on the History of Quantification in Sociology." *Isis*, Vol. 52, Part 2, No. 168 (1961).

[9] Lazarsfeld, Paul, "Latent Structure Analysis." *Psychology*, Vol. 111, S. Koch (ed.). New York, McGraw-Hill, 1959.

[10] Lazarsfeld, Paul, "Methodological Problems in Empirical Social Research." International Congress of Sociology, Stresa, 1959.

[11] Lindzey, G., "Thematic Apperception Tests." *Psychological Bulletin*, Vol. 49, No. 1 (1952).

[12] McKinney, J. C., "Procedures and Techniques in Sociology," in *Modern Sociological Theory*, Becker and Boskoff (eds.). New York, Dryden, 1957.

[13] Merton, Robert K., *Social Theory and Social Structure*, revised edition. Gencoe, Ill., The Free Press, 1957.

[14] Nagel, Ernest, "A Formalization of Functionalism," in *Logic Without Metaphysics*. Glencoe, Ill., The Free Press, 1956.

[15] Nagel, Ernest, *The Structure of Science.* New York, Harcourt, Brace, and World, 1961.

[16] Park, R. E., and F. W. Burgess, *Introduction to the Science of Sociology.* Chicago, Univ. of Chicago Press, 1933.

[17] Parsons, T., and E. Shils, *Toward a General Theory of Action.* Cambridge, Mass., Harvard Univ. Press, 1951.

[18] Tryon, Robert, "Identification of Social Areas by Cluster Analysis." *Univ. of Calif. Publications in Psychology,* Vol. 8, No. 1 (1955).

CHAPTER 14

THE OBLIGATIONS OF THE 1950 POLLSTER TO THE 1984 HISTORIAN

The meetings of the American Association for Public Opinion Research give testimony to the great progress which its members have made in two respects: Our work has shown great technical improvement over the last few years and we have tried to make it ever more useful. Those of us who work at universities, however, often have to meet the criticism that technical excellence and usefulness are not enough. The significance of our work is doubted.

It is not always easy to say exactly what critics mean by lack of significance, but in many of their comments we find them asking that research work be undertaken for other than immediate practical purposes. This "transcendency" is looked for in at least three directions. Some feel that too much polling work is done for private clients and not enough in the public interest. This is certainly true and many of us wish the availability of funds would make possible a different state of affairs. Others mean that our work does not contribute enough to general theoretical knowledge. In this respect we ourselves have started to improve matters. The program for our meetings this year shows clearly that we are looking more and more on public opinion research as part of an analysis of political behavior on the one hand, and as part of a general theory of opinion formation and decision-making on the other.

But there is at least one more aspect of this quest for significance.

Reprinted from *Public Opinion Quarterly* (1964), Columbia University Press, by permission of the publisher.

This has to do with the choice of specific topics in even the simplest opinion poll. Even if we do not work for a specific client, do we not have a tendency to ask questions which will make interesting reading in tomorrow's newspapers? Don't we overlook the fact that, in a way, the pollster writes contemporary history? Might not the 1984 historian reproach us for not having given enough thought to what he will want to know about 1950?

Here we might explain why 1984 has been chosen for our title. In the late George Orwell's novel, the hero, Winston Smith, has grave doubts whether the world of dictatorship and thought police in which he lives is really as wonderful as the tele-screens in every other corner tell him it is. He is consumed by a desire to find out how life looked forty years earlier. But he cannot find out. A Ministry of Truth operating in Orwell's nightmare employs many historians whose sole task is to change and adapt history to the vacillating needs of the dictator. Old issues of the "London Times" are continuously rewritten so that anyone who wants to consult the past will find that it supports the party line of the day. The despair of not being able to compare the present with the past is one of the most haunting features of Orwell's story.

THE HISTORIAN'S ATTITUDE TO ATTITUDES

We all hope that this picture of the future is purely fictional, and that the 1984 historian will not block the citizen of his day from understanding the past. But how much help will he be in 1984 if we do not help him in 1950? Let me begin with a more remote example in which a famous historian was confronted with exactly this problem of explaining the past to his contemporaries.

In the 15th century Machiavelli wrote what is probably one of the first examples of modern and careful analysis of political behavior. And yet, for several centuries afterward, "Machiavellian" stood for everything evil in public affairs. At the beginning of the 19th century a reaction set in, and in 1837, the English historian and statesman, Macaulay, wrote an essay to set the matter straight. He wanted to explain why Machiavelli was so misunderstood. His answer was that "The Prince" was written at a time and in a social setting where people had a very different way of looking at things. His argument runs about as follows: At the end of the Middle Ages the Italian cities had developed a middle class culture of artisans and merchants, while the countries north of the Alps, like England, France, and Germany were still in a barbarous state. In the north, courage was the main means of survival; courage to withstand the hardships of life and courage to repel hostile hordes which were incessantly threatening each other with war. In the Italian cities, ingenuity was the most cherished ability; ingenuity in improving the protective value of the community, and ingenuity in meeting the competition of their fellow citizens in an essentially democratic society.

"Hence while courage was a point of honor in other countries ingenuity became the point of honor in Italy."

The pertinence of this passage to Macaulay's main topic is obvious. He feels that a great thinker living in what we today would call "an ingenuity culture" was judged by people who lived and are still living in the aftermath of a "courage culture."

From our point of view it is important to see what evidence Macaulay tried to adduce for his thesis. The great English historian struggles hard to make his point clear and convincing to his reader. First of all he compares an English and an Italian hero. Henry V was admired by the English because he won a great battle, in spite of his personal crudeness and cruelty. Francis Sforza was admired by the Italians because he was a successful statesman, in spite of his personal treachery and faithlessness.

And still, Macaulay is not yet quite sure that the reader has seen the matter clearly. He finally hits upon what seems to him a useful literary device, and what today we can consider probably the first projective test recorded in the literature. He writes:

> We have illustrated our meaning by an instance taken from history. We will select another from fiction. Othello murders his wife; he gives orders for the murder of his lieutenant; he ends by murdering himself. *Yet he never loses the esteem and affection of Northern readers.* His intrepid and ardent spirit redeems everything. The unsuspecting confidence with which he listens to his adviser, the tempest of passion with which he commits his crimes, and the haughty fearlessness with which he avows them, give an extraordinary interest to his character. Iago, on the contrary, is the object of universal loathing. . . . *Now we suspect that an Italian audience in the fifteenth century*

would have felt very differently. Othello would have inspired
nothing but detestation and contempt. The folly with which
he trusts the friendly professions of a man whose promotion he
had obstructed, the credulity with which he takes unsupported
assertions, and trivial circumstances, for unanswerable proofs,
the violence with which he silences the exculpation till the exculpation can only aggravate his misery, would have excited the
abhorrence and disgust of the spectators. The conduct of Iago
they would assuredly have condemned; but they would have
condemned it as we condemn that of his victim. Something of
interest and respect would have mingled with their disapproba-
tion. The readiness of the traitor's wit, the clearness of his judgment, the skill with which he penetrates the dispositions of
others and conceals his own, would have ensured to him a certain portion of their esteem.

It is clear what Macaulay is striving for. He wishes someone had
conducted attitude studies in Florence and in London of the 15th
century. Let us suppose that a polling agency existed at the time, and
was hired by Macaulay to test his hypothesis. In a somewhat facetious
way, we can imagine how they might have proceeded. The Othello
story could have been written up in one or two paragraphs, without
giving either Othello or Iago any advantage. Pretests could have been
conducted to make sure that the wording was quite unbiased. (Perhaps
they might have concealed the fact that Othello was a Negro because
that might bias some respondents.) The crucial question would have
been: How many Florentines and Londoners, respectively, approve of
Iago, how many of Othello, and how many say "don't know"? Nothing less, but hardly much more, would have been needed to provide
empirical evidence for Macaulay's brilliant conjecture.

Few historians will make such elaborate efforts to document their
statements about public attitudes. It is much more likely that we shall
find statements which read like a Gallup release, except, of course,
that the tables are missing. Take, for instance, the following account
from Merle Curti's, "The Thrust of the Civil War into Intellectual
Life."

A growing number of men and women in both sections, dis-
trustful of their leaders, sympathetic with the enemy, or merely
war-weary, preferred compromise or even defeat to the continuation of the struggle. The fact of war affected the thinking not
only of these dissidents but of the great majority of people who

accepted it as inevitable and hoped that good would come from it.

Here are all the ingredients of a statement on the distribution of attitudes. We find quantitative statements like "a growing number" or "the great majority of people." There are suggestions for comparisons between men and women and between different sections of the country. The passage which we have quoted even implies certain cross-tabulations between attitudes towards the war and attitudes toward other issues of the day.

No wonder, then, that the historians of a later period for which polls were already available would eagerly incorporate them into their writings. Dixon Wecter writes about "The Age of the Great Depression." At one point he discusses the growing acceptance of birth control. To document this trend, he first uses the traditional, indirect methods of the historian, trying to derive attitudes from their manifestations. He points to the change in terms, from "race suicide" to "birth control" and finally to "planned parenthood." Then he goes at his topic more directly.

> A poll among Farm and Fireside readers early in the Depression showed two to one for giving medical advice on planned parenthood, and during the thirties the Sears, Roebuck catalogue began to list contraceptive wares. A straw vote of subscribers by the Protestant Churchman in January, 1935, revealed almost unanimous approval for birth control, while in the next year, among all sorts and conditions, a Gallup poll agreed with a Fortune survey in finding two out of three favorable. This majority, moreover, rose steadily in later years, with women outranking men in the warmth of their endorsement.

We could cite other similar examples to show further the place of attitude and opinion research in historical studies; but it might suffice instead to point out that some of the most enduring works of historiography, such as Taylor's "The Medieval Mind" and Weber's "The Protestant Ethic," are those which dealt with the attitudes, value systems, and prevailing beliefs of the period. By the historian's own testimony, there is a place for attitude and opinion research in their field, but this still leaves open the question of what kind of polling data the future historian will need. How can we fit at least some of our findings into the stream of intellectual work as it extends into the future?

We can expect guidance from three directions. For one, we can study historical writings; secondly, we can turn to certain works on the contemporary scene; finally, we can scrutinize existing speculations on the probable course of the future. It should be helpful to illustrate briefly each of these points.

THE POLLSTER READS A BOOK

It would be worthwhile for a scholar to review typical historical texts from our point of view. Where do competent writers show, either explicitly or implicitly, the need for attitude material of the kind a sampling survey can furnish? Short of a careful scrutiny we cannot know the prevailing modes of analysis. Furthermore, the specific need for opinion data will vary according to the topic under investigation. But a few expectations are rather obvious.

In at least three areas the historian will be confronted with the need for opinion data. The most obvious, of course, is when "prevailing values" are themselves the object of his study. There are a number of classical investigations of major changes in the climate of opinion such as the transition from medieval traditionalism to the individualistic thinking connected with the Protestant Reformation. During the first half of the 19th century a countertrend started, stressing public responsibility for individual welfare. This trend could be observed in the United States as well as in other countries. Curti, for instance, points out that, before the Civil War, there was considerable resistance against accepting tax supported public schools.

> Men of power and substance frequently argued that education had been, and properly so, a family matter. . . . What could be more potent than the certainty that if free schools were granted, the concession would not end short of socialism itself? To provide free schooling for the less well-to-do would result in the loss of their self-respect and initiative.

Today, hardly anyone feels this way. But how did this shift of public opinion come about? Among which groups did it start and how did it spread? How long did it take for the initial resistance to disappear? What external events precipitated or retarded the development?

Such knowledge would be of considerable practical importance today. If we substituted the words "housing" for "schooling" in the preceding quotation, we would describe the way in which many people feel about public housing projects. It is probable that this sentiment is now in the process of historical change. So far as public health insurance is concerned, the resistance is still very great. More detailed knowledge of such developments in the past would help us to predict better what turn our contemporary problems are likely to take. If we know better the patterns of past change, we can perhaps extract from them some recurrent paths of development. Therefore, incidentally, we can expect that those historians who look at history as one sector of a general social science will be most likely to welcome attitude data.

This leads to a second area in which the historian would undoubtedly need public opinion data. Wherever a new type of institution or a major legislative development was investigated, he would be greatly helped by data on the interaction between the diffusion of attitudes and the sequence of social actions. One of the most thoroughly investigated phenomena of this kind is the turn from laissez-faire to social legislation, which took place in England during the second half of the 19th century. Karl Polanyi has pointed out that the free market system never really worked well in any event. He summarizes Dicey's famous investigation of "Law and Public Opinion in England" in the following way:

> Dicey made it his task to inquire into the origins of the 'anti-laissez-faire' or, as he called it, the 'collectivist' trend in English public opinion, the existence of which was manifest since the late 1860's. He was surprised to find that no evidence of the existence of such a trend could be traced save the acts of legislation themselves. More exactly, no evidence of a 'collectivist trend' in public opinion prior to the laws which appeared to represent such a trend could be found.

Here is a challenging suggestion that major legislative events may not be preceded, but rather followed, by changes in public opinion. Before one could accept such a conclusion one would certainly want to know how safe it is to make inferences of this kind merely by examining newspapers, pamphlets and recorded speeches. Could it not be the case that there was an undercurrent of public opinion in the direction of social legislation which did not find expression in the kind of material available to the historian, but which would have been caught by systematic public opinion research at the time?

A third area of overlay between the historian and the pollster ought to be those writings in which specific events are to be explained. There is virtually no American historian, for example, who has not tried at one time or another to explain the outcome of some presidential election. Robert Bower has collected a whole folklore of stories which have arisen in connection with elections of major importance, such as those of 1840, 1882, and 1896. He analyzes these explanations of election outcomes and shows that all of them imply the type of knowledge about issues and personalities of the day which might have been obtained through polls. Even with poll data it is not easy to arrive at safe conclusions. This is known by everyone who followed the efforts to understand Truman's election in 1948. Bower's "Opinion Research and Historical Interpretation of Elections" shows how much more tenuous the conjectures are for previous periods.

Historians themselves are, of course, aware of this task. A group of medievalists started, in their professional journal, "Speculum," to appraise the status of their work. The first article, by J. L. LaMonte, was called "Some Problems in Crusading Historiography." It was of interest to read there that "the decline of the crusading ideal in spite of papal propaganda is a little known subject." One is reminded of the studies of returning veterans reported in "The American Soldier" when the author deplores how little is known about "the social effects of the change in material status of such crusaders as returned after considerably bettering their position in the East."

In such a reappraisal of historical writings, we should be sensitive to the effect which opinion surveys have had in changing the notion of a "fact." There was a time when only political documents found in archives were considered appropriate evidence for the historian. That made him focus on political events; everything else was interpretation. Then the "new history" centered attention on data such as economic and social statistics. This enlarged considerably the area of what were considered facts. Still, sentiments and attitudes remained a matter of interpretation. Now, however, they too have become facts. The result of a public opinion poll is as much a fact as the content of a political document or the crop and price statistics of a certain region.

In turn, the term "attitude and opinion research" should not be taken too narrowly. Let us remember that we have always known and discussed among ourselves that much more than simple "yes-no" questions belongs in our equipment. In connection with the historian's problem, two techniques in particular will certainly need considerable refinement on our part. One derives from the problem of saliency. The fact that a respondent answers a question which we put to him still does not tell us whether he would have asked himself this question or whether the matter is of particular concern to him. The historian will certainly want to know what issues were in the foreground of attention at various times and in various sectors of the population. Published polling material does not contain enough of such information; as a matter of fact, considerable methodological progress on this point is still needed. The diffusion of opinion in time and social space is a second problem which we do not yet handle with enough emphasis or enough technical skill. In many more of our surveys we should find out where people get their ideas and how they pass them on. All of this has thus far been a matter of conjecture for the historian; we are supposed to turn it into an enlarged array of "facts." Thus the study of historical writings will not only be a source of significant topics; it could also be a spur for methodological improvements.

SIGNS OF THE TIMES

A second source of ideas, interesting hypotheses and leads for significant field surveys may be found in many efforts to understand the meaning of what is going on around us right now. It has been said that each generation must rewrite history, because hitherto unconsidered aspects of the past become interesting in the light of the changing present. But there is certainly a limitation to this rule. If there is no data at all on certain aspects of the past, not much can be done, even under the impetus of a strong new curiosity. The pollster as a contemporary historian thus takes on considerable importance. What he considers worthy of a survey will, in later years, influence the range of possible historical inquiries.

Therefore, the question of where the pollster can get leads for significant investigations is an important one. Again, we cannot exhaust the possible choices, but a few clear avenues suggest themselves at the moment. There is, first, the critic of the contemporary scene. There are always social commentators who are especially sensitive to the shortcomings of our times; it is not unlikely that they hit on topics about which the future historian will want to know more. Let us quote passages which are characteristic of the type of statement we have in mind.

> Much too early do young people get excited and tense, much too early are they drawn away by the accelerated pace of the times. People admire wealth and velocity. Everybody strives for them. . . . Here they compete, here they surpass each other, with the result that they persevere in mediocrity. And this is the result of the general trend of the contemporary world toward an average civilization, common to all.

We can visualize translating this social comment into a research program. It would not be too difficult to develop an index of competitiveness, and to study at what age individuals exhibit a marked increase in their average scores. But that would not be enough. We are also called upon to follow the consequences of such developments for broader areas of society; for "not the external and physical alone is now managed by machinery, but the internal and spiritual also. . . ."

> Has any man, or any society of men, a truth to speak, a piece of spiritual work to do, they can nowise proceed at once and with the mere natural organs, but must first call a public meeting, appoint committees, issue prospectuses, eat a public dinner; in a word, construct or borrow machinery, wherewith to speak it and do it. Without machinery they were hopeless, helpless. . . .

Here a more sociological type of data is required; number and types of meetings, attendance figures, etc. Most of all we will want to study the statistical interrelationship between attitudes and kinds of social participation in intellectual enterprises.

Most interesting about these quotations, however, are their dates and their sources. The first is from a letter which Goethe wrote in 1825. The second is a characteristic portion of an essay written by Carlyle in 1830. Here are two leading minds in two different countries voicing the same apprehension in terms which might well be used today. Undoubtedly experts could provide us with similar statements for any other century, for we are always likely to find evidence of a feeling that matters were very different sometime ago. There are certain standbys which recur in many discussions: the tensions of daily living have become so much worse; people are now more apathetic politically than they were previously; the cultural taste of the country has been depraved. We shall not be able to decide the truth of such issues in retrospect, but we can at least lay the ground for more responsible discussion of the problem in the future.

The social critic will focus our attention primarily on certain contents and subject matters which are important for our times. There is another group of analysts who are more concerned with the kinds of dimensions which are useful in describing the social scene. They are likely to be interested mainly in comparisons[A] between various countries, for instance, or between different social groups. It should never be forgotten how difficult it is to make the social scene "visible." When we deal with nature, many objects, like trees or stones or animals, force themselves on us visually. Social entities are much more the product of creative intelligence. The notion of a clique, for instance, or of a reference group, the inner gallery for which so many of us play the drama of our lives, or the distinction between an introverted and an extroverted personality are real conceptual inventions. In social observations we are often in the position of a bird which flies across the sky with a flock of other birds. For the external observer, the flock has a clearly visible geometric shape; but does the bird within the flock even know about the shape of his "group"? By what social interrelations among the birds is the form of the group maintained?

When we translate these sketchy considerations into problems of survey research, we meet them in a familiar form. Every self-respecting pollster will report his findings nowadays "sub-classified by age, sex, and socio-economic status." We know from our studies that these are useful classifications. But are they the most significant ones? Wouldn't we be helped in the work of today, and wouldn't we help readers of the future if we were alert to additional variables according to which we might classify our samples and analyze our findings?

It is on such an issue that we can get guidance from writers who have tried to obtain the best possible view of the contemporary scene. Let us turn for a moment to the patron saint of modern public opinion research, James Bryce. He makes an effort at one point to compare the political scene in England and that prevailing in this country. To this end he distinguishes "three sets of persons, those who make opinion, those who receive and hold opinion, those who have no opinions at all." After elaborating on this distinction, he comes to the conclusion that the first group is somewhat larger in England than in the United States of 1870, while the proportion in the second group is very much larger on the American continent than in Britain. From this he draws a number of interesting conclusions. The "power of public opinion in the United States," for instance, seems to him related to the inordinately large ratio of opinion holders to opinion makers.

To find significant variables for political classifications continues to be a challenge for writers of this kind. It is quite possible that an index of political participation and interest might prove a useful instrument for a great variety of surveys, on a national as well as on an international scale. As a matter of fact, some research organizations are reported to be working on the development of such devices.

In the writings of contemporary social scientists, the pollster will find other classificatory suggestions which are worth pursuing. David Riesman, for instance, has just published a book centered on the distinction between three types of social character. One is the tradition-directed type; the person who behaves as he thinks his social group expects him to, does not believe he should change anything in his environment, and feels shame if he violates any of the rules under which he lives. The second is the inner-directed type; the person who is guided by strong moral standards, has a kind of psychological gyroscope which controls his conduct, and who feels guilt if he does something which is not right. Finally, there is the outer-directed type; the backslapper who wants to get along with everyone, who has few convictions of his own, and who feels general anxiety if he is not successful in receiving all the signals which he tries to catch on his psychological radar system. In chapter after chapter of *The Lonely Crowd* Riesman tries to spell out the political correlates of these three types. He is especially interested in the outer-directed type, which he considers characteristic of modern American life. Riesman discovers in him a dangerous kind of political apathy. He wants to get all the inside dope on politics just as on baseball, but he has lost all belief that he, individually, has any influence and therefore refrains from giving public affairs any serious thought or any active devotion. A careful reading of Riesman's chapter on politics will show how much empirical research could and should be geared in with such speculations.

Finally, the literature of the so-called cultural anthropologists belongs here. They are not only concerned with singling out significant topics or finding variables which would be useful to make more clearly visible the main character of the contemporary scene. They also want to uncover the mechanisms by which the scene develops. Distinguished equally by brilliance and by irresponsibility of factual evidence, they challenge the pollster to try to bring about effective cooperation. But the challenge is worth accepting, for from an interaction between the two groups could develop really new insights into human affairs. No newspaper reader can be unaware of the writings on "national character." The main thesis is that each society and each national subgroup develops its own way of looking at the world, and its own way of giving satisfaction to basic needs. It is the function of the family to raise children in such a way that they "want to act in the way they have to act as members of the society or as a special class within it." Like a group of expert ball players giving a public exhibition, the anthropologists toss their variations on the basic theme from one to the other. Margaret Mead describes in great detail the small American family with its lack of tradition and its uncertain goals in a quickly changing world:

> . . . while the child is learning that his whole place in the world, his name, his right to the respect of other children—everything —depends upon his parents . . . he also learns that his own acceptance by these parents, who are his only support, is conditional upon his achievements, upon the way in which he shows up against other children and against their idea of other children.

Gorer picks it up from Mead. He agrees with her that there is a strong element of uncertainty in the emotional life of the American family. The parents do not quite know what is right and therefore can love their children only if they are successful in their own peer group, the school class or the gang. But Gorer does not think that ambition or success drive develops in children as a result; he has a different notion:

> The presence, the attention, the admiration of other people thus becomes for Americans a necessary component to their selfesteem, demanded with a feeling of far greater psychological

> urgency than is usual in other countries. . . . The most satisfy-
> ing form of this assurance is not given by direct flattery or com-
> mendation (this by itself is suspect as a device to exploit the
> other) but by love.

The two writers, if confronted with their statements, would probably say that there is a strong relation between ambition and the desire to be loved. Yet how do they know that these desires are more frequent or more intense among Americans than among other people? They give many examples from Rotary meetings and from double dates in college which make their idea plausible. We pollsters are accustomed to asking for a better definition of terms and for more precise evidence; so we are inclined to criticize these anthropologists. But are we fully justified? Have they not seen here topics which are considerably more worthy of investigation than the rating of movie stars or even the attitudes of voters toward a local candidate?

Here are writers who have challenging ideas on the structure of our social relationships and their effect on attitudes and opinions. Does this not suggest that we have neglected the first link in this chain? To cite one specific example. In the writings of the social anthropologists, the authoritarian structure of the family plays a large role. Who among us, either in this country or abroad, has collected answers to questions like these: To what extent do young people make their own occupational choices and to what extent do their parents influence their decisions? In what countries and in what groups does a young suitor still ask the girl's parents for consent to marriage? How are conflicts between father and son resolved when they both want the car or both want to use the living room? Where do children still spend their holidays with their families, and where do they go off on their own? How much visiting of relatives is there, how frequent are family reunions, and so on? What would adolescents consider the main complaints as to the way they are treated by their parents? What activities are parents most eager to forbid in their young children and what principles are they most anxious to inculcate in their older ones?

Useful contributions along such lines could be made, especially by those among us who conduct international polls. But in this discussion we are not interested in the present for its own sake; we want to look at it from the point of view of tomorrow. What should we watch as the present slowly turns into the future?

GLANCING INTO THE FUTURE

Scrutinizing writings on the past will give us an idea of the kinds of data which historians have missed prior to the appearance of the pollster on the scene. Studying the literature on present-day society will give us a chance to confront theoretical thinking with empirical data. A final, and probably the most important, possibility develops when we make efforts to guess what the future will want to know about today. Quite a number of political scientists feel that the best way to study the present is to see it as a transitional stage to future events. Harold Lasswell has emphasized the need of "developmental constructs."

> In the practice of social science, . . . we are bound to be af-
> fected in some degree by our conceptions of future develop-
> ment. . . . What is the function of this picture for scientists? It
> is to stimulate the individual specialist to clarify for himself his
> expectations about the future, as a guide to the timing of scien-
> tific work.

We should form expectations of what major changes might come about within the next decades. It is in connection with these changing conditions that the historian will expect that we, today, have initiated a series of trend studies. This is undoubtedly the most difficult task. It not only requires of us pollsters that we translate more or less vague ideas into specific instruments of inquiry; there is so little thinking along this line that we shall even have to assume some responsibility for guessing what will be of importance a few decades hence. The best we can do in the present context is to give a few examples of the kind of effort which will be required.

There can be little doubt that the history of the next decades will be centered around the effects of the rapidly increasing industrialization characteristic of our times. Perhaps the reaction to contemporary mechanization will be found in strong religious movements. If this is the case, what will the future analyst, in retrospect, wish that we had ascertained today? An interesting lead for this is found in *The American Soldier*. The importance of this work lies in the fact that, for the first time, we really know something about the experiences and feelings of an important sector of the population. As far as religion goes, the following observation is reported. About three-fourths of the soldiers said that prayer was a source of strength in battle, but the minority who did not find this so had certain interesting characteristics: they experienced less fear, laid more stress on their relations with other soldiers, and seemed, in general, to be what modern psychologists would call better adjusted personalities.

Here, in one result, may lie the seeds of an important bifurcation. Increasing industrialization may lead to a compensatory dependence on religious beliefs. Or, it may create a new type of personality, differently adjusted to new social demands. We cannot tell in which direction the future will tend; as a matter of fact, we do not even know whether any really new developments will take place in the religious sphere; but general considerations and bits of research evidence seem to indicate that systematic work is called for.

At the same time that we try to answer these more general questions about the intensity of religious beliefs, we should analyze the specific character of religious movements as they develop. In this connection Julian Huxley has provided an impressive set of predictions. In his essay on "Religion as an Objective Problem," he distinguishes between the "old" religion and the "new." According to him, the old one developed as a result of fear and ignorance of the external physical environment. Modern science has given us enough insight into and control over the forces of nature so that religious beliefs as we have known them so far are likely to fade away slowly. Now we are faced with a new set of problems emerging from what he calls the "internal environment"; the disorganization of our economic and social life, war, poverty, and unemployment. New religious movements are likely to develop, centered less around the worship of a supernatural being than around the worship of a single solution for social evils.

> The process, of course, has already begun. Many observers have commented on the religious elements in Russian communism— the fanaticism, the insistence on orthodoxy, the violent 'theological' disputes, the 'worship' of Lenin, the spirit of self-dedication, the persecutions, the common enthusiasm, the puritan element, the mass-emotions, the censorship.

The new religion is now in its most primitive form, with Communism and Fascism as typical examples. But just as the old religion moved from simple paganism to a refined monotheism, so will the new religion outgrow its present crudeness.

> Accordingly, we can prophesy that in the long run the nationalistic element in socialized religion will be subordinated or adjusted to the internationalist: that the persecution of minorities will give place to toleration; that the subtler intellectual and moral virtues will find a place and will gradually oust the cruder from their present pre-eminence in the religiously-conceived social organism. We can also assert with fair assurance that this process of improvement will be a slow one, and accompanied by much violence and suffering.

Here, indeed, is a research program. First we must find appropriate indices for the various shades of belief which Huxley distinguishes. Then we shall want to get our information separately from a large number of social subgroups. Trend data will have to be assembled over a long period of time; and wherever possible, these trends should be linked with external events. If a special movement starts somewhere, if a related book becomes a best-seller, if some special legislation is passed or a voluntary association established, we shall want to study the pertinent attitudes "before and after."

This is not the place to propose a concrete study design, but we should warn against oversimplifying the whole problem. The attitudes in which the historian will be interested are certainly complex in nature; and, in order to cover one single concept, it may be necessary to employ a whole set of interlocking questions. As a matter of fact, it might very well be that future trends will be different for different dimensions of the same notion. To exemplify what this means in terms of our work, we shall choose for our second example the problem of class tensions.

There is an abundance of prophecies in the literature which can be loosely labelled as Marxist. Conflicts of interest between the working class and the influential business groups will become more acute. The workers will become more class conscious, and more aggressive towards the privileged groups. The latter, in turn, will defend more strongly their class interests and more and more neglect the democratic forms of politics. These ideas are too well known to need further elaboration. Instead, let us pick out of this whole complex the notion of class consciousness, and see whether we can develop a kind of barometer by which to measure trends in the next few decades.

In recent years, a large number of business companies have conducted surveys to determine their standing with the public, but this by no means meets the task. There could very easily be an intensification of class consciousness among workers which does not express itself immediately in invectives directed toward General Motors or Standard Oil. Not even the recently increased interest of social psychologists in this problem covers it fully. Richard Centers, in his "The Psychology of Social Classes," has developed a set of questions pertinent to two elements: readiness to accept the government as an agent in economic affairs; and a feeling that avenues of economic advancement are closing up, that social rewards are not fairly distributed.

The total picture has many additional aspects, however. We should study whether workers have a feeling of identification with their class. If a worker's son becomes a lawyer, should he work for a union rather than for a big corporation? Is there an increased interest in reading stories about workers rather than about movie stars? Is there an increased interest in leisure-time associations especially designed for workers? Another aspect of the problem would be whether workers are concerned with the power structure in the community. Do they think that the courts handle poor and rich alike? Do and can the councilmen in the city represent both poor and rich? Do they feel that the rich have special influence with the police? Even if there is growing uneasiness on this score, the question still to be raised is whether it is channeled into political reactions. Does "going into politics" become a more respected and desirable pursuit? Is voting the "right" way something which becomes an important criterion for judging people? Do political issues become a factor in one's own personal plans?

This example, incidentally, raises a serious problem of strategy for the pollster. Topics relevant to the work of the future historian are likely to come from the area of social change. Polls dealing with such areas can easily become suspect as "subversive" or "inflammatory." It will therefore be important to make clear, both to the general public and to specific clients, that the public opinion researcher is not taking sides when he focuses part of his attention on more unconventional issues. As a matter of fact, it might very well be that some of the work suggested here might best be done under the joint sponsorship of several agencies or perhaps under the aegis of a professional organization like the American Association for Public Opinion Research.

WHAT SHOULD BE DONE?

We pollsters cannot be expected to tackle the whole problem by ourselves. We should seek the assistance of a "commission for the utilization of polls in the service of future historiography," whose specific task it would be to furnish us with appropriate ideas. This commission should consist, on the one hand, of historians and other social scientists who have given thought to questions such as those we have raised, and, on the other hand, of research technicians who can translate research suggestions into actual study designs.

There certainly will be no scarcity of topics. There is much evidence to show that people in this country were inclined to shy away from concern with international relations. Suddenly we are thrust into the position of being the leading power in the world. How will people in this country adjust to this change, and what will be the mutual interaction between the distribution of attitudes and the actions of our policy-makers? At what rate will Americans really become aware of the existence of the Far Eastern people? When will they notice that the famous destruction of the "human race" by the atomic bomb might really mean the replacing of the Western sector of humanity by their Asiatic fellow men? Another element of our tradition is the belief that one man is as good as another. But in a society which becomes ever more complex, the expert plays an increasingly important role. How will this proverbial anti-authoritarian tradition adjust to the increasing, and probably unavoidable, "bureaucratization" of the modern world? Or one might turn from the political to a more personal sphere. Increasing amounts of available leisure time will force more people to review their "designs for living." How will they use the time over which they themselves have control: will they use it to have a richer personal life, to equip themselves better for competitive advancement, or will they just fritter it away? There is certainly an obvious interrelation between these questions and new technical developments such as television.

Whatever topic we select, the procedure for research will always be the same. We must first formulate clearly a number of alternative assumptions about future developments. Then we must decide on the kind of indices which are pertinent for the problem at hand; this is where the research technician can make his main contribution. To set up the machinery for collecting the data is a matter of decision and funds. As to the selection of respondents, a certain flexibility will be necessary. For some problems a national cross-section will be most appropriate. For other problems very specific population groups will have to be sampled. When it comes to studying the diffusion of attitudes, attention will have to be focused on elite groups. In other cases specific occupations or special age groups will command our interest. And at all times we shall want to collect "background information": documentation on major events, on the activities of organizations, community leaders, etc.

At this point, we should warn against a possible misunderstanding. Previously we stressed that attitude surveys provide a new type of "facts" for the historian. But this does not imply that they are more important than the more traditional kind of data. It is just the interplay between the "objective" facts and attitudes which promises a great advance in historiography. If for a given period we not only know the standard of living, but also the distribution of ratings on happiness and personal adjustment, the dynamics of social change will be much better understood. Let us add that sampling surveys will enlarge our ideas on social bookkeeping in still another way. Nothing is more characteristic of this trend than what has happened in the decennial census of the United States. As long as we thought only in terms of complete enumerations, we could afford to include only a few questions. Now that we use five percent and one percent samples on specific items, we are able to cover a much wider range of topics. This is undoubtedly only a beginning. Since small sample designs have been perfected, there is no reason why sociography should not develop on a much broader scale. Cultural activities and other living habits may soon be added to the more conventional trends in the birth rate or export trade. It is certainly no coincidence that the Kinsey reports did not begin to appear before 1948.

As early as 1908, in his "Human Nature in Politics," Graham Wallas pointed to such changes in what he called the methods of political reasoning. He compared the reports of two Royal Commissions, both of which were concerned with the reform of the English poor laws. One was established in 1834 and the other in 1905. The earlier

one dealt with "a priori deduction, illustrated, but not proved by particular instances." Now (in 1905) things are different.

> Instead of assuming half consciously that human energy is de-
> pendent solely on the working of the human will in the pres-
> ence of the ideas of pleasure and pain, the Commissioners are
> forced to tabulate and consider innumerable quantitative ob-
> servations relating to the very many factors affecting the will
> of paupers and possible paupers. They cannot, for instance,
> avoid the task of estimating the relative industrial effectiveness
> of health, which depends upon decent surroundings; of hope,
> which may be made possible by State provision for old age; and
> of the imaginative range which is the result of education; and of
> comparing all these with the 'purely economic' motive created
> by ideas of future pleasure and pain.

As can be seen, Wallas did not want to replace, but to complement, principles with social surveys. And so we too do not suggest that
attitude data are better than "hard" facts, but that they add, so to
speak, a new dimension.

There is one more suggestion for the work of the new commission
on polling and historiography. We are all aware that prediction is one
of the touchstones by which a science can justify itself. So far our predictions have been confined mainly to the outcomes of political elections; many have felt that this is a rather insignificant pursuit. There is
no reason, however, that we should not predict future sentiments and
then, later on, study whether we were right. One of the most impressive chapters in *The American Soldier* is that on "The Aftermath of Hostilities." In the summer of 1944, the Research Branch
prepared a document predicting what attitudes they expected among
soldiers at the end of the war. In 1945, many of those predictions were
tested: At some points the predictions were correct, and at others,
wrong. But no person reading this chapter can escape the feeling that
here might be the substitute for laboratory experiments, so often impossible to carry out in the social sciences. Interestingly enough, without knowing about the experience of the Research Branch, an historian,
Helen Lynd, saw this very link between her field and ours. In writing
about "The Nature of Historical Objectivity," she stated:

> . . . we know surely . . . that the future which lies ahead will
> become present, and that hypotheses which we may now make
> can be tested by the course of events. If we are in earnest about

historical objectivity, why do we not more often frame precise hypotheses about what may be the course of events in a given area in a given time? . . . With all that can be said against the recent opinion polls in this country there is this to be said in their favor: they at least made their errors public so that they could be subject to the verification of events.

It is somewhat faint praise to say that we at least make our errors public. We deserve better. But it might be our own mistake that many people are not aware of the many implications inherent in our work. Public opinion research has the unique opportunity to increase self-awareness in the community, a self-awareness which is an important factor in individual as well as in collective health. The great contribution of modern psychoanalysis is that it has given us more understanding of what is going on in ourselves. Public opinion research can do the same for the larger community if it becomes more aware of its potentialities and more eager to develop them. We want all of our intelligent fellow citizens to have respect for the kind of work we are doing. One very good way to get this respect is for us to show that we recognize our common problems and can contribute to their clarification.

CHAPTER 15

PUBLIC OPINION RESEARCH AND THE CLASSICAL TRADITION

Quite possibly the emergence of empirical social science will one day be considered an outstanding feature of the twentieth century. But its birth has not been without travail. Hardest have been its struggles with what we shall call the classical tradition. After all, for two thousand years or more people have thought and written about human and social affairs. Has the empirical trend been an enriching innovation? Has it had a pernicious effect? The matter has certainly been much discussed in recent years.

The debate over the study of public opinion probably provides the best case in point. Since about the beginning of the eighteenth century a steadily increasing amount has been written on this subject by political scientists, by historians and, recently, by sociologists. Toward the beginning of the twentieth century, however, this classical tradition was confronted by the empiricists, who rallied around the notion of attitudes.

The empirical tradition in opinion and attitude research began modestly enough in Germany with simple laboratory experiments on problem solving, in which the notion of "mental sets" was carved out. It gained strength from the work of the Chicago school of sociologists, which brought the study of attitudes and values into play. Immediately thereafter, the psychometricians under the leadership of Thurstone introduced the portentous problem of measurement. And finally came the public opinion research people who, on the one hand, narrowed the

This may be identified as publication No. A-230 of the Bureau of Applied Social Research, Columbia University. Reprinted from *Public Opinion Quarterly*, 21:1 (1957), Columbia University Press, by permission of the publisher.

conceptual range but, on the other, greatly extended the field of practical applications.[1]

About ten years ago the aspiring new science and the classical tradition confronted each other like petulant antagonists. Our professional organizations certainly took cognizance of the matter. Three presidential addresses delivered at AAPOR annual meetings since 1950 have been devoted to the discussion of the relation of public opinion research to history, political theory and social theory, respectively. Nor did exponents of the classical tradition let us forget their claims: Lindsay Rogers made violent attacks, Herbert Blumer articulated his complaints, and the historians showed their contempt for public opinion research by their neglect, speaking about it only occasionally and upon request. This contentious situation has been ably summarized by Bernard Berelson in an unusually thoughtful and informative paper.[2] Were we to review where we stand now, hardly anything could be added to Berelson's remarks, and if we want to discuss how to proceed from here his essay is still the most suggestive.

Berelson sees the present state of public opinion research as the seventh phase of an unfolding process which began with a general feeling that something called public opinion was important. As a result, prominent writers developed broad speculations about it during a second phase of development. In a third phase empirical data were drawn on wherever they were available: magazine articles, speeches, or other documents. The shortcomings of these data led, fourthly, to intense interest in the methodology of the field. At this point a fifth phase set in, during which specialized commercial agencies as well as university institutes took the lead in research. Next, contact was made with intellectual neighbors such as anthropology and psychology. This makes possible the seventh phase, into which we are just entering, a phase in which systematic propositions on public opinion are being developed: public opinion research has become an empirical social science.

If we were dealing with a field like chemistry, or any other natural science, we would be rather confident that any new phase incorporated what was of value in past work; only the historian of

---

[1] For an excellent brief history of the empirical position see Gordon Allport's essay on "Attitudes" in the *Handbook of Psychology*, edited by Carl Murchison (Worcester, Mass.: Clark University Press, 1935).

[2] In *The Study of the Social Sciences*, edited by Leonard White (Chicago: University of Chicago Press, 1956).

natural science must actually turn back to earlier stages. In the social sciences the situation is not as simple. Progress in the clarity of formulations and the respect for evidence is often accompanied, at least temporarily, by an insensitivity to the broader visions and the more general concerns characteristic of an older tradition.

The resulting clash between modern empiricists and spokesmen for the classics recurs in many other fields, and is almost always productive. This is true for three distinct reasons. First, empirical development usually furnishes sharper conceptual tools that enable us to see the classics from a new vantage point: what was only dimly perceived before can now often be discerned with clarity and, as a result, new implications of all sorts can be brought to light. Secondly, the very act of inspecting this classical material brings to our attention ideas which might otherwise have been overlooked, either because of preoccupation with the work of the day, or because empirical researchers are likely to be guided too much by what is a manageable topic at the moment, rather than by what is an important issue. Finally, the classical tradition, as exemplified by Berelson's first two phases, is by no means over. We hope that scholars will keep on thinking about problems with a broad scope, irrespective of whether data or precise modes of reasoning about these problems are available. Theorizing itself can make progress, and the logic of empirical research can contribute to it. Thus, our conceptual task is to bend Berelson's phases into a loop to see how the early phases mesh with the later ones.

COMPLEXITIES OF THE CLASSICAL NOTION

We may profitably begin by paying heed to the discussions centering around the definition of public opinion. It is no coincidence that both Blumer and Rogers make this big point: when the pollsters use the term public opinion, they do not know and cannot say what they mean. Now, in principle, this is not a picayune objection. Definitions, whether implicit or explicit, do indeed have great influence on scholarly activities. In another respect, however, the objection is a strange one. Neither of the two authors proposes a definition. And if one looks at the collection of quotations which Rogers provides in one of his chapters in *The Pollsters*, one is impressed by the fact that few of the classics offered a definition. As a matter of fact, earlier writers over-flow with comments about the mysterious and intangible character of public opinion.

Why is public opinion so difficult to define? It is generally agreed that it was the rise of the middle class, the spread of democratic institutions, the expansion of literacy, and the growth of mass media of communication which gave rise to concern with what was loosely called public opinion. By this term many authors of the classical school referred to people who did not belong to the ruling classes from which the government personnel was recruited and yet claimed a voice in public affairs.[3]

But two matters became puzzling. One is a normative problem: What is the best relation between this "public opinion" and the government? The second is a descriptive problem: How does public opinion actually exercise its influence? The term "public opinion" came into use in just the casual way in which we have introduced it now. While ostensibly a concept, it actually signified only a complicated congeries of observations, practical problems, and normative concerns. It is very much worth while to follow closely this startling piece of intellectual history: how the complexity of a developing historical situation was experienced as a linguistic difficulty because no appropriate logical categories existed to cope with it. In modern parlance one would say that there was a confusion between the subject language dealing with factual observations, and the meta-language dealing with the way the observations should be analyzed.[4]

---

[3] In a book by Emden on the people and the constitution, to which we shall come back later, an interesting appendix on this history of the term "The People" can be found. He shows that at various periods in English history the people were always those who hadn't yet the right to vote but were about to get it at the next turn of parliamentary reform. In Germany, prior to the First World War, the liberal intellectuals were, for all practical purposes, excluded from government. It is therefore not surprising that the German sociologist Toennies defined public opinion as the opinion of experts (*Gelehrte*), the men who thought about public issues but did not have direct access to the centers of power. Cecil S. Emden, *The People and the Constitution*, 2nd edition (London: Oxford University Press, 1956).

[4] Interestingly enough, at least one historian has dealt in detail with a similar difficulty for an earlier epoch. Lucien Febvre makes the point that in 16th century France it was impossible to develop a system of religious scepticism because the language did not provide the necessary intellectual base for it. See his *Le Problème de l'Incroyance en XVI° Siècle*, pp. 383–401.

We shall take our main example of this problem from an essay by the German historian Herman Oncken on "The Historian, the Statesman, and Public Opinion." According to Oncken, the statesman is concerned mainly with the enduring interests of his country; therefore when he writes history he should be mistrusted. The historian is mainly concerned with truth; he should not become too involved in politics or he runs the risk of a conflict of values. "Public opinion"—watch the personification—stands for the evershifting qualities of the human mind not encumbered by either scholastic or national responsibilities.

Oncken goes on to discuss public opinion as follows:

> The vague and fluctuating cannot be understood by being clamped into a formula; certainly not when it is a very characteristic of the concept that it embodies a thousand possibilities of variation. But when all is said and done, everyone knows, if put to it, what public opinion means. If it must be set in words, then it can only appear hedged around by many restricting clauses: public opinion is a complex of similar utterances of larger or smaller segments of society concerning public affairs (1, 2); at times spontaneous, at times artfully manipulated (3); expressed in a multitude of ways, in clubs, assemblies, above all in the press and in journals, or perhaps only in unspoken feelings of each one of us (4); of the common man in the street or of a small circle of the cultured (8); here a true power factor, which statesmen must take into account, or something of no political significance (5); something again to be evaluated differently in every country (5 or 6); sometimes united, rising up like a tidal wave against the government and the experts, sometimes divided, concealing conflicting tendencies (7); at one time bringing out the simple and natural sentiments of the people, at another time being the rowdy thoughtless manifestations of wild instincts (6); always leading and always being led (5, 3); looked down upon by the sophisticated, yet forcing the hands of men (6, 5); contagious like an epidemic (10); capricious, treacherous (9); and power mad (resembling man himself) (6); and then again only a word by which those in power are bewitched (5).[5]

We have inserted numbers after the sentences in this passage so that we can refer to them easily. Now, what is interesting about this bewildering formulation is that it can be disentangled easily as soon as one matches it against what one might call *a complete attitude distribu-*

[5]   *Essays on Politics and History* (Berlin, 1914), Vol. I, pp. 203–204.

tion. It is a commonplace for most of us that polling does not consist merely in finding out how many people are for or against something. We need to know the social and demographic characteristics of the respondents, and we take great care to distinguish between people who are informed and concerned with the problem and those who are not. In other words, a good public opinion poll ends up not with one distribution of attitudes but with many of them for different sectors of the population. In this sense, Oncken undoubtedly gives a definition of public opinion. It is a statistical distribution of utterances (No. 1 and No. 7), expressed by various segments of the population (No. 2), and these segments can and should be classified by the degree of their competence (No. 8).

But intermingled with this definition are a number of empirical problems which are encountered in investigations more complicated than cross-sectional surveys. What factors determine a given attitude distribution at any given time (No. 3)? What effect does it have on statesmen and on the legislative process in general (No. 5)? How are opinions communicated and diffused (No. 10)?

Two further elements in this passage foreshadow topics which are now of great technical concern to us. How should one choose among the various sources and devices which can be used to ascertain an attitude distribution (No. 4)? Oncken mentions only expressions at meetings and in the printed mass media. Today we would add questionnaires and other more systematic research procedures. And we would now translate the phrase "capricious, treacherous" (No. 9) into the terminology of panel techniques, distinguishing people who upon repeated interviews show constant attitudes from those whose attitudes fluctuate. Finally (No. 6), Oncken is obviously concerned with the normative problem of how certain opinions should be evaluated—a matter to which we shall return subsequently.

It is this intertwining of matters of definition and factual problems which is so characteristic of the classical tradition. We are probably faced here by an irreversible development. Now that we have the reality of public opinion polls we will undoubtedly keep on calling public opinion a well analyzed distribution of attitudes. But certainly no one denies that we still know very little about how such complete attitude distributions come into being, and what role they actually play in the governmental process. And under the general heading of the "mass society phenomenon" we certainly keep on worrying about the role it *should* play. Thus the issue of definition resolves itself in an interesting way. The critics of polling are worried that the joy of having found greater conceptual clarity will lead us to forget some of the grave philosophical and empirical problems with which the classics dealt (and well these critics might worry as far as some pollsters are concerned). But what is overlooked is something that has happened often in intellectual history: a new technique has permitted the sorting out of various aspects of a diffused concern and has prepared the way for a more rational approach to its different elements.[6]

THE "PUBLIC OPINION SYSTEM" AS A BRIDGE

There has recently been an interesting effort to find a formulation which will bridge the gap between the classical tradition and the modern turn of events. MacIver has introduced the term "public opinion system."[7] It implies a clear understanding that the multiplicity of facts and problems by which earlier writers were confused can be structured only by distinguishing different dimensions in the concept of public opinion. One is "the opinion alignment," corresponding to the type of information which modern public opinion polls provide. The second dimension is the "structure of communication." This refers to a set of questions with which many sociologists are concerned: the role of associations and leadership; the way in which the mass media and their public influence each other. The third dimension is "the ground of consensus" which takes account of a distinction that has perturbed other writers. Some of the attitudes relevant to the study of specific historical situations are of long enduring character: people are hardly conscious of them, take them for granted, and they come to the fore only in situations where these basic sentiments are some-

---

[6] An interesting parallel could be developed with the invention of the Arabic number system. This was also of a highly technical nature, but it permitted the formulation and later the solution of problems which were unmanageable with the numerical symbolism of antiquity.

[7] Robert M. McIver, *Academic Freedom in the United States* (New York: Columbia University Press, 1954). The "structure of communication" as part of the "public opinion system" is a felicitous way to bring out a feature common to many writers steeped in the classical tradition. Hans Speier, *e.g.* (in the *American Journal of Sociology*, 1950) takes an "historical approach to public opinion;" he mainly provides valuable material on ways in which opinion was formed, for instance, in coffee houses, salons, etc. Only tangentially is he concerned with "opinion alignment."

how threatened. Such "grounds of consensus" should be distinguished from opinions on current controversial issues.

The three components together form the "public opinion system." Two of them are clearly parallel to the two groups of elements we found in Oncken. The third component aims at taking care of another difficulty which has plagued writers during the last century: What aspects of popular sentiment are significant for the analysis of social events? The French social psychologist, Gabriel Tarde,[8] has proposed a three-way distinction: tradition, opinion, and fashion. The German sociologist, Toennies, has paralleled the well known distinction between *Gemeinschaft* and *Gesellschaft* by coordinating religion with the former and opinion with the latter. The problem was always to place "public opinion" somewhere between the rather permanent and subconscious value system of a society and the fleeting reaction of a people to the passing events of the day.

Probably the most productive formulation of this kind has been taken over and developed by historians under the term "climate of *opinion*."[9] This concept became fashionable in the seventeenth century, and acquired prominence through Carl Becker's analysis of the eighteenth century Enlightenment in France. It is often drawn on by historians when they explain why they are not interested in contemporary polling: they assert that we do not investigate quasi-permanent sentiments out of which grow opinions on specific events. A sociologist giving the presidential address at the annual meeting of AAPOR recently acknowledged the existence of the issue by admonishing us to pay more attention to the study of *"mentality."*

RESEARCHING THE "CLIMATE OF OPINION"

Now this is indeed a topic on which the classics have much to teach us. Here they were certainly in their element, because historical

---

[8] His book on *Opinion and the Crowd* has never been translated. It is, however, well summarized in Sorokin's *Survey of European Sociology*. Herbert Blumer's paper on "mass and opinion" is a rendition of the Tarde point of view. (See "The Mass, the Public, and Public Opinion," included in *Reader in Public Opinion and Communication*, edited by Bernard Berelson and Morris Janowitz. Glencoe, Ill.: The Free Press, 1953.)

[9] For some historical references on the term "climate of opinion" see R. K. Merton's essay on *Social Structure and Anomie* (Free Press, Glencoe, Illinois), p. 378, footnote 6.

documents, laws and customs are an important source of insight into climates of opinion. But again, the situation is rather complex. Some of our more sophisticated contemporaries like to answer that we can discover the basic values of any population group by applying methods like projective tests; anthropologists, especially, incline toward this point of view. But such procedures are costly, even on a small scale, and almost unmanageable with a reliable sample. There is, however, a possible compromise; this consists in the development of fairly simple projective *items* which can be handled within the frame of a sampling survey procedure. We have not yet made a great deal of progress along this line, and it is therefore worthwhile to review where we stand.

Some examples can be taken from current studies of *"national character."* We find considerable differences between nations if we ask such questions as: Can people be trusted? Is it possible to change human nature? Should children consult their parents before they get married? Is it dangerous to contradict one's superiors? Should clergymen or teachers be more respected in the community? Would you rather live in another country? What do you approve or disapprove of most in your neighbors?

Within a single country, class differences have been made the object of special investigation. What should children be punished for? How much do adolescents confide in their parents? What decisions does the husband made without consulting his wife? The answers indicate whether the "mores" vary between social strata. In addition, tensions between classes can be investigated using projective items. Are the courts and the police considered impartial, or do they favor the rich? Does a worker or a business man feel he has more in common with people of the same class in other countries, or with people of a different class in his own country? Is it especially interesting to read stories and books about people of one's own class?[10]

Attention should be drawn to findings which deserve to be followed up as the historical scene changes. In a survey conducted in Germany in 1946, a sample of the population was asked whether they considered physical courage an important quality in a man. More than 90 per cent said "no." This probably reflected disillusion with

[10] The general role of such questionnaire items is discussed and exemplified by Jean Stoetzel in an article on the use of polls in social anthropology (UNESCO *International Social Science Bulletin*, Vol. V, No. 3). Stoezel, incidentally, was the first, in his dissertation in France, to stress the relation of history and political science to attitude research.

the Nazi ideology, as well as an effort to guess what the American interviewer wanted to hear. It would be highly instructive to repeat this question a few years after the revival of a German army. If physical courage gains rapidly in prestige, we may have to start worrying about the consequences of German rearmament.

DICEY REVISITED: THE FEED-BACK EFFECT

Behind the battle over definitions, then, lie the serious difficulties involved in selecting problems that are important. The choice of problems, in turn, helps determine what type of techniques need development and what data should be gathered. But there is also another relationship between the style of thinking in a social science and its technical development. The propositions which the classics developed were of a broader and altogether different nature from the more microscopic findings with which we concern ourselves today. Only rarely is the discrepancy small enough to allow the problems of interest in the older tradition to be approached with the techniques and orientations of the newer one.

An exception is found in one of the most famous of the older books: Dicey's *The Relations Between Law and Public Opinion in England During the 19th Century*.[11] The title clearly presents the scope of the work. The author's main interest is in the changes which came about in England between 1840 and 1880. The earlier date represents the peak of *laissez faire*, when efforts were made to minimize governmental interference with economic affairs. By 1880 a great deal of social legislation had been enacted, and an era had started which Dicey dislikes, and interchangeably calls the era of collectivism or of socialism. He not only tries to trace the effects of prevailing trends of opinion on legislation; he also seeks to account for changes in opinion, and formulates a number of "characteristics"—generalizations purporting to explain the ways such changes come about. One of these rules covers what we today might call a feed-back effect: "laws foster or create opinion."

Now it happens that we have by now a considerable amount of data showing that Dicey was right. Cantwell and Hyman have demon-

---

[11] Second edition (London: Macmillan Co., 1920).

strated that immediately after Congress enacts a law there tends to be an increase in the number of people who approve of it. (Their examples range from the debates on enlarging the Supreme Court to the Marshall Plan.) Planck gives us similar data from France, where public opinion polls showed increasing approval of a series of international agreements right after they had been signed. But how did Dicey know this when obviously no such evidence was available to him? Again, a careful reading of his argument permits separation of the "old-fashioned" from the creative and enduring element. On the one hand, he calls his rule an "undeniable truth" and seems to think that he can derive it from basic principles. On the other hand, he supports his contention with examples, developing various interesting ideas in the course of his argument. According to him, most people are sufficiently uncertain enough about their opinion, so that when a law is enacted "its underlying principle derives prestige from its mere recognition by parliament." As a matter of fact, he says, the less clearly this underlying principle is formulated the more likely it is to be accepted. Casual legislation on marginal matters often "surreptitiously introduces ideas which would not be accepted if brought before the attention of the nation" in a more explicit form.

Here is something like the beginning of a theory of how an accomplished fact finds support. Modern notions like "legitimation," "redirection of attention" and "the nature of an unstable equilibrium in a weak opinion structure" can easily be read into Dicey's discussion. But the most interesting fact from our point of view is that in none of the modern publications presenting data on this feed-back phenomenon has there been the slightest effort to explain it. Thus "Dicey revisited" shows a serious gap in our contemporary approach and gives the first hint on ways to fill it.

EMPIRICAL VERIFICATION OF CLASSICAL INSIGHTS

Sensitized by one such episode, we can now again raise the question of where we can find further material to apply to the observations of classical authors. Obviously this material cannot come from one single public opinion poll, and the time periods covered by empirical research are usually too short to be of much help. But we are now beginning to collect *comparative* public opinion data, and these are likely to lead to broader generalizations. The impetus for this has come largely from other fields. The cross-cultural files gathered at Yale by anthropologists have yielded a number of interesting books comparing the social structure or the child rearing practices of a large number of primitive tribes. Industrial sociologists have compared the productivity of work teams under varying conditions of leadership and personal interaction among members. Political scientists have begun to use the forty-eight states as a kind of political laboratory. [A very interesting example is a study which attempts to show that the weaker the two party system is in a state the more influential are the pressure groups.[12]]

Slowly, attitude research is being included in this new movement. One of the ways in which Bryce compared England with America was in regard to political participation. He felt that in each country one could distinguish three strata: those who make political decisions; those who seriously discuss them and influence the decision makers through the press, books, meetings, and so on; and finally, the politically inert and uninterested masses. Bryce thought that the middle group was considerably larger in the United States than in Europe; but he had no evidence.[13] Today it might, however, be supplied by the "index of political activity" constructed by Julian Woodward and Elmo Roper.[14] They obtained information on their respondents' activities in parties and pressure groups, the extent to which they discussed politics with friends, their frequency of voting, etc. Finally, they divided the American population into four groups: Those who were very active (10 per cent), those who were active (17 per cent), those who were inactive (35 per cent), and those who were very inactive (38 per cent). Probably the real decision makers were not included in their sample, but reasonable reading of the questions asked by Woodward and Roper would make the active 27 per cent correspond to Bryce's second group and the inactive 73 per cent to his third. As usual, the division has to be somewhat arbitrary, but such an index, once con-

[12] *"Report of the Committee on American Legislatures,"* Belle Zeller, editor, American Political Science Association. See also P. T. David "Comparative State Politics and the Problem of Party Realignment" in *Research Frontiers in Politics and Government,* The Brookings Institution, 1955.

[13] *American Commonwealth,* Part IV, Ch. X.

[14] "Poltical Activity of American Citizens," *American Political Science Review,* Vol. XIV, December 1950, p. 872.

structed, would be suitable for making comparisons over time and space.

In the international field, our best example comes from an attitude survey which UNESCO carried out in nine countries during 1948.[15] We select one phase of this study because it relates attitudes to an economic index. The respondents in nine countries were asked which country in the world would give them the life they wanted to live. For each of the nine nations the proportion of respondents who named their own country was computed as an "index of satisfaction." This then was related to a set of statistics made available by another agency of the United States showing the "per capita calory supply." The measure of economic well-being had a correlation of .75 with the index of satisfaction. Even the deviations suggest interesting speculations. For instance, Mexico had the lowest food standard but was relatively high in the satisfaction of its citizens. Perhaps this may be explained by the high morale possibly engendered by the revolution and also by an improvement over past standards of living. The Netherlands, on the other hand, were low in satisfaction in spite of a relatively good food supply. This might be due to war devastation, the loss of Indonesia, or the high population density in Holland.

We now must return to one element in the picture which we bypassed before. The classical tradition is very much concerned with the problem of what the proper relation between public opinion and democratic government *should be*. Rogers' most valid objection against contemporary pollsters is exactly on this issue: they either do not think about it or they make naive statements to the effect that the government should actually do what the public opinion polls tell them the people want. This is a normative problem, and therefore it is important to know what the relation between the discussion of values and the factual findings of empirical research can be. The more we know about the probable consequences of various measures, the more certain can we be as to whether they will realize the values we strive for, and the more wisely can we choose among the conflicting values themselves.[16]

In the earlier writings on public opinion, value problems such as

[15] Buchanan and Cantril, *How Nations See Each Other*, Urbana: Univ. of Ill. Press, 1953.

[16] While there is agreement on the general logic of the problem, little work has been done to analyze in detail how arguments are actually supported by facts in the discussion of social affairs. Obviously this is not identical with the rule

this one were discussed in a pseudo-factual language which made communication between generations especially difficult. Consider, for example, the first major American book on the topic: A. Lawrence Lowell, *Public Opinion and Popular Government.*[17] In the initial eighty pages or so of this book, Lowell proposes to find out what "true" opinion is. The first reaction of a modern reader is to think the question absurd (what is true electricity?), and to discard the book. This, however, would be a mistake. For, upon considerable effort, one learns that by "true" Lowell means the kind of public opinion which a democratic government should take into account.

Following this lead, one discovers that Lowell has three very different criteria of "true" public opinion. In modern terminology they are: (a) opinions should count only after proper general discussion, and only those people should be included who have given the matter considerable thought. Applied to current polling practices, this means that while thoughtful persons can readily be identified by good polls, the *timing* of polls, if they are to be used by government officials, raises quite a number of important problems. (b) Neither elections nor referenda really ascertain people's attitudes properly; the former fail because they are not centered around issues, and the latter because we do not know whether the "right" (informed) people participate. Clearly, Lowell would have welcomed polls if properly analyzed and interpreted. (c) Certain topics should never be the subject of legislation and, therefore, cannot be objects of "true" public opinion; religion is an example specifically mentioned by the American constitution. Here the intricate decision of excluding certain topics confronts us. Should "true" opinion in these areas be ascertained by a public opinion poll, historical analysis of the tradition of a country, or by general philosophical consideration? Lowell does not raise or answer these questions, but he suggests interesting problems about what people consider private and what they consider public issues under various circumstances.

---

of formal logic. But we also do not mean the misuses of propaganda, which have been described by content analysts. What we have in mind is the systematic description of efforts to come to reasonable conclusions from necessarily insufficient data. The problem is similar to the question of how policy decisions are related to factual information in government and business. This has not been well investigated either.

[17] (New York, 1913.)

PUBLIC OPINION AND GOVERNMENT POLICY

The relationship of opinion to government policy has been discussed in another type of literature, to which we could profitably pay
more attention than we have previously. There are writers who try to
approach normative questions by the careful analysis of historical
events where the consequences of measure actually taken were first
described and then judged. Before considering concrete examples, attention should be drawn to the historical aspect of the problem itself.
Emden's history[18] reveals the big changes which came about in the
British climate of opinion on such matters. A century-and-a-half ago,
for instance, it was illegal to publish any reports on the debates of the
British parliament. After a while summaries were permissible, but the
votes of individual members could not be published. Only since 1845,
and after serious debate, were official reports issued. Conversely, up
to about 1880 it was considered inadmissible for politicians, including
cabinet ministers, to address the population at large. They could appeal
to their own constituencies, but otherwise only parliament itself was
thought to be the proper place for debate.[19]

Three detailed monographic studies have analyzed the relation
between governmental policy and contemporary expression of opinion
in an especially interesting way. One was published in 1886 and is often
quoted, but it is rarely read because of its inordinate length.[20] Its setting is the Russian-Turkish conflict in the late 1870's which led up to
the Congress of Berlin. The issue between the two countries was the
protection of the Christian population of the Balkans, then part of the
Turkish Empire. According to the author, the British people were for

---

[18] See footnote 3. This book contains much interesting information, for instance, the history of petitions in the 19th century (pp. 74 ff). Petitions fell out
of usage because it was impossible to know which sector of the population the
signers represented. A reading of the controversy, almost a hundred years old,
shows that everyone was groping for something like representative sampling carried out by politically neutral agencies.

[19] Even today the English tradition is quite different from the American. If
a law is under discussion in Congress radio and television overflow with panel
debates and press interviews on the issue. The British Broadcasting Corporation
does not permit a discussion of laws within a period of two weeks prior to a
parliamentary debate to prevent the influence of the public voice on the deliberations of the legislature.

[20] Geo. C. Thompson, *Public Opinion and Lord Beaconsfield 1875–1880*,
(London: Macmillan Co., 1886).

the liberation of the Balkan provinces, a wish which corresponded to the demands of the Russian Government. Disraeli (Lord Beaconsfield) feared an extension of Russian influence into Europe, and his policy was essentially to help the Turks. Thus a situation arose in which the British government acted avowedly against the advice of the majority of the British press and of most civic organizations concerned with foreign affairs. Thompson gives a vividly documented description of the dramatic interplay of the two partners to the conflict: how events sometimes strengthened the one and sometimes the other and how they reacted to each other's moves. The normative problem with which the author is concerned is whether even if a government has the majority support of its own party in parliament, it shall be required to resign when there are unmistakable signs that the population at large does not agree with its policy. In the 1880's this was not yet the British tradition; it probably would be today.

The data on which Thompson drew are speeches, resolutions, editorials, and similar documents. His contribution consists in the minute analysis of the different phases of the conflict. But he has to look at the matter, so to say, from the outside; he has no information on how the decisions were made in either the British cabinet or in the various groups which organized what he called the "agitations," the anti-Turkish movement.

A much more recent book by Lynn M. Case is outstanding because it has just this kind of information.[21] Under the second Empire the French government had a detailed system for obtaining reports on public opinion from its administrative officials in all parts of the country. These were not the usual reports of the Secret Police, denouncing individuals, but rather were detached impressions of how various social groups responded to the policy of Napoleon III.[22] In times of crisis these reports came in as often as once a week. Case not only gives a very good picture of these interesting reports; he also tells of the effect they had on the foreign policy of the Second Empire, citing minutes of cabinet meetings during which these reports were discussed and used as arguments by the participants.

---

[21] *French Opinion on War and Diplomacy During the Second Empire,* University of Pennsylvania Press, 1954.

[22] In the historical part of his book, Toennies has a section on France (pp. 375–401). He quotes there a letter by Mirabeau urging Louis XVI to set up just this kind of an organization. Whether the reporting system of Napoleon III goes back to these early stages cannot be seen from Case's book.

This book includes one dramatic episode in which the normative implication comes out with particular clarity. In 1866, Napoleon wanted to interfere in the Austro-Prussian War, in order to avoid a Prussian victory. Public opinion reports, however, indicated such a strong desire in the population for peace and so much danger of a revolution in case of war that the group in the cabinet which was against intervention prevailed. As a result, Prussia became so powerful that four years later it could provoke war with France which, in turn, led to the defeat of Napoleon III and to the end of his regime. Case calls into doubt the wisdom of having a foreign policy guided by public opinion.[23]

Finally, we have W. P. Davison's study of the Berlin Airlift. There he reports actual polling data from Berlin cross-sections and interviews with policy makers on various levels among Americans as well as Germans. He shows how public reaction went from incredulity through hesitancy to a decision to stick it out on the side of the Western powers. Davison stresses a complex interplay: American determination was strengthened by favorable German attitudes; in turn, the Airlift increased the German expectation that the Allies would not desert them and that the Russians would not be able to take over the city. This made many cautious souls willing to take part openly in anti-communist activities. The main practical applications of this study turn on the relation of leadership and public opinion in a crisis; because of the need for swift action, Davison feels that those in command of the administrative machinery have to take chances and trust that the people at large will support them eventually.[24]

NEED FOR A CLASSICAL-EMPIRICAL SYNTHESIS

In sum, valuable thinking on the relation between governmental decision and public opinion is available. It falls short of an ideal type of

---

[23] He takes a position quite similar to that of Almond and Speier in their writings on the topic.

[24] In its yet unpublished form the study is the first to combine poll data with traditional historical analysis. A preliminary summary of some of the findings is available from a paper identified as P-851, The RAND Corporation, Santa Monica, California.

research only insofar as the information on public opinion itself is more or less inferential. Undoubtedly, it will take a considerable length of time before we have a joining of the two trends: a careful analysis in the classical tradition supported by modern empirical data. Still, it does not seem unjustified to conclude these remarks in a somewhat Utopian mood. During a debate on the relation between history and public opinion, a historian remarked that even in the future his colleagues will not need attitude studies; they will know what actually has happened and from that they can infer what "effective public opinion" was at the time. However, the French economic historian Fernand Braudel provides us with the pertinent rejoinder:

> Victorious events come about as a result of many possibilities, often contradictory, among which life finally has made its choice. For one possibility which actually is realized innumerable others have drowned. These are the ones which have left little trace for the historians. And yet it is necessary to give them their place because the losing movements are forces which have at every moment affected the final outcome, sometimes by retarding and sometimes by speeding up its development. The historian should also be concerned with the opposing elements, its incipient waves which at the time were not easily arrested. Ideas which couldn't be realized at one time still might have made the subsequent victory of another idea possible.[25]

In other words, if an event is the result of several potential trends, none of which have been fully realized, then it cannot be really understood unless the "tendencies" are known. It is illogical to reverse the analysis and to derive the potential from the actual, because various combinations of trends might have led to the same outcome. Only attitude data can provide the components which produced the final result.

Thus, from all sides the need for broad gauge opinion studies becomes increasingly obvious. But the complexity of this task also becomes more evident. While modern empiricists have reason to be pleased with their progress, there is no doubt that they can gain much from close contact with the classical tradition. We should not be deterred by the classicists' sometimes out-moded style of reasoning. The essence of progress, it has been said, consists in leaving the ashes and taking the flames from the altars of one's forebears.

[25] From a discussion remark on "historical economics" contributed to the French *Revue Economique*, 1952.

Part Five

Organizational Issues

CHAPTER 16

THE SOCIOLOGY OF EMPIRICAL
SOCIAL RESEARCH

To choose a topic for a presidential address is a rather frightening experience. More irrevocable than marriage, more self-revealing than a dream, it forces one to assign priorities to a variety of interests which have long remained lazily undecided. Between the time when the American Sociological Society was organized in 1906 and the first world war, its presidents were more fortunate. Elected for two years, they could give two addresses. One was usually devoted to a specific sociological problem that concerned them, and the other to a kind of state of the union message, in which they discussed matters currently of concern to our profession at large. At first, I thought I would have to make a choice between the two types. Recently I completed a preliminary survey of organized research in this country wherein I investigated where we stand with respect to our research centers, social relations laboratories, our bureaus of applied social research. This seemed to me an urgent professional problem and a good topic for tonight's discussion. But I also had a theoretical candidate. You all know the old saying: those who can, do; those who cannot, teach; and those who have nothing to teach, become methodologists. I always felt that this is an unfair misunderstanding of methodology,

Reprinted from *American Sociological Review*, 27:6 (1962), by permission of the publisher. Presented as the presidential address at the fifty-seventh annual meeting of the American Sociological Association, Washington, D.C., September 1, 1962. The author has had the help of many friends and colleagues during the several revisions of this address. Special thanks are due to Jane Hauser, Freda von Pawloff, Professors Bailyn, Bell, and Merton, and Dr. Herbert Menzel.

and tonight's occasion seemed an opportunity for clarification. I finally decided to combine the two topics and to center my remarks on the interrelation between the organization of social research and methodology. This involves the following five points:

1) Empirical research requires a specific kind of organization which I shall call "institutes." These institutes in turn generate a bent of mind, a way of reflecting on research procedures which I shall call "methodology."

2) Such induced sensitivity to methodology can be fruitful for general sociological analysis in areas far afield from what we think of as empirical studies.

3) To understand the contemporary scene it is necessary to provide some facts and raise additional questions on the history of empirical social research in Europe, as well as in the United States.

4) Today's social research institutes in this country are a very recent development, raise interesting organizational problems of their own, and have broad implications for the teaching of sociology and, perhaps, even for the future of our university administration in general.

5) The substantive work these institutes carry out needs to, and soon will, undergo a considerable broadening which I shall specify at the end of my remarks.

There is not time enough to elaborate any of these points in detail. Consequently, I shall occasionally use, as a device for speedier communication, illustrations taken from my own academic career. I have repeatedly advocated that sociologists should give accounts of the way their interests and writings actually develop and I am ready, therefore, to take my own prescription and trace back some of the things you know I stand for. In a way, this is an effort to draw generalizations from a single case. And my first point is indeed best introduced by a personal reminiscence.

THE METHODOLOGY/—INSTITUTE SYNDROME

When I joined the staff of the University of Vienna, some thirty-five years ago, one of my first assignments was to review a large body of data on the occupational choices of young people. It was easy to see the regularities of their choices. They were linked with social stratification, and permitted one to interpret age differences in terms of a general theory of adolescence. The available studies also contained many tabulations of the *reasons* for the choices. But this material was contradictory; no sense could be made of it. My attention shifted to the problem of what was wrong with the mode of investigation. And here I noticed an ambiguity in the question "why." Some youngsters answered in terms of the influences to which they had been subjected, while others talked about the attractive features of the jobs under consideration. Still others referred to broader personal goals which they hoped would be served by a particular occupation. An investigator's lack of skill in the art of asking "why" led to meaningless statistical results.

The study was originally inspired by a program of research on adolescents laid out by my Viennese teacher, Charlotte Bühler. But, in my own biography, it led to a sequence of studies on choices: how could one find out why people bought one product rather than another, why they voted the way they did, why they listened to certain radio programs, and so forth. Ever since, I have continued to search for sound ways for making empirical studies of action. When can one use retrospective interviews? When is it better to use panel studies (repeated observations of people in the process of choice)? When are decisions best understood by considering the social context—the school, the factory or other organizations—within which the choice was made? And in all this, of course, I find myself puzzled by a theory of action where no one ever acts, and by modern mathematical decision theory where people act on probabilities of future events and utilities of outcomes, but where no one ever asks from which social and experiential background these estimates arise.

A program for the empirical study of action required a staff of collaborators trained to collect and analyze data whenever a research opportunity offered itself. I obtained permission from my academic superiors to create, in Vienna, a research center very similar to the kind of American institutes I shall discuss presently. It antedates, as far as I know, all such university institutions in this country except the one at the University of North Carolina created by Howard Odum. Now, supervising even a small research staff makes one acutely aware of the differences between various elements of a research operation and of the need to integrate them into a final product. Some assistants are best at detailed interviews, others are gifted in the handling of statistical tables, still others are especially good at searching for possible contributions from existing literature. The different roles must be made explicit; each has to know what is expected of him and how his task is related to the work of the others. Thus, staff instruction quickly turns into methodological explication. Maintaining the intellectual standards of an institute is tantamount to codifying empirical social research as an autonomous intellectual world.

But this is not the end of the story. When one is responsible for directing research, abstract sociological issues turn into down-to-earth challenges. It is not enough to develop constructive typologies; one must decide under which type a particular person or group actually should be classified. One cannot just ponder over the nature of causality; one must give concrete evidence as to why a certain election was won or lost. At this point the tables are often turned. The research operation can provide the model which helps to clarify and unify problems that arise in spheres of inquiry far removed from empirical social research in its narrower sense. And this is my second point: Methodology can often give aid to social theory.

RELATIONS BETWEEN METHODOLOGY AND SOCIAL THEORY

Permit me to consider with you one example of the relation between methodology and social theory. Many of you, I am sure, are acquainted with the notion of an attribute space. It starts with the observation that objects can be described along a number of dimensions. Think, for example, of an IBM card on which people are described by sex, race, education, etc. In such a space, regions can be combined to form typologies. Thus sex and employment status permit many combinations; but for certain purposes it makes sense to distinguish just three; men, irrespective of their work, and women according to whether they are housewives or work outside.

This reduction of a combinatorial system of attributes to a smaller number of types has a counterpart which I have called a *substruction*. Beginning with a typology, or simply a list of objects, we ask ourselves in what way they have originated from an attribute space. The linguists do that today. They take the basic sounds of languages— the phonemes—and look for the minimum number of attributes of which these phonemes are combinations. Such a "binary description" of language leads to characteristics such as nasal/oral, strident/mellow, tense/lax. Any real language occupies only certain regions of the attribute space and leaves others empty.

In empirical social research we come across this substruction whenever we wish systematically to classify people or groups according to a proposed typology. My first encounter with this problem occurred when I worked with Erich Fromm on a study of authority in European families. He had distinguished four types: complete authority, simple authority, lack of authority, and rebellion. In order to use his ideas for an empirical study, we had to introduce criteria or, more specifically, questionnaire items along two dimensions: the degree of authority the parents wanted to exercise and how much of it their children accepted. Each of the two dimensions was divided into three levels, giving nine combinations. Seven of them were easily reduced to Fromm's types, but two of them forced us to acknowledge a fifth type: families in which the children wanted more authority than the parents were inclined to impose. Substruction helped us discover a new type.

The relation between typologies and attribute spaces will be obvious to anyone who has converted people into questionnaires and finally into cross-tabulations. But what matters most now is the way such a formal observation clarifies more general sociological issues. You will remember that Max Weber gave ten criteria for a pure bureaucracy. We cannot deal tonight with a ten dimensional space, so suppose we arbitrarily select two of the ten criteria. Each officer has a clearly defined sphere of competence and he is appointed on the basis of technical qualification. This gives a two dimensional space you can visualize easily as a traditional system of x-y coordinates drawn on a piece of paper. Actual organizations will be points in this system according to the degree to which they exhibit the two characteristics, which we shall assume have been scaled from 0 to 5. And as a free gift we now know what an ideal type is: it is the region in the upper right corner, around the point with the coordinates 5/5.

How about the diagonally opposite point, the one with the coordinates 0/0? No one, as far as I know, has worked out in detail what a non-bureaucracy looks like. But in another area the relation of these two points is very familiar. I refer to Toennies' "Gemeinschaft and Gesellschaft," Durkheim's "Société Mécanique and Organique," Becker's "Sacred and Secular Society," and Redfield's "Folk and Urban Continuum." The most seminal effort to provide a substruction for this typology is Parsons' "Pattern Variables." For the sake of simplicity, let us take two of the many dimensions which have been proposed for this typology—say, isolation and social homogeneity. Assume that they are somehow measured and entered respectively on the two axes. Then the pure folk society is at 0/0 and the pure urban mass society is diagonally opposite at 5/5. Now a good model is supposed to generate more ideas than were put into it to begin with, and this one does. Our two corner points can be connected by any number of lines that can vary in shape and length. They turn out to be the paths along which the transition from the traditional to the modern social system can be found. I suggest to you an instructive parlor game. Take your favorite theory of social change—telling how one aspect of society affects other social dimensions—and translate it into lines connecting points in an attribute space. While you will not obtain an empirical answer, you will be helped by the clearer formulation of problems and by seeing unexpected connections between possible solutions.

I hope the example I have given has helped to back up the second item in the five point plan which guides me tonight. The technical and organizational nature of empirical social research leads to formal ideas, to distinctions and interconnections relevant for many sociological pursuits well beyond the realm of strictly empirical research. My position is akin to the kind of sociology of knowledge which Marxists employ when they stress that new tools of production are often reflected in new ways of intellectual analysis. I look at empirical research as an activity which is especially conductive to x-raying the anatomy, the basic logical framework of general social inquiry. This is, of course, not the only way to look at the situation. One could focus on the content of the empirical studies produced in recent years, and my concluding remarks are devoted to this substantive aspect. But let me elaborate for a moment on the context in which I see my formal emphasis—formal both in intellectual and in institutional terms. I have always been most curious about the *process* of production, the *structure* of a piece of work, the *way* people reach a specific intellectual goal. As an amateur musician, I find my enjoyment of music considerably enhanced if an expert explains the theoretical structure of a quartet. Knowing little about *belles lettres*, I am indebted to the "new criticism" because its internal analysis of a piece of writing opens an experience to which I would not otherwise have access. This interest in "explications" was reinforced during my student days. It was in that period that the theory of relativity had come to the fore. We were greatly impressed by the fact that it came about partly through the conceptual clarification of basic notions. I remember vividly the delight in discovering that it is not obviously clear what is meant when one says that two events, one on the sun and one on earth, occur "simultaneously." I should add that reading a mathematical paper reinforces this tendency. Hours are spent on one page, trying first to guess what the author is driving at, then why he is concerned with this objective, and, finally, the understanding of his proof. (Proofs are usually presented in a direction opposite from the way in which a theorem was originally discovered.)

In my teaching, I try to convey this mood to students in various ways. We read empirical research closely and try to reconstruct how the author was led from one step to the next: what data he might have inspected but not reported; how the order of his final presentation might have developed from an originally vague and quite different imagery. Often an hour is spent just on analyzing a table of contents. It comes very close to what the French call *"explication de texte,"* a training which gives them such great expressive strength. Dilthey's notion of hermeneutics, his general principles for interpreting philosophical systems, is echoed in this effort to make students understand that writing a term paper and publishing a book have more in common than they suppose. I have no evidence for the educational value of this methodological approach, but this does not keep me from being very convinced of its merits.

I now want to turn to some institutional problems and consequences which are indigenous to the way empirical studies are typically set up in contemporary American universities. This is more easily explained if I first insert some remarks on the history of social research.

A NOTE ON HISTORY OF SOCIAL RESEARCH

There are two leading facts in this history. First, its origins lay in early modern Europe (it may be dated as far back as the Seventeenth Century), but in Europe it failed to develop as a regular branch of professional sociology. Secondly, in the United States, where it was destined to flourish, it existed long before it found organizational setting in our universities. Permit me to digress sufficiently to explain some of the remarkable circumstances these bare generalizations cover.

A series of studies now under way at Columbia University shows that practically all modern empirical techniques—our Latin American friends sometimes summarize them as Yankee Sociology—were developed in Europe. Sampling methods were derived as a sequence to Booth's survey of life and labor in London. Factor analysis was invented by the Englishman, Spearman. Family research, with special emphasis on quantification, came of age with the French mineralogist, LePlay. Gabriel Tarde advocated attitude measurement and communications research. (Looking at the contemporary French scene, one might well speak of his posthumous victory in his epic battle with Durkheim.) The idea of applying mathematical models to voting was elaborately worked out by Condorcet during the French Revolution. His contemporaries, Laplace and Lavoisier, conducted social surveys for the Revolutionary Government, and their student, the Belgian, Quetelet, finally and firmly established empirical social research under the title of *"physique sociale."* He did this, incidentally, to the great regret of Comte, who claimed that he had invented the term and now had to substitute for it a much less desirable linguistic concoction, to wit, sociology. In Italy, during the first part of our century, Niceforo developed clear ideas on the use of measurement in social and psychological problems, brilliantly summarized in his book on the measurement of progress. The Germans could claim a number of founding fathers: Max Weber was periodically enthusiastic about quantification, making many computations himself; Toennies invented a correlation coefficient of his own; and, during Easter vacations, von Wiese regularly took his students to villages so that they could see his concepts about social relations acted out in peasant families.

And yet, before 1933, nowhere in Western Europe, did empirical research acquire prestige, a home in universities, financial support, textbooks, or enough devotees to form what I should like to call a critical mass: the number of people sufficient to maintain each other's interest by providing a reciprocal reference group. What accounts for this discontinuity in European sociology? All of these countries have today a large, albeit somewhat ambivalent, interest in empirical research, but why is it now experienced as an American invasion rather than what it is in reality: a revival of an autonomous European development? I do not know. Perhaps the ravages of two wars and the intervening fascist period kept western European sociology from taking the "operational jump" for which it was ready; or perhaps structural features of university life or of the general intellectual climate in Europe made it necessary for the breakthrough to come in a new country. Only a very careful analysis of the material published around 1930, here and in Western Europe, could give an answer.

In the United States another historical problem is puzzling. We know that concern with underprivileged groups led to various fact-finding efforts here, such as the work of the American Social Science Association around 1870, and the survey movement which began at the turn of the century and was later supported by the Russell Sage Foundation. But why did it take so long for the universities to find their proper place in this broad trend? The question will not be fully answered but the issue is well illustrated by the efforts of the University of Chicago to develop means by which ameliorative activities in the community and the research interests of academia could join forces. The facts I shall summarize have been assembled by Mr. Vernon Dibble as part of the Columbia University history program mentioned before.

You all know of Albion Small, the founder of the *American Journal of Sociology*, and one of our early presidents. He began his chairmanship of the Department of Sociology at the University of Chicago in 1893. One of the professors in this Department, a former minister, was appointed because of his knowledge, based on previous activities, of the needs of the Chicago community. I refer to Charles R. Henderson, who, indeed, lived up to everyone's expectations. He wrote manuals for social workers on how to collect information that would help advance social legislation; he organized networks of social informants; he trained students who later became prominent in their own right. But, at that time in Chicago, it was assumed that the role of the University was to help the community solve its problems; the sociologist was not to carry out research himself. This was not a meaningful division of labor, however, and Henderson was soon forced to collect and analyze his own data. And yet the University structure had made no provision for this turn of affairs. Consequently, one day, Henderson, in a mood of desperation, wrote Albion Small that he just had to have an assistant at $100 a month. He listed ten arguments in favor of this revolutionary idea. As a typical illustration let me quote his argument No. 8:

> My department of study suffers unjustly in comparison with those of the physical sciences, with their costly equipment and corps of permanent assistants. I do not hope to be put on an equality with them, nor do I wish for them any diminution of equipment, but I want a little chance to demonstrate what can be done for the science of human welfare and furtherance of the higher life, with even a meagre supply of help.

The typewritten letter, dated February 1902, has a handwritten postscript: "Since writing the above I have learned that a similar arrangement to this proposal has been successfully tried at Columbia by Professor Giddings."

In March, Small wrote a three page letter to President Harper supporting Henderson's request as "part of a large program which we are all feeling that it is time to work out." This large program was empirical sociological research which would entitle "the University of Chicago to the leading place in that subject in the world, at least until some of the European universities shall realize the readjustment of interests that is going on."

Henderson obtained his assistant, but Small did not realize his great design. In 1914, a committee wrote a sixty page report on the need for a "bureau of social research" in Chicago. The bureau was not visualized as a University activity. The plan was sponsored by the City Club of Chicago and signed by a committee of four, consisting of three businessmen and George Herbert Mead. As far as I can tell, it was never implemented.

In 1922, Small was willing to join forces with a man with whom he shared nothing but an institutional conviction. The then dean of the Business School at Chicago proposed a central research institute, ignoring all departmental divisions. In a letter to the president, Small not only approved the idea but stated that "It makes my heart bleed to fear that our own social science group will miss its birthright by failure to qualify for the opportunity." And he added his own version of how the system would work:

> There should be "genuine commissions of inquiry" with a hierarchical order of work: graduate students would do the "as-

sorting of materials and of organizing them in accordance with the findings of their more experienced seniors." But, so that this not become mere routine, "regular sessions of the seniors would be held with the graduate students present for thrashing out all the questions of principle involved." He wanted a cumulative continuity of such work. "The minutes of each inquiry, properly filed and indexed in the archives of the institution, would form an object lesson in the methodology of that type of inquiry and would be permanently instructive, both as to mistakes to be avoided in subsequent inquiries, and as to methods which proved to be useful. All this in addition to the substantive results of the investigation.

But even in 1922, the University was not ready for such a radical step. As a matter of fact, at about the same time, they refused a similar institute which Merriam had proposed for political science.

But, short of this, Small made great strides. He succeeded, often in the face of great resistance, in appointing men like Robert Park who introduced the guided dissertation into the Department of Sociology. Until then, the doctoral candidate followed the German pattern; he chose his topic, wrote his thesis in solitary confinement, and presented the final product to a professor who judged its intellectual merits. In Chicago in the 1920's the dissertation became part of a general program and was carried out in close contact with the sponsor. This was facilitated by Beardsley Ruml who deliberately used the Spellman Fund to make empirical research a regular part of the graduate curriculum.

That was the time when the sociological work being done at Chicago was prominent in American Sociology. But, after the initiative of the great pioneers like Park, Burgess, Thomas, and Ogburn, this dominance waned. It is my guess that a more formal organization for social research would have extended the influence of these great Chicago leaders even after other graduate schools began to make their bid.

Small always stressed that empirical research did not concern him personally, but that the future of sociology as a discipline depended upon the discovery of an appropriate institutional form for its exercise. It is interesting, incidentally, that this part of his work is nowhere mentioned in the many papers written about him. And yet, it is to his great credit, as a sociologist, that he sensed something which has since been documented by historical investigation. Turning points in higher education have often hinged on some institutional innovation. The medieval universities became permanent institutions once Paris established the disputation as a way of training students. The humanist revolution revolved around the scrutiny of classical texts. The idea of the modern university began with the Berlin seminar, a group of students who did more than just listen, who, in fact, also conducted their own research under the guidance of a master. And the contemporary sciences—of nature as well as of society—required the laboratory.

It took fifty years before we began to face this problem realistically in sociology, and much research will be needed to clarify what delayed and what finally led to the social research institute becoming imbedded in the university structure. Among the early handicaps one can easily think of are reasons like these: too few graduate students to form teams with division of labor; lack of seniors who had themselves risen from the ranks of empirical research; and, of course, lack of funds. But only monographic studies of places like North Carolina, Wisconsin, and Columbia will bring light onto the issue. Let me now turn to a review of the contemporary scene.

THE SOCIAL RESEARCH INSTITUTE IN THE AMERICAN UNIVERSITY

There are about one hundred universities in the United States which today give at least ten PhD's in all fields combined, including the natural sciences. Slightly less than two-thirds of these institutions have made arrangements to carry out social research. We draw our definition rather liberally: it can be either a unit specifically attached to a Department of Sociology; or an interdepartmental setup including the Department of Sociology; or, finally, a fairly permanent project to which at least one sociologist is attached, even though the Department does not participate officially. The programs of these agencies are either *specialized*, or they cover a broad range of topics and are, so to say, *general purpose* units. The former outnumber the latter by more than two to one. The "general purpose" units, in turn, divide rather evenly into those which are *autonomous*, in the sense that they develop their own programs, and those which see themselves mainly as *facilitating* the research activities of individual faculty members. The distinction is somewhat difficult to make because academic tradition favors the rhetoric of facilitation, while the inner dynamics of such institutes press towards increasing autonomy and self-direction.

You are all aware of the controversies which have grown up around these institutes. On the positive side, we may note the following. They provide technical training to graduate students who are empirically inclined; the projects give students opportunities for closer contact with senior sociologists; the data collected for practical purposes furnish material for dissertations through more detailed study, or what is sometimes called secondary analysis; the members of a Department with an effective institute can give substance to their lectures with an enviable array of actual data; skills of intellectual cooperation and division of labor are developed; chances for early publications by younger sociologists are enhanced.

On the other side of the debate, the argument goes about as follows. Students who receive most of their training on organized projects become one-sided; instead of developing interests of their own, they become mercenaries of their employers; where institutes become influential, important sociological problems are neglected because they do not lend themselves to study by the "research machinery"; people who work best on their own find themselves without support and are regarded as outsiders.

The situation, as I see it, is promising but confused. We allow these institutes to develop without giving them permanent support, without integrating them into the general university structure, without even really knowing what is going on outside our immediate academic environment. As a bare minimum it is imperative that a more detailed study of the current situation be carried out. This would hopefully lead to recommendations for university administrators, for members of our own Association, and for all others concerned with the basic problem of how the avalanche of empirical social research can be fitted into current educational activities without having careless institutional improvisations destroy important traditional values or hinder creative new developments. True, we have no perfect formula for incorporating institutes into our graduate education. But pluralism is not the same as anarchy, and it is anarchy with which we are faced at the moment. Some form of permanent core support, assimilation of teaching and of institute positions, a better planned division of the students' time between lectures and project research, a closer supervision of institute activities by educational officers, more explicit infusion of social theory into the work of the institutes—all this waits for a systematic discussion and for a document which may perform the service which the Flexner report rendered to medical education fifty years ago.

In such a report the role of the institute director will have to figure prominently. Let me place him in a broader framework. We are confronted, nowadays, in our universities, with a serious problem which can be classified as an "academic power vacuum." When graduate education in this country began, no one doubted that the university president was an important figure. Gilman at Johns Hopkins and White at Cornell were intellectual as well as administrative leaders. Stanley Hall at Clark was impressive both as a president and as a psychologist. Inversely, individual professors were deeply involved in organizational innovation. John W. Burgess forced the creation of a graduate faculty upon the Columbia trustees. In his autobiography he describes movingly what this meant to him as a teacher and scholar. Silliman sacrificed his private fortune to establish a chemical laboratory in his home and finally convinced the trustees at Yale that natural sciences were not a spiritual threat to young Americans.

Today, however, we witness a dangerous divergence: academic freedom is more and more interpreted in such a way as to keep the administration out of any truly academic affairs; and the faculty, in turn, has come to consider administration beneath its dignity. But educational innovations are, by definition, intellectual as well as administrative tasks. And, so, they have fallen into a no-man's land: the President and his staff wait for the faculty to take the initiative; the professors on their side consider that such matters would take time away from their true scholarly pursuits. As a result, many of our universities have a dangerously low level of institutional development.

One institutional consequence of research institutes is that they inevitably train men who are able and willing to combine intellectual and administrative leadership. An institute director, even if his unit only facilitates faculty research, must train a staff able to advise on important research functions. It is not impossible that, on specific topics, the collective experience of the institute staff exceeds the skills of the individual faculty member. One who has lived with scores of questionnaires can help write a better questionnaire on a subject matter in which he is not expert. Having helped to dig up documents and sources of data on many subjects makes for greater efficiency even on a topic not previously treated. In an autonomous unit this is even more pronounced. Here the staff carries out a self-contained work schedule. A hierarchy is needed, proceeding often from assistants to project supervisors, to program director, and, finally, to the director himself. The latter is at least responsible for reports and publications. But the director is also concerned with maintaining what is sometimes called the "image" of his operation. Its prestige, its attraction for staff and students, and its appeal for support are self-generated, not derived only from the reputation of the teaching departments. The professional staff sees its future career closely bound up with the destiny of the unit, a fact which sometimes makes for challenging problems in human organization.

At the same time, the director must develop the coordinating skills so necessary in a modern university. Often the place of his unit in the organization chart is not well defined. The novelty of the whole idea makes for instability and requires considerable institutional creativity. And, finally, we should frankly face the fact that in our system of higher education the matching of budgetary funds with substantive intellectual interests is a characteristic and enduring problem. The institute director knows the skills and interests of the faculty members, and he brings men and money together. This is not badly described as the role of "idea broker." Often he will have to work hard to obtain funds for a more unusual research idea suggested to him; at other times a possible grant looks so attractive that he will try to discover, among some of his faculty colleagues, what he would diplomatically call a "latent interest."

I am afraid this is not the appropriate forum for reforming university presidents. But I can at least try to convince some of you that directing a research institute is no more in conflict with scholarly work than is teaching. The director is faced with a variety of research problems which permit him to try out his intellectual taste and skills, while the individual scholar might find himself committed to a study prematurely chosen. The multitude of data passing through the director's hands considerably broadens his experience. Staff conferences provide a unique sounding board for new ideas. Even negotiations for grants open vistas into other worlds which a sociologist can turn to great advantage in his own work. Undoubtedly not every personality type is suited for this role, and even the right type of man needs proper training. But the opportunities for self-expression and for intellectual growth are considerable, and sociologists, in particular, should not be misled by the prevalent stereotype of administration.

I have now sketched out my main theme: empirical social research tends toward an organizational form of work which has two consequences: on an intellectual level, it forces one to be explicit about the work in hand. This, in turn, leads to a methodological awareness which radiates ideas into general fields of social inquiry. On an institutional level, institutes are, in themselves, a highly interesting innovation. They affect the organization and curriculum of departments of sociology, and they focus attention on the broader problem of what I have called the power vacuum in American universities.

This brings me to my last point. To what does all this empirical research add up? In a way, this is related to the main theme of this convention: "the uses of sociology." First, a reminder: until 1937 our annual meetings always had a central theme; then a resolution was adopted that because the field had become too diversified, this practice was no longer possible. By now, it would seem that diversification has reached such a point that the annual meetings should perhaps try to review common denominators, one by one. In any case, I used the feeble authority of the President and persuaded the Council that the problem of utilization is an urgent one. Actually, it would be better to talk of a utility spectrum. At the one end, you have the idea, most clearly represented by contemporary Soviet opinion, that the only justified use of social research is the advancement of social revolution. Having grown up in an exciting and constructive period of socialist optimism, I have never quite lost my hope for radical social change. But I do not believe that empirical social research of the type we are discussing tonight can contribute much to it.

At the other end of the spectrum, one finds utility in the narrowest sense. This includes studies for government agencies, for business firms, labor unions or other voluntary organizations which pay for them in the expectation that they will advance their purposes. But do they really help? As you know, we hope to publish the main contributions of this convention in a volume under some titles such as "Applied Sociology." From watching the period of preparation for this program, I gather that a kind of curvilinear relation exists. The greatest difficulty in providing concrete examples comes at the two extremes of the utilization spectrum: the exponents of basic social change and the people who want guidance for immediate policy and action are most often disappointed.

Within this continuum many points could be singled out for discussion. Having little time left, I want to select two of them, one because the record of the past is impressive, and the other because the needs of the future are urgent.

ACHIEVEMENTS AND HOPES OF EMPIRICAL SOCIAL RESEARCH

It has been said that the most sociologists can hope for at the moment are theories of the middle range. My colleague who coined this phrase gave his presidential address on multiple discoveries. So he will not mind if I report that fifty years ago, during the early phases of the Chicago school, the hope was expressed that their field studies would contribute to "intermediate scientific truth." And, indeed, empirical social research has proved most useful in serving this function.

Let me bring in at this point a final reminiscence. When I began to conduct studies of consumers as part of my Austrian program of research on choice, I often had to defend their scientific dignity. On one occasion, I pointed out that a series of such studies permitted important generalizations, and chose, as an example, the notion of the "proletarian consumer." Comparing him with his middle class counterpart, I described him as:

> . . . less psychologically mobile, less active, more inhibited in his behavior. The radius of stores he considers for possible purchases is smaller. He buys more often at the same store. His food habits are more rigid and less subject to seasonal variations. As part of this reduction in effective scope the interest in other than the most essential details is lost; requirements in regard to quality, appearance and other features of merchandise are the less specific and frequent the more we deal with consumers from low social strata.

Notice that this is a summary of a large number of studies, no one of which, in its own right, is very interesting. But, together, they led to the notion of effective scope. This concept became subsequently useful in many ways—be it to distinguish between local and cosmopolitan roles, between lower and better educated social strata, or just between people whose radius of interest could be small or large. Stouffer's notion of relative deprivation was similarly developed from a variety of seemingly unconnected attitude surveys. Many other examples could be given to show the possible contributions of empirical studies, however narrow, to theories of the middle range. As a matter of fact, this is almost implied in the very idea of mediating between descriptive data and higher order generalizations. Inversely, there probably would not be much theory of the middle range without the steady supply of specific studies, a growing proportion of which comes from various social research institutes.

At another segment along the utility spectrum we meet the question whether major social improvements have been facilitated by the available techniques and the existing organizational forms of empirical social research. I do not refer to the continuous efforts to improve recognized trouble spots such as delinquency or racial discrimination. The issue is rather whether it is possible to do what Robert S. Lynd once called research for the future—studies which are generated by a sociological analysis of unrecognized social needs. We have tried for years to clarify this challenging idea at Columbia University. When Allen Barton became Director of the Bureau of Applied Social Research at Columbia, he put some order into our collective thinking by developing types of studies which would satisfy Lynd's criterion. Let me give you two examples from his list. One type can be called the investigation of "*positive deviant cases.*" We take it for granted that certain types of situations usually take unfavorable turns. And yet sometimes exceptions occur: local or regional elections in which a good candidate wins in spite of the fact that his adversary has the power of the machine on his side; a really independent small town newspaper which survives in spite of opposition by the "interests"; a faculty successfully resisting infringements on academic freedom; escape of youngsters from temporary associations with criminal gangs. While the content of these examples varies from case to case, they all converge on the central task of finding generalizations centered on the problem of how to stem an undesirable social drift. It is muckraking in reverse.

Another type of study can be called the *pretesting of new social ideas*. A new notion of creative reform—especially if it has just been formulated—often needs studies to check on its assumptions and to perfect its design, partly to improve its feasibility and partly to facilitate its public acceptance. At the present moment, for example, it appears that structural unemployment can be solved only by a large-scale relocation of workers. The idea often meets great resistance from local commercial, church, and union interests. Some legislative aid for specialized re-training even precludes the use of federal funds for relocation. In addition, many workers themselves seem to resist relocation, although the extent and the relative weight and interconnection of all this is by no means known. Parallel to the need for pertinent sociological and psychological data, one must ask whether, from an economic and a technical point of view, it is easier to move people or to move factories.

The mere size of such studies might be enough to outgrow the capacity of a single research group. They require an interweaving of quantitative and qualitative technique, of simultaneous research on individual and organizational levels, together with some historical analysis. Furthermore, such inquiries are time consuming. But there is nothing prohibitive in itself about such an extension of current research practices. And yet the fact that it has not been done is by no means accidental. Having been director of an institute for some years, I cannot avoid a feeling of regret. It is a great temptation to undertake a study for which funds are available, on topics which require the kind of skills one has developed in one's staff, under sponsorship which promises continuity. My generation has had to worry a great deal about the mere survival of our organizations and their acceptance by university administrations. The new generation of directors, whom we have trained, work under better conditions. They should have the courage to strike out in the direction of some of the more complex areas that I have just tried to exemplify. I seriously hope that they will take the flames, and not the ashes, from the fires we have kindled.

As I come to the end of my remarks, I become aware that the difficulty of writing a presidential address is equalled only by the prospect of leaving the rostrum and hearing one's friends say that it was all very interesting, but the main themes were not quite clear, that the examples might have been more pointed, the organization of the points was somewhat confusing.

It is a little like the case of the man who asks for a divorce and gives, as his reason, the fact that his wife talks and talks and talks. The judge asks what she talks about and the man replies: "Your honor, that's just the problem, she doesn't say." My sympathies tonight are naturally with the woman. There are situations where one wants to express ideas that can hardly be communicated to others who have not undergone comparable experience. I have done my best to say what I am talking about. It is my conviction that, as time goes on, a growing number of sociologists will meet the problems and situations to which I have been exposed. If some of them find that, in retrospect, my observations make sense and that, as they face a concrete decision, some of my suggestions prove of help, then the purpose of this address will have been achieved.

CHAPTER 17

INTERNATIONAL SOCIOLOGY AS A SOCIOLOGICAL PROBLEM

International gatherings have repeatedly played an important role in the social sciences. At the London World's Fair in 1872 Karl Marx created the second international. The St. Louis World's Fair in 1904 brought the world's leading sociologists together and one can easily trace the profound influence this American experience had on Max Weber's subsequent writings. Today's vastly improved communications all year round make periodic face-to-face gatherings less momentous events. Still, they are important occasions and their impact can probably be increased further if one reflects on what functions they do or could perform. We offer some observations here which suggest that a systematic study of such international events could be of real service to the profession.

A NOTE ON HISTORY

The origins of formal international organizations of sociologists can probably be traced back to the International Institute of Sociology

Written with Ruth Leeds. Reprinted from *American Sociological Review*, 27:5 (1962), by permission of the publisher. To honor our foreign colleagues on the occasion of the Fifth World Congress of the International Sociological Association, held in Washington, D.C., the Editor invited the President of the American Sociological Association to prepare a statement on the significance of international sociological gatherings. We are indebted to Paul Lazarsfeld and Ruth Leeds for their thought-provoking contribution. (The Editor)

(IIS) which was created in 1893 with headquarters in Paris. It held yearly congresses until 1910, then changed to a triennial schedule. The congresses were interrupted by the first World War and not resumed until 1927. The 1939 Congress was cancelled because of the second World War. We have inspected a sample of their proceedings and several elements seemed to us interesting. The IIS had very definite working principles. The three basic ones were: (a) all order of social facts are intimately related to each other, and none should be omitted in research; (b) in studying any social fact, objective rather than subjective method should be followed; (c) the social world needs to be understood in order to be improved; "Knowledge for action but before action."[1]

One had to be elected to the Institute and the names of the members were published each year. The catholicity of the membership is striking. In addition to the leading names of sociology proper, economists and biologists were included. Thus, for instance, Galton was vice-president in 1895. Alfred Marshall, Thomas Masaryk, and several French Prime Ministers were early members. Somewhat later, Gustave Schmoller, the leader of the German historical school of economics, became president and almost every member of the Austrian marginalists was an officer. By 1913, the roster of membership seemed to include, with one notable exception, individuals of importance in any country where social sciences in the broadest sense were cultivated. The exception was the Durkheimian group in France.[2] An interesting historical study would be to find out why the flag of sociology provided this rallying point prior to the creation of more specialized professional international organizations.

The topics of the early congresses were very much the same as the ones with which we are concerned today, but they were treated in a rather broad style. Detailed empirical studies in the modern sense were not included. But one must remember that the statisticians had already

---

[1] *Annales de l'institut international de sociologie*, Paris: Vol. I (1895), pp. v–vi. An account of the First Congress of the IIS by René Worms is found in the *Revue internationale de sociologie*, Vol. II (1894), pp. 721–728.

[2] Durkheim and his followers did not join, presumably because the permanent secretary of the IIS was one of his opponents, René Worms. For references to this schism in early French sociology, see Robert K. Merton, "Recent French Sociology," *Social Forces*, 4 (May, 1934), pp. 537–545. Merton refers to the propounding of anti-Durkheimian polemics in the *Revue internationale de sociologie* (p. 537). The bearing of this feud on IIS activities remains to be investigated.

started their own international organization in the middle of the 19th century and made Quetelet their permanent president. Quetelet's notion of social physics encompassed most of what today we call quantitative social research. It would be worthwhile to compare the proceedings of the two organizations and to see to what extent they perpetuated the speculative approach of Comte, on the one hand, and the empirical bent of Quetelet, on the other.

Each Congress had its major theme, and one cannot say that the selections had a strong prophetic element. The 1913 Congress dealt with the problem of progress; ony in 1930 did war and peace appear as the featured theme. There are many topics in the proceedings of the old institute which have been reopened by speakers at the congresses of the present International Sociological Association. A comparative analysis would help us to chart the trend in our work.

The new organization, the International Sociological Association (ISA), was created under UNESCO auspices after the second World War and in definite opposition to the IIS whose activities were resumed under the leadership of the Italian Corrado Gini. The circumstances of the break have not yet been studied. As most of the participating men are still alive, a valuable piece of oral history could be provided.[3] UNESCO's position apparently was that the members of the old institute had been too involved in the political problems of the second World War so that a completely new organization was necessary. Gini has published his side of the story but the organizing committee of the ISA has not yet presented its account of the matter.[4] In modern times—since 1950—the IIS seems to have attracted those sociologists who lean more toward a humanistic social philosophy rather than to the development of empirical social research, which is emphasized by the ISA. The implications of these divergent institutional orientations

---

[3] The senior author of this paper offers the following reminiscence. In the fall of 1948, Otto Klineberg, who then directed the social science affairs of UNESCO, called a few of us together in Paris. I happened at that time to spend a term in Oslo to help in the organization of a Norwegian social research institute which in the early post-war years certainly was the most vigorous research center in Europe. I invited the leader of the Norwegian group, Rinde, to go with me to Paris. Subsequently, and properly, he was made the first secertary of ISA. As far as I can remember, the problem of the IIS was not mentioned at the 1948 planning meeting, and, I for one, became aware of the issue only many years later.

[4] *Proceedings of the Fourteenth World Congress of the International Institute of Sociology*, Rome, 1950, Vol. I, pp. 184–185.

for the progress of sociology in member countries would itself be a worthwhile topic for research.

The ISA held its first Congress in Zurich in 1950, one year after its organizing meeting in Oslo. Succeeding Congresses have been held every three years in Liège (1953), Amsterdam (1956), Stresa (1959), and Washington, D.C. (1962). ISA membership is generally not held by individuals but by national organizations. Unlike the old IIS, the ISA did not formulate specific programmatic statements. But the major themes selected for its congresses seem to be more responsive to the major problems of the times. Thus, social planning was featured in Stresa and the Washington Congress featured problems of newly developing countries. The numerical preponderance of American participants in marked, particularly in contrast to the relatively few Latin American participants.[5]

Sociologists are notorious for studying everything but their own institutional arrangements. At every stage of this historical sketch we have mentioned a worthwhile topic that has not yet found its analyst, and several more easily come to mind. Did the League of Nations foster international cooperation among social scientists after the first World War? What was the effect of that war on the work of the old IIS? Was its programming responsive to the emergence of fascism?

The ISA has not been in existence long enough to permit extensive analysis of its relations to the political scene, or of its major trends. Still, we can raise a few questions with regard to the four congresses held during a twelve-year period. A major theme at the Zurich Congress was "Sociological Aspects of Relations Between Nations." The actual papers and discussion, however, tended to be more "psychologistic." They emphasized the application of small groups research to the international level, and the need for studies of attitudes and values, since internecine strife supposedly was nourished in the main by stereotypes, prejudice, and ideological conflicts.[6] In Liège, three years later, sharper distinctions were made between psychologistic and sociologistic approaches to "Intergroup Conflict and Its Mediation." It was suggested that the real contribution of sociology to international relations lay in the study of the desire for national survival and conflict of interests. But throughout the discussion there was an undercurrent

---

[5] Our neighbors to the south, however, tend to be much more active in the IIS than we are.

[6] *International Social Science Bulletin*, 3 (Summer, 1951), pp. 203–213.

of pessimism as to whether sociology could make a contribution to international relations.[7] After the 1953 Congress this particular theme is not in evidence.

While international relations became a neglected topic at the Congresses, the concern with underdeveloped countries increased. At Zurich there appeared to be virtually no concern with the subject. The Liège Congress contained programmatic papers describing the development of our discipline in the context of rapidly changing and industrializing countries.[8] Approximately ten per cent of the papers presented at Amsterdam focused explicitly on one or another underdeveloped and now rapidly changing country.[9] One session at the Stresa Congress was devoted to a discussion of underdeveloped countries and at Washington the subject was a major theme at the Congress. Another question, then, for the researcher who would study our own work is: what accounts for the decline of one topic and the rise of another, particularly when both have been of paramount issue during the period in question? For certainly the early neglect of underdeveloped countries and the recent neglect of international relations at our World Congresses are not a reflection of the changing importance of these subjects in the world at large.

Two themes which have received attention at virtually every Congress are methodology and stratification. The analyst for our discipline might examine how papers and discussions on these two topics have changed from Congress to Congress, and whether there have been cumulative developments with an idea presented at one congress bearing fruit in research presented at a subsequent one.

SOME FUNCTIONS OF INTERNATIONAL CONGRESSES

World Congresses perform several significant services, particularly that of sensitizing us to foreign points of view. Yet, surprisingly, the

[7] *International Social Science Bulletin,* 6 (No. 1, 1954), pp. 25–32.

[8] *Transactions of the Second World Congress of Sociology,* Vol. I (1953), pp. 11–16, 22–25.

[9] For example, Hassan El Saaty, "Changes in the Industrial Organization of Egypt," *Transactions of the Third World Congress of Sociology,* Vol. II (1956), pp. 11–19.

American sociological journals do not even report on the international meetings. We went through the journals published in recent years and the only items we could find were a few perfunctory communications buried in annual reports of the American Sociological Association.[10] Our journal editors should assign special reporters to the international meetings with the instruction to pay special attention to non-American activities. We shall later make a stab at such "listening with the third ear" by briefly reviewing some parts of the four volumes in which the Stresa (1959) proceedings were published recently.[11] Our emphasis will be on papers by non-Americans. We hope thereby to give the average American sociologist a feeling for a foreign, especially Western-European, point of view.

Learning about foreign points of view is, however, only one major function of international meetings. Two others are equally important: the development of informal personal contacts and the formal provision for comparative social research. To these two other functions we shall turn first.

THE ROLE OF INFORMAL CONTACTS

General Informal Functions.[12] Meeting foreign colleagues in face-to-face situations presents a variety of benefits which cannot be had otherwise. Personal contacts often permit one to assess the merits of a man with greater ease than his published work. Such intimate knowledge becomes highly useful when one seeks collaboration or assistance from someone who shares similar interests. These contacts themselves facilitate subsequent correspondence about professional matters which otherwise could not be initiated with the same ease. Plans for joint undertakings can be more readily initiated in the relaxed atmosphere of

[10] See, however, Nels Anderson and K. J. Nijkerk, "International Seminars: An Analysis and an Evaluation," *Administrative Science Quarterly*, 3 (September, 1958), pp. 229–250. Robert C. Angell has reviewed the social research activities of UNESCO. See his "UNESCO and Social Science Research," *American Sociological Review*, 15 (April, 1950), pp. 282–287. Sociological journals abroad appear more likely to report on the ISA Congresses.

[11] Available from International Sociological Association, 116 Rue des Flamands, Louvain, Belgium.

[12] We are indebted to Herbert Menzel for ideas on this topic. We have also interviewed colleagues who have actively participated in international meetings.

a cocktail lounge than via letters. Also, in this relaxed atmosphere, one can commiserate on common occupational hazards, such as the public's penchant to confuse Sociology with other areas—in Europe with Socialism, in the United States with Social Work.

A foreign colleague can inform one about research projects which are being conducted in his country by groups that are not represented at the congress. Such information serves as a "calling card" when one wishes to contact a particular research group at a later time. The foreign colleague can also give his estimation of the work being done and the persons who are doing it. This provides one with some basis for judging whether it is worth establishing contact with a particular foreign group.

Substantive Informal Functions. Although the papers themselves are frequently subjected to recrimination because they detract from informal meetings and conversations, they do serve to facilitate the establishment of personal contacts. Their presentation draws together in the same room people who share similar interests, thus permitting them to identify one another. Secondly, the papers serve as "invitations" to start a conversation with colleagues, to break the initial barrier that exists between total strangers.

At a world congress, friendships among colleagues who have limited opportunities to see one another can be renewed. Just as new contacts serve to initiate joint research plans or the development of ideas, the renewal of friendships serves to give a fresh impetus to plans undertaken at a prior time. The cumulative value of international congresses could be assessed by the number of projects which, once initiated, are maintained through several meetings until completed.

The papers, and the professional conversations which they stimulate, permit one to gain new insights and ideas. A statement or casual remark which is "obvious" in one country might be new and seminal in another. Additional data from one country might lead to corroboration or refinement of a particular hypothesis that was developed in another country.[13] As might be expected, an international meeting is especially useful for the advancement of any comparative work. To a large extent this requires a formal apparatus, which we shall consider

[13] Andrzej Malewski, "Dwa Modele Socjologii (Two Models of Sociology)," *Studia Socjologiczne*, Warsaw, 1 (No. 3, 1961), pp. 50–51. Malewski briefly speculates on how different sociological orientations lead to variations in international cooperation among colleagues.

presently, but first let us note the ways in which the world congresses serve informally to further comparative research. Colleagues engaged in such work have found that opportunities for face-to-face contact are particularly helpful in obtaining a more accurate impression of a particular phenomenon in a given country. Because of the dearth of solid data, especially in the case of underdeveloped countries, they find themselves resorting to published material which frequently contains impressionistic accounts and incidental observations. Through conversations, foreign confreres can either corroborate or dispel impressions gained from such inadequate sources.

To express the matter on a more general plane, the international congress is unique in that it can help overcome the provincialism with which sociology in each country is unavoidably beset. For even those of us who are active in comparative research tend to view, say, an Indian village not on its own terms but with reference to another community we might have studied, thus possibly blinding us to important underlying differences. Exchanges with a colleague from India then force us to stop riding our pet horses and to straddle a new one. Moreover, through such conversations we can gain a greater respect for our foreign colleagues. We learn to view them not only as valuable assistants for our foreign based research projects but also as men of knowledge in their own right.[14]

Congress papers on similar topics provide an opportunity for comparisons which often can be conducted only informally. For those present at a congress, personal discussion permits clarification of details, which is not possible for those who must rely on the published transactions for their information. For instance, at the Second World Congress, two studies were mentioned, in passing, which dealt with the problems of college dropouts, one from Mexico and one from Germany. Similar studies from two vastly different countries immediately invite comparison, but neither Mendieta Y Núñez nor König gave particulars in their formal papers, so those interested in the subject of college dropouts were obliged to speak to them personally.[15]

[14] See R. N. Saksena, "Sociology in India," *Transactions of the Fourth World Congress of Sociology*. Vol. I (1959), pp. 64–74. These pages suggest that the theme of "ugly American" is not limited just to politics and business. See also R. N. Saksena, "Some Observations on Sociology in India," *American Sociological Review*, 27 (February, 1962), p. 97.

[15] *Transactions of the Second World Congress of Sociology*. Vol. I (1953), pp. 36–43, 63.

The significance of these informal functions for sociologists will vary from one country to another. The sharpest differences would probably be found between those countries where the discipline is well established and those countries where the "take-off point" for sociology as a self-sustaining, fully developed discipline has not yet been reached. The world congress probably serves as a functional alternative to national meetings for the sociologists of those countries where the number of sociologists stays below what might be called the "critical mass" necessary to generate their own active national associations.

The *Transactions* of the Stresa congress contain many references to the effect that in those countries where the "critical mass" has not yet been attained sociologists are unable to produce interesting work. In such instances, the international congress might serve to stimulate the development of interesting work and new ideas and help get such a country over the hump. This invites the danger, however, that the predominant influence of sociologically more advanced countries might lead not to the stimulation of a genuine national development in "sociologically underdeveloped" countries, but merely to imitations of activities from abroad. Conversely, one might ask whether a sociologically advanced country has reached a saturation point beyond which it becomes impervious to outside influences. These questions again suggest that a special study of the role of international meetings would be in order.[16]

An analysis of the informal functions of the ISA and their differential significances for various countries might suggest strategies for formalizing these functions. One such strategy would be to expand the responsibilities of the rapporteurs for the special sessions. The rapporteurs might themselves take the opportunity to speak with the authors of those papers that strike them as being particularly interesting because they suggest a new idea or invite comparison, and include the results of their discussion in their *Transactions* reports. Incidentally, the third Stresa volume shows two styles of discussion reports. One is organized around topics, mentioning in a secondary way who made a specific contribution, and the other summarizes the discussion speak-

---

[16] On the speculative level the list of possible effects can be extended endlessly. For example, another informal function of the world congress might be to make sociologists of a given country more conscious of their own national trends, which in turn might serve as a rallying point for the development of a national "platform."

ers in order of their intervention. To us the former style seems much more preferable.

The international meetings also have a problem with translations. The interpreters often are professionals who usually translate for international political and diplomatic meetings. Consequently, they employ a mode of translation which tends to de-emphasize conflict and cleavages in the discussion. An intellectual meeting unlike a political meeting, however, thrives on conflict and disagreement insofar as they stimulate clarification of thought and development of new ideas. The translators should be alerted to the import of genuine intellectual disagreements to avoid de-emphasis in the future.

THE ADVANCEMENT OF COMPARATIVE RESEARCH

Sociologists agree that our ideas must be tested in different social settings if we wish to arrive at generally valid propositions. An international organization is our obvious operating ground for such comparative research. The ISA furthers this goal through the formation of subcommittees for specialized research. To date there are nine committees, covering stratification and social mobility, industrial sociology, urban-rural sociology, sociology of the family, sociology of mass communication, political sociology, psychiatric sociolgy, sociology of religion, and sociology of leisure and popular culture.

These committees serve important functions in the development of comparative research. Some of them are of a substantive character: a) by drawing attention to a central problem, the committees can stimulate studies in some countries which otherwise would not pay attention to the topic at hand; b) by stimulating research in several countries, the committees provide data for potential cross-national analyses; c) the committees can provide a framework and install an apparatus which would facilitate such cross-national comparisons.[17]

On the methodological plane, the committees can help to eliminate or to overcome technical difficulties that often arise vis-à-vis

---

[17] The efforts of the Sub-committee on Political Sociology to collate an international bibliography and to establish an international data center exemplify the concrete services these committees can offer to make international comparisons more feasible.

cross-national work. They can provide a common conceptual framework, make suggestions regarding techniques which permit comparisons, and advise on the use of equivalent variables, as, for instance, in the measurement of socioeconomic status.[18]

Besides their research functions, the subcommittees can perform certain administrative tasks: planning special sessions for the international congresses, and coordinating the work of sociologists with other international organizations like UNESCO or the International Political Science Association.[19] Between the extremes of research and administrative functions the committees render another important service, that of publishing periodic trend reports. The work of Reuben Hill is an outstanding example of this service.[20]

SENSITIVITY TO FOREIGN VIEWPOINTS

We return now to the significance of learning foreign points of view. The second and the third volume of the Stresa proceedings permit us to catalogue four of the foreign overtones which an attentive correspondent for an American sociological journal might have caught.

The first is the way our Western European confreres explicitly or almost unconsciously link sociological issues to the political situation in their countries. A good example is provided in the report on the sociology of leisure by the Italian Ricardo Bauer. Bauer, in turn, leans heavily on the work of the Frenchman Dumazedier. The Western European countries all have strong labor parties which were the protagonists for the shortening of the work week. As a result, one central problem for these experts is whether the use of the new leisure by workers is compatible with traditional goals of labor parties. Is there a corrosion of class consciousness? Do the occupational activities of various blue-collar and white-collar groups still form the sub-stratum

---

[18] On international comparisons, see Malewski, *op. cit.*, pp 50-51

[19] The Sub-committee on Political Sociology, for example, participated in a seminar on the utilization of survey data in comparative cross-national research this summer which was sponsored by UNESCO and organized by the International Political Science Association.

[20] Reuben Hill, "Sociology of Marriage and Family Behavior, 1954-1956," *Current Sociology*, 7 (No. 1, 1958), p. 28.

from which their specific leisure-time activities can be derived? The
desire to answer such complex questions also necessitates a much more
subtle conceptualization of the notion of leisure itself. For example,
should non-working time spent on doing chores around the house be
considered leisure? The answer is in the negative because such pursuits
do not represent an "active, independent, positive response to the negative side of industrial civilization, to the sense of passivity, regimenta-
tion, and conformity that modern social life unceasingly generates."

A second characteristic of foreign contributions is their greater
emphasis on macroscopic ideas. Here Jean Floud's paper on the sociology of education is illustrative. She charges the American tradition
with looking too much at schools as self-contained social systems; the
"a-historical psycho-sociological bias" of much of our work stems
from the fact that there is "so much less variety in the United States
than in Europe in the historical antecedents and constitution of schools
in the public system." Her emphasis is on the effect which the broadest
social and economic context has on educational practices. Miss Floud
thinks not only of visible institutional changes and variations but also
of more subtle ones—for instance, the effect which the competition
with Russia has had on thinking about the functions of American high
schools. According to her, such a macroscopic approach is especially
pertinent at a time when we study underdeveloped countries where
education will have a vast impact on social and economic life. German
sociologists receive praise for being more sensitive to such problems,
but unfortunately Miss Floud nowhere gives specific references so that
one cannot easily check on and draw lessons from her general remarks.
We checked Neal Gross' instructive paper on the same topic in
Sociology Today.[21] The Gross paper is certainly inspired by broad
sociological considerations. In one respect, however, Miss Floud's ad-
monitions are brought out: while Gross explicitly describes the influence of the local community on the school system, he does not
elaborate on the more general social forces to which the British author
pays prime attention. The trend review by Hill, mentioned above,
corroborates the view that macroscopic emphasis is a major feature
distinguishing European from American work.

The third emphasis voiced by Western Europeans is a desire for

[21] Neal Gross, "The Sociology of Education," in Robert K. Merton, Leonard Broom, and Leonard S. Cottrell, Jr., editors, *Sociology Today*, New York:
Basic Books, 1959, pp. 128–152.

an historical context. Although the Stresa volumes do not contain many historically oriented papers, one can discern several variations on this theme. One is the study of long-range historical trends of a given institution; a second is the linkage between historical analysis and contemporary empirical research. The first—usually called the Weberian tradition—represents an old issue. One methodological seminar reported in the third volume was dedicated to it, but did not yield any new ideas on the subject, at least as far as the condensed reports permit one to judge. The linkage between historical analysis and empirical work presents a more challenging issue and is used in two ways in the Stresa papers. Historical analysis can help sharpen the formulation of a contemporary research problem. Halsey, in the education section, reviews the changing function of British universities from the medieval period to the present. His concern is the extent to which these institutions are responsive to the changing technological structure of society. By comparing historical trends in several countries he suggests criteria with which to evaluate contemporary educational practices. The second method of linking historical considerations to newly collected data is through interpretation. Thus, Rosenmayr, in earlier work, had explained various aspects of Viennese housing conditions in terms of the long dominance of the imperial court. In Stresa, he carried this analysis further by applying it to new findings: the desire of old people in Vienna for "family intimacy at a distance" which means they wish to have contact with their married children but do not necessarily care to live with them.

A final theme apparent in discussions between European and American colleagues is the greater sensitivity of the former to topics of social significance. Insofar as this contains an implicit criticism it is partially due to a misunderstanding. Often a topic which receives both foreign and domestic attention appears to be more significant abroad mainly because other governments, in contrast to ours, play a greater role in the management of economic and social affairs. But this very fact gives rise to discussions and observations abroad which cannot be made easily in this country. Characteristic of this is the fact that all three rapporteurs in the social planning session were non-Americans: Myrdal from Sweden, Bettelheim from France, and Ossowsky from Poland. Even in the discussion period of this section the Americans were clearly in the minority. The three main papers presented at the social planning session are laden with interesting ideas which would deserve a special review. The most sociological tack was taken by Ossowsky, who emphasized the unanticipated consequences of planning measures: the decision, for instance, to set a quota for students who had to reach a certain level of achievement led to the deterioration of high school life in Poland and had to be rescinded. An example contributed by a discussant was that groups originally brought together within Indian communities to hear educational broadcasts redefined themselves as political action groups.

In summary, then, we note that a reporter with an especially sensitive ear to non-American activities at the Stresa meeting—at least as far as the *Transactions* permit one to judge—could have made several observations: 1) Western European sociologists tend to be more sensitive to the broader political implications of their research topics; 2) they emphasize the macro-sociological aspect of their problems; and 3) they link the problems to historical antecedents, and look for their social significance. There is little doubt that Americans desire to do the same. And it is not at all clear whether these observations tend to represent the hopes of our European colleagues rather than their achievements. But the mere differences in effort and in style of writing, upon which the international congresses help us to focus, are reminders of matters which are overlooked on more than one occasion.

The students of the Eastern scene and of underdeveloped countries do not differ very much from us in the points of view they bring to social research. But the situations in which they find themselves are often quite different from those with which we are acquainted. Their reports serve either to lure us into participating in their studies or to help us see new facets in the familiar situations at home. The next section presents general observations on such situational variations.

SOME OTHER NATIONAL DIFFERENCES

Beyond such variations in points of view, any international conference is likely to call our attention to experiences which we cannot encounter in our own countries and which give us real food for thought. Take, as an example, the section on sociological knowledge as applied to race relations. The late Franklin Frazier approached the topic from an American point of view, discussing mainly the relations between a white majority and a discriminated-against black minority. The specialized papers supply additional examples, especially from England and from Indonesia. But another group of papers showed that in some countries a new aspect of race relations emerges: namely, the co-existence of several ethnic groups where there is no historical precedent for dominance by one of them. Malaya and Israel, each in a different way, are examples of this. Whether the second type of situation will lend to or require new sociological insights cannot be told from the scanty evidence given in the Stresa volume.

Other examples of topics new to the American scene can be gleaned from the section on industrial sociology. The Scandinavian and Western Germans repeatedly return to the experiences their countries have with workers' participation in the management of private industry, but they did not appear to feel that very realistic strides had yet been made toward an industrial democracy. At the same time, from a research point of view, some Western European countries allow for fascinating comparisons between the management of the privately owned factories and those which belong to the nationalized sector of the economy. A further comparison is suggested by the remarks of the Polish and the Yugoslavian participants: one between the nationalized industries in the Western countries, where state ownership is an exception and the corresponding experiences in Communist countries, where it is not only the general national practice but where it is more closely related to the political life of the country. We hope that in the future the ISA will pursue more systematically these comparisons which give a new twist to a familiar problem. Certainly opportunities for them abound: Israeli managers provide variation on the cross-pressures problem with their conflict between wanting to increase the profitability of their factories on the one hand, and, on the other, wanting to provide employment for unskilled immigrants who hope to assimilate into the new country. Undoubtedly cross-pressures between national values and economic rationality will be found in a variety of forms throughout the newly developing countries.

A topic which would deserve more detailed investigation than is afforded by the Stresa proceedings is the impact which variations in national social bookkeeping methods might have for social research. For many countries reliable census figures are still not available. Where this is the case should we introduce Western census procedures? Or could it not be that with the development of modern sampling procedures many problems usually handled by census data might be more properly and economically handled by sampling, provided census practices were not too much ingrained by law or by tradition? Inversely, are we sufficiently aware that new developments in social institutions might provide us with unexpected research opportunities? In England, for instance, the vast extension of social services gives rise to a type of study many of us hoped for but were never able to carry out. One can now select in 1962 two comparable samples of, say, delinquent and non-delinquent juveniles whose histories can be traced back to their pre-natal family situation as revealed fifteen years ago when the mothers were interviewed in order to receive family assistance. Similar information is available from the time when educational decisions were made. None of this has to be obtained from retrospective interviews because the social services cut in at crucial phases of the life cycles of all British citizens, including moments of crisis such as illness or unemployment. There can be little doubt that this will lead to important types of longitudinal research, even if initially the records still turn out to be deficient.

It is more difficult, and understandably so, to find national differences in a discussion of methodology. As a matter of fact, looking at the bibliography of the papers presented, the American observer will have to have a rather fine third ear to hear anything new. Still, a number of variations in the way the task was understood are worth noting. The French report is mainly concerned with what one might call the two extremes of the methodological spectrum. On the one end, it reviews the now-available research techniques and, on the other end, it discusses the relation between empirical research and social theory, including mathematical models. The American report concentrates more on a middle area: the explication of certain specific procedures like causal analysis of statistical correlations or the translation of concepts into indices. The German report is most interesting where it deals with a special national issue. König tries to locate the role of the Frankfurt Institute. Our colleagues at work there attempt to combine a neo-Marxist criticism of industrial society with a skeptical view of the empirical research methods with which they became acquainted during the period of exile in the United States. König proposes to distinguish between social theory and a theory of society. The former, in principle, tries to develop testable propositions even if at the moment not enough data are available to provide the necessary evidence. A critical theory of society, however, starts with certain value assumptions and uses empirical data mainly for the sake of argumentation. What the Frankfurt group calls critical theory is indeed a vexing matter, difficult to grasp. It simply rejects embarrassing counter-evidence as stemming from an ideological perversion. And yet, one has the feeling that its point of view deserves respect and attention.[22] König makes a constructive effort to clarify the issue. The examples he gives, especially if they were analyzed in more detail, would further help to sharpen the underlying issues. Space does not permit elaboration of this discussion here.

Stoetzel and his collaborators add one important topic—the organization of social research. The French are in an especially good position to highlight some of the problems involved. The French National Center for Scientific Research (CNRS) has supported social research much longer than the corresponding organization in this country and it has done it by building the social research profession into an intellectual bureaucracy. There are in fact now two academic career lines in France: one as teacher in a university and one as researcher in the CNRS.[23] The resulting problems in terms of status conflict and organizational overlapping have only recently found attention in this country. The American review, rendered by the senior author of the present paper, includes some of the controversies between the European and the American research traditions mentioned above.[24]

Since "The Uses of Sociology" was the central theme of the 1962 Washington meetings of the American Sociological Association, it

---

[22] The report in Volume One on German sociology is written by Adorno, a leading member of the Frankfurt group. The flavor of his attitude and that of his associates is very well reflected in his critical survey of the German empirical research scene. König, in his discussion of the theory of society, repeatedly refers to earlier writings of Adorno which were written in very much the same vein as his Stresa contribution.

[23] The concern of the French sociologists with organizational aspects of their work seems to be quite pervasive. Bourricaud devotes several pages in his report on substantive trends in French sociology to the problems which have been created by the double hierarchy of teaching and research. (First volume.)

[24] Paul F. Lazarsfeld, with the collaboration of Sydney S. Spivack, "Observations on the Organization of Empirical Social Research in the United States," from *"Information" Bulletin of the International Social Science Council*, 29 (December, 1961).

may be worth while to add a word on the manner in which the notion of "application" is understood in the Stresa papers. In some (for instance, the Levi and Frazier papers), application signifies the role of sociology in the clarification of a more specific intellectual problem: for example, the understanding of population development or of race relations. At the other extreme, we have the paper by Hill, who reviews in great detail how sociological family studies are used in counseling, what family problems are emphasized primarily in text books or in popular literature. He pays special attention to the "development of a corps of interpreters," specialists who would mediate between policy makers and social scientists. They would tell the former how to utilize our research findings and would guide us in the selection of research topics which would be useful for those who are charged with making decisions on practical affairs. The paper by the Dane, Henning Friis, on "social welfare planning and administration" takes a middle position. He discusses with great insight what he calls "the sociological core" of social welfare research. What are the social forces which shape the social security policy of various countries? How do they approach the conflict between humanitarianism and self-reliance, either in terms of opinion research or in terms of their actual policies? What is the intertwining between general party politics and social welfare problems? What are the special problem groups? How should existing welfare services be evaluated? Friis's bibliographical references and his general familiarity with the American situation show that on such a relatively specific topic there is international agreement on what sociology can contribute.

The Belgians who report on industrial sociology speak in terms familiar to any American colleague. But they also speculate on the factors which explain why, in certain countries, sociologists are called in as industrial consultants and in others they are not. The Dutchman Hofstee devotes most of his time to an instructive analysis of the papers on rural life which were submitted to his section. But in the beginning of his presentation he notices a pertinent and interesting difference between applied industrial and rural sociology. In the industrial field, the units are large enough so that a single factory might be studied and useful advice given either to the manager or the union president. A single farm is too small to be treated this way. The common characteristics of rural life override the differences between the various production units. Therefore, the sociologist mainly studies the effect of the rural community in its bearing either on farming habits or on difficulties during increasing industrialization.[25]

THE 1962 ISA CONGRESS IN WASHINGTON

American sociologists were very happy indeed to be the hosts to the Fifth Congress. All sorts of obstacles in terms of visas were overcome. General support by American foundations, and by the American Government itself through the National Science Foundation's Division of Social Sciences, made it easier for our foreign colleagues to join us in the national capital.

The Organizing Committee announced four major themes and each of them will permit us to clarify some of the issues we have raised.

The first theme focuses on the question of how sociological work should be communicated to policy makers and to the general public. We are certainly interested in knowing more about the various ways in which sociologists in other countries handle the relations with their "clients." The problem of research institutes, their relations to graduate teaching, the effect of available funds on the direction of research, and many other matters of this kind are still very much in flux. We can certainly learn much from the experiences of colleagues who have worked in different traditions and have discovered interesting institutional innovations.

The second theme deals with questions of growth and development in the institutional areas—especially the polity and the economy —of underdeveloped countries. It is gratifying and understandable that this topic moves from the periphery of previous congresses to the center of the present one. Many points made in this paper apply to the sessions which deal with this theme. Let us hope that it will be reported in such a way that we will obtain a better insight into the function of international congresses on a subject matter which requires international cooperation in so many forms.

The third theme is the role of social theory which, of course, can never be omitted by any gathering of sociologists, national or inter-

---

[25] This, incidentally, raises the interesting point that the study of large plantations or of large commercialized farms might provide an important counter-example.

national. Undoubtedly, the dialogue between East and West will continue. The problem to watch is whether, as we move from one congress to the next, we just repeat the old positions, or whether there is a cumulative clarifying effect from one meeting to the next. We should also be sensitive to the possibility that social theory does not consist of just Marxism and functionalism. There are undoubtedly important finer variations to which we should lend an attentive ear.

The fourth theme is sociology of knowledge. It probably grew out of the Stresa discussion where Aron and Merton commented on the various national surveys. There are interesting differences between the comments of the two men. Aron mainly stressed variations among main currents while Merton emphasized that the main debates between sociologists are really the same in all countries. Especially Merton's paper (which for technical reasons was reproduced in the third volume) gave a well-defined and exemplified list of these debates. It is hoped that the chairmen and the rapporteurs of the special sessions will look for as much continuity as possible in this area.

The participants in the fourth theme were interested in all aspects of the sociology of knowledge and not only in the sociology of the social sciences. But it is to the latter topic that the present paper intends to make a minor contribution. An international congress is an instrumentality to advance knowledge, yet we know little about how it actually does this, and therefore we are ill-equipped to know how such a congress can be handled most effectively. The goal of this paper will have been achieved if a sizable number of the participants in the Fifth Congress will view international congresses as an opportunity for organizational analysis and will transmit their ideas and observations to the colleagues who will be responsible for the next meeting.

CHAPTER 18

A PROFESSIONAL SCHOOL FOR TRAINING IN SOCIAL RESEARCH

INTRODUCTION

Within the last two decades the scope of the social sciences has been greatly enlarged; they have also undergone some very decisive changes. In the past, the social scientist had to be satisfied with data which were collected in the "natural" course of administrative book-keeping. Today, new types of data are gathered. Recent developments in sampling have greatly extended the number of items covered by the Census; business not only records its internal operations; market research has led to much information on the consumers of its products; polls register various facets of political attitudes of different population groups, where in the past only voting data were available; the Federal Reserve Board studies the saving habits of individual citizens where previously only gross figures on bank deposits were known.

Our system of social bookkeeping has thus become expanded in scope and sophisticated in technique. Many more agencies for such

Written with Robert K. Merton. This memorandum, written in 1950, was widely circulated in mimeographed form. A faculty committee at Columbia University discussed the matter but found that no funds were available to carry out the plan. The memorandum was then submitted to the Ford Foundation, which in turn appointed a committee. In the course of discussions, alternative ideas were considered which finally led to the creation of the Center for Advanced Study in the Behavioral Sciences. Its structure is quite different from the one proposed in the present memorandum. On the other hand, its ideas move parallel to the recent Report which recommends the creation of a graduate school in applied social science.

bookkeeping are in operation than before; many more areas are covered more intensively, and much more knowledge is available on the differences between various population groups. In addition, more social events are now subject to such systematic description. Not only what people do, but what they intend to do, and what they expect to happen are now objects of social inquiry. Not only the resolutions of board meetings, but the way the decisions were reached is an object of record.

The historian, three decades ago, would pick out quotations from newspapers according to his own judgment; today, systematic procedures of content analysis for mass communications have been developed. The morale of workers in a factory used to be a matter of conjecture; today it is the object of a concrete investigation. In the same way, the degree of tensions between various countries is investigated by field studies sponsored by various governments or international bodies. Projective tests, scales, indices of group cohesion, effectiveness of media of propaganda are data as realistic as population or production figures were three decades ago. Carlton Hayes once remarked that history changes its character when the nature of its data changes. As long as the historian had only state archives as his main source, his interest was political history. When social statistics became available the scope of his work grew correspondingly. This is undoubtedly true for all the social sciences.

The present memorandum naturally stresses training in research operations, but it also wants to show the close interrelationship between research operations and basic theoretical thinking. The general theory of society has always been greatly affected by new discoveries about primitive people. It is now being influenced by the development of new techniques of social investigation. The theorist who knows that new types of concepts and propositions can be tested empirically changes his mode of thinking and his focus of attention. In the same way, economic theory is certainly being influenced by the fact that the notion of utility has become an object of psychological experiment.

It so happens that the sociologist has been most concerned with the new devices of social documentation and their implications for scientific knowledge and social practice. This is not surprising to anyone who knows the way sociology came into being as an independent discipline. One of its functions was and is to study the many areas of social life left uninvestigated in the 19th century. The historian had his documents; the political scientist his voting data and the blueprints of constitutions; the economist had production, taxation, and trade figures. The sociologist, almost by definition, penetrated new areas where no systematic data were available. It is no wonder, then, that he became most sensitive to the need for new techniques in social analysis. Today, departments of sociology all over the country have become spearheads in new ways of collecting and processing the type of data now available to all social science.

But this development, in fact, has not yet been paralleled by the creation of places where systematic training in such skills can be acquired. Everyone now working in the field will probably agree with the following five deficiencies:

a) At no university can the student find a comprehensive exposition of all these new techniques.

b) Even where some of them are taught, they have not been well integrated with the older and better established procedures of, say, the historian or linguist.

c) Little scrutiny has been made by the other social sciences as to where this "sociological" research might or might not be useful to them.

d) There is nowhere established a continuing study of the relation between empirical procedures and the theoretical analysis of the workings of society as a whole, which certainly is the basic purpose of all the social sciences.

e) No provisions are made at any university for the continuous developing of devices of social bookkeeping, testing their usefulness and eliminating the wasteful ones.

These points have become a major concern for all interested in the growth of social sciences; and this concern usually is set forth as a call for better training facilities. A recent report by the Social Science Research Council on "The Training and Selection of Social Scientists" abounds in remarks like these:

> The problem of how to train better research workers deserves first place on the order of business of social science departments . . . The crucial problem at present is one of training . . . Few graduate departments of social science are able to give their students a thorough training in research . . . An immediately feasible step toward raising the standards of social science research training which now generally prevail would be

the *establishment of experimental model training programs in a few universities.*[1]

Interestingly enough, not much specification can be found in such discussions as to what is meant by "model training programs." That is what needs to be spelled out. For how can there be any training program organized if there isn't a rather clear picture of what elements it should consist of? The present memorandum is an attempt to begin such specification; it would be the task of the proposed Institute to carry it into further detail and make a reality of it.

THE OBJECTIVES OF PROFESSIONAL TRAINING IN SOCIAL RESEARCH

The man engaged in the practice of empirical social research represents a new professional type. But though he has been fulfilling a professional role for some years, this has not yet been widely recognized. The failure to regard him as a professional practitioner is well illustrated by the report of a significant conference held in 1948 and centered about "Education and Professional Responsibility." Five professions—law, medicine, engineering, business, and dentistry—were represented at the conference. Social Science was not represented. Yet, throughout the conference, there were repeated allusions to the part which the social scientist could and should play in clarifying and furthering the functions of the several other professions. He was described, for example, as having an essential role in clarifying the social relations between physicians and patient, or in clarifying the economic, social and psychological implications of public law for the lawyer. But on no occasion did members of this conference on professional education ask where and how the social scientist is to obtain the training required to apply his knowledge and skills to this range of problems. The unexpressed presumption evidently held that the social scientist was somehow being trained for these tasks.

Since then the social demand for these skilled practitioners of social research has far outrun the effective supply. As recent inquiries into

[1] Elbridge Sibley, "The Recruitment, Selection and Training of Social Scientists," *Bulletin* 58 of the Social Science Research Council, pp. 44, 104, 128, 130.

the situation have found, there exists in government, industry, labor unions, welfare organizations—in virtually every sector of American society—an expressed demand for skilled, experienced, and knowledgeable social researchers which cannot be adequately met. One gains the impression that in no other single professional group does the supply of practitioners fall so short of the demand. There is clearly *not enough personnel adequately trained to organize social research bearing on specific problems of policy and social action*, to direct the collection of needed data, to provide theoretic and policy-oriented interpretations of the data adequate to the needs of the occasion, and to communicate these findings in appropriate form. There are many academic social scientists; there are few qualified practitioners of social research.

Nor is the *shortage* of social science practitioners the sole current deficiency; there is, further and perhaps more importantly, the problem of defects in the *quality* of current training. The products of social science departments of the country are often ill-accomplished in the skills of the craft. We consider professional training to be a *supplement*, not a *substitute*, for graduate training in a substantive social science. There is no intimation here that graduate education is obsolete and should accordingly be scrapped. It is only that *graduate education is not enough to qualify a man for engaging professionally in social research*, and that his grounding in the basic knowledge of the discipline must be geared in with his acquisition of multiple research skills.

Basic academic knowledge would typically be provided by a core of courses offered by the graduate departments in the student's sphere of interests. But, as we shall see when we come to consider the *methods* of training for professional research, such a program would differ from the traditional form of graduate courses in at least three respects. First, the materials in each course would be so marshalled as to permit, more than is now commonly the case, a *graded sequence of courses*, leading to progressively advanced work. Secondly, the organization of each course must be such as to allow for the student's taking an increasingly *active part in the work of the course*, rather than being a passive and silent witness to formal lectures. And thirdly, the student would have considerably less choice of courses, since to a considerable degree he would be required to select *patterns of interlocking courses*, rather than a distantly related aggregate of scattered courses, as is so often the case in present graduate departments of social science. This more rigorous program of study is intended to lead to a basic grounding in substantive knowledge which can be later utilized as a basis for new inquiry and research. The question of how the curriculum of the training institute can be best coordinated with the work of the regular graduate departments is a serious one. The answer will depend upon a variety of circumstances; some examples will be given in the technical part of this memorandum.

The major purpose of this twin emphasis on systematic academic knowledge and on research skills is to prepare the professional student for a lifework in which he continues to learn for himself, after he has left behind him the supervision and assistance provided by the professional training center. The professional student must master both substances and skills: knowledge of the first, providing him with the *what*, and competence of the second, with the *how*. Together they comprise the foundations of knowledge and trained capacity upon which the professional student may himself later build.

THE NATURE OF PROFESSIONAL SKILLS IN SOCIAL RESEARCH

This is clearly not the place to itemize in detail the multiple skills that the professional social researcher must have at his command. But it will help identify the distinctive needs of professional, as distinct from merely academic training if some of the major *types* or *classes* of skills are, however briefly, reviewed. Among those, four important kinds of skills deserve notice because of their strategic place in the professional practice of social research:

   a)   The skills of field work,
   b)   The skills of organizing and directing a research team,
   c)   The skills of developing policy-oriented research, and
   d)   The skills of developing theory-oriented research.

THE SKILLS OF FIELD WORK

The term, field work or field experience, is traditionally applied to that first-hand experience in the collection and diagnosis of pertinent materials which comprises the core of all the professions. Whether it be the medical clinic, the court room, the building site or the tunnel site, the dental clinic or the settlement house—all the professions and near-professions recognize that the student must have sustained and considerable direct experience "in the field," if he is to be prepared for his professional tasks after graduation. To some degree, though unsystematically and sporadically, graduate departments of some of the social sciences have also provided a modicum of training in field-work skills. But what is unsystematic and sporadic for the graduate student must become systematic and sustained for the professional student. Else, lacking such disciplined and supervised experience in field work, he must enter the professional sphere innocent of the most elementary skills of his craft. To hear about field work is no substitute for experience in field work.

THE SKILLS OF DIRECTING SOCIAL RESEARCH

Much, though by no means all, of professional social research is conducted by research teams, rather than by individual scholars pursuing their separate, if not unrelated, inquiries. Cooperative or team research at once calls for the exercise of special skills in the organization and direction of research. And, this too, sets distinctive tasks for professional, as distinct from academic, training in social research. It is an important commonplace that only the man experienced in the diverse operations of a social research project can effectively direct the project. But the future director of these researches must also acquire the more difficult skills of planning and organizing the research undertaking as a whole. And this manifestly calls for special training procedures to be incorporated into the educational structure of the professional school.

THE SKILLS REQUIRED FOR POLICY-ORIENTED RESEARCH

Empirical social research is conducted for one or both of two purposes: (1) to help solve a practical problem, or (2) to help solve a theoretical problem. In the former instance, the social researcher joins with his client, the policy maker, in a common task: to provide generalized knowledge and specific data for the clarification of policy alternatives. The techniques of converting a policy problem into a form amenable to empirical research are by no means self-evident, to be improvised as the occasion arises. Basic training is required for their mastery. But it is not at the moment necessary to develop this at any length, since these problems have been sufficiently recognized for the Carnegie Corporation to provide a research grant to Columbia University in support of a study of the role of the social scientist in applying research to the formation of policy.[2]

THE SKILLS REQUIRED FOR THEORY-ORIENTED RESEARCH

The professional social researcher has another type of "client" as well—the social science theorist. What seems to be an occasionally vexing problem for the more mature sciences turns out to be a compelling and crucial difficulty for the social sciences. Theory and empirical research are not often enough consolidated. The theoretical branch of the social sciences has a history of hundreds of years—some will say, of at least two thousand. The systematically empirical branch has a comparatively short history. The continued separation of the two is an all too familiar fact. Some theorists, seeking to develop some of the critical problems in the discipline, have little first-hand acquaintance with the current potentialities of empirical research. And too many of those engaged in empirical research have not been trained to utilize a theoretical framework in their inquiries. Here again, there are communicable and transmissible skills in perceiving and working toward the effective interplay of theory and applied social research. All applied research has its potential theoretic by-product, and all sound theory has implications for the design of applied research. The professional student must be trained to gather up and to make widely available the theoretical surplus-value of his work. This is what was meant earlier in this memorandum by the observation that the development of professionally competent research will advance the development of the social science disciplines.

[2] These problems have been sketched out in a research memorandum which is the basis of a symposium recently published in the *Philosophy of Science*. From these preliminary inquiries, it appears evident that an array of skills in the formulation, focussing and conduct of applied social research represents another requirement of the professional practitioner. (See Merton's contribution to Vol. XVI, #3.)

How can these skills be imparted? This question has been the object of ten years of trial and error with those who worked at Columbia's Bureau of Applied Social Research. The next section tries to formulate some of these experiences.

THE NATURE OF PROFESSIONAL TRAINING FOR SOCIAL RESEARCH

The trained research sociologist must be systematically prepared to adapt his program of research to the requirements of the problems that confront him. No rote procedures, or, at the other extreme, no mere improvisation will do the job. He must have the equipment, gained through disciplined and, at first, closely supervised experience with a great variety of research problems to meet new research situations with an array of skills which must then be adapted to meet the contingency.

Among the various methods of instruction that have been systematically reviewed (and, in part tried), four are particularly suited to achieve this objective of an ordered flexibility of skills. Mutually supplementary and interlocking, these four methods are:

a) The case method of instruction,
b) Supervised participation in current research projects,
c) Internships and externships,
d) A cumulative series of research seminars.

These methods of instruction considered most appropriate for professional training would not displace more familiar patterns of graduate training, such as the formal lecture and the discussion course. They would, instead, supplement some of the current training methods at points of strategic importance for the professional researcher.

THE CASE METHOD OF INSTRUCTION

The use of case materials is perhaps the most characteristic feature of all professional training. Whether it be based upon the "case," as in law and advanced business education, the "instance," as in engineering, or "the clinical case," as in medicine, these systems of training have one thing in common: they require the student to engage in the disciplined, supervised, and detailed practice of diagnosing or analyzing problems of the type he will encounter in professional practice.

The case method of instruction is a possibly misleading phrase, for it seems to imply that this method of training is one and the same in the several professional fields. This is not so. *Each profession has its own kind of case material, obtained from different sources through different procedures.* The schools of medicine and of law get their cases virtually ready-made from the hospital clinics and from the appelate courts, respectively. The schools of engineering most often devise instances of professional problems, sometimes hypothetical, sometimes actual, which the student is required to work through. The business schools are in a more complex situation, for they must collect their cases in the field. For them, cases do not come readily to hand through an institution associated with the professional school, as the hospital clinic, nor are they automatically recorded by an appropriate public agency, as the appellate courts. Instead, the business schools must develop a trained staff of case-finders who gather up and assemble the case materials needed for training purposes. The Harvard Graduate School of Business Administration, for example, reports that such case-finding is a major task for its junior instructional staff, requiring a budget of some eighty thousand dollars annually.

Different kinds of case materials are variously adapted to different purposes in social research training. Of the numerous kinds, we here consider briefly only those five which the Bureau of Applied Social Research has begun to develop in a limited fashion:

a) Case materials, drawn from varied field studies, centered upon *particular strategic operations in the analysis* of research data;

b) Case materials codifying the procedures presently *implicit* in the *collection of qualitative field data;*

c) Case materials designed to afford students experience in the *"translation"* of "classical" theoretic and empirical discussions into terms of contemporary research;

d) Case materials to instruct students in feasible *methods of social diagnosis and forecasts;*

e) Case materials designed to instruct students in *comparative* sociological research.

Nothing can give a more concrete picture of the thinking and experience behind the present memorandum than a detailed discussion of the case study approach in social research. For this reason, the last part of this memorandum is completely devoted to an elaboration and exemplification of the five types of case materials mentioned above.

TRAINING THROUGH PARTICIPATION IN RESEARCH PROJECTS

Neither the student nor the instructor can anticipate the specific research posts that will be filled by the student after he enters upon professional practice. He cannot, therefore, be prepared for a particular career, say, in the Bureau of Labor Statistics, or the Congress of Industrial Organization, or the American Telephone and Telegraph Company. Not only is it unfeasible; it would, in our view, be undesirable even if possible. Preparation in such specific detail is appropriate for vocational rather than professional training.

Instead, it is the objective of this training program to prepare the student for a wide variety of research roles, many of which he will be called upon to perform, whatever the particular nature of his professional career. It is intended to train him in these diverse skills typically required by the most varied kinds of social research.

Research projects do not consist of an array of isolated research operations. Increasingly, they require a research staff, each member of which must coordinate his activities with the activities of his associates. They involve an *organization* of research staff in which the interrelations of the several parts are of decisive importance to the success of the whole. Each member of the team must know and must be equipped to play his part. It is essential, therefore, that *each student will in due course have had sustained experience in taking up every role involved in a research staff*. This experience with diverse research roles in their numerous interrelations can be provided only by participation in social research projects.

As he moves from one research role to another, he becomes aware of their complex interrelations. In periodic meetings of the research staff, he sees at first hand how specific technical operations are linked with the intellectual objectives of the inquiry. Having himself made the passage from technician roles to analyst role, he gains a sense of the intellectual enterprise as a whole.

In the realistic context of an actual research project, the *student not only acquires separate skills but learns the coordination of skills through disciplined, responsible experience* under the supervision, not only of the faculty member directing the research, but also of his fellow students engaged in the same cooperative enterprise. If he seeks approval, it is not the almost empty approval registered by a grade, periodically assigned by an instructor. In effect, he is graded daily, in terms of the judgments of his student-peers, of his instructor and, derivatively, of himself. This training program will prepare men and women for the *planning, organization and direction of research*, the very skills for which the effective social demand perhaps most outruns the available supply. For the director of research must, above all else, be thoroughly versed in the complex *connections* of the multiple roles fulfilled by a research staff, not merely conversant with the separate roles.

Preliminary experimentation with such training, suggests that *particular kinds of research projects* are especially well adapted to these several purposes. These are research projects which take an earlier research as a point of departure, in part representing substantial replication of the earlier study, and in part moving well beyond replication to deal with problems barely emerging in the initial study. Such partly replicative and partly new projects have been found to have distinct advantages for training. Students begin by critical review of the earlier study, thus ferreting out implications and provisional hypotheses which at times have not been expressly stated in the earlier work. This useful exercise sharpens their critical faculties at the same time that it keeps criticism from becoming purely captious. They do not stop with mere criticism. They are subsequently charged with responsibility for designing an inquiry which would permit a check on the validity of their inferences. Analysis of the subsequent research materials is thus sharply focussed on clearly articulated hypotheses.

Having had the actual experience of building their own research upon the solid results won by previous researches, they will be the less likely, in their later professional career, to consider each research as though it were an entirely new start, an attitude notoriously common in certain fields of social science. As a series of such researches are developed in a training center, each new generation of students will gain a sense of continuity and cumulation in social research, not easily acquired unless there is a measure of replication as well as a measure of originality in the research training projects.

Special attention should be given to the field of *social diagnosis*. In some preliminary trials the following procedure has been found useful. Case material was available on families who had been investigated prior to the depression. The students were asked to predict how these families would react to the economic and social emergencies of the depression. Actually, material was also available as to what happened to the families after 1930. The confrontation of diagnosis with actual data was especially instructive; it is somewhat similar to the use of autopsies in medical training. Obviously such material can be provided in many fields. Good use was made, for example, of case studies where the political history of individuals was well documented; a diagnosis was made as to how they would behave in the next election, and again the diagnosis was confronted with actual information originally withheld from the student. Precisely because this permits a subsequent review and comparison of expectation with actuality, it serves to sharpen the interpretive skills of students. These trial-analyses of sets of data may yield a valuable research design at the very time that they are being used as a means for instruction.

INTERNSHIPS AND EXTERNSHIPS

These represent an organized system of instruction in which the novice actually enters into practice on researches oriented toward problems of policy under the supervision of a faculty member or an experienced practitioner. The interns or research assistants receive this training in a university institution affiliated with the training center, a research bureau, or institute. The externs receive their training in research agencies in government, business, social service, and education.

So central is the *place of the intern or research assistant* in the professional training programs that their multiple functions deserve detailed review. These junior members of the staff, themselves just removed from the status of graduate student and still appreciative of the problem and outlook of the student, are essential to the day-by-day effectiveness of the training program. It is these interns, *graduated through the early stages of the training to the status of assistants to the faculty directors of research,* who bridge the gap between a relatively small senior faculty staff, and a relatively large student body Like the interns and resident physicians in hospitals associated with medical schools, they serve the functions of junior and essential members of the faculty, although formally they may sometimes be assigned status only on the research staff, and not on the teaching staff. It is they who provide the almost daily supervision required by students engaged in a training research project.

Not only do the interns and assistants take an important part in the direct supervision of students at work on research projects, but they serve a further *advantage in helping to assemble, collate and prepare the case materials* which constitute, as we have seen, a major focus of the training program. The very experience gained in the preparation of these materials prepares them the better to guide students at work on projects in the utilization and development of research skills. The interns themselves also gain appreciably from this system. Those students who remain at the training center for a year or two after they have completed their own formal training requirements achieve a maturity of mind and a degree of competence which makes them all the more effective practitioners after completion of the internship. And this practiced group of interns might well constitute *the most effective recruiting ground for teachers of research* in the future.

Externship would provide yet another kind of supplementary training. It is unlikely that the research institution attached to any one center of professional training will have so extensive a research program that all students can receive supervised experience in every significant research role. As an auxiliary arrangement, of importance particularly for those students who have definitely decided upon their future specialization, *the training institution would establish liaison and affiliations with research agencies in business, government, labor, and social welfare,* where externs might receive on-the-spot training.

Externship would clearly provide students with experience in the actual concepts of applied social research. They would come to learn at first hand the ways in which applied research problems emerge into view; they would see something of the interplay between theory, research and policy. They would learn anew that methods must be shaped to obtain the data needed for the particular problems in hand. Students would also learn something of the problems of communication between researcher and policy maker, in the course of preparing research reports, memoranda and studies. Through temporary work in the research divisions of operating agencies, students would experience the full context of applied researches in all their complexity. The extern would of course be in continuous touch with the training center. It would be somewhat like the situation in which a young psychiatrist carries on his first case himself but *reports continuously to an older and more experienced man about the progress of his work*. In his discussions with the supervisor of his externship, he reaps the best fruits of his outside experience.

A PROFESSIONAL JOURNAL OF SOCIAL RESEARCH

A forward-looking part of the program for professional training might well consist of a journal of social research, *edited by advanced professional students*. The parallel to the conspicuously successful Law Review at once comes to mind. It has been described as "educational machinery with cleanly developed techniques for rapid and amazingly effective training, machinery recognized by faculties as having peculiar value in supplementation of the standard curriculum." To a major degree, the needs of professional training in social research are such that these can also be substantially served by a journal associated with the training center. The small group of highly selected students charged with the responsibility for editing a journal—at the outset, preferably a quarterly rather than one appearing at too frequent intervals—will obtain *training in the course of working up materials for the journal which is a kind not provided by any of the other methods of training here under review*. It might be added that even well-trained research students are often very inept in reporting their results. Experience in research writing, which the journal would give, should contribute to an *all-round improvement of standards in research writing*.

Such a journal would not only discuss recent scientific developments, but would deal with problems faced by the profession in a changing society, carry notices about new techniques and research apparatus, and serve as a guide through current literature in the field. Case materials focussed on a given research problem would find a regular place in the journal. Students and practitioners would provide abstracts of research studies, thus acquiring skills in the preparation of useful abstracts, a skill not overly common in the field of social research at the present time. Not only would all this provide a major supplementary training device for the student staff, but the journal itself would help keep practitioners of social research, no matter how long they have been out of school, in *touch with current developments in the profession.*

It might be added that even well-trained research students are often very inept in reporting their results. Experience in research writing, which the journal would give, should contribute to an *all-round improvement of standards in research writing.*

SEMINARS AND WORKSHOPS

Experience in research training at universities has shown the following difficulties. A seminar is set up to develop a class project. The design of the study is carefully discussed, the instruments of inquiry are developed by pretest and discussion. Each student makes a few interviews or observations with the final instrument and at that point the term ends. At best a few hypothetical tables are considered, or a few relevant observations assembled. The state of analysis is hardly ever reached and as a matter of fact can hardly be reached in the nature of the task. If it is a quantitative study, students cannot assemble enough interviews to make a statistical analysis realistic. If it is a qualitative study based on documents or observation, there is rarely time for the many necessary moves back and forth between an individual item and induced, more general ideas (which in turn guide the search for new observations or documentary details).

The lesson is that seminars are needed specially devoted to later stages of analysis. This is, of course, possible only if appropriate material is available. In the quantitative case, one would take the punch cards and code books of studies that had already gone through the field stage. The material may come from a research bureau attached to the institute; it might derive from the study of a teacher who acted as consultant to an outside agency. The intellectual side of such *secondary analysis* is well known. The administrative side deserves rather careful preparation. The instructor has to think up specific subtopics pertinent to the material on hand. In general each student will have to report twice, once presenting his plan and then summarizing his findings. At every one of these meetings connections between the various sections have to be established. If possible, a final collective document should at least be sketched out.

In the case of qualitative material the administration is not any less complex. In field observation probably a number of students should be sent to the same or comparable sites; hopefully, they will bring back different observations, which already permits a fruitful methodological discussion. After some interpretations have been worked out, the students have to go back for two purposes: 1) to see whether the analytical ideas sharpened their observations and 2) to look for possible contradictory evidence. All this has to be done in very quick succession because the main task of the term is the writing of reports, which is a notoriously difficult thing to teach and requires endless rewrites.

It would therefore be preferable to begin such workshops with material that is already available in documentary form—reports from previous studies, diaries, letters and so on. Sometimes here too secondary analysis might be possible. The interviews from books like Angel's study of the family in the depression or Dollard's cast and class might still be available and their restudy might make the main topic of such a workshop. The division of labor and the coordination of subreports will be similar to those mentioned above.

The conducting of this kind of seminar requires special skill and might have an educational by-product. Students who showed promising talent in an earlier seminar could act as assistants in a subsequent year. To really be able to conduct such workshops requires considerable experience; by systematically providing opportunities for such specialized training the small supply of competent instructors would be increased.

CASE STUDY MATERIALS NEEDED FOR TRAINING IN SOCIAL RESEARCH

The case study approach is so important that the remaining pages will be devoted to its more detailed elaboration. Social scientists, who are interested in the details of the proposed type of instruction,

will find here concrete examples elaborating the five types of case
studies mentioned previously.

CASE MATERIALS CENTERED UPON STRATEGIC OPERATIONS IN THE ANALYSIS OF QUANTITATIVE RESEARCH DATA

Many of the problems regularly encountered by the professional
social researcher call for the use of complex analytical operations (as
distinct from routine statistical techniques). He must be skilled, for
example, in the formation of empirical indices of complex concepts;
he must know how to apply procedures for discriminating between
valid causal relations and spurious causal relations; he must be practiced in the art of so interweaving quantitative and qualitative analysis
that each supplements and enlarges the significance of the other.

Training each of these sets of complex operations requires its own
distinctive body of case materials. *Each body of case materials collected from diverse and scattered sources is assembled so that it involves
a key research problem* (e.g., spurious relationship), which can be
solved only through the application of the research operation in which
the student is being trained at that moment. Each set of material thus
requires the student to work his way through a research situation of
the kind regularly confronting the professional researcher. To solve
the problem, he must first identify the precise nature of the research
problem (known to the instructor, but not to the student); secondly,
select and bring into play the research techniques best adapted to the
solution of this problem; and thirdly, engage in repeatedly practicing
the actual application of the given research skill.

But to achieve these purposes, it is necessary to provide the materials for training. Systematic case materials of this kind are presently
lacking in the greater part of social science. They must be collected
and prepared. Each kind of case material requires the skillful piecing
together of materials, now widely scattered, which have in common a
basic research problem solvable only through certain basic operations.
Each compendium of case material is, as it were, "rigged" to require
the student to come to terms with a distinctive kind of problem by introducing the operations adequate to clarify and to resolve it.

Such training materials represent a capitalization of resources designed to obtain large savings in the time of instructor and students alike during the training program. For it would be wasteful and ineffectual to have students study an entire research report in order to identify those parts which bear strategically upon a particular research operation. For much, perhaps the greater part, of each research study inevitably involves routine operations, easily learned and assimilated by the student. Only a small part, even in researches of the first quality, consists of materials involving one or another of the complex and basic research operations. It is therefore essential for training purposes to *collect and collate from a wide array of the basic materials bearing upon each of these strategic kinds of research procedures.* Else, each student will be dissipating the all too-limited time he has available for training in seeking for himself the few grains of wheat hid in the bushels of chaff.

Nor can this type of concentrated training in strategic skills be accomplished by another traditional mode of training: by having students conduct a limited research of their own for training purposes. For here again, as is well known, the student would be devoting the greater part of his time to the essential but routine operations, which comprise the backbone of most social researches. The training enterprise would contain too large a proportion of watered stock. Given the relatively brief time available for training, it is necessary to effect a concentration in the instructive exercise of complex and important skills, rather than to have this dwindle, for want of the needed training materials, to a small part of the educational program.

Though the preparation of this kind of training material would be a sizeable task, its prospective value endorses the attempt. For the value of these training materials will multiply as they are utilized, not only in the training center where they were first developed, but in *other centers ready to make use of case materials specifically designed to produce professional social researchers* with trained imagination, ordered flexibility, and practiced research skills.[3]

[3] The budget for preparing these case materials, however substantial it may at first appear, becomes slight and inconsiderable in comparison with the costs of having large numbers of students, in effect, developing their own training materials over and over again.

CASE MATERIALS CODIFYING THE PROCEDURES
PRESENTLY IMPLICIT IN THE COLLECTION
OF QUALITATIVE FIELD DATA

Case materials for training in a wide range of statistical and quantitative techniques for the collection of statistical and quantitative field data exist in fair abundance. The Bureau of Applied Social Research, for example, has in preparation a considerable body of materials codifying experience in the design of interview schedules, questionnaires, observations of small groups, and other standardized methods of collecting statistical data.

The picture is radically different with regard to *the collection of qualitative field data*. Here, training is negligible and training materials virtually absent. Not that qualitative data fail to be recognized as of the highest importance in social research. The cogency and intellectual impact of the Lynd Middletown studies or, in another vein, of Thomas and Znaniecki's monumental volumes on The Polish Peasant is generally acknowledged to depend on their perceptive and skillful utilization, not of quantified, standardized field data—which belong to the category of important but, on the whole, routine field work operations —but of significant qualitative data, adroitly analyzed, which set forth the nature or qualities of the constituents of human behavior. These qualitative materials, typically unanticipated by the field worker before he went into the field, often represent the growing points of the discipline since they call attention to basic aspects of social behavior not caught up in the data assembled through the use of more nearly standardized procedures of data collection. (Later, of course, these often less systematic materials become the focus of standardized methods and thus enter into the systematic body of evidence which constitutes the discipline.)

Up to the present, the graduate student of social research has received little training in the collection of field materials such as these. In effect, he is told only that perceptiveness or ingenuity is a precious asset for the field worker. Deprived of systematic training in the procedures of collecting qualitative data, he is sent out into the field without preparation and is urged to exercise his ingenuity to the utmost. Given the happy circumstance that he is a gifted observer, he does, indeed, sometimes return with significant qualitative materials. But this is in spite of rather than because of his training. He happens to be among those rare few who learn how to swim by themselves, only because they have been dropped into deep water. One seldom hears from the many who fail to survive the ordeal. No one will mistake this sink-or-swim philosophy as the appropriate motif for a program of training.

It is clear enough that students vary in their native capacity for making perceptive and insightful qualitative observations, and that these differences probably cannot be erased through formal training. *But if perceptiveness cannot be induced by training, it can be enhanced.* The student's latent qualities must often remain undeveloped, if only because the aids to the development of these qualities have not been worked into a program of training. All too widely it is assumed that these qualitative procedures must remain an elusive, private, and incommunicable art. Yet it is plain that there are recurrent situations and problems in field work that can be met successfully by communicable and transmissible procedures. This basic aspect of training need not be allowed to go by default.

Such training can be provided through the use of case materials that bring together and analyze instances drawn from the literature of previously unstandardized kinds of qualitative field observations. This requires the collection of seemingly different and apparently unconnected field observations which, upon appropriate review, are found to involve the same characteristic procedures of observation. Preliminary efforts toward the preparation of such case materials show that it can be accomplished. The observations of a Lynd on the major place of the automobile in the field of Middletown, for example, are then seen by the student to involve essentially the same order of qualitative observation as the observations of a Malinowski on the functions of technological collaboration among the Trobrianders or the observations of a Thomas on the functions of fraternal organizations for Polish-Americans.

Not only does the repeated working through of such case materials provide more nearly standardized modes of observation, but it also sensitizes the student to a wider range of strategic data than that ordinarily recognized by students schooled only in the more routine techniques of collecting field data. In learning these qualitative procedures, they are also extending their sights. In due course, this may be expected to make for less narrowly confined types of studies conducted by professional researchers in the field.

One last consideration argues for the special importance of developing case materials for training in those qualitative procedures. To an increasing degree, social scientists have come to recognize that, whatever their merits and their indispensability for obtaining data about large numbers of people, the standardized quantitative procedures (involving questionnaires, interview schedules, etc.) have become too nearly the exclusive resource of the social science field worker. It is widely felt that these procedures need to be supplemented and extended. This gives all the more point to that part of a training program which aims to develop skills in the less formalized procedures for collecting qualitative field data. And this objective in turn can be approximated through the development of case materials for the general character here under discussion.

CASE MATERIALS CENTERED ON THE TRANSLATION OF 'SOCIAL SCIENCE CLASSICS' INTO TERMS OF CONTEMPORARY SOCIAL RESEARCH

As is too well known, the graduate student of social science tends toward one or the other of two opposed, and equally indefensible positions, in regard to social research. He is, at the one extreme, forever subject to the dangers of intellectual parochialism. Taught to place great store by precision of research, he may come to limit his studies to those narrowly constrained problems which have little importance for the advancement of the discipline.

At the other extreme, some students, not infrequently the more capable among them, may rebel against what they take to be the excessively confining nature of research aimed primarily at precision (even at the expense of the intellectually significant problem). These students are tempted to abandon systematic empirical research altogether. Overreacting against the threat of parochialism, they turn exclusively to the "largest" problems of the time, after the fashion of the social philosopher. They confuse the abstract importance of a problem with the prospect of advancing knowledge about the problem.

As stated periodically throughout this memorandum, it should be the object of professional training in social research to provide for that combination of skills and scholarship which exhibits the distinctive merits of both and the distinctive limitations of neither. It must provide *training in the skills of the craft needed for the effective practice of research, and education in the theory and connected factual content of the discipline.* It must produce neither mere social technicians nor mere social philosophers.

The preparation of case materials drawing upon the strategic writings of the best minds who have attended to problems of man in society is designed to curb the new barbarism, implicit in assuming that nothing of any consequence for social science has been said in the generations preceding the present day emergence of systematic empirical research. Because a Tocqueville made no use of questionnaires and attitude scales, and a Bryce fell back on his personal impressions of the American polity, the present day research-minded student fails to read Tocqueville and Bryce. What is more important, he fails to study, analyze, and reformulate some of the seminal and now researchable conceptions set forth in their works. In consequence, he emerges from his training, variously equipped to conduct social research, but not at all schooled in a range of problems to which he might most profitably apply his research skills.

Preliminary efforts have resulted in procedures for preparing the special kind of case materials which draws upon the classics of social science, and for provisionally assessing their characteristic place in the training program. *The classics in sociology*—for example, some of the writings of Simmel and Durkheim, or Weber and Spencer—*are converted into intensively examined rather than superficially scanned texts.* A single page may be the occasion for an extended reformulation. The student is brought to see that behind each significant statement in such a text, there lies a problem, more often implied than stated. For in the period antedating systematic research, these authors characteristically set forth "answers" to a problem, without stating the problem itself in strict terms. Seemingly simple conceptions—the concepts of "common will" implied by Rousseau, or the concepts of social class implied by Marx, for example—are found, upon due scrutiny, to involve multiple meanings in different contexts.

In ferreting out these multiple meanings, the student broadens his own conceptual horizons. He also converts metaphors into researchable propositions. Having extracted and operationally reformulated these multiple meanings, he returns them to their contexts in the original sources, with the intention of uncovering the central intellectual concerns of the "classical" author. Thus, Bryce becomes understood as an anthropologist of governmental structure and functions, centrally concerned with the possibility that Americans might have developed new political instrumentalities for dealing with old political problems. Simmel's "formal sociology" turns out to be a first effort to isolate variables in the description of social structures, to scale them, and to study their correlations.

Finally, the student working through these case materials considers the possible ramifications of the ideas he has unearthed in the classical sources. He asks whether the essential conception can be more rigorously and more fruitfully restated in terms now current in social research. He locates the old idea on the new map of contemporary social science.

Thus, he utilizes these case materials to trace the historical filiation of ideas: by establishing the intellectual antecedents and descendants of these germinal ideas, he may come to see his own work in a historical setting.

These case materials are intended to habituate students to the careful and intensive analysis of the classics, rather than to what has been called "the typical layman's newspaper-headline style of dealing with the printed word." At the same time they would infuse a measure of humanism—which will not, of course, be confused with humanitarianism—into training for social research. *They would curb the inadvertent tendency for a new barbarism in social science.* Above all, they would save the would-be technician from himself.

CASE MATERIALS DESIGNED TO TRAIN STUDENTS IN THE APPLICATION OF SOCIAL RESEARCH TO PROBLEMS OF PUBLIC AND PRIVATE POLICY

As we have noted earlier in this memorandum, professional training must equip the student with a variety of skills needed to conduct research oriented toward problems of policy. But, as we have also noted, the case materials for such training do not come ready-made, after the fashion of legal cases comprised of decisions handed down by appellate courts. But if the finished case materials are not readily available, the raw case materials are. Social science *has* been applied, in diverse spheres and with diverse results. Consequently, the experience is there, but it must be systematically gathered up, reviewed, collated and codified.

The actual workaday experience of professional practitioners of social research in government, business, industry, labor and welfare organizations *provides a storehouse of raw materials which can be drawn upon for the preparation of training documents.* In the previously mentioned study of the application of social research to policy, we have found that practitioners of research are altogether willing to make such experience available. Documentary records, successive drafts of research memoranda and reports, minutes of conferences between policy makers and researchers, interviews with policy makers and with researchers—these are some of the sources providing salient facts of each case.

Through case materials of this kind, students can be trained to see more than the specific practical problems in hand. Are there types of applied research in social science that are particularly likely to fructify basic theory? At which points do there characteristically arise obstacles to the utilization of research in the formation of policy? For which kinds of practical problems is the use of applied social science presently pointless, and for which kinds is it extremely useful, if not indispensable? Does the role of the research practitioner differ when he is part of a research staff attached to an operating organization, and when he is in a research agency independent of the client organization? How does the researcher come to reformulate the practical problems of the policy maker so that an investigation appropriate to the problem can be designed? These and other associated questions are among those that will be inevitably faced in actual practice. A sound training program must therefore provide for some prior disciplined experience in dealing with questions of this order.

The fact is that we are only now beginning to learn something of the actual, rather than the supposed or *ideal*, relations between basic and applied social research. As presently conceived, these would be clarified by *training seminars centered about reports of actual cases of research applied to policy by practitioners who took part in the research.* The patterns of these seminars would be somewhat as follows. Practitioners present a relatively brief and compact factual memorandum on the case including materials on the research organization, its form and informal relations with the policy makers in question, the form in which the policy problem was originally put, the limitations of size of research staff and budget, the time available for research, and the apparent expectations of the client regarding the nature of the research and the uses to which it might be put. These memoranda of the pertinent facts of the case are presented to the student members of the seminar and they, in turn, working as student-teams of two or three, prepare a research brief bearing on the case. Before any collective discussion, then, these documents represent the provisional design of research as developed by students. These documents are reviewed by the instructor and the visiting practitioner, in advance of those meetings of the seminar, which are to be devoted to the given case.

The seminar meetings themselves represent a kind of clinical session, consisting of a review of the research formulations proposed by the students. The instructor, the practitioner, and the students jointly examine the alternative proposals in the light of the actual situation. As each clinical session develops, the practitioner indicates, serially, and piecemeal, what he did in fact do, comparing this with the suggestions set forth in the briefs of the students. Students come progressively to see that *policy-oriented research involves a sequence of choices among alternative research decisions which might have been taken.* They learn something of the way in which practice differs from theory, not in the ignorant sense of that phrase (which implies that theory is somehow inferior to practicality), but in the significant sense that considerations other than those expressed in an abstract theory need to be taken into account when research is oriented toward questions of policy.

In these clinical sessions, instruction does not proceed solely from professor to student, or even from practitioner to student. Instead, there develops a more active and more varied learning situation, in which professor, practitioner and students are all diversely learning from collective examination of the case in hand. The practitioner, for example, is often required in the presence of students to clarify for himself the rationale for certain research decisions, which he actually made, particularly when these differ from suggestions advanced in the students' briefs. This has a double advantage, first for the students, who thus see the pertinence of substantive principles and methodological precepts; and second for the practitioner, who is forced to review, perhaps for the first time in some instances, the grounds for his decisions. So, too, the interaction among students themselves makes for an effective learning situation. Since different 'solutions' of the problem in hand are submitted by the student-teams, working independently, there is considerable interplay among them, as one team asks another to justify its proposed solution at a given point as against an alternative which they have advanced. An intellectually provocative kind of rivalry (rather than grade-seeking competition) develops among the student-teams with respect to reaching a seemingly most effective analysis of the case.

A series of such clinical sessions, based upon diverse cases introduced by practitioners, leads to an effective assimilation by students of basic principles of analysis in place of mere improvisations. It will undoubtedly be found, for example, that principles and precepts that are worked through in connection with a problem introduced by one practitioner will enter into the discussion of a problem subsequently presented by another practitioner. This unpremeditated experience of drawing upon general principles may be expected to give the student a healthy but not exaggerated respect for principles of analysis, and thus wean him from any tendency toward rank empiricism. But it is important to notice: these principles thus *earn* his respect; they are not authoritatively and doctrinally imposed upon him.

Through such clinical sessions, finally, *students learn of many problems and research situations which have not yet found their way into books.* They share in the intellectual excitement of being at the frontiers of certain developments in the field. By working on these first-hand cases presented by practitioners, the students gain a lively sense of being in the thick of things significant for social research, rather than being outsiders with access to problems, materials, and findings only after they have seen print. The printed materials, moreover, ordinarily do not recapture the full complexity of the actual research situation, in the degree that this is true of the clinical sessions. As everyone knows, social research as written for publication seldom includes the varied details of the various rabbit-paths, culs-de-sac, and mistaken assumptions that ordinarily enter into the actual investigation. The student merely reading reports knows nothing of the mistakes that were made, and thus learns nothing about detecting and guarding against such mistakes.

There are other potential values that could be realized by this type of training. But perhaps this is sufficient to indicate the need for case-materials on policy-oriented research, the nature of such materials, the procedures for bringing them into being, the ways in which they can be utilized for training purposes, and the distinctive training functions they would serve.

CASE MATERIALS DESIGNED TO TRAIN STUDENTS IN THE PROCEDURES OF COMPARATIVE SOCIAL RESEARCH

We have previously noted that the advanced student of social research often tends toward intellectual parochialism, through the common practice of neglecting the significant writings of an earlier day. There is another aspect of this danger, which has to be overcome. Much empirical research is being done on very specific problems, with narrowly circumscribed samples. Thus the impression is created that "little" subject matters go together with clearly defined research operations while "big" issues—for better or worse—have to be approached in a vaguer more "philosophical" way. This is a misunderstanding that can best be dispelled by studying topics for which larger social systems form a natural research unit. Such topics can be provided by the systematic comparison of different nations and different societies. Therefore, case material is needed from the field of comparative sociology, which will permit the detailed analysis of various social structures.

At the very least, *those case materials would lead the student to recognize the relativity of cultural forms and of social organization.* For what appears self-evident when regarded in a single society becomes more properly soon as problematical when examined in several societies. Thus, the student might be asked to work on case materials to determine the respects in which "the middle classes" in the United States, England, and France are functionally and structurally alike, and the respects in which they are different. In taking up this assignment, he could no longer assume that this class position has the same significance in these several societies. In the one instance, for example, it may be found that middle class position is prevalently regarded as a way-station in the journey up the ladder of ambition, whereas in another, it may be regarded as a relatively fixed and settled position with aspirations largely limited to maintaining rather than advancing one's status. Comparative studies along these lines would open the student's eyes to the possibility that social science categories (such as middle class) have different significances in different social structures.

But the recognition of cultural relativism is only the least result of such training and, in itself, hardly enough to warrant a focus on comparative study. Training would consist, not in the mere itemization of cultural differences as a collection of interesting oddities, but in the *analysis* of these differences. The student would examine, for example, the interplay between the spread of capitalism and various systems of social stratification: thus, how does capitalism fare in a society such as China with its tradition of open competition for preferred positions in the state bureaucracy as compared with India, possessing a caste system? On the basis of data about several social structures, the student might be required to analyze the probable receptivity to new forms of social organizations.

Students would also receive training in *verifiable* social and cultural diagnosis on a comparative basis. Materials can be prepared in which information about the actual social outcome is known to the instructor but withheld from the student until he has submitted his analysis. For example, drawing upon case materials for several countries of Latin America, the student might be asked to analyze the difficulties that would probably be encountered in seeking to graft democratic forms onto a quasi-feudal social structure which appears inimical to democratic organization.

In much the same fashion, training in comparative studies would provide a sounder base for the student's theoretic orientation. A body of case materials could readily be assembled, for example, showing that wage incentives operate very differently in industrially advanced societies and in societies only touched by large industry. Confronted with such data, the student would be compelled to consider the theoretic implications of the fact that piecework wages introduced in some non-industrial societies serve not as incentives for maximizing money income, but only as a means for enabling workers to quit work at that moment when they had earned what they traditionally consider "a full day's wage." That money incentives do not operate uniformly but are themselves functions of the cultural values prevailing in society can be learned only through systematic work on comparative materials. After having worked through a series of such case materials, the student would have a grounded sense of the limits to the applicability of those social theories making assumptions of fact which do not hold uniformly for different types of society.

Comparative study would also provide the student with training in the clarification of basic concepts. Comparative research exerts pressure for such clarification. For a requirement of such research is that the concepts to be defined with sufficient clarity to enable genuine comparison, a requirement which is often neither perceived nor satisfied when standardized data are drawn from a single society. An effort to compare the "standard of living" in vastly different societies, for example, would at once compel the student to clear up the concept of standard of living if only because such seemingly different elements appear to be involved in different societies.

In the course of such efforts, the student would soon learn that data on population, land tenure, migration, industrial production, etc. in different societies are far from comparable. In the attempt to determine the degree of comparability of governmental data, he would be led to a systematic review of the methods of gathering those data in different societies. This would provide him with that first-hand knowledge about source data which is indispensable to the responsible student of social research.[4]

Cases centered on comparative social materials, then, would constitute another major part of the case system for training in social research. By assembling these materials—and as the Cross-Cultural Survey illustrates, much of the material is readily accessible—the training center would further round out the professional student's methodological skills and substantive knowledge.

A CONCLUDING NOTE

These five types of case materials do not, of course, exhaust the possibilities. Various training centers may choose to focus on various

---

[4]   There is another major methodological value in this type of training. Comparative study represents the closest counterpart to the *logic* of experiment achievable in the study of large social systems (as distinct from small groups experimentally contrived in the laboratory of the social psychologist).

kinds of materials. As a matter of fact, the accumulation of the necessary documents should be one of the main contributions which professional training centers will make to the development of the social sciences at large. The budget and the personnel of the center will have to be planned in such fashion that continuous and diversified work on the collection and publication of these documents can be provided for.

Part Six

Expert Witnesses

CHAPTER 19

PAUL LAZARSFELD'S WORK IN SURVEY RESEARCH AND MATHEMATICAL SOCIOLOGY

James S. Coleman

The past thirty-five years have seen the beginning and the rapid growth of survey research for studying sociological problems; and the past twenty have seen a beginning, and somewhat slower growth, of the use of mathematics as a tool in sociology. Some see these developments as beneficial for social science; others see them as diversionary, and of little help for important problems. For good or ill, Paul Lazarsfeld has been important in the development of both these areas of work, and I want here to describe some of the ways this has been so.

But before I begin this, I want to draw attention, as a kind of comparison point, to an alternative tradition of research, based on field observation. The qualitative observations that form the basis of many community studies constitute a kind of polar extreme to the systematic surveys and statistical analysis that characterize much sociological research. And some of the qualitative field workers who practice such methods show remarkable imagination and freshness of sociological insight. A few examples from a community study will illustrate this freshness of view. In one study field workers measured the rate at which a sample of men in the town walked. They measured also the rate at which a sample of women walked. They found a curiously large discrepancy between these rates: over half the women walked at a rate of three kilometers per hour or more; over half the men walked at a rate of less than two miles per hour. These sociologists also asked some men and women to describe their daily activities. A typical woman's day went like this:

6–7   Get dressed, fix the fire, fix breakfast.
7–8   Wash and dress the children, get them off to school.
8–9   Wash dishes, shop for food.
9–10   Clean up the house.
10–11   Cook.
11–12   Finish cooking and eat.
12–1   Wash dishes, clean up the kitchen.
1–2   Bring children home from school.
2–3   Darning and sewing.
3–4   Darning and sewing.
4–5   Darning and sewing.
5–6   Get the children.
6–7   Eat supper.
7–8   Bathe children, dress them for bed, put them to bed.
8–9   Sewing.
9–10   Sewing.
10–11   Go to bed.

A typical man's day went like this:

6–7   Sleep.
7–8   Take my child to school.
8–9   Take a walk in the street.
9–10   Go back to the house.
10–11   Stand on the corner, outside the house.
11–12   Eat.
12–1   Take a nap.
1–3   Walk to the river.
3–4   Go down to the store.
4–5   Go get the milk.
5–6   Play with my child.
6–7   Eat supper.
7–8   Go to bed.

The contrast between these two days is the contrast between a person whose life is full, and a person whose life is empty: the contrast between a woman who must walk fast to accomplish her daily tasks, and a man who walks slowly so as to consume the time that would otherwise weigh on him.

These ingenious sociologists noted also that newspaper circulations had declined over the three years from 1927 to 1930 in this community—a decline that is understandable because the plant, which was the town's main employer had closed, and most men had become unemployed. But the sociologists noted another point: the decline was not uniform. The paper that concerned itself most with politics and devoted most space to political and economic issues declined 60 percent, although the price had been reduced; the paper that was largely devoted to sports and entertainment declined only 27 percent, though its price had not been reduced. This led the sociologists to suggest that the unemployment and loss of hope had reduced interest in politics and public affairs, and had led to an escape into vicarious experience of spectator sports and entertainment.

This acute sensitivity to indicators of the state of a social system is not universal among qualitative field observers; it distinguishes those with a drive to know the psychological state of a collectivity—those who can see the community as more than the sum of its parts. The sociologists with such sensitivity often scorn survey research precisely because it treats a social system as no more than the sum of its parts—as an aggregate of individuals.

Yet the man who has been perhaps most responsible for the development of survey research is indeed the man who, with his colleagues, made these sensitive observations in a small town in Austria, in one of his first empirical research activities as a sociologist—Paul Lazarsfeld.

This is a curious conjunction, for survey research has been derided by sociologists from Herbert Blumer onward, as the enemy of research on a social system or a collectivity by overlooking the very fabric of ties that constitutes this system of collective body. How did Paul Lazarsfeld move from studying the mood of Marienthal to analyzing the voting and buying and listening decisions of individual voters, consumers, and radio listeners? And did this move represent a shift from the sociologist interested in collective psychology to the psychologist interested in aggregate psychology? Did Paul Lazarsfeld, in his use and development of survey research, desert sociology for psychology? Or perhaps, because of the strength of his personality, did he divert sociology from its legitimate social concerns to spurious psychological ones? It is a mark of the importance of the man that these are not merely questions about a man's intellectual career, but questions about the development of research in sociology—for the development of systematic methods in sociology has depended greatly on both the research examples and the methodological papers of Paul Lazarsfeld.

I will not attempt here to establish the precise extent of this dependence, to argue for or against the priority of Lazarsfeld in any particular research innovation, for that is not my purpose. It is enough to recognize that there is a strong dependence of the present state of survey research upon his work, and to go on from there to the questions I've posed above: i.e., did he desert his sociological interests and by so doing help divert a whole discipline from its principal concerns? I will try to answer these questions first of all in Lazarsfeld's work generally, and secondly, in his development of mathematical sociology, where the question of forsaking sociological concerns is similar but not identical.

The first step away from Marienthal was a move to the United States and a move to mass communications research. These two moves were not unrelated. The age of radio was beginning in the U.S., and other national mass media, such as magazines, were becoming more important. But the study of the effects of mass media on a dispersed audience was quite different from the study of the effects of unemployment on a community. The research shifted from a focus on a collective body—a community, whose members simply provided indicators or cues to the collective mood of the town—to a focus on individuals as units. The impact of a radio program or a movie or a magazine ad was obviously (or so it then seemed) only upon those exposed to it. Thus, the focus shifted to individual decision making and the influences upon it. A similar individual focus was relevant for studies of voting. In all this research upon buying decisions, voting decisions, and attitude change, the research became aggregate psychology, in which the social system as a system was wholly neglected.

From this work, it was possible to go in any of several directions. One, which is illustrated by the brilliant sequence of work carried out by Hovland and his associates, is to carefully control exposure to mass communication through laboratory experiments, and thus study in much more detail the psychological mechanisms of attitude or behavior change. Lazarsfeld did not take that path. He went in precisely the opposite direction, leaving exposure to mass media uncontrolled—and thus a variable for study in its own right—and continuing to examine the effects of mass communications as it occurred in society. And in doing this, he began to drift back toward the community. The panel voting study of 1940 and that of 1948 was carried out in single communities. In the first of these, the research analysis still focussed on the individuals as isolated entities, not as part of an organic community. In the second, tentative steps away from the wholly individual focus occurred by studying the relation between a man's vote and the voting preferences of his friends and his family. Then, in the study of innovation in women's fashions—begun as a study of the effects of mass media, but finally published under the title, *Personal Influence*— the social system of the community again came back into the analysis. For the force of the data showed that in fashion decisions, the mass media were only the initial element in a sequence of communication that passed from the media to opinion leaders, and from there to others who relied on personal communication from their friends rather than the media. Thus, the individuals were no longer seen as distinct, separated elements responding in the aggregate to mass communications, but as part of a communications and influence network.

At the same time, in his methodological writings, there emerged other indications of a reemerging concern with social units such as the community. In a discussion of index formation, he introduced the idea of group variables, measures of the community or other social unit of which the individual found himself a part—variables that might affect attitudes and behavior. Later, in seminars and in a project at Columbia on "Concepts and Indices in the Social Sciences," this interest was enlarged; and several persons were set to work on problems of "global indicators," that is, indicators of the state of a community or another social unit—work which in part found its way into the methodology reader, *The Language of Social Research*, and papers published elsewhere. These indicators and the work on them were bringing Lazarsfeld full circle to the collective psychology of the Marienthal study. Significantly, one of the sources used by students in the search for global indicators was the old Marienthal research.

But this was more than a return to the past. Intervening had been the whole development of survey research in which Lazarsfeld had himself played a crucial part. Thus, the role of the global indicators and the group variables came to be used not merely to characterize the collective mood of the community, but as independent variables that could have an impact on the individuals who found themselves in those communities. The culmination of this combination of two parts of his past occurred in *The Academic Mind*. This research examined the attitudes toward academic freedom of social science faculty members in a sample of colleges throughout the country, at a period tinged with fears of internal Communist subversion. In the attitudes themselves, and in the analysis which examined influences upon them, the "attitude climate" of the particular college campus played a crucial role. Thus the community indicators and group variables were important not merely to describe the climate existing in a given college; they were important for showing how this climate affected the attitudes of faculty members within it.

With this research, Lazarsfeld had returned to his first research interest; but to it, he had added the research techniques and the analytical aims of the intervening years.

The question arises as to what brought this return to a more sociological perspective of the first research, from the aggregate psychology of the audience, consumer, and voting research. Two hypotheses are tenable; and I will mention both, without trying to determine their relative importance. One is simply that the press of his own concerns and interests in social processes, in mass behavior, and in collective (as distinct from aggregate) psychology, led him back as research techniques became able to combine those interests with his analytical ones. The second hypothesis is that the move to Columbia, and in particular the continuing dialogue with Robert Merton in seminars, in research planning, and in casual discussions, focussed Lazarsfeld's attention back toward a concern with collectivities and their impact on individuals within them.

Parallels have been drawn between the combination of Lazarsfeld and Merton at Columbia, in which there was continuing interaction between the methodological and the theorist with consequences for the work of both; and the combination of Stouffer and Parsons at Harvard, in which initial attempts at intellectual exchange were not successful. This does not, however, answer the question. For not only is there this interaction, which suggests Merton's influence; there is also earlier work which shows that these concerns did exist in latent form throughout the mass media phase of his work.[1]

Whatever the source, it is clear that if Lazarsfeld did for a time desert his initial sociological interests and did perhaps lead survey research toward aggregate psychology, he also helped bring it back as a new tool useful for studying problems that have been the concern of generations of sociologists.

From this examination of research content and methods in general, I want to turn now to the developments in mathematical sociology that Lazarsfeld fathered. Again, the same kind of question is relevant: do not the mathematical developments represent a forsaking of his earlier sociological concerns in the search for precision? It is useful to give a brief catalogue of the activities of Lazarsfeld in this area to indicate the nature of his mathematical contributions.

Lazarsfeld's influence in mathematical sociology has been through several media: through his direct contributions themselves, through organizing the efforts of others toward this goal, and through setting problems, which have been successfully pursued by others. Probably the least important of these influences has been his own direct contributions. The problem which has most fully occupied his attention is latent structure analysis, a technique for discovering and measuring the underlying structure of attitudes held by individuals, when these underlying attitudes are only probabilistically related to responses. This idea and technique has had a long and fitful history in Lazarsfeld's work. It has appeared in print as long ago as Volume IV of *The American Soldier*, published in 1949; yet it remains to this day a technique for which practical and detailed methods are unavailable to the general practitioner of social research. Thus for many sociologists, latent struc-

---

[1] This interaction with Merton indicates, however, another aspect of Lazarsfeld's personal and intellectual style which has played an important part in his impact on the discipline. This is his incessant concern with others in his immediate environment. Not only did he develop a long dialogue with Merton, played out both in joint seminars and in research, but he did so with Ernest Nagel as well—like Merton, much more a solitary scholar, who would never have initiated such interaction. Whatever the consequences of these interactions in the work of Lazarsfeld, Merton and Nagel, they were exceedingly important for some of their students, in giving a sense of the relationship between different approaches to the same problem. The others whom he drew into his intellectual arena, for shorter or longer periods, were numerous and well know: S. M. Lipset, C. Wright Mills, T. W. Anderson, Howard Raiffa, Duncan Luce, among others.

ture analysis has been more a promise than a reality; and however impressive the original conception on which it is based, it has remained principally a conceptual scheme for discussion rather than a method for use. There is, however, another idea of Lazarfeld's on the borderlines of survey analysis and mathematical models, which has had a totally different history in the discipline: a strong and continuing impact as a result of a single clear and straightforward paper published shortly after the idea was developed. This was the elaboration scheme for qualitative attributes, published in 1952 in *Social Research: The American Soldier.* This approach to cross-tabulations was the first attempt to lay out a formal procedure for discovering causal relations among qualitative attributes, to discover spurious relationships, and to determine the intervening paths through which effects took place. This paper, and an analogous paper by Herbert Simon for continuous variables constituted the first elements in sociology of the approach to quantitative analysis which lays out explicit causal structures.

Lazarsfeld's development of the elaboration scheme was an attempt to introduce causal asymmetry into cross-tabulation analysis. It was stimulated in part by Louis Guttman's introduction via scale analysis of a different type of asymmetry into cross-tabulations. Guttman's asymmetry, which led to "Guttman scaling," was a method for discovering a dimension underlying responses to a set of items; Lazarsfeld wanted an asymmetry which would reflect causal relations. The result was his elaboration scheme, which became the standard for causal interpretation of survey data for many years.

Although this work (unlike latent structure analysis) has had important and continuing effects, and although he has made other contributions, such as recent work in a general "algebra" of dichotomous attributes, I believe Lazarsfeld's principal impact in mathematical sociology has been through organizing the efforts of others in this direction. There have been three such efforts that especially stand out. The first is a series of lectures in mathematical social science at Columbia in 1950–51, which were subsequently published as *Mathematical Thinking in the Social Sciences,* in 1954. This book held for a long time an important place as the initial stimulus for sociologists interested in mathematical methods. In some respects, this book, though its chapters were diverse and of varying relevance to sociology, initiated the field.

The second milestone was the Behavioral Models Project, carried out at the Bureau of Applied Social Research. This project was highly productive and resulted in several important books: *Games and Decisions*, by Luce and Raiffa, *Developments in Mathematical Psychology*, edited by Luce, and *Mathematical Thinking in the Measurement of Behavior*, edited by Solomon. Besides these books, the project provided an intellectual milieu in which interests in mathematical sociology could prosper, both on the part of young faculty and graduate students at Columbia—a kind of starting point for careers in mathematical sociology.

The third major milestone in organizing efforts in mathematical sociology began in 1960, and is still continuing: the internationalization of mathematical methods through semi-annual UNESCO Summer Institutes, held in Europe. These institutes, organized by Lazarsfeld, have had and are continuing to have a wide impact on the new generation of sociologists in Europe.

The final medium through which Lazarsfeld's impact in mathematical sociology has been manifest is via the problems that he has posed and then left unsolved or only partially solved for others. I will examine one of the most important of these, the study of mutual effects of attitudes in panel analysis, in some detail later, and thus will not discuss this medium in detail here.

With this brief overview of Lazarsfeld's major contributions to mathematical sociology, we can restate the question: does not this work represent a forsaking of sociological concerns in the search for precision? To answer this, it is useful to examine the relation of his mathematical endeavors to other interests.

First of all, the most important observation is that Lazarsfeld's mathematical work was closely related to, and grew out of, his survey analysis. Some of his methodological contributions, such as work in index construction, comparison of indices by their "areas of ambiguity" substruction of an attribute space, the widely-used three-variable elaboration scheme in survey analysis and the development of mutual-effect indices for panel analysis are all directly derivative from problems in survey analysis, and lie in that intermediate area between survey methods and mathematical sociology. His most extensive and continuing direct contribution to mathematical sociology—latent structure analysis—also derives from measurement problems in survey analysis.

The second important point to recognize is that none of these contributions are contributions to the field of statistics, as generally defined. The use of standard statistical techniques, either descriptive statistics such as correlation coefficients, or statistical inference such as tests of significance of a difference, has been largely foreign to Lazarsfeld's methods. This is all the more striking because the concurrent development of research methods in psychology were making heavy use of standard statistical methods. Lazarsfeld's survey analysis, and most of the parallel and subsequent work by others made little use of standard statistics, and only in the past few years has survey methodology in sociology come to make widespread use of standard descriptive and inferential statistics. Does this mean that we can add a second charge: that Lazarsfeld impeded and delayed the fruitful use of statistics in sociology? Certainly that charge has been made by some methodologists, and it is reasonable to raise it here.

These two characteristics of Lazarsfeld's mathematical sociology—its close ties to survey research, and its neglect of standard statistical tools—are important for understanding both the aims of Lazarsfeld in his mathematical work and the impact it has had on systematic sociology. To understand his aims and the impact, it will be useful to examine in somewhat more detail a specific example. One of his most extensive and continuous concerns over a number of years has been the measurement of "mutual effects" of attitudes in attitude change. The problem is this: in panel or experimental data, where two dichotomous attitudes are measured at two points in time, two questions arise: Do either or both of the attitudes affect one another? and, How can one measure any effects of these attitudes upon one another? The first attempts to answer these questions were by the development of "mutual effects indices," using data tabulated in the form of 16-fold tables, that is, tables cross-tabulating the positions of a panel on both attitudes at two points in time: a $(2 \times 2) \times (2 \times 2)$ table. These were *ad hoc* indices showing which attitude dominates the other. A number of students at Columbia, most successfully Lee Wiggins, took up this problem and developed sophisticated measures of mutual effects. But this was unsatisfying to Lazarsfeld, in part because of the much more satisfactory treatment that exists for continuous variables, and in part because this index construction provided no rationale for using one index rather than another. On the other hand, an explicit mathematical model would provide a mirror or model of the process of change, and thus constitute a structural foundation and meaning for the parameter values—

and these parameter values would thus become the measures of inter-dependence between the attributes.

For continuous variables, a pair of simultaneous differential or difference equations have long been used in physics and in economics to describe the effects of two variables on one another. As a consequence, he explored with a number of persons the possibility of transforming those models for use with dichotomous attributes: William J. Baumol, who had widely used difference equations in economics; Gerald Thompson, a mathematician with social science interests; and others. None of these attempts were highly satisfactory. But the problem was a legitimate and important one, and Wiggins' work continued; my own work in mathematical sociology took that as one of its focuses; and others at other places, such as Pelz at Michigan, and Campbell at Northwestern have struggled with the problem Lazarsfeld posed.

The problem at present has been taken several steps farther. First, the analog to continuous-variable systems of equations has been developed by use of stochastic processes. Secondly, the problem as mathematically formulated at present can be and is, as has been shown, fully parallel to models of change with continuous variables, and thus is brought into the sphere of advanced statistical methods that include time series analysis, systems of differential equations, and lagged regression analysis. Thirdly, John Tukey has recently proposed (taking the stochastic model of interdependent attitude change as given) an alternative mechanism of change, which raises conceptual questions about the very nature of "effects" of attitudes upon one another.

Meanwhile, Lazarsfeld himself has returned at times to the problem, but his major contribution is already made in the steps he carried out: generating the problem, as part of the transformation of surveys from opinion polls to sophisticated tools of social analysis, developing first approximations to an answer by the construction of mutual effects indices, and pointing the way toward a mathematical model for the process. By these three important steps, Lazarsfeld helped move survey research from its primitive stages to a stage advanced enough to make use of the most powerful mathematical techniques available. And in so doing, his principal aim was not obscured: to study with precision the processes of change within the members of a population.

This example illustrates what appear to me as the benefits of Lazarsfeld's failure to use standard statistical techniques in his methodology. For if he had done so in the early development of survey research, the statistical methods that could have then been used would have been very different ones than those to which the actual course of development has led. They would have been, for example, chi-square tests of goodness of fit and of the significance of the difference between two proportions. The "style" of survey research would not be, as it has been in the Columbia tradition, one of discovering processes, but would likely have been codified into a rigid testing of hypotheses in a way more appropriate to experimental data than survey research. Thus there is a great likelihood that the study of the process of mutual attitude change would have been lost—simply because the statistical methods available at that time, and appropriate to the rather primitive state of data analysis, are not appropriate for describing a process of change. It is possible that a rigid statistical form would have been developed for describing and testing relationships in survey data, a form that would have inhibited, rather than encouraged, the development of precise instruments for studying the process of change.

This, then, is one general thesis concerning the style of Lazarsfeld's work in mathematical sociology: that by deriving his problems from survey analysis, and by avoiding the early and rigid use of standard statistical methods, Lazarsfeld encouraged the development of models for social psychological processes—models to mirror the causal relations that constitute the dynamics of a system of variables.

But this still leaves unanswered the question of whether this has not wholly neglected social processes, and led mathematical sociology into a concern with nothing beyond psychological processes. For the mathematical models of change that have developed from Lazarsfeld's interests have been wholly models of change within individuals. The unit of analysis has been the individual, the resulting statements are about effects of attributes of individuals on attributes of individuals. Processes of *social* change have been largely ignored. This is a charge that can be less easily dispensed with. It is true that Lazarsfeld has made attempts to develop mathematical models appropriate to social processes.

For example, in the early 1950's, he became very interested with the work of Nicholas Rashevsky and his group, (which included Rapoport, Landau, Shimbel, and others) in social behavior. This work involved models for social networks, authority systems, status systems, and other aspects of a social system. But some of the work did not stand up well to careful examination, and some of it could not conceivably be tested or used with data. Thus, it constituted a dead end. Similarly, in his courses on mathematical models with Ernest Nagel, he introduced students to mathematics designed to characterize societies or social groups: work by Richardson, Lanchester, Simon, Zipf, and others. Yet neither he nor his students—nor for that matter, others who have tried to build upon this work—have been successful.

The fact of the matter is that there exists little mathematical sociology that it truly sociological in character, in that it is concerned with processes of a social system or a social organization. Neither Lazarsfeld and his followers, nor practitioners from other traditions, have made much serious headway in this area. Only in a few areas such as mathematical demography, concerned with population movements and population growth, has there been development comparable to the Lazarsfeld-initiated work in mathematics of attitude and behavior change. It is significant that this mathematical demography is also based on the aggregate of individual processes, not on the functioning of social organization.

It seems quite possible that the defect is a more fundamental one in sociological theory. There appears to be little social theory that does explicitly describe processes, little social theory that could serve as a basis or a starting point for such mathematics. What passes for theory among many sociologists is nothing more than classification, a development of categories by which social organization or roles can be described. It may, then, not be an argument of serious force to claim that such mathematical work has shown little social dynamics, if nonmathematical sociology has exhibited a similar lack.

The direction of mathematical sociology derivative from Lazarsfeld can be compared to that which stems from another tradition, and constitutes the principal alternative direction of mathematics in sociology. Just as the mathematical models in sociology of Lazarsfeld are closely tied to survey research, and depend on survey research for their data, the alternative tradition is closely tied to experimentation, and depends on experiments (principally in small groups) for its data. One can inquire whether this work is more truly sociological in character, and can provide a foundation for the mathematical treatment of social organization and social systems. Unfortunately, the answer seems to be no. The largest portion of this work appears, curiously enough, to be wholly individualistic in character. The general style of the work can be described as follows: an experiment is carried out in which individuals in a group constitute a stimulus environment for one another. Then a model is developed that describes the response of a single individual to this stimulus environment. An example is the work of Bernard Cohen, which presents a model for the response of an individual to "group pressure" in an action. The mathematics describes psychological and behavioral changes of the individual in response to the group pressure, which lies outside the model. A second class of the mathematical work deriving from small-group experiments lies at the opposite extreme. The group is taken as a unit, and the mathematics describes the behavior of this unit as a single entity. Herbert Simon's work in formalyzing propositions of Homans and Festinger about small group behavior exemplifies this approach. Simon's models consist of simultaneous differential equations that describe the "group behavior." Other learning models have been applied to the group, merely substituting "the group" for the individual as the entity which is learning. It appears, altogether, that the mathematical sociology deriving from the alternative tradition of small group experiments is not more likely to provide a base for a mathematical treatment of social organization than that deriving from Lazarsfeld's tradition of survey research.

But I have painted somewhat too bleak a picture. There are certainly examples of mathematical work, deriving both from Lazarsfeld's survey research tradition and from other directions, that provide starting points for the study of social organization. Deriving directly from the survey research tradition is work on social diffusion of innovations, which have been pursued both by use of stochastic processes and by use of deterministic models using systems of differential equations. There is the early work of Volterra with his predator-prey models involving the interaction between two populations. Even Richardson's early work applied to mutual arms escalation of notions is a step in a similar direction. Harrison White's analysis of marriage rules in primitive tribes is another example. A British probability theorist, David Bartholemew, has developed a set of models derived from renewal theory for discribing the movement into, out of, and within hierarchical organizations. And recently, there has been some transfer of mathematical approaches of economics by Mancur Olson, applying the theory of public goods to interest group formation—and others applying the theory of utility under risk to collective decisions decided by voting. But these are relatively isolated cases, and it is not clear which ones, if any, can serve as starting points for mathematical theory of social organization.

The final judgment, then, concerning the mathematical sociology deriving from Lazarsfeld's own work and from his concentration on survey analysis, is that it has not provided a base for the mathematical theory of social systems.

CHAPTER 20

AN INTRODUCTION TO LAZARSFELD'S PHILOSOPHICAL PAPERS

Raymond Boudon

THE LANGUAGE OF THE SOCIAL SCIENCES

The concern that leads Lazarsfeld to raise repeated questions about the language of the social sciences and their dispersion is common to most sociologists. Durkheim undertook the same search, especially in *Les règles de la méthode sociologique* but elsewhere as well; it is found in Max Weber, in the *Aufsätze zur Wissenschaftslehre* and elsewhere; it is also found in Parsons, notably in *Towards a General Theory of Action.*

What are the origins of this persistent search? Does it come, as Dilthey and Auguste Comte believed, from the notion that the social sciences provide a new model of understanding? Does it come from the fact that the natural sciences, through the analysis that they elicited from philosophers, led to the development of an epistemological system into which it would be difficult to fit the social sciences? Does it arise because the social sciences have not yet found their philosopher or their historian?

In any case, there is one point on which it is difficult to quarrel with Lazarsfeld. Before assessing the social sciences, before claiming their identity with or difference from the natural sciences, before conceptualizing a theory of sociological knowledge or some other large-scale system, it is essential to undertake a careful analysis of the work of sociologists and a true history of the social sciences. If today we have a number of precise ideas about the logic of the natural sciences or the "structure of scientific discoveries," to use a phrase suggested by Thomas Kuhn, this is not the result of abstract speculations on the nature of experimentation or the relation between subject and object which characterize research in the natural sciences. Rather, it is because historians have given attention to a number of scientific discoveries, and because philosophers could not avoid spending several years familiarizing themselves with the language of science before extracting from it propositions of a general order.

Perhaps the social sciences suffer from a disadvantage in comparison with the natural sciences: this is their "exoteric" or common sense character. The fact that a fair number of sociological books can be read without special training perhaps discourages the philosopher from undertaking the necessary homework which he would never neglect when dealing with the natural sciences. On his part, the historian of science may be derailed by the impression of discontinuity which the social sciences give. The cumulative nature, the linearity of mathematics or physics seem to be strong contrast with the discontinuity of the social sciences. Kuhn noted that, in order to assess the difference between the two types of discipline, it is sufficient to point to a crucial indicator: while the renown of a sociologist or anthropologist is proportional to the volume of his works, rarely does a physicist write a book. Or, if he does write one, it is usually a textbook unlikely to add to his renown among the scientific community.

If the development of the natural sciences is perhaps less linear than popular history would lead us to believe, that of the social sciences, in contrast, is perhaps less discontinuous and anarchic than is claimed by a certain tradition in the history of the social sciences. According to this tradition, the social sciences have developed as a succession of doctrines or systems high individualistic works comparable to what is found in the history of philosophy.

Thus, an important task for anyone interested in the language of the social sciences is to abandon the plane of generalities, which perhaps were appropriate at the time of Dilthey but which today are not useful either to the social sciences themselves or to the philosophy of science.

For, it is the intuition of Lazarsfeld that consideration of, or more exactly, investigation of the language of the social sciences does not only serve a theoretical function. In fact, this function is secondary. The principal role of these investigations is eventually to describe conditions essential to scientific progress. That intuition, which is also an obsession, develops out of an analysis of the natural sciences. On several occasions, in his brief autobiography, and also in his presidential address on "The Sociology of Empirical Sociology," Lazarsfeld recalls how salient an experience his discovery of the theory of relativity was for him. He describes the special intellectual pleasure he felt when he realized that the notion of simultaneity was open to question when one applied it to two events, one on the moon and the other on earth. "The notion that . . .," "open to question"—these expressions are good indications that the theory of relativity was perceived by Lazarsfeld as a discovery dealing less with reality than with the language of science. Like a discovery made by a physicist concerning his own language.

In brief, from the theory of relativity Lazarsfeld derives the idea that scientific progress often rests on the same techniques employed by scholars in linguistic criticism. Naturally, this criticism has a positive goal—the clarification of language. Lazarsfeld calls such positive criticism of scientific language *methodology*.

This conviction that scientific progress requires a clarification of language is found in other sociological writings. One recalls the sense of outrage that Durkheim expressed when he discussed authors who claimed to find a relationship between suicide rates and various cosmic phenomena and who made the second a cause of the first. This sense of outrage led to a critique of the scientific *language* employed by the Italian positivists. Durkheim showed, something which had never been clarified before, that a statistical relationship could not—with some exceptions—be directly interpreted as a causal relation, but could be the result of more complex relationships.

One might note that, if the clarity of language seems an insignificant objective, the notion that the clarification of language might be a factor in scientific progress is perhaps less commonly recognized by sociologists than might be expected. Still, today the importance of methodology is often denied. It is claimed, as C. Wright Mills wrote about Lazarsfeld's work, that rigor replaces imagination, the art of proof, the art of discovery, and, finally, that research is made sterile. These objections, if carried to the extreme, allow one to substitute facile writing and discursive language for research; they do not lead to scientific progress.

Lazarsfeld shows his irritation with facile writing and with rhetoric, which often do nothing but impede the development of the social sciences. On several occasions he takes Weber to task for his notion of the "ideal type," as famous as it is obscure and unmanageable—so obscure, as a matter of fact, that Weber himself never tried to define it. The myth of the ideal type strikes Lazarsfeld as all the more annoying because one can point to important articles, usually overlooked in the traditional history of sociology, in which Max Weber spelled out the problem of constructing typologies in logical terms which are much more satisfactory. On other occasions, he is critical of those sociologists who deny that an investigation has any merit unless it takes into account the social *structure* or unless it encompasses the *totality* of a particular social situation, without being able to specify exactly what they mean by totality or structure. Remarks such as these, according to Lazarsfeld, do not lead to any progress unless one tries to define more clearly what is signified by the terms that are used.

From the comments made up to this point, it should be evident that one will not find in the Lazarsfeld's papers discussion of the great debates, pompously labelled epistemological, that keep the social sciences in a state of ferment. His inclination more often than not has been to substitute for these broad questions those which can be treated analytically. It is better, before expressing a preference for qualitative methods, to explore the logic underlying these methods, to clarify the types of situations to which they can be applied, to analyze the problem of proof in cases where statistical inference is impossible, or to distinguish types of qualitative methods. In the same way, before proclaiming oneself a structuralist, it is necessary to know just what structuralism implies. The type of analysis that Lazarsfeld favors has led to an interesting proposition: he has shown that, in effect, the phonic structuralism of Jakobson was formally—we do not dare write structurally—indistinguishable from a logical operation frequently used in sociology, an operation which Lazarsfeld called "the substruction of an attribute space" and of which one finds the outlines in the work of Max Weber himself.

Lazarsfeld's methodology is itself based on a method, a method which he sometimes describes by the French term, "explication de texte." (On this point, see, for example, his presidential address on

"The Sociology of Empirical Sociology.") Instead of asking what would *a priori* make qualitative methods preferable to quantitative methods (or the reverse), one selects a sample of studies making use of qualitative methods, and submits them to an explication de texte. Instead of inquiring in general terms whether there are limits to the application of statistics in the social sciences, it would be better to carry out an explication of text on studies making use of statistical methods, in a manner that would result in a precise diagnosis of the difficulties encountered.

An analysis, dealing with problems in the application of statistics, can be found in Lazarsfeld's introduction to the posthumous volume by Samuel Stouffer, *Social Research to Test Ideas.* Here he addresses himself to the difficulties encountered by sociologists trying to apply statistical methods literally, without recognizing that a profitable exchange between the two disciplines presupposes a clarification of sociological language as well as awareness of the logical properties of statistical instruments. Thus, some sociologists have experienced frustration when they have naively used the notion of partial correlation without recognizing that it assumes the linearity of the correlation.

This method of explication de texte, even though the term was borrowed from methods of instruction in the humanities, was perhaps suggested to Lazarsfeld by his scientific training. It invites the methodologist to proceed from the particular to the general. It is also true that the analysis of circumscribed problems or difficulties provides the impetus for progress in the natural sciences. The particle theory of light was not replaced by a better theory as the result of general discussion of its merits, but rather through the discovery of the phenomenon of interference. Similarly, it was the failure of the experiments carried out by Michelson-Morley which led to the theory of relativity. In brief, progress in scientific language most often results from the analysis of phenomena which are circumscribed, although of strategic importance.

This seemingly obvious position is rarely accepted in the social sciences; there one often finds the assumption that only general debates lead to progress and that methodological analysis hardly makes even a marginal contribution. Perhaps this tendency to handle generalities directly is the feature that differentiates the "social scientist" most clearly from his colleagues in the natural sciences. The result is a proliferation of nouns ending with "ism," a proliferation that clearly has no equivalent in the natural sciences.

The better strategy is to move in the opposite direction, from the specific to the general. This approach finds its support in the major findings of the social sciences: the Hawthorne Effect, the strange marriage rules in primitive societies, their astonishing magic practices—such observations have certainly contributed more to the progress of the disciplines than all general debates. Going from the specific to the general has also characterized progress in metasociology or methodology. The careful analysis of writings by Fromm or Redfield had led to Lazarsfeld's work on the construction of typologies. This in turn is much more helpful in clarifying the structure of other concepts than many efforts made by speculative theorists.

This emphasis on the clarification of restricted problems has another consequence: it reveals unexpected relations between research domains, which usually are approached separately. Again, the typological discussions presented in this volume provide characteristic examples. They reveal a common logic that underlies many conceptual systems in the classical tradition of sociological theory: Durkheim's organic and mechanical solidarity, Merton's types of deviancy, Toennis' *Gesellschaft* and *Gemeinschaft*, etc.; in addition they bring out, as mentioned before, an unexpected connection between structural linguistics and the research practice of sociologists.

The same is true for the theory of measurement in the social sciences. One finds unexpected links between sociology and psychology. Lazarsfeld has reminded us how radical behaviorism has lost ground. Even in the interpretation of animal behavior, the behaviorist was very soon forced to introduce the notion of intervening variables in order to understand the relation between the stimulus and the response. These variables have the triple characteristic of being hypothetical, not directly observable and to a certain degree anthropomorphic. The idea is easily understood. I observe a little insect moving across the page of my manuscript. I approach it with my finger in order to crush it. The insect moves in another direction and increases its speed. At every new effort on my part the insect behaves in the same way. Naturally, I will interpret this behavior by speaking of an act of flight or evasion, a notion that has the three characteristics of an intervening variable mentioned above. This is certainly not a profound observation, but it is enough to undermine an orthodox behaviorism and at the same time a naive scientism.

In the paper on the history of concept formation, Lazarsfeld traces how Tolman himself viewed the response as not being completely determined by the stimulus; the two had to be linked by a more or less extensive set of intervening variables. This historical perspective sets limits to a behaviorism in its most radical form and consequently makes behaviorism less isolated; at the same time it makes visible the structural kinship between the logic of the experimental psychologist and that of the sociologist. As a matter of fact, one can find a similar development in many other instances. Consider, for example, Adorno and his collaborators when they worked on *The Authoritarian Personality*. The concept of an authoritarian trait is not directly observable and is hypothetical; furthermore, it is anthropomorphic in the sense that it is rooted in the experiences and observations of everyone's life. Like the intervening variable of the animal psychologist, Adorno's authoritarianism interposes itself between a series of stimuli (the projective questions used by the authors of *The Authoritarian Personality*) and the answers of the subject. Obviously it was still necessary to prove the utility of this variable; but this is another question.

For a moment it suffices to see that the intervening variable that the behaviorists were forced to introduce (going beyond their basic doctrine) provides an instrument which is as indispensable for the sociologist as for the psychologist. Notions like intelligence, authoritarianism or bureaucracy cannot be observed directly. This certainly does not mean that they should be excluded from a research program that stresses the prime importance of observed facts; it only means that such concepts should appear within a chain of reasoning which at its beginning and at its end is linked to observable elements. Weber for instance defined his notion of bureaucracy by ten indicators and was probably aware (as can be seen from other parts of his writings) that the relation between a concept and indicators is a probabilistic one. This type of analysis makes visible the logical links between disciplines, which seem to be distant from each other, and between authors who seem at first as distinct as Max Weber and Tolman.

CONFRONTING THE HISTORY OF THE SOCIAL SCIENCES

This example should help to show why, in Lazarsfeld's work on the language of the social sciences, *history* in addition to methodology plays a prominent role. It is not the result of a hobby, as a superficial observer might think. The two approaches, methodology and history, are in fact quite strongly connected in Lazarsfeld's way of thinking. Methodology has brought him to a theory of measurement bound up in his latent structure analysis. It is a formal analysis of the methodological connection between an unobserved hypothetical variable and observable variables, the indicators. His historical work has made him aware that the problems, which latent structure analysis attempts to deal with, exist also in psychology. The same is true for his work on the construction of typologies. He makes the point that all typologies are based on Cartesian space, the dimensions of which are classifications (whether or not that space is explicitly stated or only implicitly assumed). An historical analysis permits him to show how this formalization ties together many conceptual systems in the social sciences.

His basic concern then leads Lazarsfeld simultaneously to methodology and history. In somewhat pretentious terms, one can say that he was equally interested in the *genesis* and in the *structure* of language in the social sciences. The two approaches are really two convergent ways to conceptualize a unified social science. This is why in many of his publications one often finds the same problem discussed on two levels: an historical and a methodological one. What he calls multivariate analysis reminds one of Durkheim; latent structure analysis echoes the period when notions of probability begin to be introduced in the social sciences; attitude measurement brings to the surface the first efforts to establish measurement in the social sciences, for instance with Quetelet; the methodology of typological construction has helped us see a side of Max Weber little recognized by historical sociology; probably the qualitative analysis has revived interest in Le Play and his school.

Historical texts thus have an objective, analogous to methodological writings. They seek to unravel the relations, at first glance not apparent, between steps taken in one or another discipline; they also try to weave together the links in instances where the academic history of the social sciences is more apt to see doctrinal divisions and opposition. The historical task that Lazarsfeld sets for himself is so close to his heart that he does not try to avoid the phase which is thankless, yet indispensable, to the work of the historian—namely, to uncover, assemble and read critically works that are relatively unknown or difficult to obtain. Few sociologists, or even historians of sociology, can claim that they have studied Hermann Conring, Süssmilch or Petty. Few books on Max Weber mention the fact that he himself was directly involved in large-scale empirical inquiries. Few sociologists have made it their business to analyze in detail the significance of the objections leveled by Halbwachs against the "average man" of Quetelet.

It is interesting in this connection to refer once more to a brief statement in the autobiographical fragment to which we have already alluded: there Lazarsfeld notes that he did not officially become a sociologist until relatively late, when he was named to a chair in sociology at Columbia University, which he occupied until his retirement. Before that, not in Vienna, not at Newark, not at Princeton did he have the official title of sociologist. Without doubt, this comment contains an ironic nuance, in the sense that it suggests Lazarsfeld's refusal to become enclosed in one discipline, sociology, in which, nevertheless, the limits and specific nature are more difficult to define than is the case in all other social sciences. For one of Lazarsfeld's main intuitions is that methodological similarities bring together, not only socialist voting behavior and the consumption of soap, but also theory or conceptualization and research, psychology and sociology, economics and sociology, history and sociology.

The passion of Lazarsfeld for observation, combined with the catholic spirit which his teachers, the Bühlers, communicated to him, led him always to place particular studies in a general conceptual framework. The claim that investigations seemingly of a low order and unoriginal could lead to important generalizations is illustrated by the analysis of a number of marketing studies which he undertook at a time when he was concerned with investigations of this kind. This analysis permitted him to develop the notion of the "proletarian consumer," which included a number of important characteristics. A portion of this analysis deserves to be quoted:

> The proletarian consumer is less mobile psychologically, less active, more inhibited in his behavior. He makes his purchases in a circumscribed area. He shops more often in the same place. His consumption habits are more rigid and, to a lesser degree, subject to seasonal variations. As a result of the restriction of his psychological horizons, his interest is entirely focused on essential details; to the extent that we address ourselves to the lower social classes, considerations of the quality, the packaging, and

the various characteristics of the merchandise are seen only vaguely and infrequently.

This passage is interesting for more than the concept that it introduces. On the one hand, one sees in it proof of the claim that commonplace studies can lead to general concepts and important results. On the other hand, one also sees a fundamental methodological preoccupation: the subsuming of a number of specific traits under a general category. This preoccupation leads him to the idea of a matrix formulation, to the mathematical analysis of the relation between indicators and latent variables in latent structure analysis, and to the problem of constructing typologies. Similarly, the quotation points up the interest that Lazarsfeld has always had in the historical analysis of concept formation.

But the conceptual integration of descriptive materials and the concern to develop the structure of the language of social research through methodology represent only two aspects of the need for generalization. Earlier, we noted the irony with which he observes that he became a sociologist officially because Columbia University, which wanted to appoint him, had an opening in sociology. On several occasions he comes back, with the same irony, to the difficulties of defining sociology. It is for this reason that the general framework in which he perceives his own research activities is, without doubt, less sociology—the limits of which he has some difficulty visualizing—than the field which he calls "the empirical analysis of action."

It is relevant to elaborate somewhat on this point. For, if one wants to recapture the thinking of Lazarsfeld in its most extreme generality, one could say that his effort to endow the social sciences with a single language is based on three key ideas:

a) that of inquiry into the *structure* of the language of the social sciences, which he calls methodology;
b) that of this *genesis* of this language;
c) finally, that the common denominator of a number of investigations drawn from various disciplines is the notion of *action*.

It is true that the economic theory of decision making—like the psychological theory of experimentation, like marketing studies, like political sociology—all have as their essential theme the analysis of action. The "need for generalization," found in Lazarsfeld's double interest in methodology and the history of the social sciences, also expresses itself in the hope to integrate studies carried out in the frameworks of various social sciences under the denominator of the analysis of action. This is why, we should note in passing, most of the empirical studies he has undertaken deal with the particular moment when an act, which he calls a *decision*, has taken place: the decision to make a purchase or to consume something in *Personal Influence*, the decision to vote in *The People's Choice* and *Voting*. This is also the reason why he does not find it undignified to pay attention to marketing studies, because they make possible the empirical study of decisions that are more easily observable than others since they take place in a relatively brief span of time. Other decisions, such as occupational choices, which Lazarsfeld studied in one of his first publications, *Jugend und Beruf*, pose more difficult methodological problems.

Finally, marketing studies support Lazarsfeld in two propositions, which he set forth early in his career. The first is that, as an object of research, it is not enough to observe action; one must also analyze its structure, with the assistance of theoretical schemes: "It would be unacceptable to rest content with the assertion that x percent of the observed subjects did or thought this or that. The task is to combine diverse results through the application of a small number of integrating constructs." The second proposition is that the notion of action itself plays an essential integrative function, to the extent that it transcends special disciplines and methodologies.

SOCIOLOGY YESTERDAY AND TOMORROW

Lazarsfeld's historical studies naturally led him to raise certain problems in the sociology of knowledge. Why, first of all, the disparity between academic and quasi-official social sciences—especially sociology—and that rediscovered history to which the article on Weber and the notes on the history of quantification point?[1] Why the discontinuity in European social sciences? Having been famous and having founded a school, which lasted for several generations, Le Play fell into

---

[1] P. F. Lazarsfeld, "Notes on the History of Quantification," in H. Wolff (ed.), *Quantification* (New York: Bobbs-Merrill), 1961.

a purgatory from which he has not emerged. Quetelet did not found a school; but his work was so voluminous that, even during his lifetime, a catalogue of his works was published, with cross-references from one book to another, so that the reader could find his way through the maze. In this extensive work, one finds innovations so remarkable and so much the forerunners of modern sociology that Lazarsfeld, when he received the distinction that American universities give to some of their professors, chose to be designated "Quetelet Professor of Social Science." But Quetelet is scarcely mentioned in histories of sociology. Why did Weber not appear to understand the importance of systematic observation in order to arrive at knowledge of social facts? Why did Durkheim, emulated by many contemporary sociologists, persist in artificially separating sociology from other social sciences, attributing to it a special epistemology? Lastly, why did not the innovations, which began in the 17th century and lasted throughout the 19th century, result in Europe in an institutionalization of empirical social research until much later?

Lazarsfeld offers some answers to these questions. Le Play's school was actually a sect, resting largely on the charismatic authority of its founder. When a critical spirit was introduced into the sect, Le Play's authority passed to the Abbey de Tourville, before disappearing completely. Regarding Max Weber, the explanation is perhaps that the German tradition was not prepared to deal with what Lazarsfeld calls the empirical analysis of action. Action (die Handlung) was a concept that was in the theoretical province of jurists, in the sense that the analysis of action drew mainly on the philosophy of law. The obscurity into which another ingenious innovator, Gabriel Tarde, fell resulted perhaps from the monopoly which Durkheimian sociology enjoyed in France for a time.

More generally, one can say that at the end of the 19th century, social sciences in European universities were confined to a sociology philosophical in origin and macrosciological in orientation. By preference, that sociology dealt with global units (societies, states, nations) rather than with individual units. This is the reason, without doubt, why Tarde was so poorly understood. As for the individual, one must remember that another discipline, psychology, was introspective or experimental. The paradigms of scientific research in social science were thus, on the one hand, experimentation as it is carried out by psychologists, or else the analysis of cultural products, or finally the analysis of administrative statistics. Durkheim's *Formes elementaires* is an example of the second mode of research; *Le suicide* and many other products of the Durkheimian school examples of the third. It remained to develop another paradigm, in which sociological or social-psychological investigations could be carried out on the basis of standardized observations made by the sociologist himself. More precisely, still needed was an *institutionalization* of this mode of research, for it had been glimpsed by Tarde, used by Le Play and found a beginning institutionalization in Vienna at the Institute of Psychology directed by the Bühlers.

Perhaps the principal reason why the institutionalization of "empirical sociology" took so long to come about in Europe—at least, this is what Lazarsfeld suggests in "The Sociology of Empirical Sociology" and in "An Episode in the History of Social Research"—was that it required an organizational innovation which academics, especially those in Europe, were not prepared to adopt. This "empirical sociology" requires of those who devote themselves to it as much of an aptitude for administration as for research. Neither experimental psychology nor traditional sociology had previously encountered such problems of administration in such a direct way. In traditional forms of inquiry, the organizational model resembled the organization of the university. A project director, aided by assistants, could carry out a program of experimental research. But the organization of a sociological inquiry calls for a more extensive division of work, because the talents which come into play are more diverse and range from an appreciation of human relations to competence in theoretical or statistical matters. Furthermore, an investigation of this kind is more difficult, financially as well as in the sequence of stages and the time that it requires, than an experimental work (at least in the case of psychology). Then too, the funding, the collection of data and the application of results generally involve the sociologist in relationships and negotiations with the world outside the university. These are factors that are not encountered by the experimental psychologist.

All of these reasons help to explain why empirical sociology—sociology through investigation—has encountered such great difficulties. It presupposes a new type of academic, whom Lazarsfeld has labelled the "managerial scholar." The relation between this new social "role" and the development of empirical sociology may explain to a great extent why most European innovations pointing toward the systematic observation of social behavior have had such short lives. For European universities and societies have perhaps been less ready to adopt and recognize this unfamiliar role, which appears to be contradictory to the traditional structure of academic roles. The history of French sociology is suggestive on this point: after the decline of the Durkheimian school, in which scholarly work was entirely consistent with academic structure, the development of the social sciences after the Second World War led to institutes outside the universities, such as the Centre national de la recherche scientifique or l'Ecole pratique des hautes études. These institutes were successful, because they modelled themselves as "laboratories," a structure much more appropriate to the development of "empirical sociology" than faculty positions. It is undoubtedly for this reason that, within a few years, "empirical sociology" became the ideal for the new generation of French sociologists.

The tension between the structure of academic roles and the new roles associated with empirical research may have been particularly marked in Europe, but it was also present in the United States. At several points in his presidential address to the American Sociological Association and elsewhere Lazarsfeld calls attention to the fact that, when he first arrived in the United States, there was no institute of empirical research, except that directed by Odum at the University of North Carolina. The idea for such institutes was adopted only slowly. The reader interested in this historical problem can refer to "An Episode in the History of Social Research." But what interests us here is that the difficulties of gaining acceptance for empirical sociology in the United States, like the discontinuities in the history of empirical sociology in Europe and like the rapid development of this kind of research in France after the Second World War, tend to confirm the importance, from the point of view of the sociology of knowledge, of an organizational model associated with empirical sociology.

It is not by chance that Lazarsfeld returns to this theme on numerous occasions. Sometimes it is to underline its importance for a "sociology of sociology" and for interpretation of the history of the social sciences. Sometimes it is to emphasize the relationship between the caliber of the organizational model adopted by an institute and the quality of its methodological work: for methodological success depends directly on the quality of the division of labor.

In brief, Lazarsfeld's concern with the organization of the social sciences, which is summarized in his presidential address on "the Sociology of Empirical Sociology," is closely related to his methodological works, on the one hand, and to his studies of the history of the social sciences, on the other.

It was pointed out above that "empirical sociology" developed easily and quickly in France once the institutional mechanisms were provided. This development was nonetheless accompanied by resistances and hesitations, in France and elsewhere. Lazarsfeld, for example, points to the attacks made by Arthur Vidich and his colleagues in *Reflections on Community Studies;* they criticize empirical sociology as being one-sided and restrictive. Along similar lines, one can also cite the remarks of C. Wright Mills.

But Lazarsfeld would undoubtedly be the last to insist that all research should make use of questionnaires and proceed by the route of survey research. In 1933, he published a methodological article in which he underlined the need to have diverse sources of data:

a) For any phenomenon one should have objective observations as well as introspective reports.

b) Case studies should be properly combined with statistical information.

c) Contemporary information should be supplemented by information on earlier phases of whatever is being studied.

d) One should combine 'natural and experimental data.' By experimental, I meant mainly questionnaires and solicited reports, while by natural I meant what is now called 'unobtrusive measures'—data deriving from daily life without interference from the investigator. ("An Episode in the History of Social Research," pp. 282–283).

The article on qualitative methods, written several years earlier, pointed out that statistical methods were not in principle superior to qualitative methods.

The criticism of bias and dogmatism has as little justification as the claim that Lazarsfeld's research is based on a restricted vision of the social sciences. We have dealt with this point sufficiently so that it is not necessary to return to it. On the contrary, Lazarsfeld's persistent concern has been to substitute a discipline without frontier for the hemmed-in fields that make up the landscape of the social sciences.

From this derives the importance that he attaches to perfecting the polling methods used in empirical sociology; he wants to rid them of the atomistic and individualistic character which they are often accused of having. Thus, Blumer, in a famous attack on polls, stated that they could not advance sociology because they dealt with an abstraction: the individual taken out of his social context. One could say, sticking to Blumer's line of thought, that atomistic polls have as their object a sort of *homo psycho-sociologicus* representing an abstraction analogous to the *homo oeconomicus* found in economic theory. In the polls carried out at the time that Blumer wrote, individuals were the only sampling units. As a result, the investigator had at his disposal very little information about the social milieu of the individual. One could ask whether it is useful to know about a worker's opinions of unions if one did not also know the majority opinion in the occupational setting to which he belonged.

To answer these objections, Lazarsfeld developed the notion of contextual analysis which showed that *homo psycho-sociologicus* was a result, not of polling methods in themselves, but rather of the atomistic character of the sampling designs generally followed. In contextual analysis, the respondent is defined, not only by a number of individual characteristics (age, sex, opinion on various questions, educational level, occupation, etc.), but also by variables that describe the milieu from which he comes. In this way, the investigation loses its atomistic character, and can, by means of adequate analysis, regain the macrosociological tradition typical of Durkheim.

Thus, it is wrong to say that Lazarsfeld's methodology leads to a restrictive notion of research unsuited to the preoccupations of macro-sociology. On the level of *intentions*, he always tried hard to refine this methodology to the point where empirical sociology could meet the classical requirement that sociology take into account "social structures" and the situation "as a whole." He has always tried to give precise meaning to these ideas in order to translate them into operational language. The general conclusion was that the objections raised by unconvinced sociologists could slowly be met by progress in methodological analysis. Indeed, in appropriate clarifications and translations, the language of the "holistic" sociologists can be translated into variables and their interrelations. All that is needed is enough methodological imagination to reach this goal. Thus, methodology should be a source of reconciliation and progress rather than of disagreement.

However, Lazarsfeld does not sufficiently stress that numerous

questions at the core of the sociological search cannot be analyzed using only surveys, however sophisticated they are in their design and
in the type of data they provide. How can one base macrosociology or
historical sociology merely on observation? Here are crucial questions
to which he has scarcely tried to give answers. Perhaps this is so because he has always looked at sociology through psychological lenses.
Consequently, one cannot visualize a true meeting of the mind with a
Max Weber who always viewed the same topics basically as a jurist.

Still, papers such as "For the Historian and the Pollster" and "Reflections on Business" bear witness to Lazarsfeld's catholic effort: he
shows that empirical sociology can contribute answers to the problems
raised by classical sociology; in addition it can productively collaborate
with the historian and the economist, thus enlarging the realm of all
social science disciplines.

In other words, one can certainly raise many objections about
Lazarsfeld's work. If the paradigm of action is strategically fruitful
and integrative, it also reinforces a psychologistic distortion of sociology. Quantitative methods play an important part in sociology, adding
to standards of rigor; yet, they cannot really cope with many of the
questions which sociologists rightfully raise. Consequently, we still
need a general theory of inductive research in the social sciences. What
is the logic of functionalism and structuralism? What kind of analysis
is carried out by macrosociologists and historical sociologists? These
are problems that he barely raises. Moreover, he did not probe deeply
enough when he discussed the chances that a quantitative macrosociology could result from a better type of observation and a better coordination between social and economic research institutes and the teaching
of sociology at universities. Finally, it is obvious that the positivistic
epistemology behind what he calls methodology could not really be
reduced to the problems of *conceptualization* on the one hand and the
collection and analysis of empirical data on the other hand. One must
also inquire into the significance of theory in the social sciences; what
is needed is a view of the *total system of analytical tools* of which
each special procedure is only a dependent part.

Fortunately, Lazarsfeld has himself provided ways by which
these limitations can be overcome. Nothing keeps one from developing
a concrete epistemology of macrosociology and historical sociology
which would start out with the "explication de texte," characteristic writings in this field. The same is true for the delicate question of

what really happens when one theorizes in the social sciences. The necessary first step would certainly be to make a rather precise typology of theories as they actually exist. One would want to bring to light their characteristic logic not *a priori* but, as Lazarsfeld urges, through a careful analysis of what has actually been produced. Such investigations would be of great importance for the future of sociology.

CHAPTER *21*

ABSTRACTED EMPIRICISM

C. Wright Mills

Specialists in method tend also to be specialists in one or another species of social philosophy. The important point about them, in sociology today, is not that they are specialists, but that one of the results of their specialty is to further the process of specialization within the social sciences as a whole. Moreover, they further it in accordance with the methodological inhibition and in terms of the research institute in which it may be embodied. Theirs is not a proposal for any scheme of topical specialization according to "intelligible fields of study" or a conception of problems of social structure. It is a proposed specialization based solely on use of The Method, regardless of content, problem, or area. These are not stray impressions; they are readily documented.

The most explicit and straightforward statement of abstracted empiricism as a style of work, and of the role within social science which the abstracted empiricist should perform, has been made by Paul F. Lazarsfeld, who is among the more sophisticated spokesmen of this school.[1]

[1] "What Is Sociology?" Universitets Studentkontor, Skrivemaskinstua, Oslo, September, 1948 (mimeo). This paper was written for and delivered to a group of people who sought general guidance in setting up a research institution. Accordingly it is most suitable for my present purposes, being brief, clear, and authoritative. More elaborate and elegant statements can of course be found, for example, in *The Language of Social Research*, edited by Lazarsfeld and Rosenberg (Glencoe, Illinois, The Free Press, 1955).

Lazarsfeld defines "sociology" as a speciality, not in terms of any methods peculiar to *it*, but in terms of its being the methodological speciality. In this view, the sociologist becomes the methodologist of all the social sciences.

> This then is the first function of the sociologist, which we can make fairly explicit. He is so to say the *pathfinder* of the advancing army of social scientists, when a new sector of human affairs is about to become an object of empirical scientific investigations. It is the sociologist who takes the first steps. He is the bridge between the social philosopher, the individual observer and the commentator on the one hand and the organized team work of the empirical investigators and analyzers on the other hand . . . historically speaking we then have to distinguish three major ways of looking at social subject matters: social analysis as practiced by the individual observer; organized full-fledged empirical sciences; and a transitory phase which we call the sociology of any special area of social behavior . . . It should be helpful at this point to insert some comments on what is going on at the time of such a transition from social philosophy to empirical sociology.[2]

"The individual observer," please note, is curiously equated with the "social philosopher." Note also that this is a statement not only of an intellectual program but also of an administrative plan: "Certain areas of human behavior have become the object of organized social sciences which have names, institutes, budgets, data, personnel, and so on. Other areas have been left undeveloped in this respect." Any area can be developed or "sociologized." For example: "As a matter of fact we don't even have a name for a social science which would be concerned with the happiness of the population. But there is nothing which would make such a science impossible. It would not be more difficult and not even more expensive to collect happiness ratings than to collect data on income, savings and prices."

Sociology, then, as mid-wife to a series of specialized "social sciences" stands between any topical area that has not yet become the object of The Method and "the fully developed social sciences." It is not altogether clear what are considered "the fully developed social sciences," but it is implied that only demography and economics qualify: "No one will doubt any more that it is necessary and possible

---

[2] *Ibid.*, pp. 4–5.

to deal with human affairs in a scientific way. For 100 or more years
we have had fully developed sciences like economics and demography,
which deal with various sectors of human behavior." I find no other
specifications of "full-fledged social sciences" in the twenty pages of
this essay.

When sociology is assigned the task of converting philosophy into
sciences, it is assumed or implied that the genius of The Method is such
that it does not require traditional scholarly knowledge of the area to
be converted. Surely such knowledge would require a little more time
than is implied in this statement. Perhaps what is meant is made clear
by a chance remark about political science: ". . . The Greeks had a
science of politics, the German talk of *Staatslehr* and the Anglo-Saxons
of political science. No one has yet made a good content analysis so
that one could really know what the books in this field deal with . . ."[3]

Here, then, are the organized teams of full-fledged, empirical social
scientists; there are the unorganized, individual social philosophers. As
The Methodologist, the sociologist converts the latter into the former.
He is, in short, the science-maker, at once intellectual, or rather, Scientific, and administrative.

"The transition (from "social philosophies" and "the individual
observer" to "organized, full-fledged empirical science") is usually
characterized by four turns in the work of the students concerned."

> 1) "There is first the shift of emphasis from the history
> of institutions and ideas to the concrete behavior of peoples."
> This is not quite so simple; abstracted empiricism, as we shall
> see in chapter 6, is not everyday empiricism. "The concrete be-
> havior of people" is not its unit of study. Presently I shall show
> that in practice the choice that is involved often reveals a distinct
> tendency to what is called "psychologism," and, moreover, a
> persistent avoidance of problems of structure in favor of those
> of milieux.
>
> 2) "There is secondly," Lazarsfeld continues, "a ten-
> dency not to study one sector of human affairs alone but to re-
> late it to other sectors." This I do not believe is true; to see that

[3] *Ibid.*, p. 5. "A content analysis of a set of materials consists essentially of
classifying small units of the documents (words, sentences, themes) according to
some set of *a priori categories*." Peter H. Rossi, "Methods of Social Research,
1945–55," *Sociology in the United States of America,* edited by Hans L. Zetter-
berg, Paris, France, UNESCO, 1956, p. 33.

it is not, one need only compare the productions of Marx or Spencer or Weber with those of any abstracted empiricist. What is probably meant, however, rests on a special meaning of "relate": it is confined to the statistical.

3) "There is third a preference for studying social situations and problems which repeat themselves rather than those which occur only once." This might be thought an attempt to point toward structural considerations, for "repetitions" or "regularities" of social life are, of course, anchored in established structures. That is why to understand, for example, American political campaigns one needs to understand the structure of parties, their roles within the economy, etc. But this is not what is meant by Lazarsfeld; what is meant is that elections require many people to engage in a similar act, and that elections recur: hence the voting behavior of individuals may be studied statistically, and re-studied, and re-studied.

4) "And finally there is a greater emphasis on contemporary rather than on historical social events . . ." This a-historical emphasis is due to an epistomological preference: ". . . The sociologist will therefore have a tendency to deal mainly with contemporaneous events for which he is likely to get the kind of data he needs . . ." Such an epistomological bias stands in contrast with the formulation of substantive problems as the orienting point of work in social science.[4]

Before considering these points further I must complete my report of this statement of sociology, which is conceived to have two further tasks:

> . . . sociological research consists in applying scientific procedures to new areas. They [Lazarsfeld's observations] are just designed to characterize crudely the atmosphere which is likely to prevail during the transition from social philosophy to empirical social research . . . As a sociologist starts to study new sectors of human affairs, he has to collect the data he wants all by himself . . . It is in connection with this situation that the second major function of the sociologist has developed. He is at the moment something of a *toolmaker* for the other social sciences. Let me remind you of a few of the many problems the social scientist meets when he has to collect his own data. Very often he has to ask people themselves what they did or saw or wanted. This people often won't remember easily; or they are reluctant to tell us; or they don't exactly understand what we

---

[4] All quotations in the above paragraphs are from Lazarsfeld, op. cit., pp. 5–6.

want to know. Thus the important and difficult art of interviewing has developed . . .

. . . But [the sociologist] has had historically still a third
function as an *interpreter* . . . it is helpful to distinguish
between the description and the interpretation of social relationships. On the interpretative level we would mainly raise questions which every day language covers by the word 'why.'
Why do people have less children now than before? Why do
they have a tendency to move from the country to the city?
Why are elections won or lost? . . .

The classic techniques of finding such explanations are
statistical. We have to compare families who have many and
who have few children; we have to compare workers who often
stay away from work with those who come regularly. But *what*
about them should we compare?[5]

The sociologist seems suddenly to assume a truly encyclopedic
posture: Every division of social science contains interpretations and
theories, but here we are told that "interpretation" and "theory" are
the sociologist's domain. What is meant becomes clear when we realize
that these other interpretations are not yet scientific. The kinds of "interpretations" with which the sociologist is to work, as he transforms
philosophies into sciences, are "interpretive variables" useful in statistical inquiry. Moreover, note the tendency to reduce sociological realities to psychological variables, in the immediate continuation of the
above quotation: "We have to assume that there is something in the
personality, experience and attitude of people, which makes them act
differently in what seem from the outside to be the same situations.
What is needed is explanatory ideas and conceptions which can be
tested by empirical research . . ."

"Social theory" as a whole becomes a systematic collection of
such concepts, that is, of variables useful in interpretations of statistical
findings:

We do call these concepts sociological *because* they apply
to many varieties of social behavior . . . We assign to the sociologist the task to collect and analyze these concepts, which
are useful for the interpretation of empirical results found in
specific areas like the analysis of price or crime or suicide or

[5] *Ibid.*, pp. 7–8, 12–13.

voting statistics. Sometimes the term social theory is used for a
systematic presentation of such concepts and their interrelationships.[6]

It is not, I must note in passing, altogether clear whether this statement as a whole is a theory of the historical role that sociologists have
actually played—in which case it is surely inadequate; or whether it is
merely a suggestion that sociologists ought to be technicians-as-mid-
wives and keepers of the interpretation of everything—in which case,
of course, any sociologist is free to decline the invitation in the interests of his own substantive problems. But is it fact or precept, statement or program?

Perhaps it is propaganda for a philosophy of technique and an
admiration for administrative energy, disguised as part of the natural
history of science.

This conception of the sociologist, well housed in research institutes, as science-maker, tool-maker, and keeper of the interpretations
—as well as the whole style of work, of which this is the clearest statement I know—involves several problems which I shall now take up
more systematically.

There are two current apologies for abstracted empiricism which,
if accepted, would mean that the thinness of its result is due less to any
feature inherent in The Method than to causes of an "accidental nature," namely, money and time.

It might, first, be said that as such studies are usually quite expensive, they have had to be shaped by some concern for the problems of
the interests that have paid for them; and moreover, that the aggregate
of these interests has had rather scattered problems. Accordingly, the
researchers have not been able to select problems in such a way as to
allow a true accumulation of results—that is, one that would add up
in a more significant way. They have done the best they could; they
could not be concerned with a fruitful series of substantive problems,
so they have had to specialize in developing methods that could be put
to work regardless of the substantive issues.

In brief, the economics of truth—the costs of research—seem to
conflict with the politics of truth—the use of research to clarify significant issues and to bring political controversy closer to realities. The
conclusion is that if only social research institutions had, say, 25 per-

[6] *Ibid.,* p. 17.

cent of the total scientific funds of the nation and if they were free to do with this money as they like, things would be ever so much better. I must admit that I do not know whether or not this is a reasonable expectation. Nor does anyone else, although it must be the conviction of the administrative intellectuals among us who have frankly given up work in social science for promotional activities. But to take this as *the* issue would be to eliminate the relevance of any intellectual criticism. One thing, moreover, is surely clear: because of the expensiveness of The Method, its practitioners have often become involved in the commercial and bureaucratic uses of their work, and this indeed has affected their style.

It might be thought, secondly, that critics are merely impatient, and I am aware of magisterial discourse about "the requirements of science" being on the order of centuries rather than decades. It might be said that "in due course" such studies will accumulate in such a way as to permit significant results about society to be generalized from them. This line of justification, it seems to me, assumes a view of the development of social science as a strange building-block endeavor. It assumes that such studies as these are by their nature capable of being "units" which at some point in the future can be "added up" or "fitted together" to "build up" a reliable and verified image of some whole. It is not merely an assumption; it is an explicit policy. "Empirical sciences," Lazarsfeld asserts, "have to work on specific problems and build up broader knowledge by putting together the results of many minute, careful, and time-consuming investigations. It is certainly desirable that more students turn to social sciences. But not because this will save the world overnight; it is rather because this will somewhat accelerate the hard task of developing in the end an integrated social science, which can help us to understand and control social affairs.[7]

Ignoring for the moment its political ambiguities, the program suggested is to narrow the work to "minute" investigations on the assumption that their findings can be "put together," and that this, in turn, will be "an integrated social science." To explain why this is an inadequate view, I must go beyond extrinsic reasons for the thinness of result achieved by these researchers, and turn to reasons inherent in their style and program.

My first point has to do with the relation between theory and re-

[7] Op. cit., p. 20.

search, with the policy social scientists should adopt about the priority of larger conceptions and of areas for detailed exposition.

There is of course much generous comment in all schools of social science about the blindness of empirical data without theory and the emptiness of theory without data. But we do better to examine the practice and its results, as I am trying to do here, than the philosophical embroidery. In the more forthright statements, such as Lazarsfeld's, the working ideas of "theory" and of "empirical data" are made quite plain: "Theory" becomes the variables useful in interpreting statistical findings; "empirical data," it is strongly suggested and made evident in practice, are restricted to such statistically determined facts and relations as are numerous, repeatable, measurable. With both theory and data so restricted, the generosity of comment about their interplay appears to shrink to a miserly acknowledgment, in fact, to no acknowledgment at all. There are no philosophical grounds, and certainly no grounds in the work of social science, as I have already indicated, so to restrict these terms.

To check and to re-shape a broad conception, one must have detailed expositions, but the detailed expositions cannot necessarily be put together to constitute a broad conception. What should one select for detailed exposition? What are the criteria for selection? And what does "put together" mean? It is not so mechanical a task as the easy phrase makes it seem. We speak of the interplay of broader conception and detailed information (theory and research), but we must also speak of problems. The problems of social science are stated in terms of conceptions that usually relate to social-historical structures. If we take such problems as real, then it does seem foolish to undertake any detailed studies of smaller-scale areas before we have good reason to believe that, whatever the results, they will permit us to draw inferences useful in solving or clarifying problems of structural significance. We are not "translating" such problems when we merely assume a perspective in which all problems are seen as a scatter of requests for scattered information, statistical or otherwise, about a scatter of individuals and their scattered milieux.

So far as ideas are concerned, you seldom get out of any truly detailed research more than you have put into it. What you get out of empirical research as such is information, and what you can do with this information depends a great deal upon whether or not in the course of your work you have selected your specific empirical studies as check

points of larger constructions. As the science-maker goes about transforming social philosophies into empirical sciences, and erecting research institutions in which to house them, a vast number of studies
result. There is, in truth, no principle or theory that guides the selection of what is to be the subject of these studies. "Happiness," as we
have seen, might be one; marketing behavior, another. It is merely
assumed that if only The Method is used, such studies as result—scattered from Elmira to Zagreb to Shanghai—will add up finally to a
"full-fledged, organized" science of man and society. The practice, in
the meantime, is to get on with the next study.

In contending that these studies probably cannot be "added up"
to more significant results, I am taking into account the theory of society toward which abstracted empiricism actually tends. Any style of
empiricism involves a metaphysical choice—a choice as to what is most
real—and now we must see something of the choice required by this
particular style. A rather convincing case, I believe, might be made for
the contention that these studies are very often examples of what is
known as psychologism.[8] The argument might be based on the fact
that their fundamental source of information is a sample of individuals.
The questions asked in these studies are put in terms of the psychological reaction of individuals. Accordingly, the assumption is required that
the institutional structure of society, in so far as it is to be studied in
this way, can be understood by means of such data about individuals.

To become aware of problems of structure, and of their explanatory significance for even individual behavior, requires a much broader
style of empiricism. For example, within the structure of even American society—and especially of one American town at one time, which
is usually the "sample area"—there are so many common denominators,
social and psychological, that the variety of conduct which social scientists must take into account is simply not available. That variety, and
hence the very formulation of problems, becomes available only when

---

[8] "Psychologism" refers to the attempt to explain social phenomena in terms
of facts and theories about the make-up of individuals. Historically, as a doctrine,
it rests upon an explicit metaphysical denial of the reality of social structure. At
other times, its adherents may set forth a concept of structure which reduces it,
so far as explanations are concerned, to a set of milieux. In a still more general
way, and of more direct interest to our concern with the current research policies
of social science, psychologism rests upon the idea that if we study a series of
individuals and their milieux, the result of our studies in some way can be added
up to knowledge of social structure.

our view is broadened to include comparative and historical social structures. Yet because of epistemological dogma, abstracted empiricists are systematically a-historical and non-comparative; they deal with small-scale areas and they incline to psychologism. Neither in defining their problems nor in explaining their own microscopic findings do they make any real use of the basic idea of historical social structure.

Even as studies of milieux, such research cannot be expected to be very perceptive. By definition, as well as on the basis of our studies, we know that the causes of many changes in milieux are often unknown to the people (the interviewees) in specific milieux, and that these changes can be understood only in terms of structural transformations. This general view, of course, is the polar opposite of psychologism. Its implications for our methods seem clear and simple: the selection of milieux for detailed study ought to be made in accordance with problems of structural significance. The kinds of "variables" to be isolated and observed within milieux ought to be those that have been found to be important by our examination of structure. There should of course be a two-way interaction between studies of milieux and studies of structure. The development of social science cannot very well be thought of as resulting from a scattered group of women each making a part of some great quilt: the little pieces, no matter how precisely defined, are not to be so mechanically and so externally linked.

But it is not at all unusual, in the practice of abstracted empiricists to "get the data" and "run it" through a more or less standardized statistical analysis, usually conducted by semi-skilled analysts. Then a sociologist is hired, or even a series of them, "really to analyze it." Which brings me to my next point.

Among abstracted empiricists, there is a recent tendency to preface empirical studies with a chapter or two in which they summarize "the literature of the problem." This is of course a good sign and is, I think, in some part a response to criticism from the established social disciplines. But in actual practice this work is all too often done after the data are collected and "written up." Furthermore, since it requires considerable time and patience, in the busy research institutions it is often given over to the busy assistant. The memorandum which he produces is then reshaped in an effort to surround the empirical study with "theory" and to "give it meaning," or—as is frequently said—to "get a better story out of it." Even this, perhaps, is better than nothing.

But it does often mislead the outsider who may hastily assume that this particular empirical study was selected and designed and executed in such a way as empirically to test broader conceptions or assumptions.

I do not believe that this is the usual practice. It could, in fact, become usual only in the hands of men who took seriously "the literature" of social science—on its own terms and for long enough to grasp the conceptions and theories and problems it contains. Only then would it be conceivable that, without abandonment of the problems and conceptions, their meanings could be translated into more specific and smaller scale problems readily amenable to The Method. Such translation, of course, is what all working social scientists do, although they do not confine the term "empirical" to abstracted, statistical information about a series of contemporary individuals, or "theory" to a collection of "interpretative variables."

Interesting tricks are used in such discussion. Studies of the type I am examining, when analyzed from a logical standpoint, reveal that the "interesting concepts" used to interpret and explain "the data" almost always point to: 1) structural and historical "factors" above the level made available by the interview; 2) psychological "factors" below the depth open to the interviewer. But the important point is that conceptions neither of structure nor of psychological depth are typically among the terms with which the research has been formulated and "the data" collected. These terms may point in a gross way in one or the other of these directions, but they are not among those specific and "clean" variables which are duly accredited by this style of work.

The main reason for this seems clear: in practice, the more or less set interview—the basic source of information—usually requires a curious sort of social behaviorism. Given the administrative and financial facts of research, this is almost inevitable. For is it not obvious that interviewers at best semi-skilled cannot obtain—in fact, no one regardless of skill can obtain—in a twenty-minute or even a day-long interview the kinds of depth materials which we know, from the most skilled and prolonged interviews, are there to be gotten?[9] Nor is it pos-

---

[9] In passing, I must note that one reason for the thin formality or even emptiness of these fact-cluttered studies is that they contain very little or no direct observation by those who are in charge of them. The "empirical facts" are facts collected by a bureaucratically guided set of usually semi-skilled individuals. It has been forgotten that social observation requires high skill and acute sensibility; that discovery often occurs precisely when an imaginative mind sets itself down in the middle of social realities.

sible to obtain by the usual sort of sample survey the kind of information on structure which we know is available from studies properly oriented to history.

Yet conceptions of structure and of depth psychology are dragged into studies in the abstracted empirical style. Particular observations are explained by appealing *ad hoc* to general conceptions. General conceptions are used to formulate structural or psychological problems for the "front-end" of "the write-up" of a study.

In some research shops the term "bright" is sometimes used when detailed facts or relations are persuasively "explained" by broader suppositions. When minute variables, whose meanings are stretched, are used to explain broad questions, the result may be referred to as "cute." I mention this to indicate that there is emerging a "shop language" to cover the procedures I am reporting.

What all this amounts to is the use of statistics to illustrate general points and the use of general points to illustrate statistics. The general points are neither tested nor made specific. They are adapted to the figures, as the arrangement of the figures is adapted to them. The general points and explanations can be used with other figures too; and the figures can be used with other general points. These logical tricks are used to give apparent structural and historical and psychological meaning to studies which by their very style of abstraction have eliminated such meanings. In the ways indicated, as well as in others, it is possible to cling to The Method and yet attempt to cover up the triviality of its results.

Examples of such procedures are available quite usually in the lead paragraphs of given chapters, in "the general introductions," and sometimes in an "interpretative" chapter or section which is "spliced in." My purpose here cannot be the detailed examination of given studies; I wish only to alert the reader in such a way that he will sharpen his own examination of studies.

The point is simply this: Social research of any kind is advanced by ideas; it is only disciplined by fact. That is just as true of abstracted empirical surveys of "why people vote as they do" as it is of an historian's account of the position and outlook of the nineteenth-century Russian intelligentsia. The ritual of the first is usually more elaborate and certainly more pretentious. The logical status of the result is not different.

There is, finally, one explanation of abstracted empiricism's usual thinness of result that may be put as a question: Is there any necessary tension between that which is true but unimportant, and that which is important but not necessarily true? A better way to ask the question is: For what level of verification ought workers in social science be willing to settle? We could of course become so exacting in our demands that we should necessarily have nothing but very detailed exposition; we could also become so inexacting that we should have only very grand conceptions indeed.

Those in the grip of the methodological inhibition often refuse to say anything about modern society unless it has been through the fine little mill of The Statistical Ritual. It is usual to say that what they produce is true even if unimportant. I do not agree with this; more and more I wonder how true it is. I wonder how much exactitude, or even pseudo-precision, is here confused with "truth"; and how much abstracted empiricism is taken as the only "empirical" manner of work. If you have ever seriously studied, for a year or two, some thousand hour-long interviews carefully coded and punched, you will have begun to see how very malleable the realm of "fact" may really be. Moreover, as for "importance," surely it is important when some of the most energetic minds among us use themselves up in the study of detail because The Method to which they are dogmatically committed does not allow them to study anything else. Much of such work, I am now convinced, has become the mere following of a ritual—which happens to have gained commercial and foundation value—rather than, in the words of its spokesmen, "a commitment to the hard demands of science."

Precision is not the sole criterion for choice of method; certainly precision ought not to be confused, as it so often is, with "empirical" or "true." We should be as accurate as we are able to be in our work upon the problems that concern us. But no method, as such, should be used to delimit the problems we take up, if for no other reason than that the most interesting and difficult issues of *method* usually begin where established techniques do not apply.

If we have a sense of real problems, as they arise out of history, the question of truth and significance tends to answer itself: we should work on such problems as carefully and as exactly as we can. The important work in social science has usually been, and usually is, carefully elaborated hypotheses, documented at key points by more detailed information. There is, in fact, no other way, at least as yet, to confront the topics and themes that are widely acknowledged as important.

Index

Author Index

Subject Index

A

Abstracted empiricism, 428-440
Academic freedom, 400
Academic Mind, The, 400
Accounting scheme, 80-81,
    198-202
    (*see also* Decision analysis;
    Reasons)
Ach, N., 58-59, 67, 69, 73-75, 76
Achievement, 61
Action, 53-105
    aggregation of, 96-101
    analysis of, as basis for market
      research, 78, 183-202, 419
    as unifying theme for the social
      sciences, 420
    concept of, 83 ff.
    controlled and uncontrolled
      (Lewin), 75
    determinants of, 183-202, 203
    discontinuity of the concept in
      psychology, 54-56
    empirical study of, 53-105, 323,
      419, 421
    goal-centered theory of (Bühler),
      60-63
    in jurisprudence, 83, 84, 421
    interpretation of, 201-202
    morphology of, 75
    objects of, 61
    psychology of, 53-82
    testability of, 76
    theory of, 15-16, 55, 61, 70-72,
      323
Action language, 85, 96-101
Advertising, 77-80

Ahistorical emphasis, 429, 432
Alienation, 169, 171
American Association for Public
    Opinion Research, 278, 295
    Presidential Address, 278-299
American Journal of Sociology,
    329
American Marketing Association,
    212
American Social Science Associa-
    tion, 329
American Sociological Society (As-
    sociation), 321, 357
American Soldier, The, 232, 285,
    292, 402
Anthropology,
    cultural, 290-291
    structural, 178
Anthropomorphism, 10, 415-416
Associationism, 74
Attention, 58, 190
Atomism, 425
    (*see also* Psychologism)
Attitude climate, 400
Attitudes, 57
    and social relationships, 290-291
    change of, 187, 404
    historical and cultural variations
      in, 280-286
    in international relations, 344
    latent, 401
    measurement of, 198-201, 328,
      417
    saliency of, 286
    (*see also* Reasons, Public
      opinion, Opinion polling)